"I've grown up in church my whole life but always sensed something was missing, that there was more to the story. Re_Orient connects all the dots. It's the more everyone is looking for!

~ Josiah, a college student from Michigan

I can't imagine any healthy religious leader in America not wanting to read this book and encourage everyone they know to Re_Orient. It's like a master level course in equipping people to actually do the work of ministry with supernatural results – it's simply brilliant!

~ Gary, a pastor from California

I can't even express all the ways Re_Orient has impacted me. Our family will never be the same: reorient and disciple up in holy violent love! I can attest that the results are stunning!

~ Katy, a mom from Texas

Whoa – a mind-blowing, earth shattering extrapolation of practical love based truth that will appeal to the intellectual mind and heart of both the cynic and the believer.

~ Michael, a law student and actor from California

I know what it takes to make a world class, Special Forces soldier. I now know what it takes to make a world class superhuman disciple – they must Re_Orient!

~ Michael Paul, a soldier from Maryland

# Re_Orient

by Kevin Weaver

™

Re_Orient
By Kevin Weaver

Published by
It's Feasible Publishing, L.L.C.
P.O. Box 92764 Southlake, Tx 76092
(972) 246-8931
www.itsfeasible.com

Unless otherwise noted, all Scripture quotations are Scripture taken from the HOLY BIBLE, NEW INTERNATIONAL VERSION®. Copyright © 1973, 1978, 1984 Biblica. Used by permission of Zondervan. All rights reserved.

Scripture quotations marked AMP are from the Amplified® Bible, Copyright © 1954, 1958, 1962, 1964, 1965, 1987 by The Lockman Foundation. Used by permission.

Scripture quotations marked KJV are from the King James Version of the Bible.

Scripture quotations marked NKJV are from the New King James Version of the Bible. Copyright © 1979, 1980, 1982 by Thomas Nelson, Inc., publishers. Used by permission.

Scripture quotations marked NAS are from the New American Standard Bible. Copyright © 1960, 1962, 1963, 1968, 1971, 1972, 1973, 1975, 1977 by the Lockman Foundation. Used by permission. (www.Lockman.org)

Scripture quotations marked CEV are from the Contemporary English Version®. Copyright © 1995 American Bible Society. All rights reserved.

Scripture quotations marked ESV are taken from The Holy Bible, English Standard Version® (ESV®), copyright © 2001 by Crossway, a publishing ministry of Good News Publishers. Used by permission. All rights reserved.

Scripture quotations marked NLT are taken from the Holy Bible, New Living Translation, copyright © 1996, 2004, 2007 by Tyndale House Foundation. Used by permission of Tyndale House Publishers, Inc., Carol Stream, Illinois 60188. All rights reserved.

Scripture quotations marked DARBY are taken from The Holy Scriptures: A New Translation from the Original Languages by J. N. Darby, published in 1890.

Scripture quotations marked ASV are taken from the American Standard Version of the Bible, published in 1901.

Scripture quotations marked YLT are taken from Young's Literal Translation of the Bible by Robert Young, published in 1898.

Scripture quotations marked BBE are taken from the Bible in Basic English Version of the Bible.

Scripture quotations marked ISV are taken from the International Standard Version of the Bible.

Scripture quotations marked WEB are taken from THE JESUS BOOK – The Bible in Worldwide English. Copyright SOON Educational Publications, Derby DE65 6BN, UK. Used by permission.

Scripture quotations marked GWT are taken from GOD'S WORD®, © 1995 God's Word to the Nations. Used by permission of Baker Publishing Group.

Scripture quotations marked WNT are taken from the Weymouth New Testament, published in 1903.

Scripture quotations marked AKJV are taken from the American King James Version of the Bible.

## TABLE OF CONTENTS

GRATITUDES i

FOREWORDS iii

A VISION FOR RE_ORIENT vii

LOVE 001

SIN 043

RELIGION 105

CHURCH 167

CHRISTIAN 247

DISCIPLE 313

GOSPEL 387

SAVED 479

DOER 569

REVIVE 609

ENDNOTES 615

# GRATITUDES

God, thank You! Without You and Your eternal words, I would not exist and life as we know it would be void of all meaning. Heck, without You, we wouldn't even have life! It blows me away to consider all the ways You could have designed a kingdom, but You choose to construct one by hand, call it a family, and require only voluntary lovers to participate – it's so gracious and awe-inspiringly brilliant! You are utterly awesome!

Jesus, what can I say but wow! You are the Master – the ideal man! You did what no other had the strength, courage, or resolve to do. Thank You for taking what I deserved so I could have a shot at living the kind of life You deserved! I am eternally grateful. You are the goal!

Holy Spirit, thank You for helping me to become more like Jesus and for searching the deep things of the Father's heart and endeavoring to reveal them to me. Thank You for continuing to pursue me, even when I didn't want to be found. Thank You for leading me and for comforting me in my not-always-so-elegant quest for greater truth! You are essential!

To Michelle, my wife and "Zoe life" mate: I truly do love you. You are my friend, sister warrior, armor bearer, and, of course, cheerleader. Without you, I could not have gone to the next level, but because of you, love lives!

To Olivia Joy, "Pure joy"; Noah Jeremiah, "Rest, God will exalt"; and Immanuel Asher, "God with us in abundance and happiness": each of you were God's best gifts to your mother and me. Each of you is a jewel in my crown life. I pray that when you look back, you will conclude that Mom and Dad were the real deal. May you always see congruence in us as we endeavor to model and point you to live out love's ideal. Your affection and respect will always mean more to us than receiving it from a billion others who will never know us as well as you do. May you rise and soar even higher because we lived!

To Mom: You are love personified and the very definition of what it means to be a servant leader. Thank you for giving me roots and wings!

To Dad: I know what you're thinking, and I still love you. Knowing you're pleased with me and the way I turned out settles my soul. Thanks!

To my big sister, Kelly: I love you, Kel! Thank you for encouraging me to continue and for validating your little brother! You rock!

To my Monday night men's group (a.k.a. my band of brothers): I love you guys. How did you put up with my endless questions every Monday night for thirteen years? Thank you for being broken vessels of humility, whose pieces God welded together through trials to help form my shield of faith!

To you, the reader: I want to sincerely thank you for reading this book; it was written with you in mind. As the author, I genuinely tried to picture you, as an individual, at the other end of every word written and every concept conveyed. We may or may not get the opportunity to know each other personally, but I want you to know that I hold you, the individual God created, in the highest regard. At the end of the journey to reorient together, whether we agree or disagree about anything we cover along the way, there is one thing for certain: I honor, respect, and love (in the way we are about to reorient to the word) you and God's intent for your life!

For each of you acknowledged in this section, I pray that at the end of this book and the end of my life, each of you will be able to honestly say of me, "Well done!"

# FOREWORDS

From the first day I met Kevin, he has been a truth seeker: a seeker of the Word of God, passionate for all things about God, and diligently weaving his life in such a way to produce the disciple of Jesus I admired then and today. It seemed too good to be true when I first met Kevin so many years ago sitting in an airport, but as you will read later in this book, God is all about producing too-good-to-be-true news! I have witnessed for the past fifteen years of marriage a genuine man after God's heart as a husband and father, a man of integrity, and a man I love and respect more and more with the unfolding of each day. "Love Lives" in us!

Michelle Weaver

Greetings! I truly believe this book is the first step to a worldwide revolution. Misguided and misinterpreted Christian doctrines have caused confusion and bitter divisions for far too long and have resulted in the exact opposite of Jesus' mission. Inaccurate translations from one language to another over the centuries have become enshrined. Much of what Jesus promoted has been misunderstood. Life-changing truths are reduced to clichés and traditions with zero power. Modern man has caged supernatural truths into the powerless realm of the natural mind. But this book can help reverse that and liberate countless lives.

My goal in writing this forward is simple: to provide the reader with a glimpse into Kevin's heart. What makes him tick? How intimate is his relationship with God and Jesus Christ? What's his motive for writing this book? How does he feel about you as a reader? I think these questions should be answered before you invest your time and money reading this. Believe me, the information contained in this book will challenge your views about traditional doctrines and definitions at every level. Regardless of your background, I can guarantee without hesitation the insights contained here will blow your mind.

So allow me to answer the questions I mentioned earlier. What makes Kevin tick? First, he truly loves people. Like Will Rogers, I don't think he's ever met a stranger. He loves to fight for the underdog. He's tireless when it comes to pursuing truth – I mean relentless.. In addition, he's a devoted husband, a spiritual guide to his three children, and no matter how busy the schedule, he always makes time for family and friends. When someone's in need, Kevin is one of the first to help. Even in the early years when I watched him battle for breakthrough in his own health and finances, Kevin never wavered in sharing his time and possessions with total abandon. Jesus once exclaimed, "There goes someone who has no guile." Guile means deception or corrupt motives. As a long-time friend, I'm witness to the fact that Kevin has no guile.

The next question is, "How intimate is his relationship with God and Jesus Christ?" Kevin and I met in 1994 when he responded to a request at a church we attended inviting men to gather into small groups for weekly meetings. His obvious hunger for truth and a closer walk with God was clear from the beginning. For 12+ years, he was first to arrive and last to leave. Many of our meetings began at 6:00 p.m. and ended at midnight. I watched Kevin night after night ask God to give him more of His Spirit. And God answered. During one meeting, I witnessed Kevin having an encounter with God beyond anything I've seen before or since. From that night, he walked with power and anointing. Many people were healed, including my wife. I was sitting next to Kevin when the Holy Spirit exploded His revelatory truth about God's love that he writes about in this book and how it is the secret to overcoming anything that falls short of love's ideal. So, how intimate is his relationship with God and Jesus Christ? My simple answer: more than any other I've encountered.

As for his motive in writing this book, I'll simply say it really is YOU. Kevin loves truth, and after two years of focused research, he has discovered exciting truths that will completely change the way you see God, see the church, and see mankind's role. There is a real battle raging between God and evil, but the weapons God gave to overcome evil have grown rusty over the centuries. Even worse, there has been such confusion over the battlefield that Christians sometimes use the weapons God gave us to attack and destroy each other. It's time for that to stop. We must reorient our understanding in order to effectively wage war together against evil. This book resets the compass and explains how and why the modern church is powerless.

Finally, our last question is, "How does Kevin feel about you?" Although Kevin hasn't personally met every reader, he's one of those rare individuals who truly loves people. Not in an abstract way or just because God calls for it. He sees into a person's heart and finds the good in everyone, finding ways to bring out the best in people through inspiration, never through condemnation. He walks the talk, and you will too!

Sincerely,

Chuck Frazier

# A VISION FOR RE__ORIENT

It started in a dream and in what seemed like a medieval iron-working shop.

I became aware I was standing in front of a very large work bench. The bench was about waist high, and on it were swords about three feet in length laid perfectly in a row with just their hilts advancing past the table's edge.

The swords appeared highly polished with a single discernible word written on each blade. I recognized the words to be frequently used religious words that I often wondered about and endeavored to teach because they were so often misunderstood.

I also noticed a door to my left, slightly cracked and with radiant light shining through it. The door appeared to be an exit door to a larger venue with an awaiting crowd more sizable than I could comprehend and on the verge of eruption!

As I was noticing the number of swords, the door, the rumblings of the crowd, and other details about my surroundings, I sensed someone approach from behind and to my left. I turned to see who it was and heard Him say, "Here, hone this one," as He handed me a sword.

The sword had lost its luster and appeared covered in debris, like it had been buried for thousands of years. Upon laying hold of the sword, I intuitively knew what to do. I began to sharpen it on a now rotating mill stone in front of me.

As I began honing the sword, I noticed its luster begin to return, and it became more brilliant as light reflected on it. I continued to sharpen the sword and noticed a single word emerge, emblazoned on the blade.

When I clearly discerned the word, I laid the sword with the hilt extending outward alongside the other swords lined up on the table in front of me.

It seemed as I completed one sword, the person behind me would hand me another. As I worked intensely, the swords began to multiply and ultimately stretched in a line to my right, beyond my ability to see.

After what seemed like months of work, I asked, "What are these?"

The person behind me said, "These represent every word I want you to hone in private, which I will soon ask you to hand out in public."

Then the man said, "It's important for you to understand these are not your swords. These are designed for others who will choose to use them to bring about the most glorious generational transition in the history of mankind!"

The work now seemed more significant than I could understand at that time.

I remember being overwhelmed with a sense of urgency to complete the task and an almost fearful awareness of the need for precision, sensing that each sword now being honed in private would soon be on open display and used by an emerging generation to bring about change in ways that generations before had failed to do.

As I sensed my work was finished, I turned to my left to exit the room and felt something hinder my movement. I looked down to observe two swords impaled in the ground beside me.

They were similar to the swords I had been honing that were now resting on the bench. I asked the man behind me what they were, and he replied, "These swords are for you, Kevin."

I looked more closely at the two swords, and each one had a single word written on it.

The first one said *resolve* and the second *enmity.*

I recognized the man with me as God, and He said to me, "I gave you the first sword, Kevin, the day you decided to rise up and resolve once and for all that I am good. I gave you the second when you rose up with a holy, violent enmity to love what I love and to hate what I hate. From this day forward, resolve will be your anchor and enmity will be used by you to heal and protect. Wield them carefully, and prepare to reorient!"

Hence, my charge to you, reader.

The words contained in this book were not written for me. They were written for you. They are your "swords"!

Each word explored in this book is a two-edged sword, in the sense of having dual purpose. Each can be used to cut down or to heal and restore. In the years I have spent immersed in this work, I have done my best to hone each one to a fine edge in order to make it more effective in your hands and more powerful to do both.

Because these words are also God's words, when wielded properly they possess the supernatural power to give you superhuman ability. They can cut down and destroy anything that rises up against the knowledge of God's love and His ultimate desire to heal and restore you, your family, and those entrusted to your care in every realm of life where He has called you to administer His will on earth – just as it is in heaven.

Let the uprising begin!

Until it's finished,

What if nothing was impossible

And what Jesus said was true,

That we could do greater works

Than even He could do?

PRELUDE TO
– GREATER WORKS –
Lyrics by Kevin Weaver It's Feasible Publishing, LLC

Download the complete lyrics and an .mp3 version of this
song in its entirety at www.thereorientbook.com.

Brandon,

So proud of
Excited to see
future holds!

resilient journey

you man
what your

Enjoy you
g !  Disciple up!

Kenn

10.18.12

**101**

# LOVE

# What's your REACTION to the word?

⊕ Positive

⊖ Negative

◎ Neutral

# What does the word MEAN TO YOU?

_____

_____

_____

_____

_____

_____

_____

_____

_____

Now let's see what others say. ▶

The way people surveyed
reacted to the word LOVE.

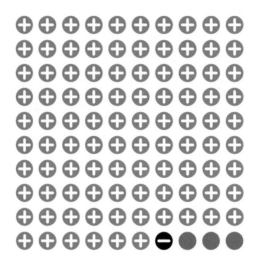

96.74%
Positive

00.36%
Negative

02.89%
Neutral

See a video of respondants in the Resource section for this chapter at www.reorientbook.com.

IAW

Common words people surveyed
associated with the word LOVE.

CARING MYSTERIOUS
MAKES SMART PEOPLE STUPID
A FLEETING EMOTION
GIVING HARD TO GRASP
STRONG FEELINGS
OVERUSED AND MISUNDERSTOOD
KINDNESS
FAMILY
UNCONTROLLABLE
GOOD
UNPREDICTABLE
NON JUDGMENTAL
EVERYONE NEEDS IT
SEX

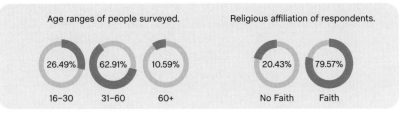

Age ranges of people surveyed.

26.49%  62.91%  10.59%

16–30    31–60    60+

Religious affiliation of respondents.

20.43%  79.57%

No Faith   Faith

# LOVE_REDISCOVER

## OLD TESTAMENT HEBREW WORDS FOR LOVE

USED    *More than 200 times*

WORD    AHAB */ah´-hab/*

DEFINITION    *To have strong affection for, beloved or friendship, to like*

---

## NEW TESTAMENT GREEK WORDS FOR LOVE

USED    *More than 280 times*

WORDS    PHILEO */fil-eh´-o/*
STORGE */stor´-jay/*
EROS */air´-ose/*
AGAPAO or AGAPE */uh-gah-pay/*

DEFINITIONS    **Phileo:** *Friendship or brotherly type affection*
**Storge:** *Natural type affection*
**Eros:** *Erotic type or sensual affection*
**Agapao** *or* **agape:** *A good will or charitable "God" kind of love*

# LOVE__RECOUNT

# LOVE

## OLD TESTAMENT VERSES USING THE HEBREW WORD

202

## NEW TESTAMENT VERSES USING THE GREEK WORD

237

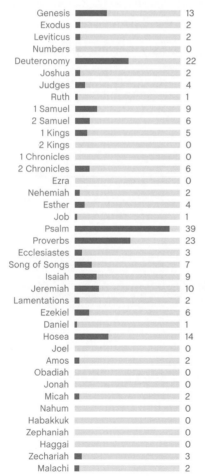

|  |  |
|---|---|
| Genesis | 13 |
| Exodus | 2 |
| Leviticus | 2 |
| Numbers | 0 |
| Deuteronomy | 22 |
| Joshua | 2 |
| Judges | 4 |
| Ruth | 1 |
| 1 Samuel | 9 |
| 2 Samuel | 6 |
| 1 Kings | 5 |
| 2 Kings | 0 |
| 1 Chronicles | 0 |
| 2 Chronicles | 6 |
| Ezra | 0 |
| Nehemiah | 2 |
| Esther | 4 |
| Job | 1 |
| Psalm | 39 |
| Proverbs | 23 |
| Ecclesiastes | 3 |
| Song of Songs | 7 |
| Isaiah | 9 |
| Jeremiah | 10 |
| Lamentations | 2 |
| Ezekiel | 6 |
| Daniel | 1 |
| Hosea | 14 |
| Joel | 0 |
| Amos | 2 |
| Obadiah | 0 |
| Jonah | 0 |
| Micah | 2 |
| Nahum | 0 |
| Habakkuk | 0 |
| Zephaniah | 0 |
| Haggai | 0 |
| Zechariah | 3 |
| Malachi | 2 |

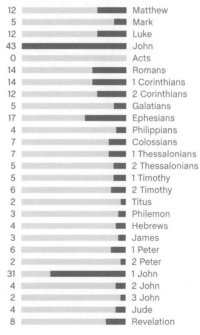

|  |  |
|---|---|
| 12 | Matthew |
| 5 | Mark |
| 12 | Luke |
| 43 | John |
| 0 | Acts |
| 14 | Romans |
| 14 | 1 Corinthians |
| 12 | 2 Corinthians |
| 5 | Galatians |
| 17 | Ephesians |
| 4 | Philippians |
| 7 | Colossians |
| 7 | 1 Thessalonians |
| 5 | 2 Thessalonians |
| 5 | 1 Timothy |
| 6 | 2 Timothy |
| 2 | Titus |
| 3 | Philemon |
| 4 | Hebrews |
| 3 | James |
| 6 | 1 Peter |
| 2 | 2 Peter |
| 31 | 1 John |
| 4 | 2 John |
| 2 | 3 John |
| 4 | Jude |
| 8 | Revelation |

*Graph is based on the highest verse use and shown visually as a percentage of the highest value.

# LOVE__REORIENT

When you hear the word *love,* what do you think about?

In a recent survey we conducted, more than ninety-seven percent of the people responding had a very positive impression of the word *love,* and the other three percent were neutral. Only one person had a negative impression of the word *love.* As our survey indicates, *love* is not as controversial or contentious a word as some of the others in this book that require our reorientation. However, it may be the most misappropriated.

Even in so-called religious circles, where love is a central theme, people rarely relate to or use the word the way the Bible actually does.

The word *love* is so commonly used in society that most people have become completely desensitized to it. We:

*Love* you!

Wonder if you *love* me?

Are certain we *love* it!

Write *love* songs,

And *love* letters,

Have *love* affairs,

Fall in *love,*

Sometimes, head over heels in *love,*

But then we may fall out of *love,*

Because we were looking for *love* in all the wrong places[1]

Or maybe we did it only for the *love* of money,

The *love* of Pete,

Or just as a labor of *love,*

So we protest for free *love,*

End up living in a *love* shack, baby,[2]

And feeling like *love* bites,[3]

Or *love* hurts,[4]

Leaving us to wonder if people are feeling the *love,*

But since all is fair in *love* and war

We decide to do it all for *love,*

Because, after all, we all need *love,*

And, in the end, *love* is all we need![5]

> " *If love is the answer, can you please rephrase the question?* "
>
> – LILY TOMLIN –

People use the word *love* ubiquitously nowadays to describe everything from their feelings about pizza to their children.

One respondent even defined *love* as "that mysterious thing that makes even really smart people do insanely stupid things."

For a lot of people, love is thought of as a fleeting emotion that comes and goes mysteriously and is as uncontrollable and unpredictable as the wind.

However, despite all the mystery and misapplication surrounding our modern-day usage of the word *love*, it unquestionably remains an essential and extremely important one. It may be even the most important word as it pertains to matters relating to God. Love – and specifically *agape* love – may qualify as the most important word in this book.

**RECONSIDER**

Fun with *love* word usages:[6]

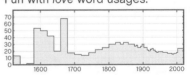

Word frequency usage from 1539 to 2007 in occurrences per 100,000 words per year

Phone Digits: (...) ... -5683
Anagram(s): vole
Scrabble Score: 7

NJW

That's partly because *agape* love is the filter, or lens, through which we must view all other notions related to God, His thoughts, and His intent for all creation and mankind.

Without first applying the lens of *agape* love, we simply cannot see God clearly, nor will we be able to correctly discern His heart, His very nature, His words, or His precepts.

Understanding the meaning of *agape* love has changed the way I see God. It changed the way I interpret His plans for my life. It changed the way I talk, the way I act, and the way I strategize every business venture.

I am now convinced that *agape* love alone, when acted upon fully, has the supernatural power to transform me, you, entire households, cities, nations, and the world as we know it!

*Agape* love, in our reoriented understanding, is the greatest force that has ever been unleashed with sufficient power to liberate mankind and is the greatest weapon ever given that, when wielded properly, has the power to transform the world for a higher kind of good.

To see why, however, and to begin to reorient, we first have to make a key distinction.

## ALL LOVE IS NOT CREATED EQUAL

**RECONSIDER**
*Agapao* or *agape* love: the primary New Testament word used in the context of God and His relationship with mankind.

All forms and expressions of love are good and fit for a purpose, but all love is not created equal.

*Agape* love is special. It has many unique characteristics that set it apart from all other forms of love and infuses it with a supernatural power that other forms of love simply don't possess.

The meaning of the Hebrew word *ahab* is fairly straightforward.

In essence, the Hebrew Old Testament definition of *love* means "to have strong affection for" something or someone.

However, when translating the word *love* from the Greek language, used in the Greek language, to English, things get much more intriguing.

Consider how the modern dictionary defines *love:*

**Love**
*noun*
1. a profoundly tender, passionate affection for another person
2. a feeling of personal attachment or deep affection, as for a parent, child, or friend
3. sexual passion or desire
4. a person toward whom love is felt; beloved person; sweetheart
5. (used in direct address as a term of endearment, affection, or the like): *Would you like to see a movie, love?*

The Greek language is more precise in its definitions and its subsequent use and application of the word *love*. The Greek language uses four specific words to express four specific kinds or expressions of love.

The first Greek word sometimes translated *love* is *phileo*. It means "a kind expression, or to have a brotherly type of affection for something." You may recognize this original Greek word as the modern-day root of the word for the city we call Philadelphia (which literally means "the city of brotherly love"). *Phileo* love is the kind of love you might have for a brother, sister, or close friend.

The second Greek word sometimes translated *love* is *storge*. A *storge* type love means "to have a natural affection or innate fondness for something." You might consider the kind of affection we naturally have for a good, long nap on a Sunday afternoon or a hot drink on a crisp, fall day.

The third Greek word sometimes translated *love* is *eros*. As you might guess, *eros* love implies a kind of "erotic or sensual love" and is the word from which we derive our modern word *erotic*.

The fourth Greek word translated *love* is where things get really exciting and meaningful for our purposes – *agape*.

*Agape* is unique and rarely used outside the Bible, but is the predominant Greek word for *love* used in the New Testament. It's also critical to note that *agape* is the only word for *love* used in the context of describing God, His intent and motivations, and especially His love toward people. *Agape* love is also the kind of love God says we are to have for all people, whether they are friends or enemies.

*Agape* love – God's kind of love – is an action word meaning:

> " *The kind of love that is always contending for the highest possible good in every situation and relentlessly contending until it's a present-tense reality!* "

Pause here.

Seriously. Don't rush past this definition.

Read it a few times if you have to.

Read it until you can quote it verbatim.

OK. Have you got it?

Why am I making such a big deal of this? Because, as you are about to see, this definition is absolutely essential for everything else requiring our reorientation in this book. Miss this definition of *love* and you will severely limit what you can receive from this book – and receive from God.

Get this, and I assure you there will be no limit to either.

This kind of love is not only the primary word and definition for love to which we are going to reorient in this chapter, but also the filter we will use to reconsider and reorient to the real meanings of every other word in this book.

So, what makes this kind of love so unique? For one thing, it's the only type of love considered to be entirely *selfless* and a *willful* choice. In contrast, all other types of love – *phileo, storge,* and *eros* – are not inherently willful or selfless, but rather involuntary reactions, reflexes, compulsions, or responses to other kinds of stimuli.

While other types of love simply cannot exist apart from the stimuli used to create them, *agape* love can.

Because of this characteristic, unlike other forms of love, there is not much chance the *agape* kind of love will ever be produced involuntarily or by random happenstance.

These characteristics make *agape* love the willful, intentional, and conscious decision to contend for the highest possible good in every situation and to keep contending until it's a present-tense reality, irrespective of feelings, emotions, or any natural instincts to the contrary.

That's why I like to call *agape* love the *choicest* of all loves – not only because it is the best of the best when it comes to love, but because it cannot exist apart from my *choice* to unleash it.

What's makes this choice attribute so liberating is that it means *agape* love can then exist apart from all outside stimuli and can be relied upon to produce itself any time, any place, and under any circumstance. Ironically, even though the choice nature of *agape* love makes it completely independent of all other things, many times choosing *agape* love is hard and seems to be a very *unnatural* choice.

The good news, however, is that because it's most often produced in such unnatural ways, it has the power to yield unnatural results – even "super" natural results and realities – when exercised effectively.

This unique ability *agape* love has to exist and continue to work outside the realm of human feelings, emotions, or dependence on other outside factors makes it an unshakable foundation that we and God can build upon.

When wielded with unwavering resolve, it also becomes an unstoppable force with the power to transform any life, any circumstance, and, ultimately, the world as we know it for a higher kind of good. Our ability to choose to contend for and obtain *agape* love in any circumstance is a uniquely human trait that separates us from every other created thing on Planet Earth.

For example, animals, as loving as they can be, cannot willingly produce it. Animals can obviously demonstrate a strong affectionate type of love, but they lack the capacity to override their natural instincts and reactionary impulses to withhold their affection or even become hostile – especially when confronted by a perceived enemy.

Our capacity to choose *agape* love, regardless of the circumstances, sets us apart from all other living things and gives us access to a kind of love and its results that is far superior to every other form of love.

## A MORE EXCELLENT WAY

My insistence that the reoriented meaning of love holds the solution to a list of perceived crises the global church is facing was met skeptically by one church leader.

He told me, "Son, your *love* thing is an idyllic notion, but we already had the love and peace movement. In the United States, it was called the seventies, and unfortunately, you missed it because of your age. Love is important, no doubt, but as a practical method for social transformation, it failed then and it won't work now."

To the leader's surprise, I actually agreed. In fact, that's my point exactly. While the love movement in the seventies emphasized a certain kind of love, it was not an *agape* love movement. And because it was not an *agape* love movement, it lacked the power to produce the highest kind of good we can think or imagine and the transcendent change that *agape,* love's ideal, promises it will deliver.

Thousands of years of so-called religious tradition and other well-intended philosophies of mankind have simply failed to produce and sustain the higher kind of good on a mass scale that all of us instinctively know is possible and which only *agape* love – the "more excellent way" – makes possible.

People get nervous when someone starts emphasizing love as the primary means of real and lasting transformation. They are afraid that too much emphasis on the love of God will lead to unconstrained behavior without proper standards – ultimately, lawlessness. That can certainly be true if *agape* love is administered sloppily. But in actuality, God says real *agape* love can constrain bad behavior without the need for external enforcements:

> The *agape* love of Christ **constrains ‹some translations say "controls"›** us.
> ~ *2 Corinthians 5:14*, WEB, ‹*emphasis added*›

This should be encouraging for every parent, teacher, leader, and those in law enforcement and the government looking for more efficient, effective, and inexpensive ways to constrain bad behavior. *Agape* love, as a method of law enforcement, while not easy to master or to choose to administer, is sure cheaper than building and staffing prisons.

When administered properly, *agape* love can be a huge supernatural force, all-encompassing in its implications and ability to not only constrain, but transform. In addition to calling *agape* love "the more excellent way", God goes as far as to guarantee that *agape* love, when done excellently, will never fail. He even says that every *law* or *precept* He ever prescribed for mankind in the entire Bible can be summed up and fulfilled by simply exercising *agape* love. In other words, if a person masters this one thing – *agape* love – they get credit for doing all the rest of His commandments by default. The traditional notions of so-called ministry gifts, like appointing apostles, prophets, teachers, pastors, preachers, and evangelists  or the working of miracles are secondary, less excellent methods when compared to the pursuit and mastery of *agape* love:

> *Now ye are the body of Christ, and members in particular. And God hath set some in the church, first apostles,*

*secondarily prophets, thirdly teachers, after that miracles, then gifts of healings, helps, governments, diversities of tongues. Are all apostles? are all prophets? are all workers of miracles? have all the gifts of healing? do all speak with tongues? do all interpret? But ‹covet› earnestly the best gifts: and yet shew I unto you a more excellent way.*
~ *1 Corinthians 12:27–31,* KJV, ‹**emphasis added**›

Notice how it says we should covet *agape* love! It's the only place in the Bible I know that God actually says to covet something. *Covet* is a strong word, and since coveting is generally not something God encouraged people to do, this notion of *agape* love must really be important.

There are hundreds of places in the Bible where God tells why *agape* love is so excellent. You wouldn't be exaggerating to say the entire book, the Bible, is actually an *agape* love story, despite how it may have been portrayed or wielded as a weapon to the contrary throughout the centuries.

Let me share twenty of my favorite passages relating to *agape* love. Before we consider them, though, I would like to suggest a reorienting strategy that helps to eliminate some of the traditional dogmas and biases that might exist in our minds around these verses. It's a simple approach and one we will use for every word we will be reorienting to in this book.

When reading each verse, read it through completely, from beginning to end – out loud, if possible. If this is not an option, at a minimum, try speaking the words silently to yourself as you read. Once you have done that, start from the beginning and reread the verse, but substitute the word *love* with the actual definition for *agape* love to which we just reoriented ourselves.

To the extent you believe the Bible is God's inspired words as spoken through man, this approach will help you better resonate with His inspiration behind the words, the actual tone and voice God intended each verse to carry.

For a little practice run, try it, using what is unarguably the most famous verse in the Bible, John 3:16:

> For God so loved the world that he gave his one and only
> Son, that whoever believes in him shall not perish but have
> eternal life.

Now, here is the same verse but with the actual definition of the word
*agape* love included and definitions of other key words expanded in
brackets for emphasis.

> For God so loved ‹**always contends for the highest kind
> of good in every situation and relentlessly contends until
> it's a present-tense reality**› the world that he gave his
> one and only Son, that whoever believes ‹**fully convinced,
> completely persuaded and have confidence**› in him shall
> not perish ‹**be destitute or have a loss in their well-being**›
> but have eternal life ‹**perpetual super abundant life now
> and forever**›.

Isn't that awesome? Isn't John 3:16 much more rich and powerful when
you consider the actual meaning of *agape* love in the context of the
verse? The next time you are watching a sporting event and you see
someone holding up the seemingly obligatory John 3:16 sign, you may
think differently about the implications!

So, with this "substitute the actual meaning and reorient" strategy
fresh in our minds, let's take a look at the top twenty reasons (starting
first with the verse we just used as our sample) about why God says
*agape* love is the more excellent way.

Remember, read each verse from start to finish, and then read it again,
replacing the word *love* with the reoriented definition of *agape* love.
*Agape* love:

> *always contends for the highest possible good in every situation and relentlessly contends until it's a present-tense reality!*

*Note: Wherever you see the word agape in all following verses, it was included by me for emphasis and was not part of the original English version of the text. Likewise, all other notations, while biblically accurate, added or emphasized by me are noted as such.*

## TWENTY REASONS, VERSES, AND BRIEF EXPLANATIONS WHY AGAPE LOVE IS MORE EXCELLENT

1. *Agape* love is God's ultimate and only motive.

   *For God so loved the world that He gave his one and only Son, that whoever believes in him shall not perish but have eternal life ‹**God kind of life**›.*

   *~ John 3:16*

   God's only motivation and intent for this planet and all it contains is *agape* love's ideal. It's the force behind everything He thinks, intends, does, provides, and requires. He even went to the greatest length imaginable to make the kind of life it could produce available to anyone who would believe in it!

2. God is *agape* love.

   *He who does not ‹**agape**› love has not become acquainted with God [does not and never did know Him], for God is ‹**agape**› love.*

   *~ 1 John 4:8, AMP*

   Did you know the word for God and the word *agape* in the Bible can be used interchangeably? In other words, if it's not *agape* love, it can't be God, and vice versa. It also says that a person has never known and cannot come to know Him apart from knowing *agape* love.

3. *Agape* love is an order, not a mere suggestion.

*A new ‹**second**› command ‹**order or prescription**› I give you: ‹**Agape**› love one another. As I have ‹**agape**› loved you, so you must ‹**agape**› love one another. By this all men will know that you are my disciples, if you ‹**agape**› love one another.*

*~ John 13:34–35*

We are actually ordered to *agape* love each other by Jesus Himself! This is not a mere *suggestion* for us to follow if we feel up to it, but an *order* – the primary prescription from the commander-in-chief Himself. He even goes so far as to say our *agape* love for each other is how the world will know we are His followers. Notice it does not say others would know we are of God by our church attendance, scriptural knowledge, theological beliefs, high moral standards, opposition to low moral standards, or even our Christian paraphernalia, like our WWJD (What Would Jesus Do) bracelets or the little *ichthus* fish symbol on our cars. It's only by our ability to do *agape* love.

4.  *Agape* love is the greatest of all commandments.

*‹**Agape**› love the Lord your God with all your heart and with all your soul and with all your mind. This is the first and greatest commandment. And the second is like it: ‹**Agape**› love your neighbor ‹**those close to you**› as yourself. All the Law and the Prophets hang on these two commandments.*

*~ Matthew 22:37–40*

Not only did Jesus say that we are to "do" and "be" *agape* love to the world, He said that every other precept contained in God's commandments hangs its entire weight on this one thing. In other words, you could get this right – perfecting *agape* love for God, others, and yourself – without even possessing knowledge of another single commandment and still fulfill every other commandment of God's by default. At least for me, that greatly simplifies things. I just want to scream out, "Yes, I can do this!"

5.  *Agape* love is light, as in the opposite of heavy.

*This is ‹**agape**› love for God: to obey his commands ‹**prescripts
or favors**›. And his commands are not burdensome.*

*~ 1 John 5:3*

Even God's most direct commandments, the Ten Commandments
in the Old Testament, were not meant to be harsh or heavy, but
rather liberating and light "prescriptions or favors" that allow us
to overcome and obtain *agape* love's ideal.

6. *Agape* love is more valuable and profitable than any other spiritual
gift we can pursue.

*If I [can] speak in the tongues of men and [even] of angels, but
have not ‹**agape**› love (that reasoning, intentional, spiritual devo-
tion such as is inspired by God's love for and in us), I am only a
noisy gong or a clanging cymbal. And if I have prophetic powers
(the gift of interpreting the divine will and purpose), and understand all the secret truths and mysteries and possess all knowledge, and if I have [sufficient] faith so that I can remove mountains, but have not ‹**agape**› love (God's love in me) I am nothing
(a useless nobody). Even if I dole out all that I have [to the poor
in providing] food, and if I surrender my body to be burned or in
order that I may glory, but have not ‹**agape**› love (God's love in
me), I gain nothing.*

*~ 1 Corinthians 13:1–3,* AMP

That verse says it all. If you really want to impress God, hone your
*agape* love skills above all else. All other rhetoric is noise. Spiritual
gifts, divine wisdom, and impressive faith without *agape* love are
nothing. All seemingly noble acts of service and acts worthy of
glory are nothing if not done with *agape* love as the motive. I think
what terrifies me most is that these things are apparently possible
to pursue and achieve with a different motive entirely.

7. *Agape* love is the only thing God says to covet.

*Eagerly pursue ‹**covet**› and seek to acquire [this] ‹**agape**› love
[make it your aim, your great quest]; and earnestly desire and
cultivate the spiritual endowments (gifts), especially that you*

*may prophesy (interpret the divine will and purpose in inspired preaching and teaching).*

*~ 1 Corinthians 14:1,* AMP

Remember, no other place in the Bible does God suggest, approve of, or command humans to have such a strong desire to eagerly pursue or even covet something. Even in the Ten Commandments, He said, "Don't covet." Yet, *agape* love is to be coveted as the primary spiritual gift we are to pursue. It is what we are to make our ultimate aim or greatest quest.

8. *Agape* love is the one thing we owe every human.

*Keep out of debt and owe no man anything, except to ‹**agape**› love one another; for he who ‹**agape**› loves his neighbor [who practices loving others] has fulfilled the Law [relating to one's fellowmen, meeting all its requirements]. ‹**Agape**› love does no wrong to one's neighbor [it never hurts anybody]. Therefore ‹**agape**› love meets all the requirements and is the fulfilling of the Law.*

*~ Romans 13:8, 10,* AMP

You may be thinking, "Really, every human? Is that even possible?" Relax. Loving someone, or, more specifically, contending for the highest possible good for someone in every situation, doesn't mean you have to agree with everyone, trust everyone without reason, or accept everything about everybody – even those who are not striving to be most excellent. But you still are expected and, as painful as it may seem, capable of loving them!

9. *Agape* love causes God to manifest Himself to us.

*Whoever [really] ‹**agape**› loves Me will be ‹**agape**› loved by My Father, and I [too] will ‹**agape**› love him and will show (reveal, manifest) Myself to him. [I will let Myself be clearly seen by him and make Myself real to him.]*

*~ John 14:21,* AMP

Spend a moment contemplating this verse. Have you ever wanted to see God and have God manifest Himself to you personally? For everyone who's ever desired this – here is the key. Engage in the practice of actually *doing agape* love, and God promises to personally manifest, exhibit, or make Himself clearly visible to you!

10. Doing *agape* love compels others to think differently.

*God's kindness is intended to lead you to repent (to change your mind and inner man to accept God's will).*

*~ Romans 2:4,* AMP

Doing *agape* love and demonstrating goodness and kindness-causes others to repent or think differently about the reality of God and His nature. Notice it doesn't say it's our ability to win a debate about the reality of God or it's our definitions of what we are for or against. It's not the fear of God's eternal judgment or even the threat of punishment that makes people repent or think differently about God. It's the literal demonstration of *agape* love's goodness. The person who inspires the most love will always have the most influence.

11. *Agape* love is the key to never being separated from God again.

*Who shall ever separate us from Christ's ‹**agape**› love? Shall suffering and affliction and tribulation? Or calamity and distress? Or persecution or hunger or destitution or peril or sword? ... Yet amid all these things we are more than conquerors and gain a surpassing victory through Him Who ‹**agape**› loved us. ... Nor height nor depth, nor anything else in all creation will be able to separate us from the ‹**agape**› love of God which is in Christ Jesus our Lord.*

*~ Romans 8:35, 37, 39,* AMP

When you are in *agape* love, you never have to doubt if you are on God's side. You can be confident and are guaranteed to be on God's side in every situation, if you are doing *agape* love! It's like supernatural glue that makes you immovable, unshakable, and completely unable to be separated from God by anyone or anything on earth or in heaven.

12. *Agape* love is the key to obtaining fullness of joy.

*If you have any encouragement from being united with Christ, if any comfort from his ‹**agape**› love, if any fellowship with the Spirit,* *if any tenderness and compassion, then make my joy complete by being like-minded, having the same ‹agape› love, being one in spirit and purpose.*

*~ Philippians 2:1–2*

Do you want to be truly unified with people and experience real joy? Better yet, do you want so much joy you are too full to have any more? I know I do. This text says that perfecting *agape* love is the key to us having the fullness of joy, to becoming fully alive with supernatural joy! And if the Bible is true when it says this kind of *agape* love – inspired joy – is our strength (Neh. 8:10), then not having *agape* love – inspired joy – causes us to be in a weakened condition!

13. *Agape* love was the goal of what we now call "church" gatherings.

*And let us consider how we may spur one another on toward ‹agape› love and good deeds. Let us not give up meeting together, as some are in the habit of doing, but let us encourage one another – and all the more as you see the Day approaching.*

*~ Hebrews 10:24–25*

Stirring up *agape* love and good works was to be the goal of church gatherings (We will reorient to the word *church* in a later chapter.). In fact, some church gatherings in Jesus' time were called *"agape* love feasts". The plural of the word *agape* in the Greek New Testament was sometimes translated "love feasts" instead of *love* (Jude 1:12).

14. *Agape* love is actually what makes faith work!

*For in Christ Jesus neither circumcision nor uncircumcision has any value. The only thing that counts is faith expressing itself through ‹agape› love.*

*~ Galatians 5:6*

Neither ritual observances and practices, nor symbols of our faith are the important thing. And even though we become completely persuaded, fully convinced, and have total confidence in every principle of God, it's not until our confidence is combined with *agape* love that faith actually works as God intended.

15. *Agape* love makes everything work together for our good.

> *And we know that in all things God works for the good of those who ‹**agape**› love him, who have been called according to his purpose.*
>
> *~ Romans 8:28*

Things may not always go "most excellently" in our lives. But as we contend for *agape* love's ideal, persisting even when things fall short, God – *who is agape love Himself* – will never cease to keep contending for and working *all* things for *our good* until *agape* love's ideal is a present-tense reality in our lives.

16. *Agape* love eliminates all fear.

> *There is no fear in ‹**agape**› love. But perfect ‹**agape**› love drives out fear, because fear has to do with punishment. The one who fears is not made perfect in ‹**agape**› love.*
>
> *~ 1 John 4:18*

When we choose fear, we undermine the supernatural power of *agape* love to make things perfect – we get fear's desire for us and not *agape* love's desire. Do you want to be fearless? Do you want to live in complete confidence, with power and a sound mind? Do you want to live in a constant state of peace and security? Well, God says that perfecting *agape* love makes all that possible.

17. *Agape* love causes us to become fully mature.

> *Instead, speaking the truth in ‹**agape**› love, we will in all things grow up into him who is the Head, that is, Christ.*
>
> *~ Ephesians 4:15*

I know that being mature may not sound all that exciting, depending on your age, but this notion of maturity is different. It is not related to age, but, rather, carries the notion of becoming whole and not lacking anything – to the extent of being conformed to the very image of Jesus Christ! This notion of maturity, God says, is the inevitable result of learning to speak the truth in a way that *agape* love would speak.

18. Where there is *agape* love, God can rule in peace.

*Aim for perfection, listen to my appeal, be of one mind, live in peace. And the God of ‹**agape**› love and peace will be with you ‹**will rule**›.*

*~ 2 Corinthians 13:11*

A person can't obtain or operate in this kind of *agape* love apart from God. But where we aim for this kind of *agape* love the highest rule of law, God is able to operate with us and rule completely in peace.

19. *Agape* love is the "most excellent way".

*And in the church God has appointed first of all apostles, second prophets, third teachers, then workers of miracles, also those having gifts of healing, those able to help others, those with gifts of administration, and those speaking in different kinds of tongues. ... But eagerly desire the greater gifts. And now I will show you the most excellent way ‹**agape love**›.*

*~ 1 Corinthians 12:28, 31*

Above all other spiritual gifts to be desired, spiritual talents and skills to be honed, or things of life to be pursued, *agape* love is the most excellent way.

20. This kind of love never fails!

*‹**Agape**› love never fails ‹**never fades away, can't be driven out or become ineffective or inefficient**›. But where there are prophecies, they will cease; where there are tongues, they will be stilled; where there is knowledge, it will pass away.*

*~ 1 Corinthians 13:8*

*Agape* love has never failed, will never fail. *Agape* love provides the power to defeat any kind of enemy, prevail in any situation, and overcome any obstacle. Even if it doesn't appear that way at a given point in time, with enough time, it never fails in the end! In a world of uncertainty, *agape* love is certain, and all those who master it are transcendent.

What a list! And these examples are by no means the entirety of what the Bible has to say on this topic. Remember, the Bible refers to the *agape* type of love more than 280 times in total.

The topic of *agape* love and the supernatural power behind the word simply cannot be discussed in a single chapter. I could easily dedicate a whole book to this topic alone.

At a minimum, we must see that *agape* love is the primary filter we must apply when endeavoring to understand God and His thoughts and intent behind the words He uses. It's the primary force behind real change for a higher kind of good.

After all, think about what the Bible says about God:

> *In the beginning was the Word, and the Word was with God, and the Word was God.*
>
> ~ *John 1:1*

And, as we've already established, it also says:

> *God is ‹**agape**› love.*
>
> ~ *1 John 4:8*

If both of these are true, then we should never separate the notions of God, His Word, and *agape* love from each other. The three are one and the same. In other words:

## God = Love = God's Word

That is why it's essential to first reorient our thinking to this God kind of love before endeavoring to reorient to God or any other word used in the context of God, especially the ones we will consider in this book.

*Agape* love is the ultimate issue behind all things and the more excellent way because God is the ultimate issue behind all things and is the way!

It's interesting to note that the Greek word translated "way," in each verse that describes *agape* love as the more excellent way, literally means "a road, a way forward, a means to navigate or mode to act."

*Agape* love is the mortar that holds everything together.

*Agape* love is the way,

the pattern,

the plumb line,

the measuring stick,

the first standard,

the chief cornerstone we must use to measure everything else against.

Let's look at one last reason why this kind of love is so fantastically extraordinary. It is so significant and so powerful that I wanted to separate it out on its own.

This final attribute turns *agape* love into a transformational force of nuclear proportions – a head-crushing force against everything that would endeavor to raise its ugly head against *agape* love's ideal. It is why I like to refer to *agape* love as "the bomb"!

## AGAPE LOVE AND THE POWER OF ENMITY

*Agape* love is the empowering force behind enmity, which is the first and most powerful weapon God initially gave mankind to reverse the state of all things evil.

To reorient to the word *enmity* – to understand its power and its relationship to *agape* love – let's go to the first place it appears in the Bible:

> *And the Lord God said to the serpent, Because you have done this, you are cursed above all [domestic] animals and above every [wild] living thing of the field; upon your belly you shall go, and you*

CORNERSTONE
is the bonus word we
discuss in the free
video download in
the online resource
section for this book!

*shall eat dust [and what it contains] all the days of your life. And I will put **enmity** between you and the woman, and between your offspring and her Offspring; He will bruise and tread your head underfoot, and you will lie in wait and only bruise His heel.*
*~ Genesis 3:14–15, AMP, **emphasis added***

A couple of things are noteworthy about this verse. The context is moments after Adam and Eve's big stumble in the Garden of Eden. God has just explained to Adam and Eve the consequences of their actions and the less-than-excellent results they can now expect going forward unless they correct their course.

God then turns His attention to His and our enemy (the serpent in this verse we just read), and in no uncertain terms, He tells the enemy what he can expect because of what he did. Notice what God says:

*Because you have done this ... I will put **enmity** between you and the woman, and between your offspring and her Offspring.*

Notice how the enemy's big punishment for the deception he just pulled off on Adam and Eve and the trouble it caused is, among other things, his future crushing at the hands of this thing called *enmity*.

God even goes so far as to ensure enmity is an ever-present force by putting it in Adam and Eve and every child (offspring) born of a woman thereafter. Also notice what enmity is designed to empower people to do: to bruise and tread upon the enemy's head while the enemy lies in wait and can only bruise the offspring's heel! Some translations actually say we will "crush" the enemy's head, while he can only bruise our heels. For what it's worth, I like *crush* better!

So, moments after this traumatic event, God puts this thing called enmity in all mankind as a weapon to remedy and to reverse the effects of what just happened. God also ensures enmity is available for all future generations as a force to crush every form of evil any time it raises its ugly head!

So, what is enmity? The word *enmity* means "a violent hostility" or "the strongest kind of hatred" that mankind can generate. It's synonymous with the word *enemy* and it's the direct opposite of the word *agape!*

It may seem shocking and maybe even contradictory to everything we have just learned about *agape* love to have God, who is *agape* love, put the direct opposite of *agape* love – *hate* – in us to be used as the greatest weapon against our enemy.

For most of my life, even the thought of being angry seemed ungodly, let alone permitting myself to be *violently angry* or downright *hostile* toward anything or anyone. If something bad happened to me or around me, my first thought was usually anger toward other people, and sometimes toward myself, but then ultimately toward God for letting it happen. Ironically, I never felt anger toward a spiritual enemy, even after I discovered that one actually existed and wasn't just metaphorical.

Can you relate? Have you ever been really angry when bad things happened to you or others? As a result, have you said or heard others say, "Why would a good God allow such a horrible thing to happen?"

Have you ever wondered why it is that we get angry at God, people, ourselves, or even circumstances before ever getting angry at the enemy, whom the Bible clearly says exists and is the father of all evil?

Natural disasters are called "acts of God", which society readily accepts there is no insurance against! If we were to go by most news reports and accepted social rhetoric, God seems to get all the blame when things go disastrously wrong, but rarely even gets an honorable mention during uneventful times or seasons of peace and prosperity.

In times likes these, enmity, which God actually designed to crush evil, gets redirected at Him, at people, at circumstances, or anywhere else but where it was intended: squarely on evil itself!

Most people don't know it, but unintelligently hating and improperly attributing blame as a result actually disempowers the full effect of the supernatural power of *agape* love. It's a phenomenon that can be to blame for most of the evil that is permitted to exist.

I would go so far as to say that *agape* love without an equal amount of enmity for what is not *agape* love, is prevented from having its intended effect. You simply can't do either one (properly love or properly hate) without doing both equally well!

Compounding the problem is the fact that we all have enmity in us from birth. It was put there by God, so we can't get rid of it, even if we tried! The best attempts to ignore it or suppress it are futile, and yet, improperly expressing it can be harmful, not to mention evil or illegal.

The good news is that we also have *agape* love in us! When it's properly combined with enmity, it can be a crushing force of nuclear proportions on all that's evil in the world. They were designed to work together and in conjunction with each other, not independent of each other. The key is learning to live comfortably within the tension between the two and learning to exercise both equally well.

*Agape* love and enmity are like two sides of the same coin. One side is designed to permit and release the highest kind of good (love's ideal) and the other side is designed to violently resist and disallow anything that's evil or falls short of love's ideal.

Said another way, *agape* love and enmity are opposite edges of the same sword. One edge is designed to heal and preserve, and the other edge is designed to cut down and destroy.

In either metaphor, you can't have one side without the other.

You simply can't always contend for *agape* love to the fullest until you learn to intelligently hate and attribute blame – have enmity for that which is not *agape* love. It's been my experience that what we don't learn to intelligently hate or have enmity for, we will not resist fully. And what we don't hate or have enmity for, we will ultimately permit.

Think about something in your life that is resulting or has resulted in less than love's ideal for you or others you know. How do you feel about it? Do you hate it enough to refuse to permit it any longer? Do you let that hatred compel you to contend for a higher kind of good now? Or has it not risen to a level that warrants immediate action, making you willing to permit it to exist, even if it's not ideal?

To realize love's ideal, we must love and hate – we must learn to properly wield both *violent love* toward people and *violent hatred* toward evil and the enemy who creates it, both at the same time and both equally well.

This application is not an isolated notion in the Bible. We are actually commanded to love God and hate evil.

> **Love** the Lord, **hate evil;** He preserves the lives of His saints (the children of God), He delivers them out of the hand of the wicked.
>
> ~ Psalm 97:10, AMP, **emphasis added**

A key to the kingdom or realm of God (which is pure *agape* love) fully manifesting itself on earth as it is in heaven, is us doing our part to only permit or allow on earth that which is *agape* love's ideal and not to permit or allow that which is not. Check out how Jesus said it:

> And I will give to you the keys of the kingdom of the heavens, and whatever **you bind** (declare to be improper and unlawful) on the earth will have been bound in the heavens; and whatever **you loose** (declare lawful) on the earth will have been loosed in the heavens.
>
> ~ Matthew 16:19, AMP, **emphasis added**

It's our part to disallow and permit something; it's God's part to empower us and to back it up.

This kind of resistance is not meant to be passive, but an active, holy, violent, militant-style force combined with a zeal for being about love's ideal. Listen to how Jesus says it just a few chapters before the one we just read:

> And from the days of John the Baptist until the present time, the kingdom of heaven has endured **violent assault, and violent men seize it by force** [as a precious prize – a share in the heavenly kingdom is sought with most ardent zeal and intense exertion].
>
> ~ Matthew 11:12, AMP, **emphasis added**

That gets me fired up! We are to be a violent force for good and to resist evil with intense zeal and exertion.

The Bible even goes so far as to say we are to *be angry* while simultane-ously *not sinning* (a word to which we will reorient in the next chapter) and to not let the sun go down on our anger. Here is the verse:

> *Be ye angry, and sin not: let not the sun go down upon your wrath ‹**enmity or anger**›.*
>
> ~ *Ephesians 4:26,* ASV

Let me be clear. Nowhere did God say, nor am I suggesting, that *people* are ever to be the recipients or the target of this kind of enmity or violent hatred. A million times, no!

We are never told by God to hate people …

Who hate us,

Who we may not like,

With whom we might disagree,

Who don't agree with us,

Who don't talk like us,

Who don't act like us,

Who don't believe like us,

Who don't live like us.

To the contrary, these are the exact times where *agape* love will most likely need to be exercised the most.

God loves people, but hates evil because it hurts people!

This kind of holy, violent hatred was designed to be directed solely at the enemy and the evil that he produces. It's critical we know the difference; prisons are full of people who misappropriated this kind of enmity.

There are no bad people *per se,* just wounded people whom the en-emy works evil through to do really bad things. So, we are not to hate people; we are to hate and resist the evil that people do. We can love people and at the same time hate and resist the enemy who does evil through them.

The key to harnessing the power of enmity and the supernatural force of *agape* love is learning to do both at the same time and in every realm of life. Again, the key to both *agape* love and enmity is learning to intelligently hate and attribute blame while simultaneously rising up and contending for *agape* love's ideal – both at the same time!

Consider Jesus hanging on the cross in Luke 25:34, and how He asks the Father to forgive them, because they don't know what they are doing. Even though they are torturing Him, He asks for forgiveness for them because He has an agape kind of love for them. It doesn't mean He loves what they are doing. He hates it. He hates the shame of being exposed to that public torture and the shame that the people were operating in that were doing it to Him. He loves them, but He hates what they were doing to Him.

What should you say to a young woman repeatedly raped by a relative who was in church leadership, ultimately conceiving a child and being forced to have an abortion and keep everything from becoming public? She is quoted in Matt. 5:43 ("Love your enemies") and that she must forgive the perpetrator, but she is dealing with feelings of intense anger, which she believes is evidence she hasn't forgiven them for what they did.

Imagine the freedom she experienced when we she heard that not only were her feelings not evidence of unforgiveness, but the anger about what she went through was put there by God and He intended her to express it – intelligently.

Here is another way in which hatred is appropriate. Imagine my child comes to me and I know they are not being entirely truthful on a small matter, like whether they made their bed or not. To leverage the power of *agape* love and enmity at the same time, I might say something like this:

"Because I am resolved to relentlessly contend with you for the highest kind of good in this situation, I must say that I love you, honey, but I absolutely hate and will not permit lying, so stop it!"

I don't hate my child, but I hate lying. I can hate lying while simultaneously contending for the best that love has for my child.

For an example of a greater consequence, let's look at how Jesus used enmity in the New Testament account of raising Lazarus from the dead and how He uses it to subdue one of the greatest evil enemies of all time – death itself.

> Then when Mary was come where Jesus was, and saw him, she fell down at his feet, saying unto him, Lord, if thou hadst been here, my brother had not died. When Jesus therefore saw her weeping, and the Jews also weeping which came with her, **he groaned ‹was deeply troubled with indignation and anger› in the spirit, and was troubled ‹stirred and agitated›.** And said, Where have ye laid him? They said unto him, Lord, come and see. **Jesus wept. Then said the Jews, Behold how he loved him!** And some of them said, Could not this man, which opened the eyes of the blind, have caused that even this man should not have died? **Jesus therefore again groaning in himself cometh to the grave.** It was a cave, and a stone lay upon it. Jesus said, Take ye away the stone. Martha, the sister of him that was dead, saith unto him, Lord, by this time he stinketh: for he hath been dead four days. Jesus saith unto her, Said I not unto thee, that, if thou wouldest believe, thou shouldest see the glory of God? Then they took away the stone from the place where the dead was laid. And Jesus lifted up his eyes, and said, Father, I thank thee that thou hast heard me. And I knew that thou hearest me always: but because of the people which stand by I said it, that they may believe that thou hast sent me. And when he thus had spoken, he cried with a loud voice, **Lazarus, come forth.** And he that was dead came forth, bound hand and foot with graveclothes:

*and his face was bound about with a napkin. Jesus saith unto them, **Loose him, and let him go.***

~ *John 11:32–44*, KJV, ***emphasis added***

Notice how the verse says twice that Jesus groaned and was deeply troubled. The word *groaned* in this verse means "to have a strength-filled expression of anger." The word *groan* is the Greek New Testament equivalent of the word *enmity*.

Also notice that Jesus' "strength-filled expression of anger" or groaning was so intense it caused Him to weep. It was apparently so intense, He did it twice. To both believers and unbelievers around Him, this expression was identified as evidence of Jesus' love for Lazarus. Think of that – Jesus' expression of hatred was called love by those around Him.

It's hard for me to express, in writing, what this may have looked like or sounded like if we had been within range to hear or see this event unfold firsthand. Imagine the sound of a mother's guttural sob at the sight of losing a child at the scene of an accident, combined with the anger a father would feel by being forced to witness his child being violated by an adversary right before his eyes.

That's the kind of emotion Jesus is expressing here. He is simultaneously expressing His immense love for Lazarus and His violent hatred for death. You might have heard His weeping and groaning for several blocks: "MMMMMMMMMMM ... I LOVE YOU LAZARUS ... MMMMMMMMMMM ... I HATE DEATH! COME HERE! BE FREE AND UNBOUND NOW!"

What a perfect example of the combined powers of enmity and love disallowing death and restoring life to any situation. We need an uprising of people who know how to administer this kind of holy, violent love in our generation!

# LOVE__RELATE

To close this chapter and provide a simple method to relate more specifically to *agape* love's ideal and to see its power invade our individual lives and realms of influence, I would like to provide a simple strategy. Try this short exercise with me.

I am going to list a few notions in the form of a few simple questions. Most everyone has thought about, is currently thinking about, or will likely think about one or all of these questions at some point in their life.

First, read each question. Next, pick the question or questions that relate most to you right now. Here are the questions:

1. What's God's will for my life?

2. What's God's will for my job?

3. What's God's will for my health?

4. What's God's will for my finances?

5. What's God's will for my marriage?

6. What's God's will for _____? (friend or enemy)

7. What's God's answer for the _____ crisis?

8. How should I respond to _____?

9. What should I be doing about _____?

10. What's God's will for this _____ situation?

11. Or maybe there's someone you need to forgive.

Now, consider your question (with the blanks filled in where appropriate to make each question your own) and write it down in the form of a statement. This time, however, leave a blank for the definition of *agape* love.

You can do this for any question on this list and as many other questions as you like. If you have other questions not included in those I suggested, feel free to use those instead.

Here is an example, using the ninth question from my list:

**Question:**

What should I do about *that argument I just had with my friend Eric that created so much tension in that meeting?*

Now, here is the same question written in the form of a statement with a blank for *agape* love's ideal.

**Statement:**

I will *(fill in this blank with the highest kind of good I can think of or imagine could result for both me and Eric if money and time were no object and it was in my power to fix this situation)* and not allow *(insert what you want to direct enmity toward specifically in this situation)* regarding that argument I just had with my friend Eric that created so much tension in that meeting.

Now, to make room for the supernatural power of *agape* love's ideal to rule in this situation and become a reality, my part is to begin relentlessly contending in every way for the highest possible good that I just wrote in the blank for *agape* love until it's a present-tense reality. Simultaneously, it is my part to hate, resist, and disallow with holy, violent enmity anything that would endeavor to suppress *agape* love's ideal in this relationship with Eric.

That's it. That's my part. Eric may not receive my love immediately; it may take time, or he may never be receptive to love's ideal in this situation. But the good news is that if I do my part and do not grow weary in pursuing the highest good I can think of or imagine in this situation, and if I ask God for it, He promises that He is able to do exceedingly, abundantly above all that I can ask, think, or imagine, according to His power (*agape* love's power) at work within me (Eph. 3:20).

If I will do my part to intensely resist evil with my thoughts, words, and actions toward Eric, God will back it up with all heaven's authority.

Of course, this was just an example. But it doesn't matter what the question is; *agape* love has an answer. *Agape* love can show the way, and *agape* love will never fail to yield the highest kind of good, if we do our part and give enough time for it to work.

The key to seeing the highest kind of good and seeing God do exceedingly above what I can think or imagine in this situation or any situation is doing my part, to love. I must do *at least* the highest good I can think of or imagine.

If I do my part, to love in every situation, I make a way for the supernatural power of *agape* love to come invade and transform any situation.

Think about all the attributes we listed earlier. When I do my part to demonstrate *agape* love in this manner:

I have the assurance I am on God's side,

I am acting most like Him,

I am fulfilling His highest order,

I am following His greatest commandment and fulfilling all other commandments,

I am creating ideal conditions where the Spirit of God can rule,

I am creating an environment for God to manifest Himself fully,

I am creating an ideal atmosphere for God to prove Himself strong,

I am causing others to think differently,

I am empowering my faith to work fully,

I am causing everything to work together for good,

I am disallowing fear to rule,

I am maturing into the very likeness of Christ and positioning myself to have the fullness of God's joy.

By following the more excellent way of *agape* love, I have God's personal guarantee that the effort will not be in vain and will never fail!

The opposite is also true. If I don't do my part to contend for the highest good I can think of or imagine, I am not guaranteed to experience any of the above and certainly will not experience God doing exceedingly and abundantly above it. In short, I can't ever do God's part, and He simply won't do my part when it comes to love. Love always takes two!

Whether starting or running a business, starting or running a ministry, authoring a book, writing a song, speaking to an audience of one or a crowd of one hundred thousand, planning time with my wife and kids or friends or enemies, it's possible to make *agape* love's ideal my pursuit and see *agape* love do the impossible!

# LOVE__REACT

**What are the top three things you are taking away from this chapter?**

.................................................................................................

.................................................................................................

.................................................................................................

.................................................................................................

.................................................................................................

.................................................................................................

.................................................................................................

.................................................................................................

**What action can you take now on what you've learned?**

.................................................................................................

.................................................................................................

.................................................................................................

.................................................................................................

.................................................................................................

.................................................................................................

.................................................................................................

.................................................................................................

.................................................................................................

.................................................................................................

Love sees hope

Love sees a future

No more lies or despair

Complete without a care

Love sees us healed

Love sees us delivered

Pursues the highest good

Oh, this is what your love sees, is us ... yeah, yeah


– WAL-MART SONG (WHAT LOVE SEES) –
*Lyrics by Kevin Weaver It's Feasible Publishing, LLC*

Download the complete lyrics and an .mp3 version of this
song in its entirety at www.thereorientbook.com.

# What's your REACTION to the word?

⊕ Positive

⊖ Negative

◎ Neutral

# What does the word MEAN TO YOU?

_____

_____

_____

_____

_____

_____

_____

_____

_____

_____          Now let's see what others say. ▶

The way people surveyed
reacted to the word SIN.

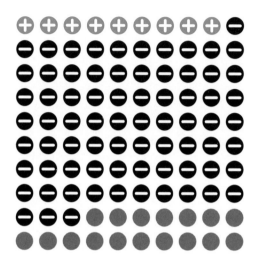

9.12%
Positive

73.68%
Negative

17.19%
Neutral

See a video of respondants in the Resource section for this chapter at www.reorientbook.com.

Common words people surveyed associated with the word SIN.

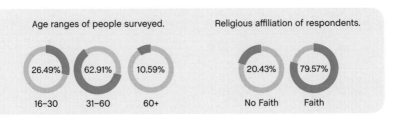

Age ranges of people surveyed.

26.49% 62.91% 10.59%

16–30 · 31–60 · 60+

Religious affiliation of respondents.

20.43% 79.57%

No Faith · Faith

# SIN__REDISCOVER

## OLD TESTAMENT HEBREW WORDS FOR SIN

USED    *More than 550 times*

WORDS    CHET */khet/*
CHATTA'AH */khat-taw-taw/*
CHATA */khaw-taw/*

DEFINITION    *Incur guilt, forfeit, purify from uncleanliness; to miss, miss the way, a wrong*

---

## NEW TESTAMENT GREEK WORDS FOR SIN

USED    *More than 230 times*

WORDS    HAMARTIA */ham-ar-tee´-ah/*
HAMARTEMA */ham-ar´-tay-mah/*
HAMARTANO */ham-ar-tan´-o/*
ANOMIA */an-om-ee´-ah/*

DEFINITION    *To be mistaken; to err or offend; to miss the mark; to be without a share in, or not to share the prize; wander from the path*

# SIN_RECOUNT

# SIN

## OLD TESTAMENT VERSES USING THE HEBREW WORD

# 527

## NEW TESTAMENT VERSES USING THE GREEK WORD

# 207

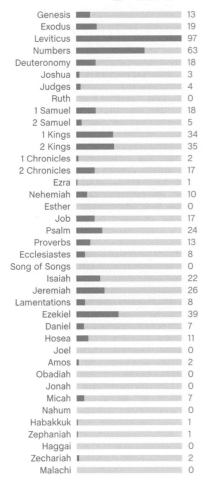

|  |  |
|---|---|
| Genesis | 13 |
| Exodus | 19 |
| Leviticus | 97 |
| Numbers | 63 |
| Deuteronomy | 18 |
| Joshua | 3 |
| Judges | 4 |
| Ruth | 0 |
| 1 Samuel | 18 |
| 2 Samuel | 5 |
| 1 Kings | 34 |
| 2 Kings | 35 |
| 1 Chronicles | 2 |
| 2 Chronicles | 17 |
| Ezra | 1 |
| Nehemiah | 10 |
| Esther | 0 |
| Job | 17 |
| Psalm | 24 |
| Proverbs | 13 |
| Ecclesiastes | 8 |
| Song of Songs | 0 |
| Isaiah | 22 |
| Jeremiah | 26 |
| Lamentations | 8 |
| Ezekiel | 39 |
| Daniel | 7 |
| Hosea | 11 |
| Joel | 0 |
| Amos | 2 |
| Obadiah | 0 |
| Jonah | 0 |
| Micah | 7 |
| Nahum | 0 |
| Habakkuk | 1 |
| Zephaniah | 1 |
| Haggai | 0 |
| Zechariah | 2 |
| Malachi | 0 |

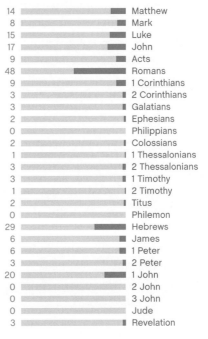

|  |  |
|---|---|
| 14 | Matthew |
| 8 | Mark |
| 15 | Luke |
| 17 | John |
| 9 | Acts |
| 48 | Romans |
| 9 | 1 Corinthians |
| 3 | 2 Corinthians |
| 3 | Galatians |
| 2 | Ephesians |
| 0 | Philippians |
| 2 | Colossians |
| 1 | 1 Thessalonians |
| 3 | 2 Thessalonians |
| 3 | 1 Timothy |
| 1 | 2 Timothy |
| 2 | Titus |
| 0 | Philemon |
| 29 | Hebrews |
| 6 | James |
| 6 | 1 Peter |
| 3 | 2 Peter |
| 20 | 1 John |
| 0 | 2 John |
| 0 | 3 John |
| 0 | Jude |
| 3 | Revelation |

*Graph is based on the highest verse use and shown visually as a percentage of the highest value.

# SIN__REORIENT

Not many words in the English language conjure up more uneasiness in the hearts and minds of us mere mortals than the word *sin*.

The majority of the civilized world has heard the word before and most people have extremely negative impressions of it. Simply asking people about it can evoke a wide range of emotions.

If you aren't sure you know what I mean, try injecting the word in a conversation the next time you're sipping coffee with friends. Something like, "Hey guys, let's talk about *sin!*" Or, "I heard there will be a great message about *sin* at church Sunday; want to check it out with me?" My guess is your religious and non-religious friends alike will become very busy all of a sudden – if they don't directly or indirectly banish you from coffee-sipping with them again!

Most people we surveyed, who consider themselves religious, were fairly assertive about the word *sin* and confident in the meanings and implications they assign to it. Others, more moderate people of faith, seemed apprehensive about the word, but agreed it was an essential part of their need for salvation.

People who didn't categorize themselves as religious seemed to care less about the word, and many others seemed angered at the mere mention of it. Still others seemed to no longer be considering a vital relationship with God because they lacked desire or confidence in mastering the *"not sinning thing."*

**RECONSIDER**

Fun with *sin* word usages:[7]

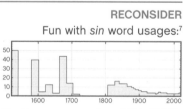

Word frequency usage from 1539 to 2007 in occurrences per 100,000 words per year

Phone Digits: (...) ... -.746

Anagram(s): isn · ins

Scrabble Score: 3

The people we surveyed could be categorized as follows:

Those in the know,

Those who didn't know,

Those who said they know, but didn't actually know,

Those who didn't know what they didn't know,

Those who no longer even cared to know what any of these words really mean.

To our surprise, those who were actually "in the know" were less than one percent, while the other categories were equally represented.

In any case, ignorance, misunderstandings, and contentions about sin abound. For such a small word, it has the power to stir up some big emotions and even bigger debates.

## COMMON IMPRESSIONS OF THE MEANING, IMPLICATIONS, AND CONSEQUENCES OF SIN

As you might guess, more than 70 percent of our survey respondents had negative impressions of the word *sin*. Six percent of those surveyed skipped the question altogether, and only twenty-six people indicated a positive impression of the word. Seventeen percent said they were neutral or had no opinion.[8]

When asked about the first thing that came to mind when they saw or heard the word *sin,* responses varied from sadness to anger disguised as sarcasm. Here's a sampling of the responses (sorted alphabetically):

A bad vice you just can't stop

A church control tactic used to strip people of self-worth

Anything that displeases God

A sin is a sin – 'nuf said

Bad, bad, bad

Darkness and demeaning

Doing something wrong

Everybody does it, so why feel bad about it?

Evildoing

God forgave me of mine, but the truth is I still struggle with sin a lot

God hates it, and most likely He is not happy with me because of it

Hell

I am full of it, no doubt

I think the Ten Commandments were punishment

I was born with it – what can I say?

Rebellion

Sin leads you to hell, if you don't put it under the blood

To offend God

When respondents were asked to be more specific about what sin actually is, most listed a specific bad behavior. Common responses included:

| | | |
|---|---|---|
| Abortion | Drunkenness | Lying |
| Adultery | Fornication | Murder |
| Anger | Homosexuality | |

Surprisingly, even Christians, whose faith is founded on the premise of the forgiveness of sins, expressed mixed views about their ongoing struggles with sin and concern about God's feelings toward them because of it. Paradoxically, phrases like "I was born in sin" and "I'm still just a sinner saved by grace" were common among the very same people who expressed confidently, "I was forgiven and set free from sin when I gave my life to Jesus."

The lack of clarity around sin and its potentially negative implications are worse when combined with the equally common impression that God is generally disappointed, angry, and intolerant toward sinners. This becomes even more muddied with the assumption that He is more than willing to send anyone to hell for eternity for even the slightest sin infraction.

There is now an entire branch of Christian theology called *hamarti-ology*[9] dedicated to the study of how sin originates and how it still affects mankind, and it categorizes what are believed to be different types of sin based on degrees of severity. This includes things like:

Mortal sins which cause spiritual death,

Venial sins, or the inability to meet the standard prescribed by God's law,

Sins of commission, which are committed against God,

Sins of omission, resulting from failing to do something God commanded,

Imputed sin, or original sin, inherited from Adam and Eve,

The seven deadly sins of anger, greed, sloth, pride, lust, envy, and gluttony.

These classifications are consistent with how the modern dictionary defines the term.

**Sin**
*noun*
1. transgression of divine law: *the sin of Adam*
2. any act regarded as such a transgression, especially a willful or deliberate violation of some religious or moral principle
3. any reprehensible or regrettable action, behavior, lapse, etc.; great fault or offense: *It's a sin to waste time*

*verb (used without object):*
1. to commit a sinful act
2. to offend against a principle, standard, etc.

This single interpretation and modern application of the word *sin* has formed and reinforced centuries of traditional thinking about mankind, and imply we:

Have been born in sin,

Have an original sin nature inherited from Adam and Eve's failures,

Have a body (flesh) referred to as our sin nature,

Have need of forgiveness of sin to escape hell and gain heaven,

Have need of a sinner's prayer to save us from our collective sin condition.

Have you heard these notions before?

Overall, how do these responses and ideas about sin compare to your ideas, impressions, and beliefs about the implications of the word?

When you encounter the word *sin*, do your worst or most recent infractions come to mind? Are you a sinner by any of the standards just listed?

Or how about an even bigger question?

What if the meaning and implications we just read about sin were wrong? I mean, all wrong! What would the implications be? Would you be willing to reorient?

## AN UNCOMMON VIEW AND ALTERNATIVE APPLICATION OF SIN

If you've never heard any of the ideas we just covered concerning sin, congratulations! You will likely have a less difficult time reorienting to the word *sin* than many others with years of religious tradition.

If you have heard these notions before, reorienting may require some extra grace and patience. Despite the traditions and common tensions around the word *sin,* I want to ask you to imagine you are hearing about it for the first time as we traverse the next few pages. While what we cover next may not be commonly known or widely accepted, it's an accurate interpretation and application of the word *sin*. In many cases, it's a much more biblically accurate interpretation than those we're used to hearing.

Contrary to the most commonly held ideas of sin, it has not always been used historically, or in the biblical context, as an evil act or an offensive behavior against God. When sin is considered a legal offense, it is technically not an act like lying, murder, abortion, homosexuality, drunkenness, fornication or adultery. While these actions qualify as fruits of sin, they are not actually sins in and of themselves.

I know we are moving in on some sacred ground for much of the organized Christian world here, but please bear with me. I'm not making a case for how God may or may not feel about any of these things individually or collectively. I do, however, want to use these simple distinctions as starting places for a new context for the word and etymology (origins and evolution) of the word. If you will remain curious, this study of the lesser-known and lesser-discussed implications of the word *sin* is immensely enlightening, not to mention immeasurably freeing. In my opinion, this is a game changer!

Are you ready?

If you research the various words in the New Testament Bible translated into English as *sin,* you will find the same Greek word at the root of each of them. It's the Greek word *hamartano*. It means:

> " *To be separated, to miss the mark, or to be estranged and/or mistaken in such a way as to not have a share in the prize.* "

Read that definition a few times.

Like we did with the word *love*, committing this definition to memory before moving forward will help you reorient much more quickly.

It bears repeating: *this is the exact definition of the Greek word used in the New Testament Bible for* sin *and from where all other words translated in English as some variation of the word* sin *derive their meanings.* Miss this meaning and it's easy to miss the original implications of each of the other words.

For example, consider these four Greek words also translated as *sin:*

1.  *Hamartano,* meaning to miss the mark and not share in the prize

2.  *Hamartema,* meaning to err or offend

3.  *Hamartia,* meaning to trespass

4.  *Anomia,* meaning to depart from, to be without law, lawless

The distinctions between the spellings of the first three Greek words translated *sin* above are subtle, but make it easy to tell they are related. The meanings are very similar. Universally and independently applying the meaning of the Greek word *hamartema* (to err or offend) without consideration of the root meaning *harmatano* (to miss the mark) would be easy to do. Then using it out of context to reinforce the common idea of *sin* as only an act that breaks the law or offends God, leads us to the present problem of the word's misinterpretation.

Conversely, when both are considered together, they imply the same thing, but from a slightly different perspective. *Trespass* can be another way of saying a person is "out of bounds", has "missed the set boundary," or has "missed the mark." *Err* can be another way of saying "to miss" or "to come up short."

These are the biblically accurate definitions and implications of the majority of the words translated into English as *sin* in the New Testament. Notice they make no mention of a specific act or a specific offense or how God feels about them.

Instead, they describe the relational state of something when compared to an ideal. In other words, a person in sin is relationally separated from the goal, which results in them obtaining less-than-excellent results and not sharing in the highest good.

The Old Testament meanings of the primary Hebrew words translated into English as *sin* are also similar in both application and implication to these New Testament words.

There are three Hebrew words most often translated *sin* in the Old Testament:

1. *Avon,* meaning iniquity or pervert

2. *Pasha,* meaning to transgress, trespass

3. *Chata,* meaning to miss, miss the way, go wrong

We will discuss the meanings and context of the first two Old Testament words in more detail later. For now, however, I only want to consider the third Hebrew word listed above. That's because the Hebrew word *chata* is the predominant word translated *sin* some 238 times in the Old Testament. As you can see, *chata* is completely consistent with the meanings of the New Testament definitions for the word *sin*.

> *To be separated, to miss the mark, or to be estranged and/or mistaken in such a way as to not have a share in the prize.*

This is the primary Old and New Testament definition of the word *sin* we desperately need to reorient to today. Looking deeper at the historical use of the word reveals this is also the meaning, context, and implication of the word *sin* that people understood for centuries prior to our more modern usage of the word.

To see what I mean, however, we need to look at the term *sin* from a different perspective, through different lens, or with new eyes.

## SIN THROUGH THE EYES OF AN OLYMPIC ARCHER, FURNITURE MERCHANT, MATHEMATICIAN, AND THE ORDERING OF SPANISH DRINKS

As most people are aware, the Greek language was the primary language of the New Testament. However, most are unaware that the word translated from Greek into English as *sin* in the Bible was widely used among Greek people and in the Greek language outside the biblical text.

In ancient Greece, and especially in the sport of Olympic archery (which the Greek culture is credited with founding), the word *sin* was prevalent. Its applied meaning in the context of competitive archery was consistent with the alternative biblical definition for *sin* we just rediscovered: "to miss the mark and not have a share in the prize" or "to miss the goal."

For a better picture of how *sin* was used in this context, imagine a bull's-eye at the center of a target. Now imagine you're an Olympic archer competing in a contest. The ultimate goal of the contest is obviously to hit the bull's-eye. Hitting the center of the target, or mark, as it was often called, is perfection. It's considered the highest good you can achieve and is, therefore, worthy of the ultimate or highest prize.

Of course, while endeavoring to hit the bull's-eye, an archer can miss in any direction. An archer can aim too high, too low, or miss to either side. In a competitive scenario, consistently missing the target, or mark, was the only sure way to erode your chances of sharing in the highest prize.

In both ancient Greece and the sport of Olympic archery, if an archer shot at a target and missed the bulls-eye, a determination was made. The distance between where the arrow struck the target and the intended bull's-eye was measured by considering the distance between the two points. That distance was called *sin*.

Just like in our biblical definition, *sin* was the term used to describe the relational state of something to an ideal!

By default, consistently missing the target would be called sinning, and I guess if you were a really bad shot, you might even be called a sinner. In either case, the miss or severity of the sin in archery was never meant to imply that the archers themselves were evil. Simply, their aim was off, resulting in an inferior outcome when compared to the ideal.

This implication of the word *sin*, in terms of missing the mark and failing to obtain the prize, is rooted in the very same word translated in the biblical text as *sin*.

The first time I discovered this history and context for the word *sin*, I was amazed, perplexed, and eventually, elated. I was initially amazed I had not been told this before. I was even more perplexed as to why. Later, I was elated because of how liberating the implications would be with respect to more often "hitting the mark" in my relationship with God.

In modern English, there is a historical application of another word that I find equally enlightening, in terms of how we are reorienting to the word *sin*. It's found in the evolution of the English word *sincere*.

In English, the word *sincere* is not a compound word, but in Latin, where the word has its roots, it is the compound *sine cere*. To say something was *sine cere* originally meant that it was "without wax."

There was a time when furniture merchants used wax to hide imperfections and fill cracks, often in flawed or damaged furniture, to obscure or minimize those flaws from unsuspecting consumers.

This became a frequent practice, but it was shunned by furniture merchants who offered higher quality merchandise, furniture void of imperfections.

Furniture from these higher quality merchants was said to be *sine cere*. Furniture from lower quality merchants, with natural or unnatural cracks or separations masked by wax, was said to be not *sine cere*. Eventually, it became common to apply the term to the actual merchants, referring to them as *sincere* or *insincere* merchants.

In this way, the evolution of the words *sincere* and *sin* are similar. They were both originally used to describe separation and the state of something as relationally compared to an ideal. Eventually, the term became used to imply a moral condition or state of a person instead.

There is one more historical and modern use of the word *sin* I find helpful in reorienting, which is the way the same word evolved and is used in the field of mathematics.

Two words commonly used in trigonometry, *sine* (abbreviated *sin*) and *cosine* (abbreviated *cos*), have roots in the same original Greek and Hebrew applications of *sin* we've been considering. The trigonometry words *sine* or *sin* are generally used to describe the relationship between two opposite angles that are – you guessed it – *separated from each other*.

Incidentally, the next time you need to order a drink in Spanish, if you prefer a drink without ice, you will need to say *sin hielo*, which is how you direct someone to *separate* the ice from the glass. *Sin hielo* means "without ice"! See, even in Spanish, the modern application of the word *sin* remains closer to the actual meaning we are reorienting to.

So, now equipped with our original Hebrew and Greek meanings and their historical backgrounds and points of references, let's apply our *agape* love lens and reorient to the most common biblical text used to support and justify more than two thousand years of the traditional beliefs and implications about *sin*.

## HAVE WE ALL REALLY SINNED AND FALLEN SHORT OF THE GLORY OF GOD, AS TRADITIONALLY THOUGHT?

There is no way we can look at all 400-plus verses that use the word *sin* in the Old and New Testament Bible. However, let's use what we have learned so far and deploy the *read and replace* strategy we learned in the first chapter on love and reconsider one of the most commonly used Bible verses regarding the topic of sin.

Remember, when you read the verse, read it once through completely. Then start from the beginning and reread it again, but this time substitute the actual definition for the word *sin* we just used to reorient.

Here is the most frequently quoted verse on sin in the Bible and what Bible Gateway ranked number twenty-eight of the one hundred most-searched verses online on any topic:

> *For all have **sinned** and fall short of the glory of God.*
> ~ *Romans 3:23,* NAS, *emphasis added*

If you applied the traditionally believed opinions of sin we just discussed in this verse, it would read like this:

> *For all have sinned ‹**committed evil transgressions and broken God's laws in such an offensive manner**› and fall short of the glory of God.*

Instead, let's take this same verse and read it again. This time, however, let's put the actual Greek definition for the word *sin* and reconsider the implications:

> *For all have sinned ‹**been separated, missed the mark, or been estranged and/or mistaken in such a way as to not have a share in the prize**› and fall short of the glory of God.*

Notice that in this verse, the Greek word translated *sin* literally means "to miss the mark" or "to be separated" and is followed by the phrase *and fall short,* which is essentially another way of saying the same thing.

But how did they miss the mark? Contrary to what has been traditionally implied, this verse does not say all people "missed it" by their offensive behavior or evil trespasses or bad deeds.

The definition of the word for *sin* used here implies, rather, that we "missed the mark" by having not yet obtained the goal or the prize or the highest kind of good that God intended us to realize. In fact, even the phrase *fall short* is another way of saying the same thing: to experience an inferior reality.

The highest goal or prize in this verse is literally the glory of God, which, of course, by implication, is a much better or superior reality than most people are experiencing.

One Bible translator, Wycliffe, uses the phrase *divine likeness* instead of *glory of God* in this verse. Personally, I like the phrase *divine likeness* because it's more precise and also consistent with what the Bible says in other places.

It should also be fairly obvious, by now, what this verse doesn't say. And based on our reoriented definition of sin, what it doesn't say is really, really important.

It does not say that due to mankind's morally corrupt behavior, we're falling short of God's expectations.

It doesn't say, as traditionally implied, that because we are falling short, He is purposely withholding His love ideal from us.

And it certainly doesn't say God is angry about our behavior and, therefore, more than prepared to eternally punish the people who are falling short.

Whether this verse and the implications of sin are very directly taught this way is irrelevant. It is hard to dispute that this is the misguided sin message the majority of people get. It dramatically affects their view of God and His thoughts and intents toward them and others.

This idea of sin, defined solely in terms of an offense toward God or a transgression of His law, has served to undermine mankind's confidence in the *agape* love of God – more so than most any other dogma I can think of.

RECONSIDER

So God created man *in his own image,* in the image of God created he him; male and female created he them.

~ Gen. 1:27, KJV, *emphasis added*

It's also one of the most significant factors preventing people from receiving fully the good news of the gospel – and specifically, grace!

This misconception has fueled for centuries what I call *sin management.* It has turned countless people away from God. They have a hard time wrapping their heads and hearts around the idea of giving themselves completely to a

God whose love for them is based largely on past or present infractions and whose future pleasure in them may be dependent on where their behavior ranks on the sin scale.

The traditional ideas around sin seemed logical to me when I first began opening up to the idea of God. After all, I was far from perfect in terms of past behaviors. So I wasn't surprised when my shortcomings were eventually labeled as sin by some well-meaning Christian friends who reinforced my gut feelings that God probably wasn't all that pleased with my performance, either.

Oddly enough, I remember being relieved when someone finally shared the traditional notion that there was nothing good in me anyway because I was "born sinful." As I understood it, their version of the gospel made a way for me to be forgiven in spite of my sinful self. It seemed to soothe my conscience and give me hope that God might cut me some slack – given that I was born that way and all.

Certainly, it made the idea of getting saved so Jesus could take away the guilt from my inherently sinful condition sound like a no-brainer. If getting rid of my sin problem was the only sure way to gain God's approval and get back into His good graces, I was in! I remember thinking that the "going to heaven" thing seemed like a bonus compared to getting a clean slate on the sin scoreboard I imagined God had been keeping.

Sadly, the initial beliefs I held about what sin was, my sin condition, how God felt about sin, and the threat of punishment for not dealing with it became a serious problem later in my relationship with God.

Subtly, these views began to take a substantial toll on the very relationship with God that I thought I gained by being forgiven of sin. As light as it seemed at the time, the singular notion of getting forgiven of sin as the primary basis for starting a relationship with God became a heavy burden and hindered my ability to connect with Him.

**REMEMBER**
Satan, who is the god of this world, *has blinded the minds of those who don't believe. They are unable to see the glorious light of the Good News.* They don't understand this message about the glory of Christ, who is the exact likeness of God.

~ 2 Cor. 4:4, NLT, *emphasis added*

Why? Because I primarily thought of sin as bad behavior, then the harder I tried to manage my sin, the more aware I became of it. The more aware I became, the more my inward thoughts reinforced that God had no reason to be pleased with me. For that matter, He didn't have any reason to even desire a relationship with me.

Even when I did well managing my behaviors, I was reminded that even thinking a thing considered to be sin was the same to God as actually doing it.

Putting down my sinful thoughts became an endless game of mental whack-a-mole. Most of the time, I simply concluded I was losing and that anything that fell short of love's ideal was likely God's punishment for my inferior performance.

Needless to say, I spent a lot of time asking for forgiveness and then doing my best to accept and agree to do what I thought God wanted in order to avoid being punished now or in eternity.

Blogger Austin Cline, a self-described atheist,[10] called this kind of logic *argumentum ad baculum,* which translated means "argument to the end of the stick" or "appeal to force," which he explains as an argument accompanied by the threat of violence if the conclusions are not accepted.

In other words, as a tactic of traditional religious conversion, religion translated into this: *If you don't accept and agree, you will be punished, either by adherents now or in some afterlife.*

In Austin's words:

> If this is how a religion treats its own adherents, why would I want to be a part of that religion? I wouldn't. If there is a god who punishes people for rational doubt, why would you want to spend an eternity with him anyway? Such a capricious, egotistical, and nasty god wouldn't be much fun. If you can't trust it to be as moral as you are, you can't trust it to keep its promises and make heaven nice or even let you stay. Not spending eternity with such a being doesn't sound like much of a loss to me.[11]

I am not an atheist, of course, but I respect Austin's viewpoint. It's sad to think that religion has brought forth such an erroneous assertion about sin. It actually compels people toward atheism as a superior alternative.

I can relate, as I considered the same option at one point while grappling intellectually with the same basic premise. The thought that God forgave me of my past sins and was now pleased with me and willing to pardon me from any punishment I deserved was initially very freeing – but the fear of repeating my sins and disappointing God all over again was an equally dreadful thought.

It wasn't until I discovered the origins and meanings of the word *sin* and began reorienting myself to the true meaning of the word that my heart became more fully alive and confident in the nature of my relationship with God. I now know there is nothing that could separate me from Him except me.

Tragically, hundreds and thousands of years of established religious traditions built around sin have made "religion" and "church" (two words we'll reorient to later on) formal practices in behavior management for people of faith. Many people on the outside simply view religion and church as institutions for sin management.

**It's clear that one of the greatest weapons the enemy uses to keep people from rising to their divine likeness is an ongoing sense of shame that produces condemnation, taken from these same traditional perceptions of how God views sin.**

Interestingly, the word *shame* implies the perception that someone in authority has examined you fully and then found you lacking when compared to an ideal.

Condemnation is shame fully conceived. Sin, as traditionally defined, can be easily misconstrued. It can then be used to fortify impermeable veils of shame and leave people with an ongoing sense of condemnation.

In reality, God despises shame (Heb. 12:2), and there should be no place for condemnation for those who are in Christ (Rom. 8:1). Shame and condemnation should be completely foreign concepts to anyone who has truly encountered the *agape* love of God.

So, why do so many people still struggle with an ongoing sense of both? There are two reasons, which involve God's feelings about sin and the established theology about man's innate sinfulness. Both are reinforced just about everywhere – in seminaries, from pulpits every Sunday, in the way religious practices and liturgies are performed, and in the lyrics of most popular Christian music.

One morning, our daughter came into my office singing a popular Christian song she had heard on the radio. The lyrics described the shame of being born in sin and bemoaned our collective need for salvation because our flesh is so dirty.

"Daddy?" she asked. "Why does God hate my flesh? Does God think I am dirty?"

Her question provoked me to rise to her defense like a sleeping soldier to the sound of an intruding enemy seeking to destroy everything he held dear!

I thought, *I may not be able to protect my children against every hurt, failure, or disappointment that life endeavors to throw at them, but I will not permit shame to define them, rule their hearts, or set limits on their obtaining a divine likeness!*

My daughter was not even eight years old, yet I was already being required to turn my enmity on shame and defend the *agape* love of God in order to fortify her mind against thoughts that her flesh was dirty and sinful and that she was not pleasing to God – worse, that she was deserving of punishment as a result of simply being alive! Incidentally, my daughter was born with eczema, a severe skin condition, so you can easily imagine the next set of dots she was likely to try and connect.

I hate that with a holy, violent enmity!

We need major mind renewal in this area. We have got to reorient or risk seeing yet another generation fail to rise to their divine potential in God because of what we call sin.

Besides, what if centuries of traditional thinking about ...

Mankind's original sin,

Mankind's innate sinfulness,

Mankind's sin nature,

Mankind's bad behavior as sin,

Mankind's need of a sinner's prayer to save them from sin

*... were wrong?*

What if how sin was really used in the Bible was more consistent with the meanings we reoriented to and the historical usage of the word outside the biblical context?

As the verse we considered at the beginning of this section says:

> *For all have sinned and fall short of the glory of God.*
> ~ *Romans 3:23,* NAS

It may be true that all of us are missing the mark, not sharing in the prize, and falling short of our divine likeness, the glory of God. But He is more interested in restoring the original glory His children were destined for than finding ways to punish their shortcomings and original sin!

Love has it covered because, above all, love covers a multitude of sins (1 Pet. 4:8).

Besides, God never said sin was all that original in the first place!

## IS IT TRUE THAT SIN IS NOT ALL
## THAT ORIGINAL ANYWAY?

We had just finished a three-day intensive we call the Re_Orient Equipping Intensive and the Supernatural Power of a Family. It's an interactive seminar we present several times a year to train and equip people.

In one of the follow-up surveys to the seminar, we asked participants what most impacted or challenged them about the experience. One couple shared that they were struggling most with reorienting to the concept of original sin.

They said they didn't doubt what had been shared about original sin was true. Instead, they felt that without the notion of their innate sinfulness and their tragically flawed nature from birth (which was there because of sin and required a grace beyond their comprehension for God to love them), then the grace or love of God they received when they were saved was devalued.

To them, God's love had been great because, in their minds, He gave it to them despite their being disqualified and unworthy to receive it – not only because of the sins they actually had committed or thought of committing throughout their lives to that point, but because they were born that way: sinful.

As we talked together, I asked the husband, "Do you love your wife?"

"Of course!" he said, emphatically.

"Do you love your children?"

"Absolutely!" he replied.

Then I asked if he felt it would make his wife's and children's hearts more alive if he explained that what made his love so great was that they were so undeserving of

**REACT**
To learn more about the Re_Orient Equipping Intensive and the Supernatural Power of a Family, visit http://www.anuprising.com/re_orient_intensive.html.

it? What if he explained to each of them that based on his standards and perspective, there was really nothing good or innately lovable about them? That from an ideal standpoint, it appeared they were tragically flawed from birth due to no fault of their own – they were just born that way?

"Then you could add that as tragically flawed as they were from birth, it paled in comparison to the way their thoughts and actions had disappointed you since," I said. "Furthermore, their sins were so egregious, they were legally deserving of nothing short of the most severe punishments – for eternity! Unless, of course, they acknowledged their condition, repented, and asked for your mercy as you explained the really good news you had for them."

What if he told them, I went on, that despite all their innate and developed shortcomings, he was going to choose to love them anyway? And that the even better news was that in spite of their less-than-desirable condition, he was going to extend mercy to them because they acknowledged their shortcomings and he was going to withhold punishment and permit them to have a relationship with him?

"Can you imagine approaching a love relationship with your spouse and children that way?" I asked.

"Of course not," he replied in almost visible disgust. "That's absurd and offensive. My love for them doesn't start from that place, and it's far superior than that."

"But isn't that the exact scenario you just told me your entire love relationship with God was originally based upon?" I asked the couple.

*They got it!*

If it's easy for people to see how devastating an approach like this would be to the health of any human relationship, why do so many people readily accept this as the default starting place for all human relationships with God? This is *God* – whose love, by the way, He says is far superior than even the best we could muster for our families!

Yet, it's the almost universally held belief among Christians and is something theologians refer to as *original sin* or *imputed sin*.

The main premise of original sin refers to two primary beliefs. First is the effect that Adam's and Eve's sin, as recorded in the book of Genesis, had and continues to have on their offspring – all mankind.

The primary effect is said to have resulted from Adam's original sin, which now causes all mankind to enter the world with a fallen or tragically flawed sin condition. The implication is that since we inherited this sin nature from mankind's original set of parents – Adam and Eve – we are morally ruined from birth.

The conclusion, as one well known author put it, is: "We are not sinners because we sin; rather, we sin because we are all sinners."

Second, it's concluded that we are then born out of favor and separated from God with an inherent need to be forgiven and then reconciled to Him from our first breath.

Most every other modern idea about sin is erected and upheld by this universally accepted and foundational assumption about sin's origin, including its effects on mankind as a whole and how we need to deal with it.

This is where the traditional process we have today of getting someone saved from their originally sinful condition came from:

1. Acknowledge you are born into and lost in sin.

2. Agree to repent from your sins.

3. Agree to accept Jesus as your personal Lord and Savior.

4. Recite what is traditionally called the "sinner's prayer."

5. Once you recite the sinner's prayer, your sins are said to be forgiven and you are officially saved.

To be saved, then, traditionally means that you are reconciled to God and will not go to hell or be eternally separated from Him with no hope of reconciliation.

I realize we are approaching some of the most sacred ground we have traversed so far. For this reason, I want to stress a couple things:

I am not trying to be intentionally controversial,

I am not making light of this process,

I am not demeaning these practices,

I am not saying they are invalid in and of themselves,

And even more importantly,

I am not being critical of people who use these methods!

That's not the spirit behind anything in this book. That's not what *agape* love would do – and I am most interested in being on *agape* love's side.

Remember: *my issue is never with people.* We are examining these *traditions only* in the context of the commonly held views of sin. We are not examining the people who practice them. So with that disclaimer, let's get back to the concept of original sin.

## THE ORIGINS OF ORIGINAL SIN

The first thing you notice when you go to the Bible to look at the verses that use the phrase *original sin* is – they don't exist!

The Bible never uses the phrase *original sin* – not even one time! Does that surprise you, like it did me?

The second thing you notice when you begin reading the Old Testament verses that use the word *sin* as related to Adam and Eve is – you can't find any!

Why? Because like the phrase *original sin,* there are no verses in the Old Testament that say Adam and Eve sinned.

Again, surprised?

It never says in the Old Testament that Adam and Eve were removed from the garden because of their sin.

It does say, however, that Adam and Eve's access to the garden was restricted by God so that they would not eat of the Tree of Life that He placed eastward in the midst of the garden (Gen. 2). Their access was not restricted because of sin, as traditionally defined, but rather so they would not eat from the Tree of Life and live forever in their current condition, now far below what God had intended for them.

As you read the whole story in the first three chapters of Genesis, it may surprise you to learn that the Bible doesn't technically say that death entered the world because of Adam and Eve's sin.

It does indicate, however, that death was resulting from their actions, because they were *separating* themselves from the source of life. The same is true for all of us today. The source of this "God kind of life" was the Tree of Life; literally, it was and is the thing God created to supply the very substance for the God kind of life Adam and Eve were intended to walk in.

Certainly, it was devastating for Adam and Eve to be separated from the very source of this higher kind of life they were created to have. It's also a bummer for the rest of us to be born into a world where we are ignorant that a God kind of life even exists – or, if we do know it exists, to believe that it's not accessible this side of heaven because of our "fallen nature."

The good news is that none of that is true. The separation from a higher kind of life in God was never meant to be the permanent state of Adam and Eve or the permanent, irreversible plight of all mankind.

It has always been God's desire that we eat regularly from the Tree of Life again and overcome separation, to be restored to our divine likeness and realize the highest kind of good He intended for us.

It really is true. You can read it for yourself right here:

> He who is having an ear – let him hear what the Spirit saith to the assemblies: **To him who is overcoming ‹rises up and is victorious› – I will give to him to eat of the tree of life** that is in the midst of the paradise of God.
>
> ~ *Revelation 2:7*, YLT, **emphasis added**

The very idea that death was God's punishment for Adam and Eve's sinning is a traditional dogmatic inference, not a direct quote from a specific place in the Bible. More accurately, sin (or being separated, missing the mark, or being estranged and/or mistaken in such a way as to not have a share in the prize) leads to death, but that does not mean that God's punishment for people who sin is death.

Notably, the first place sin is mentioned in the Bible is not in reference to Adam and Eve or their behavior, but rather in a conversation God has with one of Adam and Eve's children, Cain. And even more amazing, the discussion of sin related to Cain is not in the context we traditionally think.

Here is the verse where sin first appears in the Old Testament:

> And the Lord said to Cain, Why are you angry? And why do you look sad and depressed and dejected? If you do well, will you not be accepted? And if you do wrong, **sin** is waiting at the door, desiring to have you, **but do not let it be your master ‹what rules you›.**
> ~ Genesis 4:6–7, BBE, **emphasis added**

Obviously, God was not chastising Cain in this verse because of Cain's sin. To the contrary, God was warning Cain that he was drawing the wrong conclusions about his relationship with God, in that if Cain did well, God would accept him and if Cain didn't do well, sin was at the door, ready to make itself Cain's master – or, in other words, make Cain a slave to sin.

Sadly, millions of people draw this same "Cain-like" conclusion: if we do well, God is pleased and will accept us, and if we've not done well, we are unacceptable to God.

It's the inevitable and seemingly most logical conclusion we can draw about our relationship with God when sin is only viewed and interpreted from a performance viewpoint. The entire health of our relationship with God is then ruled by our sin condition, not love. Managing the sin is then the only way we can keep the relationship intact.

In an even more dramatic twist on the traditional way sin is perceived, let's consider the same story of Cain a few verses later. God is still trying to get Cain to change his perspective and even goes as far as putting a protective mark on Cain (despite Cain's perspective) to protect him from harm by others. Here is the text, starting with the consequences God describes resulted from Cain's perceived sin condition – in this case, the murder of his own brother:

> The Lord said, "What have you done? Listen! Your brother's blood cries out to me from the ground. **Now you are under a curse** and driven from the ground, which opened its mouth to receive your brother's blood from your hand. When you work the ground, it will no longer yield its crops for you. You will be a restless wanderer on the earth."
> ~ Genesis 4:10–12, NIV, **emphasis added**

Notice how God is speaking only of the result of Cain's actions and is not cursing Cain directly because of his actions. But Cain's perspective doesn't change, and he even blames God, as the verse continues, for what Cain believes will be the ultimate "punishment" for his actions:

> Cain said to the Lord, "My punishment is more than I can bear. **Today you are driving me from the land, and I will be hidden from your presence; I will be a restless wanderer on the earth, and whoever finds me will kill me."** But the Lord said to him, "**Not so;** if anyone kills Cain, he will suffer vengeance seven times over." **Then the Lord put a mark on Cain so that no one who found him would kill him.**
> ~ Genesis 4:13–15, NIV, **emphasis added**

See what I mean? That's the love of God, always trying to work things for our good, even when we refuse to receive it.

In the context of the story of Cain, keep in mind that prior to this incident, nobody had ever died. There had never been a murder. Cain may have not intended to kill his brother when he, as the text reads, "rose up against Abel his brother and slew [or killed] him" (Gen. 4:8, KJV). It's clear that Cain immediately felt ashamed of his actions and, in guilt, buried his brother to hide the evidence.

What may not be so obvious, however, is that what was driving Cain's actions after this event was the same perspective that drove him to be angry with God and his brother to begin with. It was the same skewed perspective that made Cain perceive how God felt about him. In Cain's eyes, God had rejected him by pointing out the less-than-excellent nature of Cain's initial offering when compared to that of his brother's.

It was Cain's original perception of God's feelings about what he offered that was the catalyst for his actions that created the even more serious events that followed.

God's love and protection of Cain never changed. Likewise, His initial correction of Cain and His later mark of protection on Cain is evidence of God's continued desire that Cain experience a higher kind of good than Cain's perspective and subsequent actions were going to yield him.

Sadly, nothing much has changed for many people today.

Much of what people do that is called sin is the fruit of feeling rejected by God and separated from Him in the first place. They feel that their original condition is less than excellent and so they are easily convinced that God has rejected them.

Nothing could be further from the truth.

---

REACT

For centuries, people have debated whether Cain's "mark" was a curse or a blessing. If you are interested, there is a program available on the National Geographic channel called Cain and Abel: Brothers at War. It does a fantastic job conveying the historical impacts of the various theological interpretations of the "mark of Cain," many of which have been hijacked throughout history to justify evil and prejudice against groups of people whom they called cursed of God because they were said to be originally cursed for being descendants of Cain. I just can't see how you can draw such conclusions from the verses we just read. I don't know about you, but marking me so that someone cannot murder me seems like a blessing, not a curse!

" Since the beginning, God has been
more interested in restoring man
to his original glory than simply
pointing out how he is missing it
and then punishing him for it. "

## REJECTING ORIGINAL SIN

Not only did the concept of original sin not appear in the actual biblical accounts we have of mankind's earliest interactions with God, but
original sin was not a concept in the Hebrew language at all.

Even in Hebrew Jewish tradition today, the idea of original sin is widely
rejected. It is generally considered, by Jewish people, to be a uniquely
Christian doctrine and, ironically, was not a term that Jesus ever used,
alluded to, or reinforced in His teachings.

This is vitally important because the Bible is essentially a Jewish
book from Genesis to Revelation, and Jesus Himself was Hebrew and
Jewish and was educated and trained in the Hebrew Jewish tradition.

If you are fairly familiar with the Old Testament, you may be wondering:
What about that text from the book of Psalms that seems to support,
and is regularly used as, the basis for original sin, or at least mankind's
innate evil tendencies? Here it is:

> Truly, I was **formed in evil,** and in **sin ‹offense›** did my
> mother give me birth.
>
> ~ Psalm 51:5, BBE, **emphasis added**

It would appear at first glance – and certainly when you pull this verse
out to stand on its own, void of context – that David is stating that he
was born evil and in sin.

For most Christians, this verse alone settles the issue. But should it?

Just looking around Planet Earth and the overall state of things, it's
certainly not a stretch to believe there is evil potential in us from birth.

I am not convinced, however, it was supposed to be that way, nor am I convinced this verse is making that claim.

I might believe that, however, if I accepted that this verse was intended to be taken literally. But I believe David was using figurative language. Real-life experience and a huge body of other scriptures would indicate this is the case.

To illustrate, let's take a single verse from the book of Job and apply the same logic traditionally applied to David's statement in the Psalms:

> "Naked I came out of my mother's womb, and naked I shall
> return there."
>
> ~ Job 1:21, NAS

Obviously, Job did not plan to literally go back into his mother's womb when he died. He was using figurative language, just as I believe David was in Psalm 51:5.

Furthermore, the idea that mankind is formed as evil in the womb doesn't seem plausible in light of other well known scriptures about God's formation of man.

David himself said that God has fashioned us (Ps. 119:73). And again, when speaking about his time in the womb, David said:

> For you formed my inward parts; you knitted me together
> in my mother's womb.
>
> ~ Psalm 139:13, ESV

And:

> It is he hath made us, and not we ourselves.
>
> ~ Psalm 100:3, KJV

Surely, God did not fashion us as evil. Did He?

The Bible clearly says that God created us in His very own image and all that He created was good (Gen. 1:26, 31).

Unless God is originally sinful, too, it can't be that He created us as evil. If it were, even Jesus, who, according to the Bible, was born fully man and fully God, would have been fully evil and fully in sin while in His mother Mary's womb. Right?

I don't know any sincere and rational person who believes that.

Still, many people argue Jesus had unique advantages over the rest of us, after all, He was miraculously conceived so He didn't have original sin in His bloodline like we do.

Well, even if that were the case, Jesus again leveled the playing field for all mankind when He made a way for everyone to be "born again," giving us the same "sinless" advantage He had. Isn't the idea of being born again the whole premise of becoming a so-called Christian anyway? So, if that is the case ...

Where do modern-day Christians get these notions about original sin?

Why do these ideas persist if they're not in the original Old Testament?

Why has original sin become so central to the modern-day sin discussion?

Why are Christians so adamant about defending their original sin nature?

I think I understand where these ideas come from, at least in part.

## REORIENTING TO THE GOLDEN TEXT ON ORIGINAL SIN

Though the New Testament never says it directly, at first glance, there seems to be a few verses that imply original sin. I want to highlight one in particular as we begin our reorientation to original sin.

Because my goal in this book is to discuss these words in more broad terms and not overwhelm people with excessive verse-by-verse commentary, I am a bit hesitant to dive into this verse in this manner because it is so long. But because it mentions sin so many times and is so prominent in modern-day discussions about original sin, I don't feel at liberty to ignore it.

For many people, this next verse is regarded as one of the more difficult ones in the entire Bible. It certainly has that potential as it relates to the topic of sin. And so, for what it's worth, this will be the most extensive verse-by-verse commentary we do in this book.

With that said, you may want to go get a cup of coffee and let the caffeine kick in just a bit before beginning the next section. At the very least, get your own Bible out, if you can, and read each section there first. That will help distinguish my commentary from the original text and make for a smoother read.

Here is the first part of the verse:

> Therefore, **just as sin entered the world through one man,** and death through sin, **and in this way** death came to all men, because all sinned.
> ~ Romans 5:12, NIV, **emphasis added**

At first glance, this verse alone may seem to make the case for original sin. However, when you consider the verses before and after it, I am not sure it's so cut and dry. Expanding the actual meanings of the words within the text paints a very different picture.

So, let's take a look at the entirety of the key verses before and after, starting with Romans 5:8 and ending thirteen verses later.

*Note: If you simply don't feel up to the verse-by-verse approach to this text, feel free to skip to the end of this chapter for a summary of the main conclusions.*

In keeping with the formatting precedent we have already set, my commentary and the actual expanded definitions of key words are in ‹brackets›.

Here are the verses, beginning at Romans 5:8:

> But God commendeth his love ‹**the kind that contends for the highest kind of good until it's a present tense reality**› toward us, in that, while we were yet sinners ‹**missing the mark and not having a share in God's highest good**›, Christ died for us. Much more then, being now justified ‹**rendered completely innocent**› by His blood, we shall be saved

*‹preserved, healed, delivered, made whole to do well in the present tense›* from wrath *‹any punishment›* through Him. For if, when we were enemies *‹even adversaries or in a hostile stance toward God›*, we were reconciled to God through the death of his Son, much more, being reconciled, we shall be saved *‹preserved, healed, delivered, made whole to do well in the present tense›* by his life *‹the super abundant, God kind of life He provides – in other words, fully alive›*. And not only so ...

~ Romans 5:8–11, KJV

As if that weren't enough good news already, it continues:

*... but we also joy in God through our Lord Jesus Christ, by whom we have now received the atonement ‹**the reconciliation, the great exchange – in other words, He took the punishment we deserved for being separated and gave us the life He deserved for never being separated**›. Wherefore, as by one man sin ‹**missing the mark so as not to share in the prize, which is God's highest good**› entered into the world, and death by sin ‹**in this case, offense**›; and so death ‹**not just immediate physical death, but death in the sense of not being fully alive**› passed upon all men, for that all have sinned ‹**missed the mark so as not to share in the prize, which is God's highest good**›: (for until the law ‹**according to Strong's concordance, the word translated law means "like food that is handed out," or in this case, "like a prescription for something that ails you"**› sin ‹**missing the mark so as not to share in the prize, which is God's highest good**› was in the world: but sin ‹**missing the mark**› is not imputed ‹**attributed to a person**› when there is no law. Nevertheless death ‹**according to Thayer's Greek-English lexicon, death here means a separation of the soul and body**› reigned from Adam to Moses, even over them that had not sinned ‹**missed the mark so as not to share in the prize, which is God's highest good**› after*

*the similitude ‹in similar fashion› of Adam's transgression,*
*who is the figure ‹type› of him that was to come.*
*~ Romans 5:11–14, KJV, emphasis added*

Notice, at the end of the verse above, it doesn't say "because of disobeying a specific command," but rather "because of disobeying in a similar pattern or similar way" – so it was not in action, but in "likeness or type" that their approach was an example or made a way for many who followed in their paths.

Let's continue on now in verse fifteen:

*But not as the offense ‹in this case, the error of coming*
*short, like missing the mark›, so also is the free gift ‹free*
*assistance or endowment›. For if through the offense of*
*one many ‹in a similar fashion as the one, not necessarily*
*because of the one – and not "all" but "many"› be dead*
*‹not fully alive›, much more the grace of God, and the gift*
*in grace ‹note that it's a gift which is received, and not*
*a status earned through not sinning› ...*
*~ Romans 5:15, KJV*

And continuing on:

*... which is by one Man ‹again, not literally but as in similar*
*fashion›, Jesus Christ, hath abounded ‹literally super-*
*abounded› unto many ‹note that, again, it does not say*
*automatically to "all" but rather to "many"›. And not as*
*it was by one that sinned ‹missed the mark, so as not*
*to share in the prize or the highest good›, so is the gift:*
*for the judgment ‹meaning, the decision› was by one to*
*condemnation ...*
*~ Romans 5:15–16, KJV, emphasis added*

Note that this verse is not saying that God condemned them, but rather that condemnation – literally, an adverse consequence or verdict – was the result of having missed the mark. In other places, it says our own hearts condemn us and convict us of sin, not just God.

And continuing forward:

> *... but the free gift is of many offenses ‹**misses**› unto justi-*
> *fication. For if by one man's offence death reigned ‹**ruled**›*
> *by one; much more they which receive abundance of grace*
> *and of the gift of righteousness shall reign in life by one,*
> *Jesus Christ ‹**or in a similar fashion as the one**›.) Therefore*
> *as by the offence of one judgment came upon all men to*
> *condemnation; even so by the righteousness of one the free*
> *gift came upon all men unto justification of life.*
>
> ~ Romans 5:16–18, KJV

Note here that using this verse to apply the notion that by one man's actions, Adam, we are all born evil at birth, you would now have to apply the same logic to say that by one man, Jesus, we are all made righteous at birth.

The passage continues:

> *For as by one man's disobedience ‹**disagreement or to**
> **disagree with**› many were made sinners ...*
>
> ~ Romans 5:19, KJV

In the verse above, the disagreement is in reference to the right pre-scription that we noted earlier in verse thirteen. Then the passage continues:

> *... so by the obedience ‹**to agree with, again as in the pre-**
> **scription or path**› of one shall many be made righteous.*
> *Moreover the law entered, that the offence ‹**missing the**
> **mark, so as not to share in God's highest good**› might*
> *abound. But where sin abounded, grace did much more*
> *abound ...*
>
> ~ Romans 5:19–20, KJV

In other words, grace abounded so that it might be made clear how much we were missing it – through a lot of offenses and missing the mark, so as not to have a share in God's highest good, even more divine favor was provided to make up for it.

> *... that as sin ‹**missing the mark, so as not to have a share**
> **in God's highest good**› hath reigned unto death ‹**leads to**

*death›, even so might grace reign through righteousness
unto eternal life by Jesus Christ our Lord.*

~ Romans 5:21, KJV

In this last verse, it's grace that leads and empowers us to righteousness and to live super-abundantly. Grace was not designed only to
cover up our inadequacies or sins to appease an angry God (as it is
traditionally viewed to do).

Also, the word *righteousness* in this verse literally means "to be in right
standing with" or "to no longer be separated from God."

Again, this last verse is saying that God established our righteousness
so that we might obtain the super-abundant life – love's ideal – which
is the kind of life He has always intended for those of us who choose
to believe Him and are willing to receive His offer.

Do you see what I mean? There is a lot contained in these verses!

**If you skipped ahead to avoid the verse-by-verse commentary, re-
sume reading here for the summary points!**

Are you beginning to see how the verses we just read are not intended
to make the case that "since one man sinned, we are all now sinners,"
in the traditional sense. Rather, it seems to suggest that through one
man, Adam, entered a way of thinking and living that leads to sin, or
literally, separation from God and
death. Through another man, Jesus,
came another way of thinking and
living that leads to no sin or no separation from God, and, therefore, life
– a more abundant, God kind of life!

It's liberating to know we do have a
choice in the matter. It's not a default condition forced upon us and
against our will by a capricious God
at birth.

He gives us a free-will choice to
think, to choose, and to act in a way

RECONSIDER
I like this verse where God describes
the choice He puts before us all:

*I call heaven and earth as witnesses
today against you, that I have set
before you life and death, blessing
and cursing; therefore choose life, that
both you and your descendants may
live; that you may love the Lord your
God, that you may obey ‹agree with›
His voice, and that you may cling
‹not be separated› to Him, for He is
your life and the length of your days.*

~ Deut. 30:19–20, NKJV

083

that leads to our being more fully alive – and, likewise, a choice to think, to choose, and to act in a way that doesn't.

## EVEN IF SIN ISN'T ORIGINAL, IS IT OFFENSIVE AND LAWFUL IN THE EYES OF GOD?

What about when *sin* doesn't mean separation or missing the mark and implies, in a legal sense, an offense towards God? Well, it turns out even then the spirit behind the word is exactly the same: love.

Even when there has been an offense that results in negative consequences (i.e., that a law of God was broken), it does not automatically mean God is offended by the person who broke the law.

It also doesn't imply that God finds the one who committed the offense (Adam and Eve, in our verses above) offensive. The negative consequences of sin are just that – negative consequences. They are not technically the judgment of God and intended to condemn. There is no condemnation for those who are in Christ (Rom. 8:1).

For example, just because I break a law and realize a negative consequence from it, does that mean I am out of favor with the person who created the law or that they are personally offended by me and judging me harshly?

Believe it or not, laws are favors in their purest form and are not meant to be punishment in and of themselves. Just laws are guidelines for safety and are designed to support freedom. They are ultimately designed to facilitate a better life.

In fact, in the New Testament, the Hebrew word for law, *mitzvah*, many times means "favor."

Wow! Now that requires reorienting! Instead of the Ten Commandments, as traditionally thought, God gave us the Ten Favors.

Believe it or not, laws are favors in their purest form and are not meant to be punishment. Just laws are guidelines for safety and are designed to support freedom. They are ultimately designed to facilitate a better life.

Like the Ten Commandments, just laws were made to protect people from harm, not to harm them or arbitrarily restrict them in ways that make them err and come up short in life. This is even truer for God's laws, which are ultimately just and always in our favor. God's laws are favors designed to lead us to a super-abundant, God kind of life.

Think about it in the context of stoplights on modern roads. They are called "stoplights," but were never meant to restrict the flow of traffic. Instead, they are to make traffic go smoother. Nonetheless, more than one time, I have been tempted to curse a stoplight for being restrictive and impeding my sense of personal freedom. Maybe, had they been called "go lights," I would have looked at them more favorably and considered them a blessing instead of a curse!

Which brings me to an interesting point. The Old Testament book of Deuteronomy uses a term which is often translated as "the curse of the law." But if it's supposed to be a blessing or a favor, not dissimilar to our stoplight example, why is the law a curse?

Well, the following insight helped me immensely. In some translations, the phrase "the curses of disobedience" is used instead of "the curse of the law."

Remember, the word *curse* in that context means "consequence" and the word *law* means "precept or prescription." Surprisingly, the word *disobedience* literally means "disagreement."

With those definitions in mind, instead of saying *the curse of the law*, you could say it this way and not be adding to the Bible:

"The *consequence* of *disagreeing* with the *precepts* or not using the *prescription God has prescribed* results in *separation* from Him and *not being fully alive*."

To elaborate, consider this analogy – going to a doctor to get help with a disease you have contracted.

What if he gave you a prescription that you disagreed with? You rejected the path to health the doctor prescribed and refused the prescription. Would you say the doctor had cursed you if you remained less than healthy?

It's the same with the laws, or prescriptions, of God. He makes them available to us to add to our pleasure and give us a better life, not to curse us and create an inferior reality for us. They are meant to be a blessing, not a curse.

It's our choice to follow His prescription or not. He doesn't force His prescriptions on anyone.

The Bible says God's Word is health or like medicine (Prov.4:21–22).

Furthermore, there is an equally amazing list of "blessings" (Blessing, by the way, means "to prosper or to succeed in reaching the goal" in the New Testament.) for anyone who will simply follow God's prescription.

The entire list of blessings is in Deuteronomy 28:1–14. When you read it, you will find it's almost the direct opposite of the list of apparent negative consequences listed in Deuteronomy 28:15–68.

The even better news is this: Even when we miss the mark and fail to realize God's highest good by knowingly or unknowingly failing to follow His prescriptions, there is a little jewel of a text tucked away in the New Testament to renew our hope:

> Christ redeemed us from the curse ‹**consequences**› of the law by becoming the curse for us.
>
> ~ Galatians 3:13

How about that?

Even when we blow it or miss it, God's love has got us covered!

Even when we rightfully deserve less than excellent consequences, love has made a way out!

## SOME GOOD NEWS FOR THE DRUNKS, FORNICATORS, ADULTERERS, AND ALL THE OTHER GENERALLY UNRIGHTEOUS TYPES TRADTIONALLY LABELED "SINNERS"

But what about those who might ask:

*I get the whole "missing the mark" thing, but if sin is not technically drunkenness, fornication, adultery, etc., what do you do with the verse where Paul plainly says people who do these things will not inherit the kingdom of God, or the verse that says that all unrighteousness is sin?*

I am glad you asked! Let's look at those verses quickly and see if the filters we have applied so far in our reorientation to sin still hold up.

First, let's check that one verse spoken by Paul most often used to indicate that people who do those "bad things" will not inherit the kingdom of God:

> *Do you not know that **the unrighteous** will **not** inherit ‹**result or obtain**› the kingdom of God? Do not be deceived ‹**to roam, go astray or err, wander from the path**›; neither fornicators, nor idolaters, nor adulterers, nor effeminate, nor homosexuals, nor thieves, nor the covetous, nor drunkards, nor revilers, nor swindlers, will inherit the kingdom of God.*
> ~ *1 Corinthians 6:9–10*, NAS, **emphasis added**

I used to read that and conclude it was pretty straightforward: do bad stuff; go to hell!

Without dissecting the whole verse word-by-word, let me highlight a few things:

Nowhere in this verse does Paul use the word *sin*.

Nowhere does he say that sinners, *per se*, won't inherit the kingdom of God.

He does, however, say the unrighteous will not.

It's an important point because the word *unrighteous*, just like *sin,* is a relational term, meaning "to be in right standing" (righteous) or "not in right standing" (unrighteous).

In light of this definition of unrighteousness, even this verse takes on new meaning:

> *All unrighteousness is sin.*
> ~ *1 John 5:17,* NAS

In other words, if you're not in right standing, you are technically separated.

Now, with that notion of what it means to be righteous or unrighteous in mind, consider the phrase *the kingdom of God*.

Notice how Paul did not use the phrase *kingdom of heaven*. He said *kingdom of God*. Did you know there is a difference?

We will discuss both of these concepts in more detail in the "Gospel" chapter. For now, it's important to distinguish; the kingdom of God is a realm of rule and is meant to refer to a current reality that, when present, produces a certain kind of atmosphere or fruit. Typically, however, the kingdom of heaven is defined as eternity with God – His eternal abode, His eternal house and so on.

The distinction is huge.

Paul is not saying in 1 Corinthians 6:9–10 that people who have done or who are doing the things he listed there are not going to heaven, *per se*, and will be eternally separated from God for what they have done. That issue will be settled by another matter altogether.

What he *is* saying is that the activities he listed will result in not obtaining the kingdom of God, which is, as he defines it in Romans 14:17, righteousness, peace (and by implication prosperity), and the fullness of joy in the Holy Spirit.

Look at another verse where Paul actually defines what the kingdom of God is exactly:

> The kingdom of God is not meat and drink; but **righteousness,** and **peace** ‹*literally, peace, and by implication, **prosperity***›, and **joy** in the Holy Ghost.
> ~ *Romans 14:17, KJV, **emphasis added***

It is interesting that Paul's use of the word *inherit* in the 1 Corinthians 6 verses is similar in meaning and implication to the concepts of sin that we are reorienting to – the idea of not sharing in the prize.

In Romans 14:17, Paul is saying the activities will not produce the highest kind of good. They will not bring people into right standing with

God. Thus, they will not be able to obtain the peace and fullness of joy they are seeking. These activities, in other words, cause people to "miss the mark entirely and cause them to not share in the highest prize God intended for them to have" now – in this life!

He is not saying God doesn't love people who do these things. He is saying these activities will restrict people from receiving the kind of love and the highest good God has in store for them. He is saying these activities result in inferior pleasures. This is consistent with the *agape* love of God.

We simply must reorient our thinking to the love behind everything God does or says, especially regarding the concept of sin. We must always examine verses, especially those that seem to contradict His love, from the starting place that God is good and God is love. Everything He is and everything He does, He does in love and for our good, not just for His!

## SO, IF WE DON'T REALLY HAVE A SIN PROBLEM ANYMORE, THEN WHAT'S THE PROBLEM?

Regardless of what side you "fall" on regarding original sin, did you know that, either way, we no longer technically have a sin problem in the world, anyway?

At least according to John the Baptist, who, when he saw Jesus coming up to him at the river Jordan, declared:

> *Look, the Lamb of God, who takes away the **sin** of the world!*
> *~ John 1:29, NIV, **emphasis added***

If you took this verse and added some brackets to expand the definitions of the actual words in it, the text would read like this:

> *Look ‹**Surprise**›, the Lamb of God, who takes ‹**lifts or takes the burden**› away the sin ‹**offense**› of the world ‹**the whole decorated planet**›!*

If this verse is true, it prompts some important questions. What in the world is going on with all this focus on mankind's sin problem?

Why, if Jesus actually took away the sin of the world, is the goal of the majority of religious activities sin management?

Why did the goal of getting saved become eliminating sin?

Why, if Jesus took away the sin of the world, does the world (especially those who are "born again") still labor under the weight and burden of sin?

Why do people (even Christians) still identify themselves by their innate sinfulness?

Why do Christians feel like they never hit the mark? Why don't they sense God's good pleasure with them, and still view themselves as a sinner saved by grace?

Is it because of the misapplication of the word *sin*? Could it be that what Jesus took away was not all the bad behavior, but rather the barriers that separated us and continued to make us err and come up short again and again?

Could it be by the life He lived and the way He lived it, Jesus was sinless? Sinless in the sense of never once being separated from God the Father. Sinless in that He never allowed anything, even His thoughts, to exalt itself above His knowledge of His Father's love for Him?

Could it be that because He did what He did and lived the way that He did, He made it possible for us to live the way He did and do even greater works than He did? The answer is yes. He said so Himself:

> *Most assuredly, I say to you, he who believes ‹**has faith**› in Me, the works that I do he will do also; and greater works than these will he do, because I go ‹**traverse the distance, eliminate distance between**› to My Father.*
> *~ John 14:12, NKJV*

Jesus took away the sin of the world so we could fulfill everything He spoke in this verse. He showed the way. If He hadn't, we would just keep erring, coming up short again and again. But He made the way. The prize that sin put out of reach is now attainable! Paul said it this way:

> *I press toward the mark for the prize of the high calling ‹**the invitation**› of God in Christ Jesus.*
>
> ~ *Philippians 3:14*, KJV

Now, it doesn't take a rocket scientist to see that there is still a lot of bad behavior and a lot of people (Christians and others) living lives separated from what God ideally intended for them.

In the literal sense, I guess you could say there are a lot of people still living in sin, in terms of being separated from God. The tragedy is that it doesn't have to be that way.

In fact, Jesus made a way that ensures it doesn't have to be that way. However, He certainly does not make anyone choose His way.

Out of love, He made it a choice for those who want to believe it and not a requirement for those who don't. But like gravity, the consequences of it are very real whether someone chooses to believe in it His way or not.

## SO, IF SIN IS NO LONGER A PROBLEM, THEN WHY DO WE NEED A SINNER'S PRAYER?

If we technically no longer have a sin problem after Jesus took it away, why do we still use a sinner's prayer as the primary means of getting the world saved from their sin condition? It seems redundant.

Since, we are going to reorient to the word *saved* later, we are not going to dive into it right now. Like *sin*, *saved* is in massive need of reorientation. But a more detailed examination of it is going to have to wait for now. You have doubtless heard the sinner's prayer before – maybe even been asked to recite it, like the majority of people who have become so-called Christians in the last half-century or so. It traditionally goes something like this:

> *Lord Jesus, I need You. Thank You for dying on the cross for my sins. I open the door of my life and receive You as my Savior and Lord. Thank You for forgiving my sins and giving me eternal life. Take control of the throne of my life. Make me the kind of person You want me to be. Amen.*

091

My wife, Michelle, says she prayed the sinner's prayer, or some variation of it, at least twelve times from sixth to tenth grade. When I asked her why so often, she said, "I was not sure it worked. I didn't feel the assurance of my salvation until much later in life."

Unfortunately, Michelle's experience is not uncommon. My own experience was not dissimilar.

When thinking back about how real and active God was in our lives, I wondered why we were so unsure of our salvation that we felt the need to repeat the sinner's prayer so many times.

After reorienting and subsequently researching and examining the actual sinner's prayer more closely, I think I now understand what may have been happening. I have a better sense of why there seems to be such a disconnect for so many people between the prayer and the transformative experience and assurance they are looking for when they pray it.

Here are some surprising discoveries:

The sinner's prayer is not in the Bible. Not even once!

Furthermore, neither Jesus nor His disciples ever suggested saying a prayer saves anyone.

So, where did this tradition come from? Why do we do it?

---

REMEMBER

We're commenting on the tradition of the sinner's prayer.

We're not attacking it.

We're not being critical of people who use it.

We're not discounting those who have said it.

We're just looking at the tradition and process.

We're not critical of the prayer itself or the organizations that use it.

We're happy when people pray.

We're happy for any method that ultimately connects people to God.

We should, however, be willing to examine and abandon any tradition that doesn't connect us to God.

As George Barna and Frank Viola discuss in the book *Pagan Christianity*,[12] the sinner's prayer was influenced by D. L. Moody (1837–1899). His primary focus was the salvation of the sinner in the traditional sense of the word and he is credited with developing the approach of giving a sermon followed by the question, "Who wants to be saved?" as well as the modern use of "decision cards" to record these salvations.

By the late 1800s, Moody's methods had spread across the United States and the United Kingdom, and it was at this time that what we now call the sinner's prayer began to emerge – though it was not specifically called that until a later time.

Enter Billy Sunday.

He was a well-known baseball player from Iowa who became an influential evangelist in his time. He popularized the crusade-style evangelism that would heavily influence Billy Graham (who, by the way, was "saved" in a Billy Sunday–style crusade in 1936).

By the 1950s, Billy Graham and his team began using a prayer derived from his tract "Four Steps to Peace with God." The original four-step formula for salvation originated from a Billy Sunday tract called "Four Things God Wants You to Know."

In the late 1950s, Bill Bright, who founded Campus Crusade for Christ, developed the form of the prayer we know as the sinner's prayer today. This was later included at the end of a so-called gospel tract still prevalent today called "The Four Spiritual Laws," which promises eternal life for all who receive Christ by reciting the sinner's prayer.

Later, in 1977, Billy Graham published the now-famous book *How to Be Born Again,* which would further reinforce the concept.

But I am convinced that the sinner's prayer, many times, translates into very little assurance for the person repeating it because there is no belief or faith required to simply recite or repeat something after another person.

Conversely, thank God, it is just as possible to say a prayer like the sinner's prayer in faith and obtain the benefits of salvation and the assurance promised to those who believe.

> **While it is certainly God's will and good pleasure to convey the benefits of salvation to us, it is our part to believe to receive them, not just to pray to receive them!**

Which brings me to two important observations:

1. God can have a will for a matter that never gets accomplished.

2. God will not do our part and we can't do His for things He wants accomplished.

What do these two observations have to do with sin, and especially the sinner's prayer?

Concerning the first observation, consider the question *Can God have a will for a matter that never gets accomplished?* For the answer, consider the concept of salvation as the ultimate objective of the sinner's prayer.

Is it God's will that everyone be saved?

If the answer is yes, as the following verse says it is …

> The Lord is not slack concerning His promise ‹**assurance**›, as some men count slackness; but is longsuffering to us-ward, **not willing that any should perish ‹be destroyed in any way, lose, or miss out›**, but that all should come to repentance.
>
> ~ *2 Peter 3:9*, KJV, **emphasis added**

why would anyone ever perish, if this verse indicates it's clearly not God's will?

It is because He gives every person a choice. God never says that people perish because of sin, because, again, Jesus took care of the sin problem. Mankind's root problem is not sin or lack of prayer for that matter. Mankind's problems are not realizing the benefits of salvation are doubt, unbelief, and lack of faith in God – not in prayer to Him.

It's why Jesus said, "All things are possible to those who believe" (Mark 9:23). He didn't say, "All things are possible to those who pray, or to all those who don't sin."

Which brings me to my second point – God won't do our part and we can't do His part for things He has asked us to do. In other words, God won't believe for us (that's our part), and we can't do the impossible without God (that's God's part).

Our part is to be confident and live with assurance (faith) in Him to do the highest good in every situation. It's always His part to actually do it.

We can't do His part, and He won't do ours.

He won't believe for us or choose for us because that's our part.

He won't have faith for us because that's our part.

He'll eliminate all the barriers that separate us from Him, but won't make us connect to Him because that's our part.

Technically, the Bible says we get saved by faith through grace. It says we get saved by praying and being sinless. It's a *huge* distinction, especially in the context of the sinner's prayer.

Jesus never prayed for anyone to be healed, and He never prayed for anyone to be saved.

> For by **grace** you have been **saved through faith;** and that
> not of yourselves, it is the gift from God; not as a result of
> works, so that no one may boast.
> ~ Ephesians 2:8–9, NAS, **emphasis added**

"Faith" saves people, not simply saying a prayer to acknowledge you are a sinner. If you still think this is a minor issue or an exercise in splitting hairs over the language of one verse, I provided an extensive list of Scriptures as a free resource online.

Are you starting to reorient? Are you starting to relate differently to the word *sin*? Are you ready for a fun sin exercise?

# SIN_RELATE

If you feel you still haven't fully reoriented to the word *sin* yet, don't worry. It will happen eventually. Remember, these ideas have been woven into the fabric of our minds for so long, it takes time to really renew them.

Maybe that's why Paul says later in the book of Romans:

> And do not be conformed to this world, but be transformed ‹*literally, like a metamorphosis*› by the renewing ‹*literally, renovating*› of your **mind** ‹*the way you think*›, that you may prove what is that good and acceptable ‹*most agreeable*› and perfect ‹*complete and highest possible good*› will of God.
>
> ~ Romans 12:2, NKJV, **emphasis added**

I like Paul's language: We must *renovate* the images we have formed in our minds and constantly renew them by bringing them into agreement with the perfect will of God, the highest kind of good, you might say love. It's a longer way of saying *reorient*.

Are you ready to start relating differently to the word *sin*?

Get away by yourself for moment. When you are comfortable, sit back, relax, and close your eyes.

Next, imagine for a moment there's nothing else going on around you. With your eyes closed, think to yourself:

*Where is God right now?*

Where is He in proximity to you?

Does He seem far or near?

Can you imagine Him at all?

If you're like most people, you might say something like:

He's with me, or

He's in me, or

He's everywhere!

If that's you, good. It's as it should be!

That's a biblically accurate description of the New Testament relationship with God: He is with us!

That's the whole goal and why Jesus was called Immanuel, which means "God with us."

Now, with that understanding in the forefront of your mind, I want you to do the same exercise, but now I want to vary the question slightly.

Think about:

Your biggest need.

Your greatest desire.

Asking God for a miracle.

Now ask yourself the same question as before:

*Where is God now?*

Is He still with you?

Is He still in you?

Is He still ever-present?

Be honest. Where does it seem God is when you are praying and when you need something?

The majority of people tell me, "If I am honest, He seems kind of distant."

God, the Bible says, is omnipresent, or everywhere, but our perception of our relationship and proximity to Him changes based on circumstance.

For most of us, when a need arises, we relate to God as a distant, somewhat unconcerned entity. It's not a matter of reality but of our relational perspective or belief.

Think about it – imagine what this looks like from God's perspective.

When He looks upon us and our hearts are separated from Him, He calls that relational distance, that separation – sin.

He's not really separated, but our view of the distance changes our relationship dynamic. He's really present, but seems distant.

Consider marriage. Imagine the greatest moments of intimacy between you and your spouse, being one with each other.

Now, imagine a moment when you went to bed angry. Maybe an argument happened earlier in the evening. Notice how the dynamic of your relationship changes. The same person can be lying beside you in bed, in the same proximity as before during your greatest moment of intimacy, but the person now seems distant.

See how that dynamic works? It's not the physical distance that creates intimacy, but the perceived health of the relationship that creates deep connections!

That kind of relational distance – sin – is what Jesus came to destroy. Jesus came to restore our relationship, or proximity, to God the Father.

Not that God ever left or was any more distant after the fall of man than before. What changed is our perception of that distance, and the enemy of our souls constantly reinforces this misperception.

Consider how Adam and Eve were in the garden visiting with God and in relationship with Him every day. The Bible says they walked together as friends, co-laboring together. There was no separation. Life was ideal. Then, after the fall, Adam and Eve hid from God the Father in shame, feeling a sense of condemnation for their performance when compared to His instruction, which they knew to be ideal.

But God showed up the next morning for their usual walk anyway. He already knew that Adam and Eve had missed the mark, in terms of what He had laid out as the highest good for them – for their benefit, mind you, and not His.

Then God asked, "Adam, where are you?" (Gen. 3:9)

Was God just trying to be cute? Didn't He know?

Maybe He really couldn't see them in that condition. Or maybe He was asking Adam to describe his own perception of where he was in relationship with God.

What I find interesting about this story is that despite how Adam and Eve missed it, nothing had technically changed about the relationship between Adam and Eve and God – especially in terms of actual distance, separation, or His desire to connect to them.

Even the list of things Adam and Eve were given by God to administer, or have dominion over, was exactly the same, after they missed the mark, as it was before.

Nothing changed except Adam and Eve's perception of their relationship with God. As a result, everything they had done before with ease and freedom and joy now had toil and drudgery attached. How sad.

But the good news is that it didn't – and still doesn't – have to be that way.

Sin (separation) is no longer a problem!

It's the same in the context of our relationship with a spouse. When things are good, notice how it's a joy to serve one another, to co-labor together, and to believe in each other. During those times, we just naturally give each other our confidence, and we believe that the other is for us, not against us.

However, notice how the dynamic changes after an offense (real or imagined). Notice how it changes after an argument. How separation is created. The very tasks that were easy to do to serve one another before now seem like hard labor. Our confidence that the other has our best interest at heart becomes impaired. The only way to remove the drudgery and reestablish the joy is to forgive one another and reconcile the relationship back into right standing.

It's no different with God and His relationship with us. When we are established and in right standing with Him (which, by the way, is what the word *righteous* actually means), things seem easier. There is more joy, there is more peace, and we are more fully alive!

Remember that verse we looked at in the book of Romans at the beginning of this chapter?

> We also joy in God through our Lord Jesus Christ, by whom we have now received the **atonement.**
> ~ *Romans 5:11,* KJV, ***emphasis added***

The word *atonement* in this verse literally means "to exchange" or "to have an adjustment of the difference or separation between two parties". It also carries the idea of restoring a relationship to divine favor or to reconcile.

What Jesus did to take away the sin of the world is called atonement. He restored the relationship possibilities to a divinely favored and reconciled state!

Atonement (at-one-ment). Jesus came:


Not to judge,

But to reconcile.

Not to separate the good and bad,

But to make us one again.

Jesus came so we could be unhindered in our relationship with Him, so that we could be empowered again to live fully in complete confidence and power to administer everything He once entrusted to us and put under our charge.

He came to restore our relational state to God. He came to set us free from the effects of feeling separate. It was for this freedom that Jesus set us free! (Gal. 5:1)

> *So if the Son sets you free, you will be free indeed.*
> *~ John 8:36*

Beautifully, the word *free* in this verse literally means "to go fully after pleasure."

Did you catch that?

Everything that Jesus came to do was in order to ...

Eliminate separation,

Make us one again with His Father,

Empower us to be fully alive,

To go fully after pleasure,

Restore us to our divine likeness,

Free us to experience and enjoy life in terms of love's ideal,

Restore us back to original glory,

Where sin is not a problem

And where we can soar!

Are you ready to reconnect?

# SIN_REACT

What are the top three things you are taking away from this chapter?

........................................................................................................................................

........................................................................................................................................

........................................................................................................................................

........................................................................................................................................

........................................................................................................................................

........................................................................................................................................

........................................................................................................................................

........................................................................................................................................

........................................................................................................................................

What action can you take now on what you've learned?

........................................................................................................................................

........................................................................................................................................

........................................................................................................................................

........................................................................................................................................

........................................................................................................................................

........................................................................................................................................

........................................................................................................................................

........................................................................................................................................

........................................................................................................................................

........................................................................................................................................

I was born in flesh

And dressed in skin

Its limits are familiar

I'm reminded again and again

I know there's more to this story

More of you to see

I know my original sin

Show me my original glory

And I will soar ...

- SOAR -

*Lyrics by Kevin Weaver It's Feasible Publishing, LLC*

Download the complete lyrics and an .mp3 version of this
song in its entirety at www.thereorientbook.com.

003

# RELIGION

# RELIGION__REVEAL

## What's your REACTION to the word?

⊕ Positive

⊖ Negative

◎ Neutral

## What does the word MEAN TO YOU?

_____

_____

_____

_____

_____

_____

_____

_____

_____

Now let's see what others say. ▶

The way people surveyed
reacted to the word RELIGION.

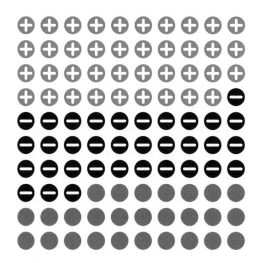

# 38.69%
Positive

# 34.24%
Negative

# 27.05%
Neutral

See a video of respondants in the Resource section for this chapter at www.reorientbook.com.

Common words people surveyed
associated with the word RELIGION.

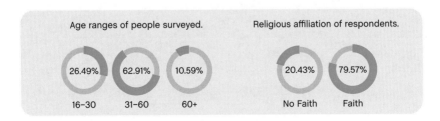

Age ranges of people surveyed.

26.49%  62.91%  10.59%

16–30    31–60    60+

Religious affiliation of respondents.

20.43%  79.57%

No Faith   Faith

# RELIGION__REDISCOVER

## OLD TESTAMENT
## HEBREW WORDS FOR RELIGION

USED  0 *times*

WORDS

DEFINITION

---

## NEW TESTAMENT
## GREEK WORDS FOR RELIGION

USED  6 *times*

WORDS  THRESKEIA */thrace-ki´-ah/*
IOUDAISMOS */ee-oo-dah-is-mos/*

DEFINITION  *To observe, as viewed from a third party*

# RELIGION

| OLD TESTAMENT VERSES USING THE HEBREW WORD | NEW TESTAMENT VERSES USING THE GREEK WORD |
|:---:|:---:|
| 0 | 6 |

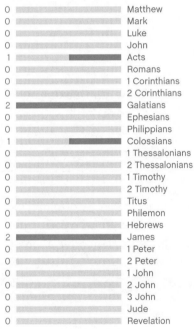

| Old Testament | | | New Testament |
|---|---|---|---|
| Genesis | 0 | 0 | Matthew |
| Exodus | 0 | 0 | Mark |
| Leviticus | 0 | 0 | Luke |
| Numbers | 0 | 0 | John |
| Deuteronomy | 0 | 1 | Acts |
| Joshua | 0 | 0 | Romans |
| Judges | 0 | 0 | 1 Corinthians |
| Ruth | 0 | 0 | 2 Corinthians |
| 1 Samuel | 0 | 2 | Galatians |
| 2 Samuel | 0 | 0 | Ephesians |
| 1 Kings | 0 | 0 | Philippians |
| 2 Kings | 0 | 1 | Colossians |
| 1 Chronicles | 0 | 0 | 1 Thessalonians |
| 2 Chronicles | 0 | 0 | 2 Thessalonians |
| Ezra | 0 | 0 | 1 Timothy |
| Nehemiah | 0 | 0 | 2 Timothy |
| Esther | 0 | 0 | Titus |
| Job | 0 | 0 | Philemon |
| Psalm | 0 | 0 | Hebrews |
| Proverbs | 0 | 2 | James |
| Ecclesiastes | 0 | 0 | 1 Peter |
| Song of Songs | 0 | 0 | 2 Peter |
| Isaiah | 0 | 0 | 1 John |
| Jeremiah | 0 | 0 | 2 John |
| Lamentations | 0 | 0 | 3 John |
| Ezekiel | 0 | 0 | Jude |
| Daniel | 0 | 0 | Revelation |
| Hosea | 0 | | |
| Joel | 0 | | |
| Amos | 0 | | |
| Obadiah | 0 | | |
| Jonah | 0 | | |
| Micah | 0 | | |
| Nahum | 0 | | |
| Habakkuk | 0 | | |
| Zephaniah | 0 | | |
| Haggai | 0 | | |
| Zechariah | 0 | | |
| Malachi | 0 | | |

*Graph is based on the highest verse use and shown visually as a percentage of the highest value.

# RELIGION_REORIENT

Don't talk about politics and religion! It's a common warning concerning the danger of discussing either subject with people with whom you desire a non-contentious relationship. But, as I overheard one radio personality say:

> ❝*Politics determine how we live on earth, and religion determines how we live forever, so it is probably time we talk about it.*❞
>
> – IRVIN BAXTER –

I don't know Irvin Baxter personally, but I couldn't agree more. It *is* time we talk about it.

But before we do, we should probably reorient to what the word *religion* means. Like the word *sin,* the traditional dogmas around religion have caused it to fall from favor.

Now that we've determined sin is no longer a problem, talking about religion should be easier, right? Most people I encounter would say no. Instead, they offer another approach to lighten the load and unburden the word *religion* from its traditional baggage. They say:

"It's not about religion, anyway. It's about relationship!"

It's the response I learned to use. It's a kind of verbal sleight of hand in conversation to shift the focus from the collective bad behavior and legalistic practices done in the name of religion throughout the centuries.

---

**RECONSIDER**

Fun with *religion* word usages:[13]

Word frequency usage from 1539–2007 in occurrences per 100,000 words per year

Phone Digits: (..7) 735-4466

Rhymes: pigeon, smidgen

Scrabble Score: 9

In the world I grew up in, when someone was said to have "found religion" or became "overly religious" or needed some of that "old-time
religion"[14] (said with tongue inserted firmly in cheek), it was rarely – if
ever – meant to be a compliment. I recall a conversation with a friend
of my father's where the topic of God came up. Almost instinctively
and without provocation, the man began expressing ill feelings toward
church, so-called church people, and, by default, religion, as though
they were all synonymous. He clearly had a sour taste in his mouth
as he asserted, "I just don't have much use for organized religion!"

In an attempt to lighten the mood and neutralize his vitriol, I replied,
"You mean, you prefer *unorganized* religion?"

We both got a laugh as he clarified by saying his problem was not with
God, *per se;* he just hated religion and wanted no part of it.

The irony for me was that, for the most part, I knew this man to be
fairly amenable, likable, and easy to be around. He wasn't a "hater"
in general. Why does the simple mention of *religion* bring up such
visceral reactions in some people? I wish I could say reactions like
these were uncommon.

Most of the people we surveyed shared some aversion to the word
*religion.* Many said it is to blame for most of the world's conflicts.
Others felt religion mainly consists of judgmental hypocrites who are
known more for what they're against than what they're for. People we
encountered were usually quick to provide a long list of people who
in their minds failed to model the love of God or lived in a way that
was inconsistent with their "religious" rhetoric.

What about you? Can you relate? Have you been burned a few times,
too? Have you been hurt by people who knowingly or unknowingly
harmed you in the name of religion?

Even if they believed in God, most people hesitated to characterize
themselves as religious, requesting instead to be referred to as believers, people of faith, Christians, etc. We had to go so far as changing
our survey to ask, "Are you a person of faith?" rather than "Are you
religious?" to even get someone to answer the question. And when

they did answer, only 38 percent indicated they held any sort of positive impression of the word.

When we asked respondents to share the first thing that came to mind when they heard or saw the word *religion,* they shared things like this:

| | | |
|---|---|---|
| A catalyst for war | Dogmatic | Ritualistic |
| An opiate | Do it or die | Rules and laws |
| Anti-gay | How sad | Sipping the Kool-Aid |
| Boring | Hypocrites | Strict |
| Catholic | I never confuse religion with faith | Structured |
| Christian | | The way someone believes |
| Church | Intolerance | |
| Devoted | It's all relative | Which one? |
| | Jesus | Wisdom |

So, what's going on with the word *religion*? What's causing it to get such a bad rap?

Should we just make it all about "relationship," as is often proposed, and forget religion altogether?

## IS IT REALLY ABOUT RELIGION OR RELATIONSHIP?

After yet another conversation with a friend who had shared their unprovoked frustrations about religion with me, I noticed something a little bit different as that familiar phrase about "relationship" rolled off my tongue. Something seemed amiss. I sensed a check this time, an unsettledness that gave me pause.

As the day progressed and I continued to roll the phrase around in my mind, I became even more unsettled. Eventually, I asked out loud,

"God, why do I feel so uneasy about that statement? What is wrong with saying, 'It's not about religion; it's about relationship'?"

His reply shocked me.

I didn't hear an audible voice, but something even louder inside of me said, "Because it's all about religion, and relationship without it is a really poor substitute!"

It rocked me. Personally, I had heard the word *religion* so often, in the traditional context, it had come to mean something sacred. It had become synonymous with so-called church, even God Himself. I just assumed it must be important somehow to God, and so I tolerated it. Yet all the while, I consistently tried giving it another relational context in order to feel comfortable about it.

In retrospect, I wonder why, if I felt religion was so important to God, I wasn't more compelled to search the matter? If religion was so important to God, why did I show such disdain for it? Why did I con-sistently try to relate my own experiences with God as being anything but "religious" in nature?

I discovered that not only does God care about religion, it's actually the "real solution" to the "real sin problem" we reoriented to in the last chapter.

Are you ready to reorient?

## WHAT IS RELIGION ABOUT REALLY?

Here's how the modern dictionary defines the word *religion.*

**Religion**
*noun*
1. a set of beliefs concerning the cause, nature, and purpose of the universe, especially when considered as the creation of a super-human agency or agencies, usually involving devotional and ritual observances, and often containing a moral code governing the conduct of human affairs

2. a specific fundamental set of beliefs and practices generally agreed upon by a number of persons or sects: *the Christian religion; the Buddhist religion*
3. the body of persons adhering to a particular set of beliefs and practices: *a world council of religions*
4. the life or state of a monk, nun, etc.: *to enter religion*
5. the practice of religious beliefs; ritual observance of faith

*Origin(s):*
1150–1200; Middle English *religioun* (< Old French *religion*) < Latin *religiōn-* (stem of *religiō*) conscientiousness, piety, equivalent to *relig* (*āre*) to tie, fasten (*re-* re- + *ligāre* to bind, tie; compare ligament) + *-iōn-* -ion; compare *rely*

As you can see, the dictionary defines *religion* as we might traditionally think of the term today. But a modern dictionary meaning does not imply the word always meant that. Hence, the "origins" section included at the bottom of most words in the dictionary.

This is especially apparent in the case of the word *religion,* which held several surprises for me as I began to research the term as originally defined.

The first surprise was how little the word appeared in the English Bible, which only uses *religion* about six times, depending on the translation.

The second surprise was the way the term was historically used when compared to the way the modern dictionary defines the term and the way most people have come to relate to it.

Originally, and contrary to the traditional meanings ascribed to it, religion is not:

| | | |
|---|---|---|
| Christianity | Islam | Buddhism |
| Judaism | Hinduism | Sikhism |

And religion was not meant to imply a denomination of any of those belief systems, like:

| | | |
|---|---|---|
| Catholic | Methodist | Episcopalian |
| Protestant | Lutheran | Pentecostal |
| Baptist | Presbyterian | Mormon |

The term *religion* also has nothing to do with:

| | | |
|---|---|---|
| Belief systems | Leaders | Methods of worship |
| Buildings | Liturgies | Tradition |

It turns out that all of the things commonly associated with religion are not religion at all. Instead, they are mankind's attempts to facilitate or bring about what is true religion.

Like sin, which was meant to describe the relational state of something or someone to an ideal and later got applied to the something or someone instead, religion was never used in a Hebrew or Greek culture to refer any of the things we just listed.

When considering the etymology of *religion*, you have to first know the word itself is not of Hebrew or Greek origin. It was originally Latin – a compound word derived from *re-ligio,* meaning "to revere," and *ligare,* meaning "to connect or bind together." Together, they are *re-connect* or *re-bind*.

For a modern English context and applicable use of the same word, think about the

**RECONSIDER**
For the Word that God speaks is alive and full of power [making it active, operative, energizing, and effective]; it is sharper than any two-edged sword, penetrating to the dividing line of the breath of life (soul) and [the immortal] spirit, and of *joints and marrow* [of the deepest parts of our nature], exposing and sifting and analyzing and judging the very thoughts and purposes of the heart.

– Heb. 4:12, AMP, *emphasis added*

117

preposition *re-* and the modern word for *ligament* used to describe the connecting tissue between a joint and bone. This literal definition and etymology of the word *religion* is why the institutions, systems, people, or places normally associated with religion are not technically religion, nor are they even the ultimate aim of real religion. They are, at best, only a means by which to facilitate a true religious experience – or, literally, a *re-connection* experience – to God!

Without the end result of actually reconnecting a person to God, all the buildings, observances, traditional practices of worship, sermons of inspired leaders, and relationships with other people are poor substitutes for experiencing God directly.

It's what God meant when He told me, "It's all about religion and relationship alone is a poor substitute." Personal connections and subsequent reconnections between God and individuals are absolutely and unequivocally a must to be considered pure religion.

And in religion, like in any authentic relationship, the goal is not just learning about each other or doing activities together. The goal is actually connecting with each other. Religion, by very definition, is a tangible, meaningful, and direct encounter and relational connection.

In both relationship and religion, the actual connection or reconnection is the goal by which everything else is measured, not the activity or method by which the connection is made.

## TRUE RELIGION SHOULD BE FUN, EFFECTIVE, AND BETTER THAN SEX

If that heading seems provocative, it may indicate we have more reorienting to do. Don't feel bad, though. I don't know many people who relate to religion as fun, effective, and better than sex.

To the contrary, I've heard it said religion, at least in the traditional view, is nothing more than hard work and that work is its only reward.

Traditional religious activities can be work. That's because even at their best, they only serve to temporarily soothe a conscience without actually reconnecting us to God. They do little or nothing to transform us and make our hearts more fully alive.

Even what are considered the most sacred of traditional religious activities:

| Reading the Bible | Church | Fellowship |
|---|---|---|
| Praying | Mass | Giving |
| Meditating | Temple | Serving |
| Fasting | Worship | |

All eventually become drudgery and unfulfilling if they are practiced apart from God or fail to produce a genuine "religious experience" or "reconnection" with God Himself.

That's because all learned methods and rituals without actual intimate connections with the Spirit of God serve only to make us more rigid, not religious.

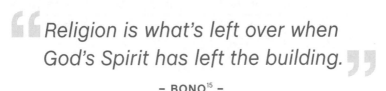

> *Religion is what's left over when God's Spirit has left the building.*
>
> – BONO[15] –

It's sad, but we have the capacity to often allow ritual or routine to slowly take the place of genuine relational connections. Even worse is considering the commitment to the routine and the endurance of the ritual as evidence of the depth and health of the relationship.

To draw again from the metaphor of marriage, consider how couples often say, "For years, we have just been going through the motions" or, "We just stay together because it's the right thing to do, or because of the kids, but we haven't had a real connection between us in years."

I can't begin to recount the number of times I've heard similar statements from people about their so-called religious activities.

Such comments are often followed by the standard admonishment from more mature religious people, "You're not supposed to get anything; you're supposed to go for what you can give, not what you can get."

**RECONSIDER**

Sixty-plus times in the New Testament alone, it says things like:

They received the word with joy. (Matt. 13:20)

For joy, a man will sell everything. (Matt. 13:44)

With good tidings and great joy ... (Luke 2:10)

There is joy in the presence of God. (Luke 15:10)

I pray that your joy be complete. (John 15:11)

The disciples were filled with joy. (Acts 13:52)

The kingdom of God is ... joy. (Rom. 14:17)

The fruit of the Spirit of God is love, joy ... (Gal. 5:22)

That our joy may be full. (1 John 1:4)

But is this right? Why is it assumed in both relationships and religion that desiring a real connection and getting something out of it is perceived as immature, shallow, or, even worse, selfish? Why is obligation and duty to serve often perceived as more godly only when it's void of any personal fulfillment or joy? Certainly, selfless commitment is honorable, and serving others dutifully is godly – but it is not religion!.

In fact, personal joy and fulfillment is the goal of pure religion, not its opposition. Authentically religious people should be the happiest, most fulfilled people on earth. The fullness of a person's joy should be the inevitable result of any truly religious experience with God. Even Jesus Himself said He did what He did for *joy!*

*Looking away [from all that will distract] to Jesus, Who is the Leader and the Source of our faith [giving the first incentive for our belief] and is also its Finisher [bringing it to maturity and perfection]. He, for the **joy** [of obtaining the prize] **that was set before Him,** endured the cross, despising and ignoring the shame, and is now seated at the right hand of the throne of God.*
    *~ Hebrews 12:2,* AMP, ***emphasis added***

Did you catch that? Jesus says He did it for *joy*, not:

Duty,

Honor,

Obligation,

Approval from God,

Or even love,

But for *joy!*

It turns out, joy is one of the greatest fruits of true religion – not drudgery – and the Bible has a lot to say about joy in connection with encountering God.

When we have lost our joy, it should be one of the first indicators that we have lost our connection with God and are having an inferior religious experience. When we have lost our joy, it's essential to reconnect with God to get it back. Getting re-ligious is how a person "re-joices"! And a continual state of rejoicing is the inevitable fruit of true religion!

True religion should always add to our joy, not subtract from it.

True religion lifts burdens; it doesn't add to them.

True religion should be fun!

True religion should be a joy!

Aren't all of us more effective at something when we're happy about doing it instead of feeling obligated? God knows that. Which is why He takes such interest in our joy being complete.

Without a real connection with God, our joy will always be incomplete. It's why anything that is done in sin (in a reoriented way) eventually yields decreased rewards, benefits, and joy while what is not sin (again, in a reoriented way) has ever-increasing rewards, benefits, and joy.

For example, compare drugs as a means of obtaining joy versus love. Drugs produce ever-increasing desires to obtain the temporary joy or delight they provide but yield ever-decreasing rewards and benefits from trying to obtain them by those methods. There is always sorrow attached. In contrast, love can be pursued without limit with an ever-increasing desire. Love only yields more joy for obtaining it, with ever-increasing rewards and benefits – and no sorrow attached.

Taking morality out of the equation, the choice becomes not just right versus wrong but one of superior versus inferior pleasures!

Any tradition (especially religious traditions) void of real connection with God robs joy and actually makes God's Word ineffective in our lives. And without authentic connections resulting in superior joy, all religious tradition becomes void of power, making those claiming to be religious look like hypocrites to the outside world.

Jesus said it this way:

> [We] make the word of God of no effect by [our] **tradition.**
> ~ Mark 7:13, NKJV, **emphasis added**

It's worth noting that Jesus did not say only "religious" traditions can make the Word of God to no effect; He simply said *tradition.*

Jesus is not saying, of course, that all traditions are bad – nor am I. A tradition is simply a learned way of doing things. Our basic paradigms, our learned ways of doing things, and our universally accepted precepts about them can many times take the place of the very things they were meant to facilitate.

Jesus is saying that when religious traditions take the place of the religious connection they were intended to facilitate, they need to be adjusted, refined, or done away.

**RECONSIDER**
The English word *tradition* comes from the Greek word *paradosis,* meaning "an oral, written, or cultural ritual or transmission of a precept." The English words *paradox* and *paradigm* are rooted in the same Greek word.

To the extent that a religious tradition produces a connection with God and results in tangible and observable fruit, it should be practiced.

The key is being able to tell the difference. How can you distinguish between the two?

There are a few simple questions that can help:

1. Does it facilitate a direct connection with God or detract from it?

2. Does it produce love's ideal or detract from it?

3. Does it add to a person's joy or detract from it?

4. Does it lift burdens from people or add to them (Is it heavy or light)?

5. Does it increase people's power to transform things or minimize it?

It's more difficult to perpetrate deception in the name of religion when people have a direct religious experience with God, as opposed to only encountering or learning of Him through the religious experience of others (who may or may not be directly connecting to God themselves).

Real or not, someone else's experience or encounter will always be an inferior reality to your own. The best way to know something is experientially from God is to know Him experientially – not just to know about God intellectually but to know Him experientially, like Adam was said to "know" Eve.

The Bible says a husband can *know* (the biblical word used for sexual relations) his wife in such an intimate way that it connects them in body, soul, and spirit – and they become one flesh (Gen. 2:24).

In the same way, we can connect with God, know God, and became one in spirit with Him (Eph. 2:18; 1 Cor. 6:17), just as God and Jesus were one (John 17:21).

That is why I say pure religion should be better than sex. The best sex can do is provide physical joy, procreate and serve to make a man and woman more like one. A religious experience, on the other hand, can make a man or woman's physical and spiritual joy complete, recreate them and serve to make them and God more like one!

For those who have yet to encounter God or know Him intimately, this may sound like a stretch. However, it is possible and reorienting more to what pure religion is will help make it reality.

Spotting truly religious people should be easy. There is evidence. Just like people who are connecting in

RECONSIDER
And Adam knew
‹had sexual
relations with› Eve
his wife; and she
conceived, and bare
Cain, and said, I
have gotten a man
from the Lord.

~ Gen. 4:1, KJV

a healthy physical and spiritual relationship with each other, a healthy spiritual and physical connection with God:

Always produces more of love's ideal and doesn't detract from it.

Always adds to a person's joy and doesn't detract from it.

Always lifts burdens from people and doesn't weigh them down.

Always empowers people to be more powerful!

It is easy to tell when religious activities are practiced and revered in the absence of real connections with God. These activities give the appearance of godliness but are completely void of any real miracle-working power to prove it:

> They will act **religious,** but they will **reject** the **power** that could make them godly. **Stay away from people like that!**
> ~ *2 Timothy 3:5,* NLT, **emphasis added**

The word *power* in this amazing verse is the Greek word *dunamis* and where we get the modern word for *dynamite*. It literally means "a disruptive, miracle-working kind of power!"

Did you catch that?

The Bible says it's possible for something or someone to seem religious but yet reject the miracle-working power that makes people more God-like or divine in nature. If people reject the miracle-working power of Jesus, it's not real religion and you should stay away!

Even Jesus Himself said that if He didn't do the miracles and demonstrate this supernatural power, we did not have to believe He was who He said He was (John 10:37).

In other words, the miracles, signs, and wonders Jesus did validated that He was really of God and that His connection with God was authentic.

It's the same with us. Just like you can't fake legitimate miracles, you can't fake legitimate religion because there is evidence. Real religion will produce miracles, what the Bible calls signs and wonders. They point to the greater reality of God so people don't have to wonder.

It doesn't matter how much knowledge people possess about God or how many traditions they practice in order to produce godliness and godly forms of power. If they don't have a genuine connection with God and the self-evident signs His Spirit produces, they are pretending!

Without authentic connection to God, what we do becomes ineffective and void of real miracle-working power to transform. Religion and subsequent religious practices then become what both the world and God call disingenuous or hypocritical and serve to distort and shut up heaven's reality to people truly seeking it.

Consider how Jesus said it:

> But woe ‹*grief*› to you, scribes ‹*writers*› and Pharisees ‹*religious leaders*›, hypocrites ‹*actors or pretenders*›! For you shut up the kingdom of heaven ‹*the realm of God, His dwelling place*› against men; for you neither go in yourselves ‹*go there and connect yourselves*›, nor do you allow those who are entering to go in.
>
> ~ Matthew 23:13, NKJV

Ignorance is not the issue in the verse we just read. These leaders Jesus is speaking to know better. This is why He calls them hypocrites, not ignorant ones.

The word *hypocrite* means "actor" or "pretender." In other words, these people are knowingly and intentionally acting a part or pretending to connect with God – but really aren't.

They are knowingly not experiencing God to the extent they know is possible. They are also withholding what they know is possible in that experience with God from an unknowing people who need it desperately.

Worse yet, they are pretending they are personally experiencing something and pretending that others are experiencing it, as well, when neither is the case. They are frauds! They know there is more, but they are denying it – publicly!

In this case, the "more" is access to the very dwelling place of God – heaven.

It's a connection everyone could have directly with God on their own terms, without the need of the Pharisees (ironically, a word that means "separatists") to mediate, control, or dictate the rules of engagement. Even worse, these Pharisees impose religious requirements on people by their doctrines and teachings that add to people's burdens. This is always the end result of any tradition that's void of authentic connection with God. It's unacceptable!

> Observe and practice all they tell you; but do not do what they do, **for they preach, but do not practice.** They tie up heavy loads, hard to bear, and place them on men's shoulders, but they themselves will not lift a finger to help bear them.
>
> ~ Matthew 23:3–4, AMP, **emphasis added**

God has gone to great lengths since the beginning of time to make Himself easy to connect with. Reconnecting with Him should add to our joy, lift our burdens, and authentically demonstrate His power to transform the world around us for a higher kind for good.

That is the goal of true religion and it's not supposed to be hard.

## SO, WHY THE DISCONNECT?

If the word religion defines a very connection with God, why are most so called Christians then hesitant to identify themselves as being religious? Why the disconnect?

Do you find it ironic that people say they are not religious in their relationship with God when the word religion actually means "to connect with God"?

Given the original sense of the word, being religious should be the goal of every person of faith.

Having a religious experience should be the goal of any religious activity.

Having religious experiences should be a regular ongoing daily occurrence for those who claim to have a relationship with God.

So, how did the concept of religion get reduced to rigid sets of practice?

After all, it's hard to deny that the entire Bible is a story about God's desire to intimately *connect, reconnect,* and *stay connected* to a people who desire the same with Him.

In the literal sense of the word *religion*, God's single, unwavering desire has been and still is to have an ongoing "religious experience" with all of mankind. Despite the disconnect, true religion is the solution to the real sin problem!

It's fascinating that God chose the family as the structure and the metaphor to describe the nature of the relational connection He had in mind to share with us.

Of all the terms He could have chosen, God:

Refers to Himself as Father,

Refers to people as His children,

Refers to their connection to each other as brothers and sisters,

Refers to the church as a mother,

Refers to Jesus in terms of a bridegroom,

Refers to the place where God gathers His people as the house of God.

The family metaphor goes to the very heart of the kind of relational connection God desires with us and

**RECONSIDER**
According to Jesus, His entire mission was to restore what centuries of unnecessary sin or separation had produced in us (Luke 19:10), to destroy the works evil had produced, and to "religion," or reconnect, those who had lost their connection with God as Father (1 Tim. 1:15) so that we could experience a more abundant life (John 10:10).

for us with each other. What other human structure is inherently more intimate than the family unit?

The high mark, the prize, the target for all authentic religious activity should serve to do three things:

1. Connect to God

2. Connect other people to God

3. Connect God's people to each other

And it should do these things in an intimate family way that lifts burdens, produces real joy, and bears tangible fruit that something actually happened. So, the aim of all pure religion is to create an *agape love* connection consistently and in all directions – between ourselves, God, and others in the family of God.

Jesus goes so far as to call this kind of religion the first and second greatest of all other God's commandments:

> *Jesus replied: "'Love the Lord your God with all your heart and with all your soul and with all your mind.' This is the first and great commandment. And the second is just like it: 'Love your neighbor as yourself.' All the Law and the Prophets hang on these two commandments."*
> ~ Matthew 22:37–40

It's simply unacceptable that so much of what is traditionally called religion (or done in the name of religion) is reduced to rigid sets of rights and wrongs, principles and precepts, observances and practices, with an "us versus them" undertone – which often separates people.

We've got to reorient!

Why would anyone settle for the inferior pleasure of tradition over the superior pleasure of actually connecting with God? Why do we keep missing the mark and not sharing in the prize that awaits all who refuse to be separated from God?

There are at least three main reasons:

1. For many, they don't know it's possible, and don't contend for it.

2. For those who know it's possible, they've never seen it and don't know how to begin the pursuit.

3. For those who do pursue it, the road to real religious experience has ditches of weirdness and sensationalism on each side, and so they often abandon the pursuit for fear they will get off the path.

But what if it's possible?

What if you don't have to settle?

What if you don't have to go crazy?

What if you don't have to be weird?

What if you don't have to be overly sensational?

What if you can authentically experience and connect with God?

What if that connection alone transforms you into His very likeness?

What if you can then connect others to Him, anytime or anyplace?

What if despite your current condition, you were born for this?

What if the fullness of joy is possible?

What if the experience and demonstration of the authentic, supernatural power of God's love is within arm's reach and could be a daily, present-tense reality?

If the answer to all of these questions is yes,

## THEN LET'S GET RELIGIOUS, SHALL WE?

Does that heading seem uninviting? If so, we may still need some mind renewal on the word *religion*.

RECONSIDER

Do not conform to the pattern of this world, but be transformed ‹*literally, the Greek word metamorphoo, where the word metamorphism comes from, as in the process of a caterpillar turning to a butterfly*› by the renewing ‹*you might say reorienting*› of your mind. Then you will be able to test and approve what God's will is – his good, pleasing, and perfect will.

~ Rom. 12:2

129

For me, I am not sure what's more disconcerting: the traditional notion of religion or the implications of the original meanings of religion – what we might now more accurately call "that old-time religion."

It seems in the postmodern, Western world, to speak of actually connecting with God in a real and tangible way is considered sensational, fringe, or, at the very least, suspect.

> " *When you talk to God,*
> *it's called prayer. If He talks back,*
> *it's called schizophrenia!* "
>
> – LILY TOMLIN –

A good friend of mine tells of a discussion he had with the dean of a well known theological seminary.

My friend was asked by the admissions board if he felt "called by God" to go to this theological seminary. When my friend replied that God had actually spoken audibly to him about that very thing, the dean explained they didn't believe God actually spoke to people in that manner any longer. The dean then suggested their institution would likely not be a good fit.

My friend was stupefied by the response. Apparently the qualification for acceptance to this theological institution was "being called by God," but actually being "called by God" was, at the same time, a disqualification.

As funny and almost unbelievable as that story sounds, it really did happen. And scenarios like his are more common than you might think.

As I travel, I frequently encounter people who hold similar beliefs.

They pray and never really expect to hear God speak back to them.

They fast and never expect to encounter God experientially.

They study to know God but never expect inspired revelation about Him.

They attend services where God is discussed but never expect Him to show up.

They labor for God but never expect Him to personally reward them for their labor.

They accept a relationship with God based on a supernatural premise – a virgin birth and the resurrection of the dead – but once they believe, they no longer expect those same kind of miracles to be a part of their relationship with God.

They read and believe stories in their Bibles about every significant person in the text having direct encounters with God and His angels, and they readily believe in a future eternal reality called heaven where God is clearly seen and experienced, but they dare not consider any of those things possible now or in this life as a present-tense reality.

When people claim to actually connect with God, receive divine revelation from Him, or manifest the extraordinary realities of the kingdom of God, they are immediately judged and ridiculed by many as heretics.

Sadly, many abandon their pursuit and end up judging those that judged them. As a result, the fires of passion that could have revived them and others are quickly extinguished.

It too often seems that as someone starts to rise up in real freedom, they are quickly attacked and pulled back down. It's a phenomenon I call "crabs in the bucket," from a story related by my friend Chuck Frazier.

He told of crab-fishing as a young boy with his grandfather. Whenever they would catch the first crab of the day, his grandfather would always hurry to put it in a five-gallon bucket and quickly secure a lid for safekeeping.

That seemed logical enough, until Chuck noticed that once they caught the second crab, his grandfather never seemed to worry much about getting the lid back on the bucket.

So Chuck asked, "Grandpa, why do you always put the lid on the bucket when we have one crab but leave it off most of the time after we catch the second?"

"It's simple," the old man replied. "Any crab can easily scale the side of the bucket. So when you only have one crab in the bucket, he will head straight for the top every time and be out in a matter of seconds. But I noticed one day that whenever you have other crabs in the bucket, as one begins to make his way to the top ahead of everyone else – to freedom – the others always attack it and pull it back down!"

The analogy is indicative of the historical plight and unfortunate end result of many of the real religious revivalists and subsequent revivals that have started and stopped over the generations. While many of them have done great things and enhanced human existence, they have all failed to permanently take the lid off of our collective human experience.

This sad history can make the pursuit of authentic encounter and freedom from tradition seem extremely difficult, even futile.

Maybe that's why so many divine encounters between man and God in the Bible started with God or an angel showing up with words like:

Don't be afraid.

Be strong.

Be of good courage.

Peace be with you.

Goodwill toward men.

Rejoice!

Why would they say those things? Could it be because actually encountering God or His angels for the first time is actually pretty scary, intimidating, or even terrifying to most people?

Sure it can be, but be assured, the reward of overcoming these fears and insecurities is a direct encounter with God that always leaves you wanting more.

# TRUE RELIGION IS KNOWING WHAT YOU ENCOUNTER, NOT ONLY WHAT YOU KNOW ABOUT OTHER PEOPLE'S ENCOUNTERS

Even more amazing than our capacity to pray, fast, study, attend, serve, and labor in the pursuit of God while never actually expecting to encounter Him is our ability to convince ourselves we should be satisfied with the results.

Initially, it seems as long as nobody challenges the protocol and nobody breaks the tradition, then nobody will get hurt. If we stick with the rules and operate under people who know them, then people are less likely to err and end up in a worse condition.

But actually,  it's just the opposite. If we don't challenge some of the traditions that fail to produce authentic religious connections, then people will continue to get hurt by experiencing inferior realities.

We must seek to know God and His ways in more than just an intellectual way. We must add wisdom to knowledge – the kind of wisdom that only comes from experiencing God and directly connecting with Him.

Just because we know about God and even begin to demonstrate some of His works, that doesn't mean we really *know* God and are actually connecting with Him. You can only identify whether the experiential knowledge and wisdom is from God by the fruit it produces. Jesus said it this way:

*Many will say to Me on that day, Lord, Lord, have we not prophesied in Your name and driven out demons in Your name and done many mighty works in Your name? And then I will say to them openly (publicly), I never* **knew** *‹literally* **meaning in an experiential way**› *you.*
*~ Matthew 7:22–23,* AMP, **emphasis added**

RESOURCE
I was reorienting to this concept myself, and I wrote a song about this kind of experiential wisdom and the fruit it produces. The song is called "Wisdom." You can download an .mp3 of this song on our website at www.thereorientbook.com.

133

Before I had actually experienced God in a tangible way, this verse terrified me. I would think, "Lord, if these guys don't know you and they've done all those things, where does that leave me?"

Like many people, I was familiar with the acts of God, but I didn't know Him. I had never really connected with Him in any real, tangible, or meaningful way.

But even people that God has chosen struggled in this area. Consider Moses and his generation:

> He [God] made known His ways to Moses, but the children
> of Israel only know of His acts.
>
> ~ Psalm 103:7, author's paraphrase

So, how could someone tell if they actually knew God beyond mere knowledge? Well, simply put, if you have to ask, the answer is that you probably don't. The good news, however, is that it is easy to fix..

To illustrate the difference between knowing someone and knowing someone experientially, consider these questions:

Do you know who the current president of the United States is?

Have you ever seen what he looks like?

Have you ever heard him speak?

Have you ever read his words?

Have you ever heard others describe what he is like?

Most would answer yes to all of those questions. But how do they know him? Mostly because:

They've heard his name many times,

They've seen his pictures,

They've heard him speak (in person, on television, on the radio),

They've read his words (in newspapers, online),

They've heard others provide commentary on what he is like,

They've heard what he's like from those who've had direct encounters with him.


But do they really *know* him?


Have they ever really met him?

Have they ever talked with him directly?

Have they ever spent time with him one on one?

Have they seen him with his children?

Have they been with him in the comfort of his own home?

Have they ever seen how he treats his wife in private?

Have they seen how he makes decisions?


In other words, the key question is not "Does someone know him?" but rather "Do they have a real, experiential connection with him, and was it meaningful enough to reconnect again?"

The answer for the majority of us is most likely no. Yet, we still feel like we know the president of the United States, and, if asked, most would say – emphatically – that they know him. Of course, what they mean is that they are familiar with him and his acts, not that they actually know him or his ways intimately.

It's the same way with God and how people often characterize their relationship with Him. Many people have heard His name. They have read His words and have heard lots of commentary about what He is like. However, most don't really know Him and have never experienced a meaningful connection with Him.

So, how would you know if you actually know God? How would you be able to tell if someone who claims to know God actually does?

It's simple. There's evidence of the relationship. The Bible calls it *fruit!*

If you knew God intimately enough and had sufficient relational capital, you could even facilitate a personal introduction for others to connect to Him themselves.

Consider an example from my business life. Imagine that I know a significant business leader very well and have credibility with him from having spent quality time with him. Our relationship is strong and has produced tangible fruit over many years. We have become close friends.

Now imagine that you want to meet this business leader. It's not a problem. I just pick up the phone and call him and say, "Hey, this is Kevin. I have come to know someone whom I would like you to connect with. I don't know them well yet, but they have a strong desire to meet you and connect directly with you."

Because of the credibility I have already established from having known this business associate closely, you would get all the initial benefits of my relationship capital with him translated to you. You would get the chance to connect with them in a way you otherwise had no way of doing, and it would all be based on the credibility of my personal connection with him.

To the extent you actually do connect and are able to maintain the relationship, I'm not needed to facilitate the next meeting. The two of you would then be friends and able to get acquainted further all on your own.

Sure, I might be asked on occasion to comment on certain things related to your relationship, but ultimately, the health of the ongoing relationship would be between the two of you!

This is the gospel in a nutshell and how true religion is supposed to work!

Jesus called us all friends (John 15:15). Then He used His own connection and relational history and accomplishments with His Father, whom He then called *"our* Father" (Matt. 6:9–13; Luke 11:2–4) to facilitate the same connection for us He enjoys. He allowed us to trade on His good name to establish our own relationship with His Father directly – one on one!

The same relational, sinless, right standing with God the Father that Jesus enjoyed is now available to us and in the same capacity. We get to approach the Father under the shadow of Jesus' own credibility and receive the same treatment – just as if we were Jesus Himself.

What a friend we have in Jesus! Literally, we all have a friend in high places!

Once we have connected and reconnect with God regularly and establish our personal relationship with Him over time, we have the ability to do what Jesus did on our behalf – we are like family.

To the extent my relationship bears fruit, I may be asked to facilitate connections for others with God who desire to know Him in the same way. The Bible calls this the ministry of reconciliation, which means to restore to divine favor – literally, atonement. (think at-one-ment)

> All this is from God, who reconciled us to himself through
> Christ and gave us the ministry of reconciliation ‹**to restore
> to divine favor or atonement**›.
>
> ~ *2 Corinthians 5:18*

This is religion in the truest sense of the word. It was never God's intention for only a select few to enjoy this kind of intimacy and connection with Him. And as we read earlier, it is certainly never God's heart for the few that do enjoy this kind of intimacy to use the access they enjoy to control or limit other people's access – or, even worse, to parade the favor they enjoy as a banner of their own worth.

## REORIENTING TO RELIGION THROUGH
## THE LENS OF FAMILY

Let's consider another analogy, again using the family metaphor, to parallel and contrast the traditional view and evolution of religion from the real heart of God.

Imagine living in the same house with your father your entire life but only having your mother and siblings tell you about him.

Can you imagine your brothers and sisters explaining how your father speaks to them and reveals personal things about his character to them, but you never see or hear him speak directly to you?

Can you imagine them telling you how your father feels about you, how he longs to be with you, how he wants the best for you and loves you, and yet a personal connection between the two of you never happens? How would that make you feel?

What if your siblings even shared words your father had written to you in letters, which you can read, but you never meet your father to hear his voice for yourself?

Imagine our whole family gets together regularly and talks about your father. They sing his praises and talk about how great he is, but he never reveals himself in those gatherings because nobody in the family goes to him or seeks to engage him or connect with him in any way. Instead, they choose to live separated from him so that you never learn it's even possible to connect with him personally.

**REMEMBER**
The Bible uses the family as a primary metaphor for relating to God:

God as Father,

Us as His children,

And us as siblings (brothers and sisters),

The church as a mother,

The great body of children as a family,

Jesus as a bridegroom,

And our dwelling places as houses of God.

What would you conclude? Would you decide your father is holding out on you for some reason? Would you think he is just mysterious and enigmatic and can't be known intimately for reasons you don't understand? Would you believe your siblings are lying, deceived, or just hypocrites? Would you conclude your father doesn't really exist – or if he does, he certainly doesn't appear to care about you much?

In the same way, because most people have never really connected with God the Father in a meaningful way, it's easy for them to conclude:

God is holding out on them.

God is just too mysterious to fully understand or ever know.

He's not real, and therefore, people who claim to actually connect with God are either deceived, lying, or hypocritical.

As bad as this analogy of the family would be to personally experience, imagine the relational implications that would ensue if your immediate and extended family members disagreed about the kind of relationship they each had with your father.

Can you picture your siblings arguing over your father's intents? Can you imagine them arguing over the meaning behind your father's words or why he does or does not do certain things, based on their own perceptions of him?

Imagine how certain aspects of your father's character would end up getting debated because each family member felt strongly about the nature of their personal relationship with him. Imagine if your family separated from each other to relieve the tension from the constant strife and lack of agreement they had about your father's ways. Imagine them choosing to disconnect from each other altogether or siding with each other, even to the extent a new family is created to accommodate those with shared perspectives!

In an extreme case, imagine that some of your family members go on to build their own families apart from you and your siblings, emphasizing only "their truth" about your father to their offspring. Imagine this is done for generations to the complete exclusion of you and your siblings, creating further relational distance.

This causes your extended family's offspring to have no real relationship or meaningful connections with the other family members. The entire family becomes defined by their differences instead of their common father. The whole family becomes driven by an "us versus them" mentality.

Eventually, if the disagreements continue, each family unit may turn on the other family units and go to whatever extent necessary to defend their own views about your father. They resolve to defend their truth above all else, even if it means hurting you and your brothers and sisters.

Socially, at least from the perspective of the outside world, you all still share the family name and resemble each other. Outsiders become confused by the infighting, and the family status is weakened among outsiders. And while the family's honor is slowly eroded, the fighting seems justified because to each family member they are defending their version of the truth and, "it's all for the love of the father."

It has become all too common for different denominations to frame the relationship with Father God and His intent for mankind through their own perception of Him or by emphasizing certain aspects of His character over others.

Unfortunately, individuals on the outside of these denominational debates get confused and can't really tell who is right and who is wrong. Since they themselves have no real connection with the Father, discerning real fruit from such relationships becomes difficult for them. They don't know what real fruit should look like.

If there are enough points of agreement about their image of the Father, they may begin to gather regularly with like-minded members of the family. They may call it their "new family" or new "church family."

If all goes well and agreement continues, the parties may formally adopt each other as "official family members," with membership documentation to follow.

On the surface, this all seems good, but there is a problem brewing. Since the nature of the entire relationship these "family members" share is based mainly on agreement and shared interpretations about the Father, their relationship and new "family unit" can only last as long as that agreement continues. If a disagreement occurs and agreement can't be reestablished, a schism forms and the family unit begins to separate.

The whole family is now in jeopardy. In most cases, separating from each other becomes the remedy. Separation then becomes the primary means individuals and families use to relieve the relational tension disagreements create.

This is especially difficult because whether we're "adopted in" or part of the family "by birth," we are still family at core. Regardless of how much someone disagrees with or refuses to accept their family, they will forever be family. There is no way to undo that fact – unless, of course, you go back into your mother's womb and are born again into a new family.

The good news (or the "gospel," as the Bible calls it) is that being born again into a new family is possible.

Jesus called it being born again or born from above. He knew we all had father and family issues. Most of us were born with an improper perspective of the Father from the start, based on our own family experiences.

Jesus knew that our personal connection to the Father, not just knowledge about Him, was critical to the health of the greater family. It's the inward groan of everyone to be adopted as true sons and daughters of the Father:

> And not only the creation, but we ourselves, who have the
> firstfruits of the Spirit, groan inwardly as we wait eagerly
> for adoption as sons, the redemption of our bodies.
> ~ Romans 8:23, ESV

Jesus knew the expansion of the family's business, which He called the kingdom of God, was dependent upon this adoption process. He believed in it so much that He sent the Holy Spirit to confirm to each of us that we could be reconciled (reconnected) to His Father as joint heirs or co-heirs with Him, and have the benefit of sharing in His future glory.

> The Spirit himself bears witness with our spirit that we are
> children of God, and if children, then heirs – heirs of God
> and fellow heirs with Christ, provided we suffer with him in
> order that we may also be glorified with him.
> ~ Romans 8:16–17, ESV

Everything He did was done to restore this relationship and reconnect each of us – His brothers and sisters – experientially to His Father – collectively our Father (1 Tim. 1:15).

He wanted this so much for us, He was willing to give His own life for it.

Jesus modeled firsthand for all to see the perfect way, the perfect truth, and the perfect life for what life with the Father looked like and the fruit that it produced.

Jesus was so connected to the Father, He became the divine likeness of the Father Himself. As such:

Jesus is perfect religious theology.

Jesus is the perfect image of the Father.

Jesus is the perfect image of what the Father would do.

Jesus is the perfect image of what the Father would say.

Jesus is the perfect image of what the Father valued.

Jesus is the perfect demonstration of how to connect with the Father.

Jesus is the perfect example of the fruit that connection should produce.

Jesus is the perfect cornerstone upon which all foundations of real religion are built.

Jesus became glorified, just like His Father is glorious.

And it is Jesus' desire that as many of us as possible enjoy being brought back to the same original glory.

We must see reestablishing the family to its original glory and allowing every child's heart to be

**RECONSIDER**

God is the one for whom and through whom everything exists. Therefore, while God was bringing *many sons and daughters to glory,* it was the right time to bring Jesus, the source of their salvation, to the end of his work through suffering.

~ Heb. 2:10, GWT, *emphasis added*

directly connected to God holds the power to restore all creation. It has the power to free it from the unnecessary perception that sin is still a problem. If we fail to do so, the curse remains:

> He will turn the **hearts of the fathers to their children, and the hearts of the children to their fathers;** or else I will come and strike the land with a curse.
> ~ *Malachi 4:6*, NIV, ***emphasis added***

There is supernatural power in an ideal family that cannot be possessed any other way. In a perfect family environment, everyone is loved and free to become fully alive. In the ideal family:

No one is disconnected,

No one is left out,

No one is second best,

No one lacks,

No one is overburdened,

No one is sick,

No one is diseased,

No one is widowed,

No one is orphaned.

The ideal family is the picture of what pure religion should look like, and contending for the ideal family is how pure religion is perfected.

So, when this kind of family-style religion is perfected and done well, how does God say it should it look?

## HOW PURE RELIGION SHOULD LOOK FROM THE PERSPECTIVE OF PEOPLE WHO AREN'T RELIGIOUS

One of the few places where the word *religion* is actually used in the Bible – and likely the most well-known Scripture that uses the word – is in the New Testament book of James.

It's a definitive statement about what pure religion is and how it should look from the outside.:

> *Religion that is pure and undefiled before God, the Father,*
> *is this: to **visit orphans** and **widows** in their **affliction,** and*
> *to keep oneself unstained from the world.*
>                          *~ James 1:27,* ESV, ***emphasis added***

Pure religion – in other words, the way we observe and connect with God – undefiled before God is for us to visit the fatherless and the widow in their affliction.

I want to highlight five words in this verse: :

1. Religion

2. Visit

3. Orphans

4. Widows

5. Affliction

*Religion*, according to the Amplified Bible as used in this verse, implies a kind of religious worship as it is expressed in outward acts and observed by others. In other words, it's the fruit others should see.

*Visit* conveys the idea of going to "see about" someone, but also the idea of relieving or providing relief. The goal of pure religion is not to just visit or socialize but to actually accomplish something. In this case, it means to relieve burdens – specifically those of what the verse calls orphans and widows.

The words translated *orphan* and *widow* in this text can be used both literally and figuratively. *Orphan* can mean a person who is literally without an earthly father or parent, or it can imply someone who is figuratively without a father or parent. *Widow* can mean a person without a literal earthly husband or someone who is figuratively without a husband.

The Bible says anyone who does not know God as their Father is a spiritual orphan. And those who have not yet come into a relationship with Jesus Christ (whom the Bible calls the bridegroom) it correlates to spiritual widows.

It is hard for males to grasp the idea of being a bride, since we consider it a uniquely feminine role.

In the same way, some women find it difficult to relate to the Bible's recurring use of the word *son* when referring to God's children or offspring.

However, it's not uncommon for the Bible to use the terms *son* or *bride* in a way that is not gender specific.

By definition, the word *son* means "one who bears the family name." The word *bride* is used and compared to the Latin word *nupto* and is from where we get the English word *nuptial*. It simply means "one who is to be joined or connected by marriage." By implication, this can certainly mean female brides, of course, but in a generic sense, it's not a uniquely feminine term.

With this distinction in mind, let's again consider the idea of the figurative or spiritual use of the word *widow* as those who have not yet come into a relationship with Jesus as the Son of God, or bridegroom.

A person with an *orphan-* and *widow*-type spirit can become easily dominated by and labor under a real sense of abandonment. Even though they're not literal orphans or literal widows, they may as well be – the end result is the same.

With respect to spiritual orphans, there are people who have earthly parents but never felt accepted or connected to their parents in any meaningful way. Worse, their earthly parents may have hurt them severely or abandoned them literally or relationally. For a person in this scenario, it's sometimes difficult for them to relate to a biblical concept of God as their heavenly Father. The idea of encountering God as a loving parent who wants the best for them can seem out of reach.

It's common for a person in this situation to become captive to an overwhelming sense of abandonment by their parents. This can affect how they think and how they interpret life and the intentions of others around them. They develop an orphan spirit.

With respect to spiritual widows, consider someone who is married but whose spouse is distant and they share no meaningful connection or relationship with them – or even worse, the spouse is hurtful and they never feel safe.

For a person in this scenario, it can be very difficult for them to relate to a biblical concept of Jesus as their spouse or as a loving partner who wants the best for them when their own experience with their earthly spouse did not result in a good connection.

It's common for a person in this scenario to be held captive by an overwhelming sense of abandonment by their spouse. They can develop what we call a "widow spirit" or a "spirit of abandonment."

The good news is that in either scenario, the reverse can also be true. There is restoration available for literal, figurative, and spiritual orphans and widows.

It's the charge and mission of all pure religion to overcome, and help others overcome, the sense of affliction that results from being literal, figurative, or spiritual orphans and widows.

Which brings me to the last word in the verse I wanted to look at – the word *affliction*.

Remember James 1:27 says that pure religion (the way it's observed that the family of God connects with God) that God accepts as completely undefiled before Him is to "visit the fatherless and the widow "in their affliction"?

The word *affliction* in this verse carries the idea of "pressure, burden, anguish, tribulation, or trouble."

Used in the context of James 1:27, relieving affliction is the end result of all religious pursuits that God Himself accepts as perfect.

So, though God loves us all the same, He takes greater pleasure in, delights in, and favors those most who make this mission their focus:

1. Connect with God.

2. Connect others to God.

3. Make it easy on those not yet connected.

True religion connects people to God and the realm of God in a way that lifts burdens – it doesn't add to them.

True religion relieves anguish – it doesn't create it.

True religion dispels tribulation – it doesn't create it.

True religion eliminates all trouble – it doesn't open the door to it!

Jesus said it this way:

> *"Come to me, all you who are weary ‹**fatigued**› and burdened, and I will give you rest ‹**ease, relief, refresh**›. Take my yoke ‹**that thing that couples us or connects us together**› upon you and learn from me, for I am gentle and humble in heart, and you will find rest ‹**ease, relief, refreshment**› for your souls. For my yoke is easy ‹**useful, good – not harsh, hard, sharp, or pressing, but comfortable, gracious, and pleasant**› and my burden is light."*
>
> ~ *Matthew 11:28–30,* NIV

I like to say it this way: "If it isn't light, as in the opposite of heavy, it isn't God and it isn't real religion."

# RELIGION__RELATE

Relating to religion in the ways we have been discussing often requires overcoming cultural paradigms that emphasize knowledge, concepts, principles, and liturgies above wisdom, experience, and personal mastery.

The ability to become like the Master (Jesus) in our connecting with God can only result from actually doing something, not just hearing or learning about it.

It's often hard for people to relate to this kind of experiential learning in our Western culture where we equate the ability to recite something with knowing something. But the Bible never equates the two. Lectures and information transfer was not the biblical concept or aim of learning, and especially not the aim of pure religion.

Knowing about or even reorienting to the word *religion,* for example, will leave you no better off than completing any other religious exercise if you fail to actually take what you've learned and do it, act on it, and actually reconnect to God in an experiential way as a result.

Remember, as we stressed earlier, it's possible to do certain traditional religious activities like prayer, fasting, study, and service without real expectation of divine encounter with God.? It's possible to learn certain precepts about God but then remain unchanged without a real experience with Him. It's possible to acknowledge His reality and express a desire to have a relationship with Him based on a supernatural premise but then not expect His miraculous intervention in your own life. It's possible to read and even relate to stories of significant people in the biblical text having direct, divine encounters with God and His messengers, the angels, and yet never expect that reality in your own life.

To reorient and relate to religion in the way it was originally intended, we need to acknowledge these biblical accounts as real stories, that actually happened to real people who had real connections and encounters with God.

To reorient, initially, we must see them as object lessons or how-to examples for how we can connect to God – not just inspirational stories of what is possible.

We simply cannot reduce religion to knowledge without experience, enlightenment without encounter, routine without results, or faith in traditions that don't produce tangible fruit! I like the way a text from the book of Ephesians says it:

> That you may be able to comprehend ‹to eagerly seize now and possess› with all the saints ‹called-out ones› what is the width and length and depth and height – to know ‹be mentally aware of and experiencing› the love of Christ which passes knowledge ‹the science of knowing›; that you may be filled with all the fullness of God.
> ~ Ephesians 3:18–19, KJV, emphasis added

What an awesome verse and when you amplify the meanings of the words within the text, it's so rich in implication. It literally says that it's God's desire that we eagerly seize and possess now an encounter with Him and in an experiential way like the "called-out ones" before us. Wow!

## RELATING TO THE RELIGION OF OUR RELATIVES

Let's considersome well-known Bible characters, our spiritual forefathers – the ones who came before us. Those God highlighted to illustrate the way we should connect to Him and the way He connects to us.

Let's consider, their religious encounters with God. Let's reorient our thinking, and begin to relate their experience to our own.

Remember, the Bible says:

God is not a respecter of persons (Acts 10:34).

God does not show favoritism (Rom. 2:11).

God never changes (Jas. 1:17).

God is the same yesterday, today, and forever (Heb. 13:8).

So then the connection and encounters between God and man that were possible then and are considered possible in the future are possible now!

So, let's look at the kinds of experiences the people had with God, and the kinds of experiences God had with them and see if we can relate.

1.  Consider Adam and Eve:

    How they walked intimately with God,

    How they connected experientially with Him each day,

    How they saw Him in the flesh,

    How they talked with Him face to face …

    *Can you relate?*

2.  Consider Noah:

    How he found divine favor with God,

    How he spoke directly with God,

    How God spoke directly back,

    How he thought this was normal, yet others did not experience it and even mocked him,

    How God confided in him,

    How God told him to build the ark,

    How God shared His personal desire for Noah's family,

    How God shared His personal desire to preserve, protect, revive, and restore mankind,

    How God shared His personal desire to save every other living thing …

    *Can you relate?*

3. Consider Moses:

How he had direct experiential encounters with God,

How he heard God audibly speak and identify Himself as "I Am That I Am,"

How he heard God audibly direct him to connect to the children of Israel,

How he heard God instruct him to convey to them that God is also their Father,

How he feared being taken seriously and God used a supernatural sign to validate him,

How God turned Moses' staff into a snake,

How Moses then picked it up by the tail and God turned it back into a staff,

How God then performed what the Bible calls "minor" miracles,

How God suspended the laws of nature for Moses,

How God sent the famines,

How God transformed the water,

How God transformed the sun,

How God sent plagues to turn Pharaoh's heart and assist Moses in his mission,

How God parted the Red Sea to bring freedom,

How God sustained Moses and millions of other people for forty years,

How they had supernatural provision of food,

How they had divine health,

How they never had to toil to provide for themselves ...

*Can you relate?*

4. Consider Joshua:

How he heard God audibly speak about becoming Moses' successor,

How he heard God audibly say how Moses had led them out of Egypt,

How he heard God audibly tell him to lead the people into the Promised Land,

How he heard God audibly say that everywhere his foot treads would be his,

How God did everything He promised,

How God instructed and empowered them to overcome every enemy ...

*Can you relate?*

5. Consider Abraham:

How he interacted with and received direct instruction from God,

How he heard God speak to him, declaring him the father of many nations,

How God gave him the desire of his heart – a son – when he was over ninety years old,

How God manifested Himself to Abraham on the mountain ...

*Can you relate?*

Can you see a pattern emerging how God continually manifests Himself and supernaturally provides for people who are willing to encounter and connect with Him? We could continue with person after person in the Old Testament, considering people like:

| Isaac | David | Joel | Jeremiah |
|-------|---------|--------|----------|
| Jacob | Solomon | Hosea | Obadiah |
| Job | Elijah | Isaiah | Daniel |
| Jonah | Elisha | Esther | Ezekiel |

These accounts – and more – of people who encountered God, spoke with God, and/or experienced divine providence in ways that surpassed simple head knowledge are just too numerous to list here.

And that was just in the Old Testament!

Let's look now at some examples from the New Testament.

6. Consider Mary:

How, as a teenager, she was asked directly by God to be the mother of Jesus,

How she was visited by an angel of the Lord to announce His plan,

How she agreed to receive divine impartation to conceive Jesus,

How her experiences were supernaturally confirmed by others,

How, despite the shame and threats she received, God guided and protected her,

How she was supernaturally provided with the means to raise Jesus,

How she found favor even with the kings and wise men of the earth ...

*Can you relate?*

7. Consider Joseph:

   How he was supernaturally visited in the same manner as Mary,

   How God gave Joseph the assurance he needed,

   How he was supernaturally provided with the means to raise Jesus,

   How he found favor with the kings and wise men of the earth,

   How he was divinely protected to complete his assignment to raise Jesus,

   How he was entrusted to instruct Jesus – the Son of God – in the things of God,

   How he was entrusted to teach Jesus – the Son of God – a trade ...

   *Can you relate?*

8. Consider the wise men:

   How they weren't believers but were visited by angels,

   How they followed a divine leading to Jesus,

   How they found divine favor to make the journey to Jesus,

   How they were used by God to provide for Jesus and His family ...

   *Can you relate?*

9. Consider the disciples:

   How they connected others to God,

   How they relieved the burdens of those not yet connected to God,

   How they had divine encounters personal to them and their mission in God,

   How they couldn't have accomplished what they did without those divine encounters,

How their faith, confidence, and assurance came from personal, divine experience with God,

How they didn't consider it heresy to be considered one with or equal to God ...

*Can you relate?*

10. Consider Jesus:

How He didn't do a single miracle of note until age thirty-three, after He had an experiential encounter,

How the heavens opened up and God spoke loud enough for everyone to hear,

How God said of Jesus, "This is my Son, whom I love, and with whom I am well pleased!"

How from that day forth – and for the next three years – miracles were daily occurrences,

How this was our example ...

*Can you relate?*

---

**RECONSIDER**

People are sometimes uncomfortable emphasizing supernatural experiences with angels, but remember, these are real biblical accounts.

*Are they not all ministering spirits, sent out to render service*
*for the sake of those who will inherit salvation?*
                                        *~ Heb. 1:14,* NAS

We are not to worship angels, but it would be equally ignorant to ignore the role the Bible says they play in our lives, both in being sent to minister to us and on our behalf.

11.  Consider Paul:

How he began to minister following His own divine encounter with God,

How he didn't consider the gospel fully preached without divine encounter,

How the extraordinary demonstration of God's power were regular experiences,

How he did not demonstrate anything publicly that he had not first encountered privately,

How he was certainly no hypocrite,

How he practiced what he preached – literally,

How, unlike other religious separatists (Pharisees and Sadducees), he connected to God,

How he shared that experience to connect with God with others,

How he demonstrated the fruit of direct experience and put it on open display,

How he didn't just point out how everyone else was missing the mark,

How he instead connected anyone who would listen, believe, and receive ...

*Can you relate?*


From the opening book of the Old Testament to the last book of the New Testament, the stories are the same.

They were not meant just to inspire us. They are what the Bible calls "signs and wonders" for all of mankind, in order to show us the way.

We should not allow anything to come between us and God or to separate us from Him or to keep us from contending for more until these kind of encounters are a present-tense reality in our own life.

If we can't relate to these religious stories from personal experience, then our personal religious experience is inferior.

Learning about God should always lead to a religious experience with God,

Experience with God should always lead to a deeper understanding of God's love,

Understanding God's love should always cause transformation,

Transformation should always lead to more religious activity,

More religious activity should always produce better fruit,

Good religious fruit should always produce love's ideal in every situation,

And love's ideal should be the evidence that inspires others to get religious!

Authentic religious theology should lead people to divine encounters, and divine encounters should lead to changed lives, not just more religious knowledge and traditions.

Face to face and one on one has always been – and will always be – God's will for His creation, and especially His children, who are called by His name.

It's His will that we all come to know Him and experience Him as Father in an intimate and personal way. This is the high call for all humanity. It's His will that no child ever live his or her life devoid of hearing Him say to them personally, "You are my child, in whom I am well pleased."

True religion needs no continual mediator; it only initially needs a facilitator. Once a person connects with God the Father and is able to hear Him speak and declare His love over them, the facilitator's role should decrease.

I am so thankful for a few men that God put in my life who modeled this. I remember my father in the faith, Chuck Frazier, saying, "Kevin, my job is to answer your questions about God only until you learn to hear Him answer them for yourself." I am so thankful Chuck did not "shut up heaven" to me by limiting my experience to his own but rather "opened up heaven" to me by sharing his experience, making an introduction to God, and then championing me to go for more.

As good as Jesus' teachers were, even Jesus could not have lived the extraordinary life He didwithout a direct encounter with God and the stunning declaration God made over Him that He was indeed His Son, "in whom I am well-pleased."

I am convinced that the same words spoken over Jesus would have had less impact if His family conveyed them to Him on God's behalf and had He not heard them directly from God Himself. They would have still been true words, but Jesus needed to experience it directly from the Father Himself, not secondhand. So do we.

God knows that. It's why Jesus went to such great lengths to make a way for us to encounter the Father. Jesus eliminated the separation between us and God once and for all and then sat down at the right hand of God to make constant intercession for us to be where He is. He desires us to enjoy the same kind of ongoing relationship He enjoys (Rom. 8:34). He even sent His Spirit to help in our weakness (vv. 26–27) and be the constant witness to us that it's possible (v. 16).

If we are honest with ourselves, we know this is our calling. It's a knowing, deep inside each of us, that there is more. It's always calling us out to more – calling us up to Him.

This is the hope of our calling and the earnest expectation of all of creation! We are all called according to this purpose – to experientially connect with God on a continual basis.

We can be ignorant of it, deny it, or lower our expectations to exclude it, but that will not make it any less true or any less possible. We are the only limitation to a personal, divine encounter with God.

We must answer the call. We must rise up and answer love's call!

## STAYING CONNECTED AND AVOIDING
## THE RELIGIOUS DITCHES

I certainly understand there have been abuses and a long history of bad behavior among individuals, sects, or movements that have emphasized experiences over knowledge or good works.

Equally, however, there is a similarly long list of bad fruit produced by those who relegate the Bible to only a written document void of experience. They shut up access to the heavenly realm, relegating it to the history or a future reality.

Regardless, centuries filled with those that have "missed the mark" on either side are not evidence of God's will on the matter. There is simply no way for people to be transformed into our divine likeness without direct encounter with the Divine.

There are ditches on both sides of every road. There is the ditch of charismatic types who tend to focus only on spiritual experiences and divine connections with God. In the pursuit of experience, they sometimes fail to balance experience with knowledge of the Word of God. It's critical to do both, as a true experience of God will never contradict the Word of God, and the Word of God will never hinder direct experience. They are one and the same, and you can't put one above the other or emphasize one apart from the other.

The other ditch, however, catches the more rigid types. They have a tendency to emphasize the Word of God as void of power and connection with God in any tangible way. They put more stock in memorizing a New Testament Bible, which Jesus didn't have, instead of learning to model the connection with God He did have!

There is a healthy balance between these two extremes. It is possible to have a healthy knowledge of the Word of God while operating in the supernatural ways of God, void of weirdness and sensationalism. While doing so, our job is not to judge people in either camp but only endeavor to judge or discern fruit – to be the change we want to see in others and not be critical of others who miss the mark we are aiming for.

Which brings me to the last verse I would like to consider on the subject of religion. It's back in the book of James, just before the verse explaining that "pure and undefiled religion" as visiting widows and orphans in their affliction.

This prior verse contains a key insight into at least one of the ways the Bible says we can tell if someone is authentically religious. It also contains the key to maturing and growing up into the kind of love we have laid as the foundation of this book and of religion in its purest form:

> If anyone considers himself religious ‹**the way he observes and connects with God**› and yet does not keep a tight rein ‹**have control over like a bridle and bit in a horse's mouth**› on his tongue ‹**how he speaks**›, he deceives ‹**cheats and deludes**› himself ‹**his thoughts, feelings, and emotions**› and his religion ‹**the way he observes and connects with God**› is worthless ‹**empty and profitless**›.
>
> ~ James 1:26

One way to tell if a person is authentically religious is to examine their speech. If what I am conveying about true religion is resonating with you, the first way you will be able to tell if you are religious is that the way you talk will change. The Bible says that how a person talks can reveal much about what's in their heart (Luke 6:45), and what's in a person's heart reveals the true nature of their connection with God.

Notice how the religious people you know speak of God or the things of God:

Is it mostly in a historical context?

Is it mostly in future tense?

Is it mostly conceptual?

Is it weird?

Is it sensational?

Is it always abstract?

Or ...

Is it more present-tense?

Is it literal?

Is it personal?

Is it practical?

Is it actionable?

Is it consistent?

Is it powerful?

Jesus only did what He saw His Father do and said only what He heard His Father say. His "religion" was not theoretical – He acted in a way that was consistent with His encounter. It should be the same with us. When we have truly connected with God and that connection has sufficiently transformed our heart, it will affect the way we speak and act.

I've heard it said that we can measure the level of our religious maturity by our ability to not allow anything to become bigger than our perspective of heaven, the realm of God – *agape* love's ideal. Our religious success should only be measured by our ability to align our actions and our words with that reality.

Even when the reality we see or our current level of experience or encounter competes with *agape* love's reality, a mature and authentically religious person will contend with confidence and continue on until it's a current and present-tense reality.

To the extent each of us individually is successful in living out true religion's mandate, we can do everything Jesus did – and more – to see entire realms on earth transformed.

This is the ultimate goal of all true religious pursuit. The Bible actually says we can grow up into the very likeness of Christ Himself:

*... to prepare God's people for works of service, so that the body of Christ may be built up until we all reach unity in the faith and in the knowledge of the Son of God and become mature, attaining to the whole measure of the fullness of Christ. Then we will no longer be infants, tossed back and forth by the waves, and blown here and there by every wind of teaching and by the cunning and craftiness of men in their deceitful scheming. Instead, speaking the truth in love, we will in all things grow up into him who is the Head, that is, Christ. From him the whole body, joined and held together by every supporting ligament, grows and builds itself up in love, as each part does its work.*

*~ Ephesians 4:12–15*

Living out the will of God and advancing His kingdom is such an important concept. Jesus said that every other law of God and the prophets hang on this one concept. He said it another way here:

*Jesus replied: "'Love the Lord your God with all your heart and with all your soul and with all your mind.' This is the first and greatest commandment. And the second is like it: 'Love your neighbor ‹**those in close proximity to you**› as yourself.' All the Law ‹**the precepts of God**› and the Prophets ‹**those who speak inspired truth**› hang on these two commandments."*

*~ Matthew 22:37–40*

This doesn't mean that you have to agree with everybody, trust everybody, or believe everybody. However, we are commanded to love everybody. That means we are to do our part to facilitate peace and do our part to stay connected and to contend for the highest possible good in every situation for people, even those divided against us.

Too often religion, in the traditional sense, has been used as a tool to divide, and yet one of our greatest mandates in the kingdom is to gather together and reconnect. True religion connects!

Literally, we "re-member" His broken body when we prefer each other, when we love each other, and when we endeavor to stay connected in relationship with each other. Jesus said that if two of us would "come together" and agree as touching anything, it's the same as Him being there and doing it Himself (Matt. 18:20). Wow. Let's get religious!

# RELIGION__REACT

What are the top three things you are taking away from this chapter?

_____

_____

_____

_____

_____

_____

_____

What action can you take now on what you've learned?

_____

_____

_____

_____

_____

_____

_____

_____

_____

The wisdom of God is peaceable

Full of mercy, gentle, and pure

It lifts the burdens of heavy hearts

And imparts love where there is hurt

– WISDOM –

*Lyrics by Kevin Weaver It's Feasible Publishing, LLC*

Download the complete lyrics and an .mp3 version of this
song in its entirety at www.thereorientbook.com.

004

# CHURCH

# What's your REACTION to the word?

⊕ Positive

⊖ Negative

◎ Neutral

# What does the word MEAN TO YOU?

_____

_____

_____

_____

_____

_____

_____

_____

_____

Now let's see what others say. ▶

The way people surveyed
reacted to the word CHURCH.

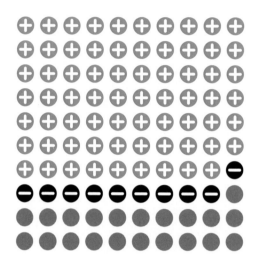

69.17%
Positive

10.27%
Negative

20.54%
Neutral

See a video of respondants in the Resource section for this chapter at www.reorientbook.com.

Common words people surveyed associated with the word CHURCH.

COMMUNITY
**HOUSE**
**OF GOD**
PEOPLE
**GATHERING PLACE**
FELLOWSHIP
COMFORT
BUSINESS
**CONFORMITY** FAMILY
**RELIGIOUS** MOTIVE
SAFE HYPOCRISY
MONEY
**MORALITY** WORSHIP
BODY OF
CHRIST
GATHERING

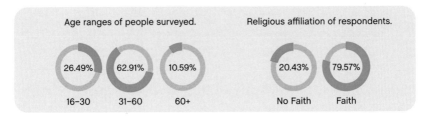

Age ranges of people surveyed.

26.49%    62.91%    10.59%

16–30    31–60    60+

Religious affiliation of respondents.

20.43%    79.57%

No Faith    Faith

# CHURCH_REDISCOVER

## OLD TESTAMENT
## HEBREW WORDS FOR CHURCH

USED  0 *times*

WORDS

DEFINITION

---

## NEW TESTAMENT
## GREEK WORDS FOR CHURCH

USED  *About* 115 *times*

WORDS  EKKLESIA */ek-klay-see´-ah/*

DEFINITION  *Calling out, called out ones, assembly*

# CHURCH_RECOUNT

# CHURCH

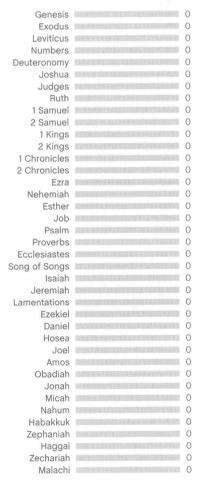

## OLD TESTAMENT VERSES USING THE HEBREW WORD

# 0

|  |  |
|---|---|
| Genesis | 0 |
| Exodus | 0 |
| Leviticus | 0 |
| Numbers | 0 |
| Deuteronomy | 0 |
| Joshua | 0 |
| Judges | 0 |
| Ruth | 0 |
| 1 Samuel | 0 |
| 2 Samuel | 0 |
| 1 Kings | 0 |
| 2 Kings | 0 |
| 1 Chronicles | 0 |
| 2 Chronicles | 0 |
| Ezra | 0 |
| Nehemiah | 0 |
| Esther | 0 |
| Job | 0 |
| Psalm | 0 |
| Proverbs | 0 |
| Ecclesiastes | 0 |
| Song of Songs | 0 |
| Isaiah | 0 |
| Jeremiah | 0 |
| Lamentations | 0 |
| Ezekiel | 0 |
| Daniel | 0 |
| Hosea | 0 |
| Joel | 0 |
| Amos | 0 |
| Obadiah | 0 |
| Jonah | 0 |
| Micah | 0 |
| Nahum | 0 |
| Habakkuk | 0 |
| Zephaniah | 0 |
| Haggai | 0 |
| Zechariah | 0 |
| Malachi | 0 |

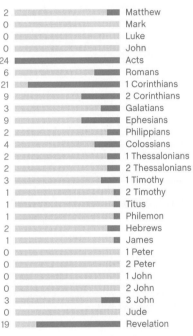

## NEW TESTAMENT VERSES USING THE GREEK WORD

# 115

|  |  |
|---|---|
| 2 | Matthew |
| 0 | Mark |
| 0 | Luke |
| 0 | John |
| 24 | Acts |
| 6 | Romans |
| 21 | 1 Corinthians |
| 9 | 2 Corinthians |
| 3 | Galatians |
| 9 | Ephesians |
| 2 | Philippians |
| 4 | Colossians |
| 2 | 1 Thessalonians |
| 2 | 2 Thessalonians |
| 3 | 1 Timothy |
| 1 | 2 Timothy |
| 1 | Titus |
| 1 | Philemon |
| 2 | Hebrews |
| 1 | James |
| 0 | 1 Peter |
| 0 | 2 Peter |
| 0 | 1 John |
| 0 | 2 John |
| 3 | 3 John |
| 0 | Jude |
| 19 | Revelation |

*Graph is based on the highest verse use and shown visually as a percentage of the highest value.

173

# CHURCH_REORIENT

Have you ever been asked if you go to church or to become a member of a church? Have you ever heard someone say "I grew up in church" or refer to the local church or the global church? When you see the word *church*, what comes to mind?

Do you imagine:

| | | |
|---|---|---|
| A building | A pew | A priest |
| A stained-glass window | A choir | A pulpit |
| A steeple | A pastor | A sermon |

Answering yes to any of the above wouldn't be uncommon. Here's a sampling of what people we surveyed said in response to the word *church* (sorted alphabetically):

| | | |
|---|---|---|
| A big gathering | A place for people who believe in God | A structured religion |
| A building | | Boring |
| A community of people | A place of worship | Catholic |
| | A place to meet with God | Conservative |
| A congregation | | |
| A fellowship of Christians | A place where God's Spirit dwells | Don't forsake gathering together |
| A gathering place | A religious structure | God |
| A holy place | A safe haven | The bride of Christ |
| A parish | A small part of a larger denomination | The governmental branch of God's kingdom on earth |

The house of God

The only way, truth, and life

There is one on every corner

The worldwide body of Christians

Where do you go?

Numerous survey respondents listed the actual name of their local church, like, for example, the First Church of _____ (fill in the blank).

We also received some humorous and/or sad responses, depending on your perspective. We heard things like:

A church is a euphemism for tax evasion

An outlet for selling furniture with really bad fabrics

Are you in or are you out?

A synonym for the word *hypocrite*

A training ground for con-artists

Come join the club – our club

The most inefficient use of prime real estate on the planet

For me, the word causes a flood of childhood images. I envision wooden podiums encircled by plastic flowers on a carpeted stage appointed with imitation Benjamin Ficus trees. I remember the chill of the holy water in the church baptismal water bowl. I recall the musty smell of the church hymnals, the creaking sound and hardness of the church kneeling bench and the

**RECONSIDER**

Fun with church word usages:[16]

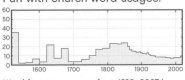

*Word frequency usage from 1539–2007 in occurrences per 100,000 words per year*

Phone Digits: (...) .24-8724
Rhymes: birch, lurch, research, search
Scrabble Score: 16

little plastic piggy bank shaped like a loaf of bread in which I saved money for Vacation Bible School.

When you were a child, were you ever asked to learn the little rhyme and hand-gesture game called "Here Is the Church"? It went something like this:

1. Here is the church (both fists together, fingers interlocking downward)

2. Here is the steeple (raise only index fingers and pointing them up)

3. Open the doors (rotate wrists and hands upward, fingers still interlocked)

4. See all the people? (indicated by moving fingers back and forth)

These examples may seem like trivial associations, but they serve to underscore how ingrained images like these can become in our collective conscious, reinforcing around what we think of and call church.

Opinions are even formed by people who have no idea what I've just been talking about, whose personal history with church is limited to weddings and funerals.

But what is church, really? How closely do these impressions and modern representations of church compare to what the biblical writers knew of church?


## A WAKE-UP CALL AND WHY WE DON'T NEED ANOTHER CHURCH

It was 4:00 a.m., sometime in January 2006, and I was awakened by a single phrase:

"Wake up! I don't need another church. I want an uprising – a call to battle in this generation!"

My wife and I had no way of knowing how drastically this short phrase would alter the course of our lives – and the lives of many others around the world – in the weeks and months that followed. It set us on a journey that ultimately reformed the foundation of our family, how we thought about and connected with God, the fruit of our connections with God, and virtually everything we thought we knew about church.

This phrase was the catalyst for reforming our ideas about co-laboring with God to supernaturally bring about love's ideal on earth, and how we began to equip others to rise up to do the same.

Though our reoriented religious activity looks nothing like it did when our life with God and the people of God revolved around what is traditionally considered church, our hearts are more fully alive. The fruit of our life with God is also exponentially more intimate, fulfilling, supernatural, visible, plentiful, and impacting than when we thought of church as the center of God's universe and the hub of His activities.

Some years later, while researching the word *church* for this book, I better saw why God was so adamant when He said, "I don't need another church!"

It's because He never wanted to build a church in the first place. In fact, the very thing we call church today may be the biggest obstacle to the world seeing what God intended to build!

To understand why, we need to look at the actual meaning and history of the word *church* and reorient. Are you ready?

## REASSEMBLING THE WORD CHURCH

It's fairly common knowledge that the Greek word *ekklesia* is the one most often translated to English as *church* in modern versions of the New Testament.

What's not so well known is that for nearly sixteen hundred years after Jesus' time on earth, this wasn't the case. More surprising is the number of experts arguing that the word *church* should have never been considered a good translation of the Greek word *ekklesia*. Given the disparity between the etymology and meaning of the words, it's understandable.

**RESOURCE**
To learn more about An Uprising and get your free copy of a two-hour equipping and teaching session called "An Introduction to An Uprising – Call to Battle," visit www.anuprising.com.

To see what I mean, let's compare the two words, starting with the generally accepted definition.

## Church

*noun*

1. a building for public Christian worship
2. public worship of God or a religious service in such a building
3. the whole body of Christian believers; Christendom
4. any division of this body professing the same creed and acknowledging the same ecclesiastical authority; a Christian denomination: *the Methodist church*
5. that part of the whole Christian body, or of a particular denomination, belonging to the same city, country, nation, etc.
6. a body of Christians worshipping in a particular building or constituting one congregation
7. ecclesiastical organization, power, and affairs, as distinguished from the state
8. the clergy and religious officials of a Christian denomination

*Origin(s):*

Before 900; Middle English *chir(i)che,* Old English *cir(i)ce* « Greek *ky ri(a)kón (dôma)* the Lord's (house), neuter of *ky riakós* of the master, equivalent to *ky ri(os)* master (*kŷr(os)* power + *-ios* noun suffix) + *-akos,* variant of *-ikos* -ic; akin to Dutch *kerk,* German *Kirche,* Old Norse *kirkja.* See *kirk.*

When this modern definition of the word *church* is compared to the modern definition of the Greek word *ekklesia,* the association of the two words seems logical enough.

## Ekklesia

*noun*

1. a gathering of citizens called out from their homes into some public place; an assembly
2. an assembly of the people convened at the public place of the council for the purpose of deliberating
3. the assembly of the Israelites
4. any gathering or throng of men assembled by chance, tumultuously

*Origin(s):*

Latin *ecclesia,* <*Greek ekklesia* from the compound word(s) *ek,* meaning "out of, from, by, away from," and *kaleo',* meaning "to call out, to call aloud, to utter in a strong voice, to summon, to be called by a name or title, to salute."

As the dictionary definition indicates, most people think of church as a place where religious people gather, congregate, or assemble outside their homes. Further, since the word *ekklesia* was also used to describe an assembly of people outside their homes, it's then thought that the two words *church* and *ekklesia* are synonymous. To reinforce the notion, *ekklesia* is sometimes translated *assembly* instead of church (Acts 19:32, 39, 41, NKJV).

But are *church* and *ekklesia* really describing the same thing? Would Jesus or other New Testament writers have thought of a church and an *ekklesia* the same way?

The answer is no.

These two words are very different and were used for centuries before and after Jesus' time on earth to describe two very different kinds of assemblies. It's only our modern paradigm and religious traditions that prejudice our thinking to the idea that an *ekklesia* assembly or congregation is the same thing as a church type assembly or congregation. The contrast between the two kinds of assemblies these words were used to describe is stunning, and the impact of historically linking the two words, in terms of Jesus' mission, is immeasurable.

To see what I mean, we need to reassemble the word *church* by considering its origins and then compare it to the origins of *ekklesia.* As we do, you'll see Jesus:

Didn't want to build a church,

Didn't advocate meeting in a church,

Didn't advocate constructing church buildings,

Didn't prescribe routine methods of church worship,

**REMEMBER**
Remember, I am not making a case for how God may or may not feel about any of these things, nor am I being critical of people who advocate them.

Didn't use the local church to describe groups of Christians,

Didn't use *church* to refer to a global body of Christians,

Didn't even know what a church was!

The word *church* is one of only a couple examples where translators chose to not directly translate a word to English from a Hebrew or Greek counterpart – and this was done with full knowledge that a known English alternative with similar connotations existed.

This is even more perplexing in the case of the word *church* as the English translation of the word *ekklesia,* since there was already an established precedent for translating the word *ekklesia* as assembly, not church.

So why not continue with the established precedent? Why choose the word *church* over the word *assembly?* And why would this be allowed, considering that the origins, definitions, evolution, and implications of the word *church* had so little in common with the word *ekklesia?* The answer can be seen, in part, by looking at the etymology of each word.

Our modern word *church* evolved from an old English word, circe. It's from which other modern English words like *circus, circle, circuit,* and *circulate* have their roots.

In the Middle Ages, the Old English word *circe* was sometimes written and pronounced *kirk* or *kirke* and since the 1400s, has been the Scottish English word for church.[17]

The Greek root word for our modern-day word *church* is actually *kurakon,* not *ekklesia.*

Even the old universal Oxford English Dictionary lists the origins of the word *church* as follows:

Old English circe, Middle English cereche, chirche, churche, cherche, etc.: Greek Kurakon

This is where things began to get really interesting.

You can readily see the Greek word *kurakon* evolving to the modern word we know as church today by looking at various iterations of the same word evolving in other languages. Likewise, you can see how the Latin word *ecclesia* became the Greek word *ekklesia,* the modern French word *église,* the Spanish word *iglesia,* and the English words we know today as *ecclesiastical* and *ecclesiastes.*

Though both Greek words eventually became used to describe an assembly, the question is should a church assembly ever be related to an ecclesiastical assembly? After all, nowhere in the history or evolution of the Greek word *kurakon* into the modern word *church* is the word *ekklesia* found. Nowhere in the evolution of the Greek word *ekklesia* into the English word *assembly* do you find the word *church!*

This is of critical importance because not only do the etymology of the two words *kurakon* and *ekklesia* differ drastically, so do their meanings and connotations.

The Greek word *kurakon* means "pertaining to the lord or belonging to a lord." The word *lord* was used throughout history to describe someone high in rank, like kings, princes, dukes, and various other magistrates. In this context, the word was historically:[18]

Used to describe a building owned by a lord,

Used to describe property owned by a lord,

Used to describe something used in the service of a lord,

Used to describe something set aside for a lord's use,

Used to describe certain days set aside to honor a lord,

Used to describe gatherings or assemblies given in honor of a lord.

RECONSIDER
*Evolution of church assembly:*
kurakon (Greek)
circe (Old English)
kirk (Scottish English)
kirche (German)
church (Modern English)
church assembly
assembly

*Evolution of ekklesia assembly:*
ecclesia (Latin)
ekklesia (Greek)
église (French)
iglesia (Spanish)
ecclesiastes (English)
ecclesiastical assembly
assembly

It was this use of the word that gave rise to the word *kurakon* being associated in a traditional religious context to describe the things of God, since both Jesus and God were referred to as Lord. The word then became historically:

Used to describe religious things pertaining to God,

Used to describe a building for religious activity,

Used to describe property used for religious purposes,

Used to describe anything used in service of the Lord,

Used to describe religious ceremonies,

Used to describe religious gatherings and assemblies.

If the original New Testament writers had used the word *kurakon* to describe their gatherings, the word *church* would have been a fitting translation.

Ironically, in the two instances in the Bible where the original writers of the New Testament did use the Greek word *kurakon,* it is not translated into English as *church,* but instead as *Lord.* Here are the two verses:

> *When you come together, it is not the* **Lord's ‹kurakon›** *Supper you eat ...*
> > *~ 1 Corinthians 11:20,* **emphasis added**

> *On the* **Lord's ‹kurakon›** *Day I was in the Spirit, and I heard behind me a loud voice like a trumpet ...*
> > *~ Revelation 1:10,* **emphasis added**

See how, in both verses, the word *kurakon* is translated *Lord,* the first referring to the Lord's Supper and the second to the Lord's Day? This would certainly make sense, since the day or meal was pertaining to a lord – in this case, the Lord's supper or day.

If ever there was a perfect opportunity to use the word *church* derived directly from the Greek word *kurakon,* this was it. But amazingly, instead of "the church's supper" or "the church's day," modern Bibles read "the Lord's Supper" or "the Lord's Day."

If that weren't confusing enough, in 115 places in the New Testament where the word *ekklesia* is used, it is translated as *church* 112 times and only three times as *assembly*.

Why the obvious disconnect? When and why did the word *church* become a suitable and acceptable translation of the word *ekklesia*? And, more importantly, what are the implications?

Some sources trace the use of the word *church* back as far as AD 190 to Clement of Alexandria.[19] Others credit the first use of the word *church* in the Bible to Theodore Beza, a Protestant follower of John Calvin in Geneva, Switzerland.[20] Beza is said to be the first person to formally change a precedent set by William Tyndale when he translated the first Bible from Greek to English some thirty years earlier. Tyndale was the first to translate the word *ekklesia* as assembly or congregation, not church.[21]

The decision by Beza and others to abandon Tyndale's translation of *ekklesia* as "assembly" or "congregation", opting instead for the word *church,* appear to be heavily influenced by Universal Catholic Church doctrines and other hierarchal forms of religious governance.

The next major iteration of the Bible into English was the King James Version of the Bible, commissioned around 1611. This version, and other subsequent translations, apparently followed Beza's precedent and used the word *church* for the meaning of *ekklesia* instead of *assembly* or *congregation,* as preferred by Tyndale.

Unlike the biblical word *ekklesia,* which can be traced back to nearly 500 BC, the word *church* was not initially used until approximately AD 1556. It did not become popularized until the early part of AD 1600.

You have to let this sink in before we reorient further.

This distinction is really important in order to reconsider the word *ekklesia* and the way the New Testament writers used the term. Even though both *ekklesia* and *kurakon*

REMEMBER
Did you catch that? It was nearly 1600 years after Jesus' time on the earth before the word *church* began appearing in English Bibles!

183

were eventually used to describe a type of assembly, it's essential that we disassociate the two words to understand how Jesus and His followers were assembling!

As you look closer, you'll see Jesus and His followers were extremely consistent and apparently intentional in their extensive use of the word *ekklesia* to describe their assemblies. However, the way they used the word *ekklesia* is inconsistent with the meaning, origin, and modern use of the word *kurakon* to which we just reoriented.

So what kind of assembly did Jesus have in mind when using the term *ekklesia*?

## A LITTLE HISTORY ON THE WORD *EKKLESIA* AND A FRESH APPLICATION OF THE INTENT BEHIND ASSEMBLING TOGETHER

Are you curious to discover whether reorienting to the real meaning of *ekklesia* would have practical implications in our world today? How it might change how and why we assemble in what's called church today? And if changing how and why people gather or assemble in churches could impact our culture?

Let's take a closer look at the word *ekklesia*.

The first thing you must understand is this: unlike the Greek word *kurakon,* which became church in English, the Greek word *ekklesia,* as commonly used for more than five centuries before Jesus, did not have a religious connotation.

If you had asked someone in first-century Athens, "Where is the *ekklesia*?", they would not have directed you to any of the following:

A building owned by a lord,

A property owned by a lord,

A thing placed in the service of a lord,

A thing set aside for a lord's use,

A day set aside to honor a lord,

A gathering or assembly in honor of a lord.

Nor would they have directed you to:

A building for religious activity,

A property used for religious purposes,

A prayer meeting,

A worship service,

A religious ceremony,

A religious gathering or assembly.

A religious notion would simply not have even come to mind. If you were looking for a religious gathering, you would have needed to ask, "Where is the *thiasos?*" or "Where is the synagogue?" That's because the word *thiasos* was a word used to describe cultic or religious-type group gatherings and *synagogue* was the word used to describe Jewish religious gatherings. These were also words widely known in Jesus' day that He could have used if His intent was to build a religious movement, organization, or assembly in the traditional sense of the word.

This begs the question: where were these non-religious assemblies happening if not in what we think of as churches? What was the purpose of these assemblies if they weren't religious in the traditional sense of the word? What in the world would the people in Greece think you meant when you used the word *ekklesia?*

An *ekklesia* suggested something civil, political, or militaristic in nature.

Did you catch that?

> ❝ *For more than five hundred years before Christ, an ekklesia had a civil, political, or militaristic connotation – not a religious or spiritual one!* ❞

Jesus and His followers intentionally used the word that had civil, political, and militaristic implications some 115 times to describe their intents. Yet, in every instance, except the three we referenced earlier (Acts 19:32, 39, 41), translators intentionally chose a more religious word, *church,* which had no such civil, political, or militaristic implications.

Why did the writers of the New Testament, and especially Jesus, use the word *ekklesia?* Did they understand the implications?

Tyndale was right – *assembly* or *congregation* was a more accurate translation of *ekklesia* than *church.* However, I am not convinced changing the word *church* to *assembly* or *congregation* would make that much difference. At least in modern times, the words *assembly* and *congregation* often carry the same religious connotation as the word *church.* Furthermore, the words *assembly* or *congregation* are not precise enough to convey the real power behind the word *ekklesia* and the reasons the original writers chose that word.

That's because the word *ekklesia* is more precisely defined as "a calling out," "called out," or, when applied directly to a group of people, "called-out ones." The word is a compound one derived from two Greek root words, *ekk* or *ecc,* meaning "out," and the Greek word *kaleo,* meaning "call" from the Greek verb *ek-kaleo* meaning "to summon."[22]

The same etymology and definition of the word *ekklesia* is used in Strong's *Hebrew and Greek Concordance* and is cited in the origins section of the dictionary definition at the beginning of this chapter. Yet still, because of the modern interchangeable use of the words *church* and *assembly,* the most often implied application of the word is in the context of a religious assembly.

However, the understood meaning at the time of the New Testament writings was to call or summon a body of people out of their homes into a local public gathering, or assembly, of a civil, political, or military nature in a public square.

Again, did you catch that? An *ekklesia* was a public gathering of citizens to govern a city.

> **The purpose of an ekklesia was to "call people out" or "summon them" to assemble or to congregate in a public place primarily to deal with civil, political, or military matters – not religious matters!**

Did Jesus and His followers know what they were implying by choosing to use the word *ekklesia,* or was it coincidental?

It was quite intentional. Jesus and His followers knew exactly what they were doing. They were not inviting a few Christians over for a potluck dinner and a peaceful Bible study at a building they had rented. They were not asking people to join them and withdraw from the social and political arenas of life to worship in private and pray nobody would notice.

By using the word *ekklesia,* these writers were summoning people to come from their homes, which at the time was the predominant place people had religious connections with God, to assemble in the public square. The goal of these assemblies was not simply to worship or instruct people about the things of God, but to rise up in the power of God to confront the civil and political issues and powers of the day that oppressed them.

You could say, and not add to the Bible, that by using the word *ekklesia,* Jesus and His followers were calling people out of their homes to *battle* – to rise up and fight for a higher kind of good in their communities.

An *ekklesia* was not a church, it was an uprising!

An uprising – a call to battle – was actually the intent behind an *ekklesia!* How cool is that?

By using the word *ekklesia,* you might say Jesus and His followers were making:

A declaration of independence,

A declaration of war,

A statement to the world,

A statement to the governmental powers,

A new civil and political community,

A new King – of Jesus – not Caesar,

A public statement they no longer acknowledged Caesar as Lord.

Jesus and His followers understood these implications and knew very well it may cost them their lives – and in many cases, it did. Unlike the free exchange of political and civil ideas we enjoy in the United States today, the world under Caesar's rule was not so accommodating of this kind of dissension.

This may partially explain why early translators were so eager to provide a more benign word like *church* as an alternative to the more inflammatory and politically and socially charged word *ekklesia.*

But Jesus and His followers were intent on sending a clear public message to the political, social, and cultural powers of their day.

By using the word *ekklesia* to describe their public gatherings, they were calling people to battle; to rise up; to form small, local, civil, and political bodies under new leadership. They were calling people to emerge from their homes and to establish civil outposts made up of small groups of people that would no longer look to the government as their source.

This call to battle, this uprising, was to summon a new kind of revolutionary army designed to usher in a new kingdom under a new rule: the kingdom of heaven under love's rule.

By intentionally using the word *ekklesia,* they were using military terms to describe their aim to destroy the strongholds of their day. As such, they began to use ecclesiastical language to describe their methods of warfare. They were clear that their weapons were not natural military weapons and that their enemy was not people, but they were declaring war just the same.

You can see this clearly in Paul's rhetoric in the following verses:

> We are human, but we don't wage war as humans do. We use God's mighty weapons, not worldly weapons, to knock down the strongholds of human reasoning and to destroy false arguments. We destroy every proud obstacle that keeps people from knowing God. We capture their rebellious thoughts and teach them to obey Christ. And after you have become fully obedient, we will punish everyone who remains disobedient.
> ~ *2 Corinthians 10:3–6,* NLT

Their mission was an uprising of individuals and small groups who would wage war against and subdue the prevailing thoughts and arguments of the day that were suppressing love's ideal.

Unlike the way we think about churches of our day, Jesus and His followers were not asking the government to sanction their mission or even give them special tax exemption to fund their efforts.

To the contrary, they were fully prepared to continue to render to Caesar what was Caesar's (Matt. 22:21), but were unwilling to acknowledge him any longer as their Lord.

An *ekklesia,* in terms of how Jesus and His followers intended it, consisted of a growing number of true cultural and kingdom revolutionaries who would go into all the

**REMEMBER**
Jesus and His followers knew that by using such rhetoric and such a politically charged word as *ekklesia,* they were likely inviting conflict that may very well cost them their own lives. For many, it literally did – but not without starting a global movement with such impact that we are still talking about it today!

189

world with a message and a mission that was better than anyone was imagining or experiencing in their time. They were being transformed by the good news of this message and wanted everyone to hear about it and to be a part of it.

In case you think I am taking liberty with this word and its connotations in the context of our theoretical trip back to Athens and application of the word, check out how these other sources define the word *ekklesia*.

The *Encyclopedia Britannica* defines it this way: "the name given to a political or governmental assembly in the city of Athens, duly convoked [called out] by proper officers and the possessing of all political power, including juridical functions."

Quoting from the *Oxford Universal Dictionary:*

> "Medieval Latin and Greek – from: *summoned:* a regularly convoked [political] assembly of Athenians."

The massive difference between the original spirit and intent behind an *ekklesia* and that of a church may explain why centuries of religious church tradition have failed to produce the kind of revolutionary social, political, and cultural change Jesus and His followers envisioned!

## " *You might even say the only way to stop the kind of uprising Jesus and His followers had in mind was to call it a church.* "

The world still desperately needs an *ekklesia* movement, not a church movement!

The world doesn't need larger and larger audiences to attend church gatherings – it needs an army of revolutionary individuals and small groups with experience connecting with God and administering the reality of His kingdom.

Just as in Jesus' day, the world needs to see the reality of His kingdom impacting every area of an individual's life first and then expanding to every sphere of life on Planet Earth – the family, business, the economy, the government, education, entertainment, and the media.

This is the Great Commission (or Co-Mission) from the Master Himself – Jesus.

Jesus didn't give us a great co-mission to go and tell the world, "Come to a church gathering." He said to go and declare the good news of the kingdom to the world, announcing the time is at hand for God's will to be done on earth, just as it is in heaven.

To those who would master the ability to administer Jesus' authority, He charged them to make the transforming power of His love a tangible reality in every aspect of life and culture:

> He said to them, *"Go into all the world* and preach ‹*herald; be a public crier*› the *good news* to all creation. Whoever believes and is baptized ‹*to make whelmed or immersed*› will be saved ‹*healed, preserved, made well, made whole*›, but whoever does not believe will be condemned. *And these signs* will accompany *those who believe: In my name they will drive out demons; they will speak in new tongues* ‹*utter fresh words*›; *they will pick up snakes with their hands; and when they drink deadly poison, it will not hurt them at all; they will place their hands on sick people, and they will get well."*
>
> ~ *Mark 16:15–18,* **emphasis added**

Apparently, this great co-mission was really good news, unless for some reason you:


Liked oppression,

Liked living with demons,

Liked dealing with snakes in your life,

Liked being sick,

Liked being broken,

Liked being unwell and not whole.


If you were in any of these categories, Jesus' message may have seemed threatening and maybe even condemnatory.

Jesus' charge was to go into all these realms, get involved, live fully alive in every area of life, and be a sign for a higher kind of good, to be a herald for a more excellent kind of news.

He wanted His followers to become the "go-to" people, not the "come-here" people! He wanted a go-to person in every realm of society – a go-to person who was a carrier of the kingdom with the proven ability to demonstrate and administer its reality.

Jesus knew that for kingdoms to truly change, men must change first. He didn't call us out to live separated lives from the world like the religious leaders of His day. Rather, He called us out first to be transformed and then to go back into the world and transform it!

He didn't tell us to go tell everyone to *come to us*. He said, *"Come to Me,"* and then ...


Go heal people,

Go preserve people,

Go make people well,

Go make people whole,

Go declare good news,

Go declare that it doesn't have to be this way anymore,

Go proclaim anything less than love's ideal is unacceptable,

Go declare anything less than love's ideal is an inferior and unnecessary reality,

Go extend His rule on earth, just as it is in heaven,

Go declare the end of oppression under a new type of government,

Go declare the end of poverty under the government of heaven,

Go administer love's rule with the authority of a King above all kings,

Go with supernatural power and authority to transform all voluntarily committed to Him,

Go, and all who believe will have certain kinds of signs follow them (not on sticks),

Go, and He will validate true believers with a song (the supernatural kind).

Jesus promised that if people would go in this manner, He would personally confirm their words with accompanying signs of miraculous nature. These would validate those who were true representatives of His kingdom with the very real, delegated authority to administer it on earth.

> Then the disciples went out and preached everywhere, and the Lord worked with them and confirmed his word by the signs that accompanied it.
>
> ~ Mark 16:20

The emphasis was not on the gathering or the actual meeting, but on the going in order to accomplish the mission. It's the Great *Commission*, not the great conference!

Reorienting to this original intent behind the word *ekklesia*, instead of the ubiquitous term we now use, *church*, can be revolutionary in and of itself and the beginning of an uprising – a call to battle in our generation. An authentic uprising and movement of this nature can accomplish more in a couple generations than two thousand years of church movements have achieved.

To answer this call, we must reorient and repurpose the idea of church to be consistent with an *ekklesia*. We must stop going to church and begin an *ekklesia* uprising – a call to battle in this generation!

193

## ARE YOU READY TO STOP GOING TO CHURCH AND START AN UPRISING?

Do you feel something stirring in your spirit? Is beginning to reorient to the word *ekklesia* changing the way you think about how and why people gathered in Jesus' time? Is reorienting to the word *ekklesia* changing the way you think about how we gather in what we call church today? Does the heading to this section sound heretical?

If so, we may need to reorient some more.

Recently, my wife and I were asked by the well-meaning spouse of a megachurch pastor, "Where do you go to church?"

I replied, "Well, I went to a great church for about thirteen years and still have a relational connection there. The last couple years, however, my family and I have traveled a lot, ministering in other churches, so we don't attend there as often anymore. Actually, sometimes we even attend *your* church. In fact, we taught in your church several times last year with great fruit. We are really grateful for your leadership and for allowing us to be there."

The pastor's spouse asked if we were members of her church and I replied no.

"So, what church are you members of, and what church do you consider your church home?" they wanted to know.

"We don't have a church home, *per se,* as we travel a lot on the weekends," I replied. "You might say we consider our home, home," I added with a laugh.

"I understand that you travel," they persisted. "But when you are in town, where do you actually attend church?"

I answered: "Well, when we are in town, we don't. We often minister to our family at home, which usually includes watching a service online, but we don't regularly attend a local church."

**REMEMBER** If you are involved in a church or in church leadership in some capacity, don't check out – hang in there. I have no intention of suggesting that people forsake gathering together or leave their local congregation. However, we do need to repurpose our gatherings and the meaning we assign to them.

The pastor's spouse seemed concerned. "So, you don't attend a local church at all?"

"Not regularly, no," I said. "But we have a relational connection to several churches. In all honestly, I am not sure how you want me to answer your question. Can you define church?"

They were getting increasingly frustrated. "I know what church is, Kevin," they said. "Church is not the building; it's the people – *we* are the church! You know what I'm asking!"

I wasn't sure that I did. I said. "If, as you say, church is not the building, it's the people, why do you keep asking me where do I go to church? How can I accurately answer your question?" I laughed in an effort to keep the mood light. "Would you like me to answer a question you already know to be inaccurate with an equally inaccurate response?" (Again, laughing to keep the mood light)

The pastor's spouse did not seem to appreciate my answer. "That's all great, Kevin, but you know the Bible clearly says to not forsake the assembling of yourselves together. I am very surprised you were even allowed to teach at our church without being submitted to a local pastor and with no record of regular attendance and tithing to a local church. I really think you should get plugged in somewhere and serve when you are in town."

I wish I could say conversations like this weren't common, but they occur all too frequently. The simple question, "Where do you go to church?" is so loaded with tradition, assumptions, and connotations that you need to redefine the entire conversation to even begin to accurately answer the question.

On another occasion, I was invited to a fairly large church setting with my family to help equip people in the miraculous through our movement, An Uprising. I began the session with a show of hands from people who had personally seen or been part of a miracle, sign, or wonder that day. No hands went up. I then asked the same question in regards to that week, that month, and that year. Only when I then asked "ever" did three people raise their hands.

Ironically, this church was part of a large charismatic-type denomination that, at least theologically, embraced these kinds of supernatural endowments of grace. But, apparently, nobody in the audience was walking in them as a present-tense reality.

I taught our "Introduction to an Uprising, a Call to Battle" for about an hour and then welcomed my family to the stage to administer the love of God and bring about the kinds of signs that we resolved should accompany all of us who believe. The result was more than thirty minutes of signs and wonders – blind eyes opened and deaf ears healed, among many other things God did that day.

Following the session, I was asked by one of the leaders what church we attended as a family. When I failed to answer the question to their satisfaction, I was warned, in a concerned and loving tone, that unless we were sanctioned by a local church to do what we were doing and focused our efforts on building up the local church, God's favor would never be on us, our ministry, or anything we did – we would be cursed!

I told him that I wouldn't want to lose the favor of God and asked what would be evidence of God's favor and how would you know if you lost it?

He paused a moment before asserting; "Well, I guess there would be certain fruit, signs and wonders that follow those who believe and for those God is with."

How ironic: We were being warned that God's favor would not be on us and could not expect to operate in the very signs and wonders we had just demonstrated if we were not sanctioned by a local church and yet, the very local church we were in had no evidence of these things even though they believed in them.

In recounting these two scenarios, I am not trying to make these local leaders look bad – they were well intentioned. I have no intention of suggesting that people forsake gathering together or leave a church congregation, *per se*. To the contrary, gathering and assembling to-gether is certainly biblical.

But I want to take a fresh look at the reasons why we gather together and the outcomes we should expect from those occasions. While there is a biblical precedent for a church-type gathering, it's equally true that *ekklesia* gatherings were never intended to take the form of church gatherings or inherit the meanings we so commonly ascribe to church gatherings today.

Does this verse sound familiar?

> *And let us consider how to **stimulate** one another to **love** and good deeds, not forsaking our own **assembling togeth- er,** as is the habit of some, but **encouraging** one another; and all the more as you see the day drawing near.*
> *~ Hebrews 10:24–25, NAS, **emphasis added***

This verse is frequently quoted and used to support our modern idea of regular church attendance and membership in a local church. It's regurgitated almost automatically as the definitive verse to uphold the tradition.

The spoken or unspoken implication of "forsaking to assemble" – which to most people means not going to church – instills fear of being apos- tate or, at the very least, out of God's will. The unspoken, but implied, communication is often, "If you dare choose to not be a member or regular attendee at a local church, you are at odds with God and rebel- ling against the plan of God – you're no longer considered one of us."

Does it have to be either-or?

I don't know if you noticed or not, but ironically, the word *church* is not even mentioned in the verse just referenced. Now, if ever there was a place where the translators could have used the word *church,* you'd think it would be this one!

After all, they had no problem using the word *church* instead of *ekkle- sia* about 115 times in the New Testament to describe the collective "gathering" of believers. Yet, in this verse, the most frequently quoted verse to support the idea of our collective gathering and subsequent church involvement, the word *church* is never mentioned.

Instead, the phrase *assembling together* was used.

Before I comment further, let's look at this verse one more time. This time, however, let's read it with the actual definitions of some key words expanded:

> And let us consider ‹**discover one another**› how to **stimu-late** ‹**provoke or incite with a kind of anger**› one another to **love** ‹**agape – to always contend for the highest good in every situation until it's a present-tense reality**› and good deeds ‹**deeds here is the Greek word for work, ergo, meaning to labor, like in your occupation**›, not forsaking our own **assembling together** ‹**meeting**›, as in the habit of some, but encouraging ‹**to call out, help contend, invoke, implore, beseech, or entreat**› one another; and all the more as you see the day drawing near.

Is this verse saying "Go to church" or "Do not quit going to church" as is typically implied? Doesn't it sound more like this verse is charging us to do pretty much everything we have discussed so far in this book – to not be separated from God or each other, to connect to each other, and to help each other cultivate and put into action the power of God's love in everyday life and our realms of influence, even at work?

Using this verse to support our traditional model of church is problematic. It's not that going to a church in and of itself is a bad thing. The problem is that church gatherings, by the nature of what church actually means, are simply not conducive to facilitating the kind of "assembling together" this verse describes. Again, it's not that:

Church is, in and of itself, ungodly,

Church is unbiblical,

Church leaders are bad or ill-intentioned,

Church people are incapable of "getting it,"

Church people are uninterested in connecting with God.

It's that:

Church is the wrong kind of structure to facilitate this end result,

Church is not the most excellent way to facilitate this kind of interaction,

Church will never have the same ability an *ekklesia* does to bring about these things.

Remember, church, by definition, is *a physical place or a building where people gather en masse for religious activities.* So, if you want to get together and encourage "each other," as this verse suggests, a church gathering with lots of people worshiping will likely not help you connect that way. It's certainly not conducive to helping you discover much about "one another" or inciting "each other" to love, while you sit shoulder to shoulder with a central figure speaking at you for an hour.

I'm not saying there is not a place for the kind of interaction and connection that the traditional understanding of church provides. It's just not conducive to produce the kind of fruit in this verse.

If you and others want to live this verse out in real life, you would likely need to take your interactions outside the normal church gathering. You would need to go somewhere more intimate and more conducive for discovering one another and provoking each other to greater works. This was the custom for thousands of years before there were church or synagogue buildings designated for this purpose.

In conclusion, I am not sure this verse makes the case for our modern idea of church as much as it does paint a solid picture of exactly the kind of fruit that an *ekklesia* was designed to produce.

Despite this limitation of church gatherings, and in contrast to what some critics of the church think, there is still valid biblical precedence for gathering in churches.

The word *church* was never used in the original biblical text, and its Greek counterpart has no relationship to the *ekklesia* that Jesus and His followers intended to build. However, there were structures considered equivalent to a church in Jesus' day.

One example might be a synagogue or temple, which even Jesus attended on occasion for prayers, special feasts, and to celebrate and even teach on occasion.

Though Jesus and His followers never used the word *synagogue* or *church* or its Greek counterpart *kurakon* to describe their gatherings, they did use the word *ekklesia* about 115 times.

That's because neither Jesus nor His followers were trying to build a network of religious edifices or physical structures to hold religious meetings or perform religious activities.

If Jesus or His followers intended to build buildings for God to dwell in and to connect with God, they might have used a word like synagogue or temple to describe their intent. That still wouldn't be clear, however, because even the word *synagogue,* like the word *ekklesia,* means "assembly."

Isn't that interesting? Even in Jesus' day, the word *synagogue* was often used in place of the Hebrew word *qahal,* meaning "congregation." But unfortunately, just like the evolution of the word *church,* the word *synagogue,* which originally referred to the people, over time evolved to refer to the physical place of their assembly – where people would go to worship, study, pray, and eventually learn.

See, even Jesus observed the same phenomenon we are discussing about the word *church* in His day – and by His intentional choice of the word *ekklesia,* expressed no interest in building a synagogue or church in the evolved sense of the word.

Why is this such a big deal? Because the only way a church or a synagogue was similar to an *ekklesia* was by being inherently local and, for the most part, regional in focus. That's pretty much where the similarities end.

**RECONSIDER**
When Jesus taught in a synagogue or temple, it was not a formal ceremony and took place in the temple court, or what would be considered a public area. In fact, it was so public, many other teachers and scribes of His day were often gathering and teaching at the same time. Jesus was never a pastor of a local church or synagogue where He taught at a regular place and time each week to a designated group of members.

A church or a synagogue, by definition, is limited to a physical place and has organized and programmed meeting times and agendas. *Ekklesias* do not.

Like churches, synagogues consisted mainly of private religious gatherings and were typically set apart from other social and political realms of life. *Ekklesias,* by definition, are public in nature, with the specific intent to engage social and political realms of society.

Churches are organized around meetings, whereas *ekklesias* are convened around a mission. Churches can easily become distracted by the pursuit of successful meetings instead of measuring the fruit of successfully accomplishing the mission.

When are the meetings?

Where are the meetings?

Who leads the meetings?

How long are the meetings?

How many people attend the meetings?

How much do the meetings cost?

Are people contributing to cover the cost of the meetings?

These become important questions to determine if church meetings are successful. But outcomes and impact on the mission are the only effective measurements of a successful *ekklesia* or uprising.

The contrasts don't end there.

Churches and synagogues revolve around central leaders who speak, instruct, and administer the things of the kingdom to and on behalf of increasing numbers – people.

An *ekklesia* is smaller by design, administered one to another, with elders or more experienced people leading by example.

Churches and synagogues are places where people go to connect with God and require very little participation on the part of the member other than attendance.

An *ekklesia,* by design, requires every person attending to participate in advancing the mission. Each one is expected to have connected with God by learning to administer the kingdom in their own home and is confirmed by the evidence or signs that follow them in public life.

Churches and synagogues are limited in scalability and impact based on their physical size and location constraints.

An *ekklesia* is infinitely scalable and mobile and can have influence and impact wherever two or more are gathered for that purpose.

The mission of a church and synagogue is impacted by the number of people in their local part of the world regularly coming to their physical locations or buildings.

The focus of an *ekklesia,* by contrast, is on "going into all parts of the world" and is inherently smaller, more mobile, and infinitely scalable.

People go to church to be taught, to be inspired by special knowledge or music, to connect with others in the community, and to gain a sense of belonging – in other words, to have the benefit of others feeding them these things.

People of an *ekklesia,* however, have a much different purpose for meeting. They come to the gathering able to teach, with an inspired song, to impart special knowledge or information, and for the benefit of others. Consider this verse:

> *What then shall we say, brothers? When you come together, everyone has a hymn, or a word of instruction, a revelation, a tongue or an interpretation. All of these must be done for the strengthening of the church ‹**ekklesia**›.*
> ~ 1 Corinthians 14:26

You don't have to quit going to church; you just need to quit thinking of church as a sufficient metaphor or replacement for an *ekklesia!*

Are you beginning to see why it's so important to disconnect the two concepts from each other? Do you feel like you are starting to get a better sense of just a few of the distinctions between a church and an *ekklesia?*

---

**RECONSIDER**

| *Church* | *Ekklesia* |
| --- | --- |
| A building | Assembly of called-out ones |
| A physical place | Anywhere |
| Set gathering times | Anytime |
| Private events | Publicly demonstrated |
| One to many | One to another |
| Religious assembly | Citizen assembly |
| Religious purpose | Social, political purpose |
| 5 percent participate | 100 percent participate |
| Leader-led instruction | Elders inspire by example |
| Meetings programmed | Open and spontaneous |
| Passive attendees | Engaged army |
| Successful by size | Smaller by design |
| Stationary | Infinitely mobile |
| Emphasis on coming | Emphasis on going |
| Limited scalability | Infinitely scalable |
| Member-focused | Fruit-focused |
| Meeting-focused | Mission-focused |
| Method-focused | Evidence-focused |

## RE-LAYING THE FOUNDATION FOR AN UPRISING AND A FRESH LOOK AT SOME OTHER FAMILIAR VERSES ON CHURCH

With the distinctions between a church and an *ekklesia* fresh in our understanding, let's reorient more and re-lay a biblical foundation for an *ekklesia.* To do so, we will use the most familiar verses from the Bible on the topic of church.

Before we begin, however, I want to make a couple suggestions.

1.  If you are familiar with a verse we highlight, try and imagine you're seeing it for the first time and try to look at it with a fresh perspective.

2. Each time we encounter the word *church* in a verse, following our previous precedent, physically and mentally replace the word church with the actual definition of an *ekklesia*.

3. Reorient by considering the impact that changing the connotations of *church* back to the connotations of *ekklesia* has on your understanding of each verse.

Probably the most famous verse in our modern translations of the Bible to use the word *church* is found in a discussion between Jesus and one of His disciples, Peter, in the Gospel of Matthew:

> *Now when Jesus went into the region of Caesarea Philippi, He asked His disciples, Who do people say that the Son of Man is? And they answered, Some say John the Baptist; others say Elijah; and others Jeremiah or one of the prophets. He said to them, But who do you [yourselves] say that I am? Simon Peter replied, You are the* **Christ, the Son of the living God.** *Then Jesus answered him, Blessed (happy, fortunate, and to be envied) are you, Simon Bar-Jonah. For flesh and blood [men] have not revealed this to you, but My Father Who is in heaven.* **And I tell you, you are Peter [Greek, Petros – a large piece of rock], and on this rock [Greek, petra – a huge rock like Gibraltar] I will build My church ‹ekklesia – "called-out ones"›,** *and the gates of Hades (the powers of the infernal region) shall not overpower it [or be strong to its detriment or hold out against it].* **I will give you the keys of the kingdom of heaven; and whatever you bind (declare to be improper and unlawful) on earth must be what is already bound in heaven; and whatever you loose (declare lawful) on earth must be what is already loosed in heaven.**
>
> ~ *Matthew 16:13–19,* AMP, **emphasis added**

It's important for the purpose of context to understand that this discussion with Peter follows an equally powerful verse. In Matthew 16:5–12, which you may want to read, Jesus warns the disciples that in order to understand what He was saying, they needed to be careful of the leaven of the Pharisees and Sadducees.

What is leaven? It is a living organism, a yeast-like substance that, when added to dough in very small amounts, ferments to make bread rise dramatically. Leaven was commonly used in Jesus' day and was a well-known metaphor. He used it to describe the power of something so small and seemingly inconsequential having a rapid and dramatic influence. Jesus specifically references the ability of only a small amount of leaven to affect a whole lump of bread(Gal. 5:9).

Immediately before Jesus began speaking to the disciples about the *ekklesia* He desired to build, He warned them about the leaven of the Pharisees and Sadducees – but why?

Jesus used the term leaven and its ability to make bread rise quickly to describe the false doctrine of the Pharisees and Sadducees and its power to influence the *ekklesia* He desired to build.

Apparently, the doctrine of the Pharisees and Sadducees had the power to create an uprising of a seemingly religious nature that had power to overtake the kind of uprising Jesus had in mind.

Jesus had a lot to say, none of it good, about the approach, methods, and subsequent doctrines of the Pharisees and Sadducees. For now, however, let's just consider Jesus' statement to Peter about building the church in our focus verse referenced earlier.

At first glance, it may seem like symbolic or cryptic religious language, but it's not – it's much, much more!

Jesus is using kingdom language, governmental language, revolutionary language, and transformational language, and He is being very intentional about it.

Understanding what Jesus is charging in this verse is an essential foundation for reorienting to every other verse that uses the word church – or rather, *ekklesia*.

**RECONSIDER**
What was the doctrine of the Pharisees and Sadducees?

Pharisees were religious leaders in Jesus' day with a well-known history of reducing religion to rigid sets of forms, ceremony, and liturgy. Sadducees were equally legalistic and known for denying the supernatural elements of religion. Both enforced and closely managed extreme sets of rules and traditions for religious observance, festivals, rites of passage, and other temple protocols. The word Pharisee actually means "separatist" in the Greek language.

Once you begin to see the major concepts in this verse through an *ekklesia* lens, instead of a church lens, all the other verses we will touch on in this chapter fall into place easily and take on new meaning. For this reason, I am spending a bit more time on this verse than the others, which we will reference more quickly.

Let's consider the main concepts that Jesus is emphasizing in this verse one by one and in the order they appear:

1. The knowledge that Jesus is the Christ.

2. The idea that this knowledge is the rock, or foundation, of His *ekklesia.*

3. That the *ekklesia* is the primary thing Jesus is interested in building.

4. That the gates of hell won't prevail against a real *ekklesia.*

5. That Jesus gives two keys to the kingdom of heaven to empower the *ekklesia.*

So, let's consider this first portion of our focus text:

> *He said to them, But who do you [yourselves] say that I am? Simon Peter replied, You are the* **Christ, the Son of the living God.**
>
> *~ verses 15–16,* **emphasis added**

**REMEMBER**
An *ekklesia* is primarily used in context of a political and social assembly, not a religious one. Inasmuch, Jesus just finished warning the disciples about the religious doctrine of the Pharisees and Sadducees, who were well-seasoned in building and maintaining religious assemblies.

Why was it so crucial that Peter acknowledge Jesus as the Christ? Apparently, many others didn't see Jesus that way. Some saw Him as a good teacher or a prophet or maybe even the spiritual reincarnation of Elijah, Jeremiah, or one of the other prophets.

The key distinction here is the definition of the word *Christ,* and especially the emphasis on Christ as the Son of the Living God.

The word *Christ* is the Greek word *khristos,* meaning "anointed." Today, people assign the word *Christ* to Jesus' name without thinking much about it – as if it were a part of His actual name.

This was not the case in Jesus' time. The word *Christ* was a descriptive word with significant, even explosive, political and social ramifications. Calling Jesus the Christ and then using the phrase *Son of the Living God* in conjunction with it had equally explosive religious ramifications. Used together, these two phrases were a linguistic recipe for inviting serious, if not deadly, political and religious conflict.

Here is why.

*The Christ* meant "the Anointed." We use the word *anointing* or *anointed* in a primarily religious context today. But it was not always used this way.

The word *anointing* technically implies a smearing on or pouring on of oil or perfumed substance as an outward symbolic act or acknowledgment of being given the divine right or power to rule.

An anointing, in this context, has been observed as a rite of passage for kingly or priestly rule for thousands of years. *Anointing* was a term reserved for royalty, for kings, and especially for the descendants of kings who were to be consecrated or set in place to rule or govern a realm and a people. An anointing was often the final ceremonial act in the divine rite of kings to transition rulership and authority to the next in command. Anointing someone was the equivalent to crowning them as king.

> *Publicly acknowledging Jesus as the Christ or, in other words, the Anointed, was a political and social act of treason that would have made you an enemy of the state and in direct rebellion to the sitting king in that day, Caesar.*

It was also an offense to his descendants, who would be considered next in line to be crowned and anointed king.

Jesus used this very description of Himself when asked by Pilate if He was, in fact, a King (John 18:37).

Adding the phrase *Son of the Living God* to the idea of Jesus being the Anointed would have been an equally inflammatory statement to the religious community of the day.

The religious community in Jesus' time, especially the Pharisees and Sadducees, would have considered this declaration the highest act of divine heresy. For a human being to be considered in the same sentence as God, let alone be called the *Anointed Son of God,* would be worthy of the death sentence in their minds.

In publicly acknowledging Jesus as the Christ, the Anointed Son of the Living God, Peter knew he was committing an extremely treacherous act. He likely understood this proclamation would be a significantly inflammatory political, social, and religious proclamation that would be met with the most severe resistance and punishment from both the political and religious leaders of his day.

However, Peter demonstrated his conviction by acknowledging that Jesus was the King who would usher in a revolutionary new kingdom to be established on earth as it already was established by His Father in heaven.

According to our focus text, this understanding of who Jesus was is the primary foundational understanding for the rest of what Jesus was going to do. Jesus intended, as the newly anointed King, to go about building His new kingdom (not church) structure upon this foundation.

Let's read it again from our focus text:

> *And I tell you, you are Peter ‹**Greek, Petros – a large piece of rock**›, and on this rock ‹**Greek, petra – a huge rock like Gibraltar**› I will build My church ‹**ekklesia – "called-out ones"**› ...*
>
> ~ *verse 18,* ***emphasis added***

Notice the Greek word for Peter in this Amplified Version of our focused text, *Petros,* means "a large piece of rock" where the word translated *rock* that Jesus uses to describe the revelation about Him being the Christ means "a huge rock."

This massive rock is likened to the Rock of Gibraltar or a boulder. It's upon this massive boulder-type rock that this living *ekklesia,* which is made up of smaller living stone–type rocks, is built upon.

By this unique use of contrasting terms, Jesus is literally saying that Peter (*Petros*) is a type of small living stone. The revelation that Jesus was, in fact, the Christ, meaning the Anointed One of the Living God, is the massive stone (*petra*) upon which His *ekklesia,* or called-out ones (not church), will build a new kingdom.

This is such a powerful verse. Jesus is changing an entire cultural paradigm that thinks in terms of structures made of stone or structures made with hands as the primary means to connect to God and manage His kingdom. Sound familiar? He is reorienting people to a completely different way of thinking – to thinking in terms of living stones and spiritual temples instead of literal physical ones.

Peter is the first to be called a stone, which eventually becomes a term applied to all those who would voluntarily join the movement and acknowledge Jesus – the *Chief Cornerstone* – as their King!

Jesus is clearly saying that an authentic *ekklesia* established on this rock-solid premise and immovable foundation will not be prevailed against and will not be overpowered by the forces or gates of the enemy.

Even though the term *ekklesia* was not used in a religious context like church or, specifically, its Greek counterpart *kurakon* was, Jesus is most certainly using or repurposing the term for spiritual and kingdom use.

He clearly intends to use this spiritual or kingdom *ekklesia* to embolden an uprising to establish a new kind of government on earth that has dominion in all realms of society. It will one day look identical to the one His Father has already established in heaven.

Jesus is primarily interested in building the kingdom and His primary method for expanding it to all parts of the earth is the *ekklesia,* not a church.

Only an *ekklesia,* not a church, has the power to keep the enemy (which He calls *the gates of hell)* from prevailing against this kingdom.

But what are these *gates of hell* that Jesus is referring to in this portion of our focus text?

> *... and the gates ‹**portal, gateway, or entrance**› of Hades (the powers of the infernal region) shall not overpower it [or be strong to its detriment or hold out against it].*
>
> *~ verse 18*

What does Jesus mean by using the word *gate*? To answer that question, I want to use an Old Testament verse as a point of reference. It uses the word *gate* in an altogether different way that brings clarity to our focus text and the power of an *ekklesia.*

**RECONSIDER**
The word *build* that Jesus used when He said "I will build my *ekklesia*" literally means "to construct a figurative house, to confirm, to build up, or to embolden." Jesus is not referring to constructing an actual building but of building up, edifying, or emboldening a group of people.

*Lift your **heads, you gates. Be lifted, you ancient doors,** so that the king of glory may come in. Who is the king of glory? The LORD, strong and mighty! The LORD, heroic in battle! **Lift your heads, you gates! Be lifted, you ancient doors,** so that the king of glory may come in. Who, then, is this king of glory? The LORD of Armies is the king of glory!*
*~ Psalm 24:7–10, GWT, **emphasis added***

The word *gates* is not referring to a physical barrier like we might imagine today, with a lock and key designed to keep something in or out. The word *gates* in both of these texts literally means "a kind of portal or entry point" that something goes through.

We are the gates. People – human beings – are the conduits, portals, or entry points that make way for the reality of one kingdom – of God or of His enemy – to manifest on earth.

In this way, every person is a walking ambassador of one kingdom or another. As submitted followers of the Christ, the Son of the Living God, we are called to be citizen ambassadors of the kingdom of heaven, operating under Christ's authority to be gates and conduits that manifest His will on earth, just as it is in heaven, wherever we go!

Likewise, there are gates – people – who are conduits, portals, or entry points that are knowingly or unknowingly agreeing to advance or manifest an opposing kingdom's agenda. The goal of this kingdom is to prevail against the establishment of the kingdom of heaven on earth.

Whether we acknowledge it or not, every person is knowingly or unknowingly living in the context of a conflict between these two opposing kingdom ideals.

People aren't technically the problem. But they are and always will be the primary conduits, portals, and entry points – gates, if you will – that create the dominant culture in any region on earth. The culture that prevails depends on the attributes of either kingdom that the people permit, allow, resist, or prohibit from becoming reality.

Unlike other traditional forms of civil government that endeavor to exert power over people, the purpose of an *ekklesia* is to enlist people to exert power over the enemy – not power over the people. The goal of an *ekklesia* is to make known the wisdom and power of God to the rulers and authorities of an opposing kingdom who endeavor to accomplish their purposes through people:

> *[The purpose is] that through the church ‹**ekklesia**› the complicated, many-sided wisdom of God in all its infinite variety and innumerable aspects might now be made known to the angelic rulers and authorities (principalities and powers) in the heavenly sphere.*
>
> *~ Ephesians 3:10,* AMP

As a practical example, let's take what we have learned so far about God and love and apply it here. Heaven is love's ideal – the highest good anyone can possibly think or imagine with the supernatural power to transform any situation or realm for a higher kind of good.

211

As you begin to contend for love's ideal, it's common to meet with resistance or opposition. Sometimes the conflict is an obvious good-versus-evil scenario, say in the case of someone wanting to enter my home and harm my family or steal our belongings. Love's ideal compels me to stop them, but an evil intent has compelled this individual to prevail against me. This is a classic good-versus-evil conflict.

But often, the greatest opposition to love's ideal comes from well-meaning people with other agendas. These agendas don't appear outright evil, but will result in inferior results just the same. An example might be a social or political conflict.

In either scenario, at the point of opposition, kingdoms are colliding and people become gates for the reality or culture of one kingdom or the other. Love is always the superior force, but love's ideal will only prevail in the end if people, as a gate for it, yield, submit, and keep contending for love until it's a present-tense reality.

This is a key distinction to understanding how the kingdom of heaven manifests on earth. It's our part, as gates, to contend for and allow the will of God to manifest and determine the culture, not God's willingness to manifest His love through us. God is always willing. The greatest common denominator is whether people are open (pun intended). This is the *key* to understanding the power we have as gates!

In fact, in the closing part of our focus text, Jesus said it this way:

> *I will give you the keys of the kingdom of heaven; and whatever you bind (declare to be improper and unlawful) on earth must be what is already bound in heaven; and whatever you loose (declare lawful) on earth must be what is already loosed in heaven.*
>
> *~ verse 19*

Notice that Jesus says, "I give *you* the keys," and that whatever *you* bind and whatever *you loose* must be already bound and loosed in heaven. The emphasis is on *you*.

Jesus gave us *the collective you* in this text – the power to bind and loose things. He did not say, "Pray to me, and I will bind and loose things for you." No. Binding and loosing is our part, and doing our part is the key to seeing the kingdom of heaven manifested on earth. God will not do our part, and we cannot do His part. If we fail to do our part, we will fail and we will not see God do His part in our lives. However, if we do our part, God never has failed and never will fail to do His part!

What is binding and loosing? The word *bind* means "to disallow something, to declare it as improper and unlawful" – in other words, to not permit it. The word *loose* means just the opposite – "to allow something, to declare it as proper and lawful."

The responsibility and power to do both has been delegated to us by God. However, as the Amplified Version of the Bible makes clear in this text, this power is limited to that which is already "permitted" and "allowed" or "not permitted" and "not allowed" in heaven.

## THE GREATNESS OF SMALLNESS AND THE POWER TO CREATE AN UPRISING THAT CAN CHANGE THE WORLD

It's clear by what we have covered so far that Jesus' mission was to establish His kingdom on earth through individuals and small groups – citizen-led *ekklesias,* not churches.

But what about the ones who followed Jesus to accomplish His great co-mission, like Paul, the other disciples, the initial seventy they commissioned, and so on? Did they understand the distinction between what we call a church and an *ekklesia?*

The answer is yes, but as we begin to look at how Jesus and His followers implemented the *ekklesia* model for world transformation, it's important to first understand something I call *the greatness of smallness!*

Jesus said we would do *greater works* in terms of impact and power, not *bigger works* in terms of the size of our structures or audience.

Even though Jesus' mission was to establish heaven on earth and empower an uprising of followers to do it, His strategy was implemented on a much, much smaller scale with an intensely individual and local focus. His mission was global, but His focus, execution and implementation was intentionally small and local.

One of the keys to the effectiveness of Jesus' uprising was His understanding of the greatness of this smallness. He was able to avoid being seduced by illusions of bigness and delusions of grandeur that result from measuring fruit by the size of gatherings alone.

Consider how Jesus Himself executed His Father's will and administrated His Father's kingdom on earth. The results are simply spectacular and awe-inspiring, especially when you consider the greatness of the ongoing impact that came from such small beginnings.

As one man:

Jesus lived His whole life within a small geographic area,

Jesus lived only thirty-three short years,

Jesus lived thirty of those years working in a small family business as a carpenter,

Jesus assembled a small group of twelve people to execute His mission,

Jesus had only three years of focused effort to change the world,

Jesus changed the entire known world as we know it,

Jesus did all this in such an extraordinary way that we are still talking about it and feeling the impact of it more than two thousand years later!

Even more stunning is how Jesus did all He did without many of the things we take for granted today:

He had no earthly birthright to prequalify Him to lead,

He had no inherited earthly throne to wield political power,

He had no social or political affiliations to wield influence,

He had no globally significant town from which to base His mission,

He had no noted accomplishments before age thirty,

He never focused on persuading the elite, but freeing the oppressed,

He never took up arms against the opposition,

He never used violence to force submission,

He never amassed a traditional military or army,

He never required anything but voluntary allegiance to His leadership,

He never required anything but voluntary involvement in His mission,

He never constructed an operational headquarters,

He never commissioned the building of satellite offices,

He had no mass communications platform,

He had no TV,

He had no radio,

He had no Internet,

He had no cars or motorized means of transportation,

He had no airplanes,

He had no cell phones,

He had no computers,

He had no real-time social network to communicate His mission, mobilize His followers, or enforce His mandates.

Do you know anyone who has accomplished so much with so little earthly resources to mobilize their vision? Considering Jesus only as a man and setting aside His divine attributes, can you think of another human being with results as significant – even with all we have at our disposal – today?

> ## *One plus God always equals a majority.*
>
> – BILL JOHNSON –

Jesus chose the God-inspired *ekklesia* model as the best means to establish God's kingdom of heaven on all the earth and to mobilize an uprising of His followers to do it – and it worked! As small as its beginnings were, its impact was massive!

Don't get me wrong. This supernatural *ekklesia* movement certainly wasn't without opposition and wasn't always easy – quite the opposite. Both the religious and political powers of Jesus' day were dead-set against this uprising and seemed determined to go to any length to stop the formation of *ekklesias*.

Even the Apostle Paul started out as one of the most adamant religious opponents of this movement, but he went on to become one of the most prolific followers of Jesus, leader of the *ekklesia,* and writer of much of the New Testament.

I was struck by how, before his conversion, Paul went house to house to attack the *ekklesia* with violence and cruelty and commit its members to prison. Notice he did not go synagogue to synagogue.

In fact, for the first three hundred years after Jesus' death, the *ekklesia* was very much a house to house movement.

Consider the following verses that mention houses where *ekklesias* met:

> *Give my greetings to the brethren at Laodicea, and to Nympha and the assembly (the church)* ‹**ekklesia**› *which meets in her* **house.**
>
> *~ Colossians 4:15,* AMP, **emphasis added**

> *[Remember me] also to the church* ‹**ekklesia**› *[that meets]* **in their house.** *Greet my beloved Epaenetus, who was a firstfruit (first convert) to Christ in Asia.*
>
> *~ Romans 16:5,* AMP, **emphasis added**

*The churches ‹ekklesia – plural› of Asia send greetings and best wishes. Aquila and Prisca, together with the church ‹ekklesia› [that meets] in their house, send you their hearty greetings in the Lord. All the brethren wish to be remembered to you and wish you well. Greet one another with a holy kiss ‹strengthen with weapons›.*

~ *1 Corinthians 16:19–20,* AMP, **emphasis added**

*And to Apphia our sister and Archippus **our fellow soldier** [in the Christian warfare], and to the church [assembly that meets] **in your house.***

~ *Philemon 1:2,* AMP, *emphasis added*

The person-to-person, house-to-house, region-by-region nature of an *ekklesia* made it the original social network. As such, *ekklesias* were able to expand and grow quickly – so much so that the Bible says thousands were being added daily. (Acts 2:41).

*The ekklesia was unstoppable, spreading like wildfire and impacting every aspect of society – to the extent it wasn't only the traditional religious community that was threatened. King Herod himself took notice and stretched out his hand to afflict, oppress, and torment all the called-out ones who were assembling: About that time Herod the king stretched forth his hands to afflict and oppress and torment some [certain] who belonged to the church (assembly) ‹ekklesia›.*

~ *Acts 12:1,* AMP

Not only was Jesus ultimately crucified for claiming to be the Christ, the Anointed Son of God and the head of the *ekklesia,* but the individuals and leaders who were following His mandate became the focus of increasing religious and political concern. Many involved in the *ekklesia* experienced severe persecution:

*And Saul was [not only] consenting to [Stephen's] death [he was pleased and entirely approving]. On that day **a great and severe persecution broke out against the church** ‹ekklesia› which was in Jerusalem; and they were all scat-*

*tered throughout the regions of Judea and Samaria, except the apostles (special messengers).*

*~ Acts 8:1, AMP, **emphasis added***

Even Peter was eventually imprisoned for his activities in this regard:

*So Peter was kept in prison, but fervent prayer for him was persistently made to God by the church ‹**the called-out ones, the ekklesia**› (assembly).*

*~ Acts 12:5, AMP*

But why were these traditional religious and political leaders so set on stopping the *ekklesia?*

After all, these called-out ones were going about doing good, paying their taxes, obeying the laws, not endeavoring to mass an armed force against anybody.

The answer lies in the rapidly expanding social, political, and religious impact these *ekklesias* were having.

They were not being attacked because they had a desire to build religious places of worship – churches – and live their lives separated from society. Just the opposite was true.

It's not dissimilar in Western society today. Most state governments don't oppose the building of churches. Most governments don't endeavor to get involved or even much care what members of churches believe or practice in private, if they operate within the confines of the law every citizen must observe.

Even in the United States of America, many in government support and sanction the right for churches to exist and even thrive as long as those activities remain "separated" from the role of the state or ruling governmental party. Most in social and governmental positions of power throughout the world don't care how heavenly directed church activities become or how heavenly minded individuals who attend church become. It's when their ideas invade the realm of earth they become problematic.

In Jesus' time and now, it's not when people agree to follow Jesus with only the intent to go to heaven that the greatest impact on earth is achieved. It's when individuals and small groups begin to live out heaven's mandate and contend for its reality on earth that real transformation begins to take place. It's only when an individual takes heaven's mandate and learns to administer it in every area of their life that society begins to take notice.

Even though the aim of the *ekklesia* never intended to bring contentions, their impact couldn't be ignored and had to be contended with.

The message of a new kind of kingdom, and subsequently the *ekklesia* Jesus commissioned to build on earth, was such good news to those who would hear it that it attracted followers in unprecedented measure.

Jesus' form of kingdom governance was so inspired and so supernatural in its ability to deliver what it promised in the here and now while not sacrificing the eternal, all lesser forms of religious and political governance were quickly losing their appeal and ability to govern.

The same is true today. The real message of the kingdom will always reorient people of any age, gender, or background to a higher kind of good (love's ideal) and confronts inferior realities.

The real message of the kingdom will always be a trumpet call to people everywhere to rise up and abandon less excellent pursuits and systems which separate them from God and His will for their lives.

Real freedom will always cause lesser pursuits and inferior systems to lose their appeal and ability to contain and control.

When called-out people are allowed to directly and experientially reconnect with God and others, it frees them to experience more freedom and empowers them to produce a higher kind of good.

When called-out people are free to recover sufficient levels of freedom, evidenced by their ability to administer the reality of the kingdom in their own houses, they will call more people out by example.

When called-out people begin organically assembling in small groups with others to be led by God (to strategically administer the same reality in every other social and political realm of society), the transformation is so viral that the world takes notice.

History has shown that the only way to stop the supernatural power of an *ekklesia* is to relegate the activities of an *ekklesia* to a church building alone!

In the book *Pagan Christianity,* Frank Viola and George Barna do a magnificent job of documenting the rise of the church-building program, as commissioned by Constantine around AD 300:

> Ancient Judaism was focused around sacred temples, priests, and ritual sacrifices.
>
> Greco-Roman paganism had the same three elements: sacred temples, priests, and ritual sacrifices.
>
> Early Christianity was the only religion on the planet that had no sacred places, sacred people, or sacred objects.
>
> In AD 312, Constantine became emperor and in 324 began a program to elevate Christianity's minority status by designating sacred buildings (churches) and sacred rituals (Sunday services, for example) to make it more familiar, appealing, and acceptable to Jews and pagans.
>
> Sunday was designated a sacred day in honor of the pagan sun god Mithras, and Sunday was described as "the day of the sun."
>
> Constantine was designated as the sacred high priest of paganism and given the title *Pontifex Maximus,* which was the same title given to the Roman Catholic pope in the fifteenth century.
>
> In AD 327, Constantine began a prolific church-building program, and, constituent with the pagan traditions they were derived from, the buildings were constructed as sacred places to worship God and designed accordingly.

By the third century, *sacred objects* were being designated and used to carry out *sacred worship* by *sacred people* in *sacred places,* which eventually gave birth to the *sacred priesthood* and the death of an individual, spontaneous connection with God for the average person.

It's easy to see how the basic structure of it all could bring the spontaneous, organic, and fluid nature of the *ekklesia* to a screeching halt.

It's not that these practices or the people who administer them are bad. It has much more to do with the cumulative effect of the traditions themselves and what they have historically reinforced about the nature of God, the relationship He desires with man, and His intent for this present world.

But it doesn't have to be that way!

## A CHOSEN GENERATION AND AN UPRISING OF INDIVIDUALS, MINYANS, AND COLUMNS THAT WILL CHANGE THE WORLD

It was almost a year after I heard God tell me that He didn't need another church, but that He wanted a call to battle, that someone asked me, "What do you think God meant? What's 'not' a church?"

I had to admit, I hadn't really thought about it that way. Until that moment, I was really only focused on starting an uprising.

For days afterward, I couldn't get that question out of my mind. Just before falling sleep, I asked God what He meant by "not a church or ministry." That night, I had a dream.

In it, I was taken to an exceedingly high place above the earth. From this elevated vantage point, I could behold entire continents, like a parade of land masses before me.

As the earth turned, North America, and specifically the United States, came into focus. I began to see what looked like massive columns breaking through the heavens and rising up from the earth like giant streams of liquid-filled light.

First, one appeared and then another and another until the entire United States seemed to be dotted with thousands of these magnificent columns of light.

I remember being mesmerized by their beauty, but equally intrigued by their apparent combination of lightness (as in the opposite of heavy) and seemingly unshakable strength. Like giant cumulonimbus clouds, they appeared substantive enough to hold great weight, yet equally transparent and light as a feather.

When the columns of light multiplied and rose from what seemed like every part of the land mass we call the United States, the globe stopped turning, as if suspended in mid-air.

*"What do you think, Kevin?"*

Intuitively, I knew in the dream it was God speaking. I replied, *"God, this is so awe-inspiringly beautiful. What is it? What are those streams of light, and how many are there?"*

The directness of His response startled me, but the terminology He used intrigued and perplexed me at the same time. *"Oh, those. Those are minyans, and there are about three thousand of them. Where there is more than one minyan in a geographic area, I call it a column. Where there is more than one column, I call it a realm where the kingdom of heaven has legal jurisdiction to manifest on earth, just as in heaven."*

Minyans, columns, and realms – what in the world did that mean? As if reading my thoughts, but with no intent of answering them directly, He said, *"I don't need another ministry or church. I want an uprising of individuals and small groups – minyans, Kevin."*

Immediately, I woke up.

The following day, I couldn't shake the dream. The imagery of those magnificent columns lingered and the term *minyan* seemed etched in my mind. I began to research the term.

Here's a summary of what I found.

The word *minyan* can be found in the first five books of the Old Testament, or the Books of Moses, according to Jewish tradition – collectively referred to as the Torah.

There, the Hebrew root of the word *minyan* is *menah,* meaning literally "to count or number" and the Aramaic word *mene,* meaning "numbered," as used later in the book of Daniel (5:25).

I learned that it was synonymous with both the Jewish word *quorum*, meaning "ten," and the Hebrew word *edah,* meaning "a family, company, or assemblage of people" or as translated in English, "a congregation."

In Jewish terms, a minyan was a small group of ten (a quorum) considered to be a legal congregation.

In the Jewish community, minyans were required, among other things, to:

Have someone open the sacred scrolls in public,

Have the ability to declare God's Word in public,

Have public worship services,

Have legally binding prayers,

Have legally binding contracts.

The generally accepted attributes of a minyan gathering and qualifications for participating in a minyan were as follows:

Gatherings generally took place in one room,

Gatherings in adjoining rooms were permitted if within hearing distance,

Gatherings required ten heads of families or qualified representatives be present,

Gatherings required participants to be of accountable age (at least thirteen years),

Gatherings required participants to have been through a *bar mitzvah* or *bat mitzvah*,

Gatherings required male participants to be circumcised.

Besides these basic attributes and qualifications, the key distinction between a minyan and a general assembly of people was their purpose.

Minyans were locally assembled to conduct kingdom business and to help govern the affairs of a local community. A modern equivalent would be a town council.

A minyan and a town council are similar in that they are made up of volunteers and citizens of the local community with vested interests in overseeing the affairs of that local community.

It's important to point out, however, that minyans differ from most legislative-type gatherings we know today in that they don't endeavor to rule over a community of people and are not made up of rulers, *per se*.

Minyans are assemblies of representatives of a local community whose intent it is to allow the kingdom of God to rule in their community and over His people. This is a huge distinction!

Minyans were not intended to be places to gather and establish rules, but rather minyans were assembled to allow God to dwell among His people and let love rule.

In terms of the basic attributes, mission, and qualifications to participate, you could say a minyan was the Old Testament version of the New Testament *ekklesia.*

Like an *ekklesia,* minyans were local gatherings of citizens called together to deliberate and to govern themselves and their communities in such a way as to permit the kingdom of God to manifest on earth just as it is in heaven.


They both were small,

They both met in local gatherings,

They both were often conducted in homes,

They both encouraged open deliberation,

They both encouraged open prayer,

They both encouraged open worship,

They both involved voluntary participation,

They both required participants to be called according to the purpose,

They both had a maturity requirement,

They both required evidence of transformation to continue gathering.

In the case of a minyan, this involved being at least thirteen years of age, completing a rite of passage such as a *bat mitzvah* (for girls) or *bar mitzvah* (for boys), and evidence of physical circumcision.

In the case of an *ekklesia,* the qualifications involved being born again, demonstrable evidence you were a believer in the mission (Mark 16:17), proof you could rule your own house well (1 Tim. 3:5), and a circumcision of the heart (Rom. 2:29).

In one other amazing similarity, in the very same way that a minyan was viewed as a legal congregation and participants were tasked with administrating legally binding prayers and contracts for their local community, Jesus gave the *ekklesia* the very same mandate: to bind and loose on earth just as it is in heaven.

It's just another amazing example of ways the Old Testament provides a glimpse of what is later revealed in the New Testament.

Like the *ekklesia,* minyans always played a critical role in shaping communities and fates of entire regions and groups of people in the Old Testament.

Here's two dramatic examples.

Consider the story in the book of Numbers where Moses was instructed to send spies into the land of Canaan, their promised land. A total of twelve spies were sent, and upon their return, "ten" of them – a minyan, a legal congregation – came back with their

**REMEMBER**

... I will give you the keys of the kingdom of heaven; and whatever you bind (declare to be improper and unlawful) on earth must be what is already bound in heaven; and whatever you loose (declare lawful) on earth must be what is already loosed in heaven.

~ Matt. 16:19, AMP

bad report and influenced the entire culture to oppose the good report provided by the two others, Joshua and Caleb.. Ten people, a minyan, kept an entire generation of people from entering their promised land!

A more dramatic example of the power of a minyan at work is to be found in the story of Sodom and Gomorrah. (Gen. 18).

Consider the following text and notice how Abraham intercedes for Sodom and Gomorrah after learning of God's intent to destroy it, based apparently on the prolific amount of evil reaching a point of no return:

> And the Lord said, Because the shriek [of the sins] of Sodom and Gomorrah is great and their sin is exceedingly griev-ous, I will go down now and see whether they have done altogether [as vilely and wickedly] as is the cry of it which has come to Me; and if not, I will know. Now the [two] men turned from there and went toward Sodom, but Abraham still stood before the Lord. And Abraham came close and said, Will You destroy the righteous (those upright and in right standing with God) together with the wicked? **Suppose there are in the city fifty righteous; will You destroy the place and not spare it for [the sake of] the fifty righteous in it?** Far be it from You to do such a thing – to slay the righteous with the wicked, so that the righteous fare as do the wicked! Far be it from You! Shall not the Judge of all the earth execute judgment and do righteously? **And the Lord said, If I find in the city of Sodom fifty righteous (upright and in right standing with God), I will spare the whole place for their sake.**
>
> ~ Genesis 18:20–26, AMP, **emphasis added**

Notice how God agrees that this city will be spared if Abraham can find only fifty who are righteous (in right standing) with God and with heaven.

The very idea that God would spare an entire region based upon the request of one man and the right standing of only fifty people is amazing. But what's even more amazing is that Abraham couldn't even find fifty!

So, Abraham continues to petition God, and God agrees to spare the region based on a continuously decreasing righteous requirement.

Here is the conversation in an abbreviated form, starting with Genesis 18:28.

Abraham: "Suppose there were five less than fifty?"

God: "If I find forty-five, I will not destroy it."


Abraham: "Suppose there were forty found there?"

God: "I will not destroy it for the sake of forty."

Abraham: "Suppose thirty should be found there?"

God: "I will not do it if I find thirty there."

Abraham: "Suppose twenty should be found there?"

God: "I will not destroy it for the sake of twenty."

Abraham: "I will speak but once more; suppose ten should be found there?"

God: "I will not destroy it for the sake of ten."


A few things really stand out in this exchange. One, how awe-inspiring it is that Abraham was close enough to God to undertake such a bargaining process on behalf of Sodom and Gomorrah; two, that God was so gracious to be continually entreated by Abraham; three, that the very presence of a minyan, ten people, the smallest legal congregation, would have given God what He needed to get a beachhead in the region and see heaven invade earth to transform it.

Think about that for a moment.

It wasn't the overwhelming presence of evil in this region that caused its demise. The demise of Sodom

**RECONSIDER**
I'm not sure exactly why ten is the magic number to qualify a minyan as a legal congregation, but I find it more than ironic that ten is always the number for redemption in the Bible.

227

and Gomorrah was caused by the absence of even a handful of people God could work through to change its destiny!

Apply this to today. It isn't the overwhelming presence of evil in a region that causes its destruction. The destruction is a direct result of the absence of even a handful of people God can work through to change its destiny.

God is always looking to strengthen those whose hearts are fully committed to Him and His purposes on earth:

> For the eyes of the Lord run to and fro throughout the whole earth to show Himself strong in behalf of those whose hearts are blameless toward Him. You have done foolishly in this; therefore, from now on you shall have wars.
>
> ~ 2 Chronicles 16:9, AMP

God will always endeavor to manifest greater where two or more are gathered for this purpose. In fact, it's exactly what Jesus said at the end of the very passage we used as our core text to begin our reorientation to the word *church:*

> Again I tell you, if two of you on earth agree (harmonize together, make a symphony together) about whatever [anything and everything] they may ask, it will come to pass and be done for them by My Father in heaven. For wherever two or three are gathered (drawn together as My followers) in (into) My name, there I AM in the midst of them.
>
> ~ Matthew 18:19–20, AMP

It's always been this way – and even greater where there is a minyan, or legal congregation. God has always manifested greater in the midst of the congregation – not churches, but congregations.

> God takes His stand in His own congregation; He judges in the midst of the rulers.
>
> ~ Psalm 82:1, NAS

Even the most adversarial enemy of God covets the seat He had chosen for Himself in the midst of the true congregation.

Remember how Lucifer declared to God that he himself would sit upon the mount of the congregation?

> How art thou fallen from heaven, O Lucifer, son of the morning! how art thou cut down to the ground, which didst weaken the nations! For thou hast said in thine heart, I will ascend into heaven, I will exalt my throne above the stars of God: I will sit also upon the mount of the congregation, in the sides of the north. I will ascend above the heights of the clouds; I will be like the most High.
>
> ~ Isaiah 14:12–14, KJV

Like a relationship between a husband and wife, God's heart, His love, and the most intimate attributes of His nature are always directed toward and reserved for the private relationship He has with an individual. The genuine connection at the individual level is His primary focus.

The corporate display of His presence in the midst of a congregation can never take the place of that individual connection. Likewise, the individual follower alone was never designed to wield the transformative influence that a true gathering of likeminded individuals (a minyan or *ekklesia*) was commissioned to wield.

Transformed individuals are always God's primary focus, but it is transformed individuals working in concert together (minyans) with God that collectively provide the supporting infrastructure (columns) God desires to establish His kingdom and see it manifesting on earth (realms).

This is my interpretation of the purpose of individuals, minyans, columns, and realms I saw from heaven's perspective in the dream I shared. To me, this dream was a blueprint – a model and example of the greatness of smallness and the key to seeing entire regions transformed.

The answer is not more churches. The Midwest town I grew up in, with a population of fewer than sixty thousand, has almost one hundred churches listed in its local directory. Even with all these churches, not by a single standard that I can think of, could you say there has been a transformative effect by heaven's reality on that region.

That's because more churches is never the answer. The answer is an uprising of individuals who are capable of administering well the reality of the kingdom in their own homes first and who reorient and act on the power of the *ekklesia* to begin to publicly transform their neighborhoods.

How evil or dark a region has become is not what will determine its outcome or whether it will enjoy all that God has promised. The difference will be made by the presence of handfuls of genuinely righteous people organized in small increments or local assemblies who are capable of teaching and publicly demonstrating by example a more excellent way to rule!

Consider just a few of the verses where Paul writes to the *ekklesia* in various regions. Remember that he knew nothing of the word *church* as we know it today, but only the word *ekklesia*. Everywhere you see the word *church* in these verses, substitute the word *ekklesia* and give it the connotation we have been discussing:

> *News of this reached the ears of the church <ekklesia> at Jerusalem, and they sent Barnabas to Antioch.*
> ~ *Acts 11:22*

> *In the church <ekklesia> at Antioch there were prophets and teachers.*
> ~ *Acts 13:1*

> *To the church <ekklesia> of God in Corinth, to those sanctified in Christ Jesus and called to be holy, together with all those everywhere who call on the name of our Lord Jesus Christ – their Lord and ours.*
> ~ *1 Corinthians 1:2*

> *Paul, Silas and Timothy, to the church <ekklesia> of the Thessalonians in God the Father and the Lord Jesus Christ: Grace and peace to you.*
> ~ *1 Thessalonians 1:1*

Notice how Paul always addresses the *ekklesia* as a whole in these verses, not individual leaders of the *ekklesia*. If these *ekklesia* were anything like a church in our modern time, Paul would have likely addressed the pastor over the church in Antioch or the priest over the parish of laypeople in Corinth. Instead, the individual people assembled in a local region were the *ekklesia* in that region, but people of the *ekklesia* were never the church.

We've got to reorient!

# CHURCH__RELATE

I understand it's difficult, if not seemingly impossible, for many people in the Western world to dissociate the things of God from our modern concepts of church.

It certainly doesn't help matters any that we have centuries of church tradition that continually reinforce these associations.

For many people involved in church, the very idea that a person can have a vibrant, legitimate, and highly impactful relationship with God that is not lived out in the context of a local church seems suspect.

The problem is not that a church itself or church structure, *per se,* is bad. As we have already firmly established, church, in terms of a building, like a synagogue, where some religious activities take place, is as biblical as an *ekklesia.* The key distinction between an *ekklesia* and a church is primarily that of form, function, and mission.

So, what's the answer? Should we just change the form, function, and reasons for meeting together in churches? Would that alone get us closer to the original intent and produce the results an *ekklesia* was intended to produce?

I don't think so. Many churches have small groups, cell groups, home groups, home fellowships, and so on. What some call house church, simple church, parachurch, or emerging church models have been offered as traditional church alternatives for decades. Most of these models are built around simple home fellowships or extensions of church meetings. While there are benefits to these models, having a small group meeting or having people gather at your home, even for religious purposes, does not make it a minyan or an *ekklesia* any more than inviting ten of my buddies over to talk about football would make the group a football team. Altering the meeting format alone will not produce the kind of change necessary to make a church an *ekklesia* with similar results. In fact, it may be that the very focus on the meeting causes the problem.

Imagine that you get together with your church leadership team or a small group of friends at your church and suggest beginning a small group. Inevitably, the discussion will produce the all-too-familiar where, what, and who questions:

Where to meet?

When to meet?

When we meet, how many should be involved?

Who will lead the meeting?

Who decides what topics get covered?

Who will sing at the meeting?

Who will be allowed to teach at the meeting?

Who will take up the offering to cover the cost of the meeting?

Who will provide pastoral oversight of the meetings?

Who will report back to the church about who attended the meetings?

All of a sudden, these little home fellowships look just like miniature versions of Sunday morning church meetings, but in a living room setting.

An *ekklesia,* by contrast, is focused only on the mission for gathering, not on the methods of gathering.

Unless we reorient, viewing an *ekklesia* through the lens of a traditional church meeting will simply produce the same results as church meetings have over time.

In China, where house churches are the norm, not the exception, the Chinese symbol and meaning of the word they use for *house church* is 地下天國, translated literally as "underground heaven"! I like how the term they use to describe their gathering and the mission of their gathering is one and the same.

The only thing an *ekklesia* and a church have in common is people. Those who assemble in an *ekklesia* and those that gather in a church can be the same people. From that point, the differences are greater than the similarities.

People can choose to start and belong to small groups and churches for many reasons that have nothing to do with their calling:

Because of friends,

Because of location,

Because of the frequency or duration of the meetings,

Because of the size,

Because of the facilities,

Because of the style of music they play or don't play,

Because of the existence or lack of certain programs,

Because of the personality dynamics of the leaders,

Because of the amount of agreement there is with one's own convictions.

The problem is that none of these things, in and of themselves, have anything directly to do with being part of the calling and the purpose that God has for a specific minyan or *ekklesia*.

In Jesus' time and shortly thereafter, His followers knew they did not choose their calling, but that God chose them to delegate a specific part of His kingdom business and to *go into the world to produce a specific kind of fruit for Him*:

> *I no longer call you servants, because a servant does not know his master's business. Instead, I have called you friends, for everything that I learned from my Father I have made known to you. You did not choose me, but I chose you and appointed you to go and bear fruit – fruit that will*

*last. Then the Father will give you whatever you ask in my name. This is my command: Love each other.*

*~ John 15:15–17*

When a minyan or an *ekklesia* comes together, it is not a social event. Yes, we must love each other in that context, but fellowship is not the ultimate goal – the goal is the mission. The goal is to go and produce fruit in the world, fruit that is specific to each individual realm of influence based upon the direction God provides

It's fine to go to church or even a small group, but it's critical not to associate that activity, in and of itself, with the intended outcome of an *ekklesia*. The methodology by which we gather can never dominate the association we make to God and our part in manifesting them.

Learning to grow up and relate to God outside the context of a church or any type of religious gathering is critical. It's the absolute, essential first step in reorienting to the ultimate aim of an *ekklesia* – to see the kingdom manifested in all the earth, not just in your meeting!

Remember how Jesus said it at the end of the core text that started our reorientation to the word *church* in this chapter?

*I will give you the keys of the kingdom of heaven; and whatever you bind (declare to be improper and unlawful) on earth **must be what is already bound in heaven;** and whatever you loose (declare lawful) on earth **must be what is already loosed in heaven.***

*~ Matthew 16:19*, AMP, ***emphasis added***

I love the way the Amplified Bible says this verse. Instead of "what you bind or loose on earth will be bound or loosed in heaven," it adds the notion that "what you bind and loose on earth *must already be bound and loosed in heaven.*"

This is a huge distinction. Since binding and loosing was a key part of a minyan and an *ekklesia,* knowing how to do it has to be a key part of our gathering and everyday life outside the gathering.

We must see what a matter is like in heaven first, before we can agree to bind (disallow) or permit (loose) it on the earth. We can only do that one of two ways, in addition to what is already written in the Word of God where He makes His will clearly known. We can go to heaven and see, or we can have the King of heaven come here and manifest it Himself.

If your primary associations, the way you *see* and *hear* God, the things of God, and the activities of the kingdom of God are in the context of church, you may rarely perceive God doing anything significant outside that context.

Ask yourself:

Do you sense the presence of God the same way at the checkout line at Wal-Mart as you do while singing your favorite worship song at church on Sunday morning?

Do you associate and relate to God while waiting in line to get your morning coffee the same way you do having a snack in your home with a small group of fellow believers from church?

Do you expect to see as many miracles or examples of heaven invading earth while filling your car with fuel at your local gas station as you expect to see at the altar on Sunday morning in church?

Recently, I was asked to teach on "The Supernatural Power of a Family" at a men's leadership event. It was an all-male gathering, but the organizers graciously allowed me to bring my entire family for the session. My wife, Michelle; daughter, Olivia (who was nine); son, Noah (who was seven); and son, Immanuel (who was two); they all joined me just moments before my time to speak.

Prior to the event, I had asked Michelle and the kids to do three things:

1. Connect with God before coming to the session.

2. Consider love's ideal, asking God to highlight people He would like us to treasure.

3. Prepare to do it.

Each of them wrote down the specific impressions they received from heaven's perspective and handed them to me on small sheets of paper right before I took the stage to introduce them.

The teaching part of the session was going great, but about forty-five minutes into it, my son Noah approached me and squeezed my hand, indicating he wanted to talk. I looked down at him and said, "Buddy, Daddy is teaching right now." He whispered in my ear as I knelt down, "I know, Dad, but one of the men that God highlighted to us is sitting in the front row. God wants to heal him. See, we wrote it down right here." He pointed to the small sheet of scrap paper they had given me earlier, which had the following words on it: *"Man, balding, purple shirt, tan pants, 48, healing from back pain."*

As I glanced at the man, he certainly seemed to match the physical descriptions, except at that point, I didn't know his age or if he had back pain. Either way, by now, I noticed everyone was waiting to hear what my son had whispered to me. Rather than go back to what I was teaching, I decided to share.

After all, it was supposed to be "the supernatural power of a family" session, not the "supernatural power of a lecture" session.

I asked the man to stand up, and I asked his name. I asked his age, and he said forty-eight.

I said, "Do you have a back pain?" He said yes!

I asked him what had happened, and he shared an extensive history of back surgeries that left him in constant pain.

Before going further, I decided to let the kids share with the audience what they had written on the sheet before coming to the event.

The kids told how the night before, while I was at the hotel, Michelle asked them to focus their imaginations on what God wanted to do at the session.

She asked them to close their eyes and share any impressions they saw in their mind's eye . Olivia described a man she saw who was balding, wearing a purple shirt. Noah added that he had an impression of a man that looked similar and was wearing tan pants. Michelle said that she sensed he had back pain.

As they were writing down the impressions, Immanuel pulled his cup from his mouth and yelled out, "Fordy ate!" Everyone laughed and asked, "What did you say, Buddy?" He yelled out again, "Fordy ate!"

Nobody knew exactly what that meant. In their best attempt to interpret his proclamation, they repeated, "Forty-eight?" He said "La" – his word for yeah, or yes. So they jotted down the number forty-eight with their previous impressions and recorded several other impressions unrelated to this man.

So now, here they were, in front of a large audience, experiencing in reality the exact vision they had received in private. The man who was balding, wearing a purple shirt and tan pants. He had back pain, and yes, he was "fordy ate!" Simply amazing!

I know it might sound sensational to some, but it really happened, in front of at least three hundred witnesses. Would you agree this is far more than what coincidence and good intentions alone could have ever produced?

For the kids and all of us watching, it was confirmation they had heard from God. What's even more amazing is that when my son spoke over the man's back to be healed, just as they saw in the vision, years of pain were eradicated in a single second, through the hands of children under the age of ten who simply asked, received, and did what they imagined love – God – would do.

It would be the first of dozens of miracles and other things that would make even the most cynical mind wonder that day. As supernatural as it was for everyone involved, it did not seem abnormal to us or our children. In fact, they would not call it supernatural at all, but just an everyday occurrence. The more unnatural thing to them would have been to not find any of the people based upon the impressions they had written down the night before.

My point in sharing this story with you is not to brag on Michelle and the kids. It is to highlight a powerful insight we had that day about how our associations with the things of God can dramatically influence our relationship with God and our ability to manifest the reality of His kingdom in every realm of life.

After seeing Michelle and the kids administer the reality of the kingdom that day, many of those in attendance approached us to say thanks. They seemed especially grateful for the way the kids operated in the supernatural in such an effortless and seemingly casual and normal way.

Though we were all humbled and honored at the kind expressions of gratitude, we stumbled trying to answer what became a recurring question, "Where did your kids learn how to do that? What church did they attend?"

It was difficult, in retrospect, because until that moment, it hadn't really occurred to us that our children had never really been in church!

Sure, they had traveled with us when we spoke in churches and knew many of our friends who were pastors of churches, but they had never been regular attendees at a local church. To them, church is not something they even associate with God, *per se*. The primary association they have with church is that it's a place mom and dad go on occasion to share about the God stuff they see every day at home, at my office, at their school, as we shop, as we eat dinner at a restaurant, at one of their sporting events, or, in general, as we go about what they think of as *normal life*.

Michelle and I have never been angry at church, subsequently choosing to opt out. To the contrary, our church associations, for the most part, have been fairly positive.

It just so happened that near the time we gave birth to our second child, eighteen months after our first, we were taking a break from a great church we had attended for more than thirteen years. That season of our life was transitional on many fronts: our routines were shifting with the addition of the children, my business was in flux and, simultaneously, we sensed God pulling us aside for a season to get more clear direction.

It was during this time that we began limiting our involvement in several of our routine church activities to privately focus our time as a family with God and to see greater manifestations of the reality of the kingdom in our lives.

Significant encounters with God followed, and eventually, so did the start of the movement I referenced earlier: An Uprising, a Call to Battle.

It was during that time that we began training the kids regularly at home and sharing with them, directly, everything we were getting from God on a daily basis. Sundays were family "training days."

Individual private encounters led to great times of sharing as a family and were followed by what we later called *treasure hunts* in public with the kids as a simple outlet to act on and do what we were learning.

Treasure hunts were like little field trips for us as a family to practice loving people, doing our part to exercise what we were learning in public to make miracles seem recreational.

The results, over time, were nothing less than supernatural as the reality of the *Great Commission* – the blind seeing, the lame walking, the deaf hearing – became almost daily occurrences for us and our children. They call it simply "God stuff."

It wasn't until we began getting the "Where do your kids go to church to learn this stuff?" question that we realized our children had no association between going to church and the *God stuff* they were now experiencing as a part of their everyday life.

Our children had no traditions in associating with God and connecting to Him, or in limiting His activities to only certain kinds of ...

| | | |
|---|---|---|
| Activities | Feelings | Music |
| Ambiance | Kinds of clothing | Preaching |
| Architectures | Leaders | Sects of people |
| Buildings | Lighting | |
| Days of the week | Locations | |

Again, there is nothing inherently wrong with these traditions specifically. But if you only associate the activities of God with a certain place, time, and atmosphere or with a select group of people and a sufficiently holy kind of ambiance, then God's activities are going to be wholly absent from the parts of your life where those things don't coexist.

If all these things listed above are required for you to discern the presence or to feel anointed by God to administer His activities, then you will never feel anointed standing in the line at your local retail store when someone beside you needs to connect with God.

Maybe that's why God was so adamant in saying we should not make elaborate images to represent Him and not associate His dwelling among men with a building made with hands.

God doesn't dwell there:

> However, the Most High does not live in houses made by men. As the prophet says: Heaven is my throne, and the earth is my footstool. What kind of house will you build for me? says the Lord. Or where will my resting place be?
>
> ~ Acts 7:48–49

The people of God are the temple of God:

> For we are God's fellow workers; you are God's field, God's building.
>
> ~ 1 Corinthians 3:9

> Don't you know that you yourselves are God's temple and that God's Spirit lives in you? If anyone destroys God's temple, God will destroy him; for God's temple is sacred, and you are that temple.
>
> ~ 1 Corinthians 3:16–17

> And you are living stones that God is building into his spiritual temple. What's more, you are his holy priests. Through the mediation of Jesus Christ, you offer spiritual sacrifices that please God.
>
> ~ 1 Peter 2:5, NLT

These are just a few verses of many I could share, but you get the idea – we are God's living stones or, in other words, the rocks upon which He is building His *ekklesia,* not His church.

If every church in the world was destroyed and another church was never constructed, it would not limit God's ability to manifest His kingdom on earth one bit. A willing heart is the only requirement for God to work through us, not elaborate or sacred structures or institutions.

That's good news because it means you take God and the power of His kingdom wherever you go, without limitation. You can safely say, "Wherever 'I Am,' there God and His Kingdom can be also!"

It's for this reason we like to call the minyan-style *ekklesias* that are now forming around the world "I Am" groups.

I Am groups are simply small groups of ten individuals or five couples that are assembling together, as Jesus and His followers were in the habit of doing. They meet together in order to reorient and incite, provoke and equip each other to bring about love's ideal in every area of their lives and realms of influence. (Heb. 10:24–25).

Take a moment to consider who you may feel led to assemble with in similar fashion. If you're an individual, do you know nine others who can rise up and reorient like you are? Consider writing their names down now. You don't have to have all nine people to begin – even one or two others besides yourself is sufficient to start.

Remember Jesus said:

> *"For where **two or three gather together** as my followers,*
> ***I am there** among them."*
> > *~ Matthew 18:20,* NLT, ***emphasis added***

God will lead you. Remember:


It doesn't have to be weekly,

It doesn't have to have a leader,

It doesn't have to be at a religious place,

It doesn't have to be organized around a religious topic,

It doesn't have to be big to be effective.

Maybe just begin by going through the *Re_Orient* book and related resources together as a small I Am group, and then focus on integrating and practicing what you are learning into your own lives and homes first. Measure the fruit. As each of you begin getting some "wins" and bringing about love's ideal in private, prepare and equip each other to rise up and battle anything that is less than love's ideal in other public realms of life where you have influence, such as:

| | | |
|---|---|---|
| Civil government | The financial community | Social services |
| Arts and media | | The family structure |
| Education | Social communication | Religion |

Just whatever you do, rise up and do something – as you are about to see in the next chapter, the whole world is waiting!

**RESOURCE**
If you want more resources on how to start an I Am group, plus a reoriented look at what the Bible really says about the qualifications for I Am group leadership, visit the online resource section for this chapter. Or if you want to share your results or see what others are doing to rise up and reorient the world, visit our I Am Group video channel at www.thereorientbook.com

# CHURCH__REACT

Top three things you are taking away from this chapter:

........................................................................................................................

........................................................................................................................

........................................................................................................................

........................................................................................................................

........................................................................................................................

........................................................................................................................

........................................................................................................................

........................................................................................................................

........................................................................................................................

What action can you take now on what you've learned?

........................................................................................................................

........................................................................................................................

........................................................................................................................

........................................................................................................................

........................................................................................................................

........................................................................................................................

........................................................................................................................

........................................................................................................................

........................................................................................................................

He's our God and He's a warrior

He surveys all the earth

Come, all who have obtained mercy

Who have tasted of His great love

Hear the call to our generation

The call to battle, to rise above

– CALL TO BATTLE –

*Lyrics by Kevin Weaver It's Feasible Publishing, LLC*

Download the complete lyrics and an .mp3 version of this
song in its entirety at www.thereorientbook.com.

# CHRISTIAN

# What's your REACTION to the word?

$\oplus$ Positive

$\ominus$ Negative

$\bigcirc$ Neutral

# What does the word MEAN TO YOU?

Now let's see what others say. ▶

The way people surveyed
reacted to the word CHRISTIAN.

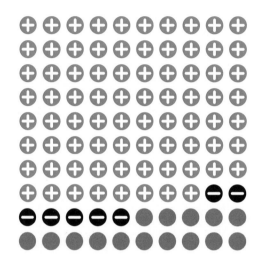

# 78.01%
Positive

# 06.53%
Negative

# 15.46%
Neutral

See a video of respondants in the Resource section for this chapter at www.reorientbook.com.

Common words people surveyed
associated with the word CHRISTIAN.

JESUS BORN AGAIN HYPOCRITE
BELIEVER
MISUSED
KINDNESS
GOOD CHRISTLIKE FOLLOWER OF CHRIST
PERSON
RIGHT-WING FAITHFUL ANOINTED
ARROGANT RELIGIOUS
SAVED LOVE
INTOLERANCE

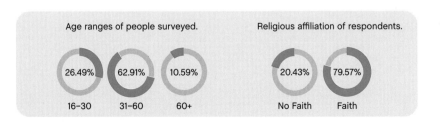

Age ranges of people surveyed.

26.49% | 62.91% | 10.59%
16–30 | 31–60 | 60+

Religious affiliation of respondents.

20.43% | 79.57%
No Faith | Faith

# CHRISTIAN__REDISCOVER

## OLD TESTAMENT HEBREW WORDS FOR CHRISTIAN

USED  *0 times*

WORDS

DEFINITION

---

## NEW TESTAMENT GREEK WORDS FOR CHRISTIAN

USED  *3 times*

WORDS  CHRISTIANOS */khrist-tee-an-os/*

DEFINITION  *Little Christs or little anointed ones*

# CHRISTIAN_RECOUNT

# CHRISTIAN

OLD TESTAMENT VERSES
USING THE HEBREW WORD

NEW TESTAMENT VERSES
USING THE GREEK WORD

0 | 3

|  | |
|---|---|
| Genesis | 0 |
| Exodus | 0 |
| Leviticus | 0 |
| Numbers | 0 |
| Deuteronomy | 0 |
| Joshua | 0 |
| Judges | 0 |
| Ruth | 0 |
| 1 Samuel | 0 |
| 2 Samuel | 0 |
| 1 Kings | 0 |
| 2 Kings | 0 |
| 1 Chronicles | 0 |
| 2 Chronicles | 0 |
| Ezra | 0 |
| Nehemiah | 0 |
| Esther | 0 |
| Job | 0 |
| Psalm | 0 |
| Proverbs | 0 |
| Ecclesiastes | 0 |
| Song of Songs | 0 |
| Isaiah | 0 |
| Jeremiah | 0 |
| Lamentations | 0 |
| Ezekiel | 0 |
| Daniel | 0 |
| Hosea | 0 |
| Joel | 0 |
| Amos | 0 |
| Obadiah | 0 |
| Jonah | 0 |
| Micah | 0 |
| Nahum | 0 |
| Habakkuk | 0 |
| Zephaniah | 0 |
| Haggai | 0 |
| Zechariah | 0 |
| Malachi | 0 |

| New Testament | |
|---|---|
| 0 | Matthew |
| 0 | Mark |
| 0 | Luke |
| 0 | John |
| 2 | Acts |
| 0 | Romans |
| 0 | 1 Corinthians |
| 0 | 2 Corinthians |
| 0 | Galatians |
| 0 | Ephesians |
| 0 | Philippians |
| 0 | Colossians |
| 0 | 1 Thessalonians |
| 0 | 2 Thessalonians |
| 0 | 1 Timothy |
| 0 | 2 Timothy |
| 0 | Titus |
| 0 | Philemon |
| 0 | Hebrews |
| 0 | James |
| 1 | 1 Peter |
| 0 | 2 Peter |
| 0 | 1 John |
| 0 | 2 John |
| 0 | 3 John |
| 0 | Jude |
| 0 | Revelation |

*Graph is based on the highest
verse use and shown visually as
a percentage of the highest value.

# CHRISTIAN_REORIENT

Are you a Christian? If not, why not? If so, how do you know for sure? After all, who is a Christian anyway? What does it really mean to be Christian? It's a simple question, but the answers you get when you ask someone are varied, and consensus is rare. The word is applied to everything from churches, schools, and movies to businesses and the people who run them.

According to recent statistics, more than 33 percent of people in the world, or 2.2 billion people,[24] identify themselves as Christians. That includes more than 75 percent of adults in the United States, or more than 224 million people.[25]

When asked to be more specific, however, about what it actually means to be a Christian, consensus is harder to achieve. Several sources, relying mostly on a 2001 edition of the *World Christian Encyclopedia,* estimate the number of different denominations of Christians in the world to be in excess of 38,000. There are more than 1,500 different denominations of Christians in the United States.[26]

The same sources group these 38,000 Christian denominations into what they call major ecclesiastical megablocks. These six megablocks (and approximate number of denominations within those megablocks) are said to be:

1. Independents (22,000)

2. Protestants (9,000)

3. Marginals (1,600)

4. Orthodox (781)

5. Roman Catholic (242)

6. Anglicans (168)

If that weren't confusing enough, each of these six major megablocks of Christian denominations is further subdivided into

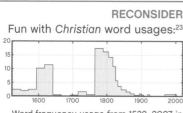

**RECONSIDER**

Fun with *Christian* word usages:[23]

Word frequency usage from 1539–2007 in occurrences per 100,000 words per year

Phone Digits: (.24) 477-8426

Antonym: Unchristian

Anagram: Christina

Scrabble Score: 14

hundreds of different subgroups[27] that vary, based on application of the word Christian.

Independent denominations, for example, might identify themselves as being apostolic, charismatic, or full-gospel Christians. Protestant denominations may identify themselves as Adventists, Baptists, or Lutheran Christians. Marginal denominations might use distinctions like Jehovah's Witnesses or Latter-Day Saints, and so on.

The number of individual members within each division and subdivision varies greatly. The Roman Catholic block, for example, with only 242 of the total 38,000 denominations worldwide, makes up the largest portion of the world's population identifying themselves as Christians. More than 50 percent, or in excess of one billion people worldwide, who identify themselves as Christian are Catholic.

Do you identify the term *Christian* with one of these major denominations?

Here's what the people we surveyed thought when they were asked about the term (sorted alphabetically):

| | | |
|---|---|---|
| A believer in God | Born again | Nice person |
| A godly person | Child of God | One who believes Jesus died for them |
| A major religion derived from Judaism | Christlike | Right-winged |
| | Confessed Christ as Lord | Servant-type person |
| An anointed person | Conservative | Soldier |
| A saved person | Follower of Christ | Way of Christ |
| A witness to the gospel | King's kids | Which kind? |
| Bible-believing people | Loves God | Zealot |
| | Made a confession of faith in Christ | |

Though their definitions were not consistent or always accurate, 78 percent of those we surveyed had positive impressions of the word *Christian.* Only 22 percent shared neutral or negative impressions of the word.

A few of the more humorous, cynical, but nonetheless common responses included things like:

| | | |
|---|---|---|
| A religion that excludes all others | Intolerant | Sheeple |
| | Overused term to gain trust | Skeptical |
| Haters | | So you say so |
| Hypocritical | Overzealous | Yeah, right |

Why are there so many opinions about what it means to be a Christian? Why are there so many different denominations of Christians in the world, and why do they all have different plans to evangelize the world and make more Christians?

For their book *Seven Hundred Plans to Evangelize the World,* David Barrett and James W. Reapsome surveyed 788 plans produced by Christian denominations over the last nineteen hundred years to evangelize the world by spreading the gospel and converting others to Christianity.

The sheer existence of so many different plans or missions for Christian evangelism plays a huge part in creating variation in the definition and confusion about what it actually means to become or to be a Christian. And worse, all indications are that the number of plans is increasing exponentially.

According to Barrett and Reapsome, in the 66 gen-

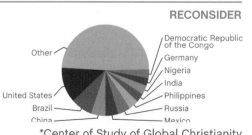

**RECONSIDER**

*Center of Study of Global Christianity, World Christian Database

erations that have passed since Jesus issued the so-called Great Commission ...

Christians in the first 55 generations averaged 2.6 plans per generation,

Christians in the beginning of the nineteenth century averaged 28 plans per generation,

Christians in the first decade of the twentieth century averaged 69 plans per generation,

Christians in the early 1970s averaged 321 plans per generation,

Christians in the present generation are on pace to yield 1,200 plans.

As cited by the authors, the average budget per plan was more than $100 million per decade, and the biggest plan at the time of their survey spent $550 million per year on its "Christian mission."

With all the effort and resources being dedicated to these Christian missions around the world, how is it working? Are people getting the message? And if so, what is the Christian message they're getting?

The book *unChristian: What a New Generation Really Thinks About Christianity,* by David Kinnaman and Gabe Lyons, published in 2007, argues that to the majority of non-Christian people, Christians no longer represent what Jesus had in mind and the Christian message has lost its meaning.

"It's clear that Christians are primarily perceived for what they stand against," they go on.[28] Christians, they say, are perceived by the majority of outsiders to be:

Anti-gay,

Anti-choice,

Anti-social,

Anti-peace,

Non-inclusive,

Not open-minded,

And generally only focused on converting or saving people who are not like them or who disagree with them.

In other words, people think Christians are only focused on fighting against something or converting someone they perceive or define as non-Christian.

Is this mixed message what Jesus hoped people would get from His followers?

For those who believe becoming a Christian and then converting others to become Christians was the primary mission of the Great Commission, wouldn't a more exact definition of what it means to be a Christian be helpful?

## SO, WHAT IS A CHRISTIAN, HOW WOULD YOU KNOW FOR SURE IF YOU ARE ONE, AND IS BEING ONE REALLY THE GOAL ANYWAY?

Did you know Jesus never once referred to Himself or His followers as Christians? Did you know His followers never referred to themselves as Christians?

Did you know the first time the word translated *Christian* was used in the biblical text, it was approximately fifty years after Jesus' time on earth?

Did you know the so-called Great Commission never once mentions converting people to become Christians?

And did you know (before you read this chapter) the word *Christian* was only used three times in the entire Bible and that the word as we know it today wasn't popularized until nearly 350 years later?

Most people are surprised to discover that all the above statements are true, especially given the consistent emphasis on the word *Christian* among people and organizations that identify with the term.

Even more astonishing to most is the context in which the word *Christian* was used in the first place and its connotation when originally applied to Jesus' followers. Both were in stark contrast to how the majority of the world thinks of the word today.

To see what I mean, let's look at where all this Christian labeling began, and where the term was first applied to the followers of Jesus, specifically the disciples. It's found in a single verse in the book of Acts:

> For **a whole year they ‹the disciples› assembled together
> ‹led together and convened›** with and were **guests of the
> church ‹ekklesia›** and instructed a large number of people;
> and in Antioch the disciples were **first called Christians**.
> ~ *Acts 11:26, AMP, **emphasis added***

Before we dive into a brief history of the word *Christian* and its connotation in this verse, I want to use this verse to make some observations and validate some of what we learned in the last chapter about church.

1. You probably noticed right away that this verse says the disciples were "assembled together" and were guests of a local *ekklesia* in Antioch. This is consistent with our reorientation to the words *ekklesia* and *church*.

2. This assembling together lasted a whole year! I don't know about you, but to me, a year would make for an extremely long gathering or series of gatherings if anything like a traditional church meeting today.

3. It was in the context of an *ekklesia* that they, together or collectively, were instructing a "large number of people." Like everywhere else you see the word *ekklesia* in the New Testament, there's no mention of:

A single large event or meeting,

A single formal location where meetings were held,

A single building or synagogue,

A single leader that officiated meetings,

A single senior pastor of the local meetings,

A single person as the spiritual covering of the meetings,

A single distinction between classes of Christians within the *ekklesia,*

A single distinction between leaders, clergy, laity, or laypeople,

A single goal of converting people to become Christians.

You will see this "ecclesiastical" pattern reinforced over and over again as we reorient to the word *Christian.* It was in the context of an *ekklesia* that people were first called Christians.

Notice in our focus verse that the disciples were first called Christians. But why? Apparently, this initial small group of revolutionary followers of Jesus began to believe in, declare, and demonstrate His new kingdom mandate so well in the context of frequent, public, citizen assemblies that they earned the distinction of being called Christians.

Ironically, the term *Christian* was not a term given to them by Jesus, nor was it a term they called themselves, nor was it a term they acknowledged as an accurate description.

So, what did it mean to be called one?

Today, the word *Christian* is almost universally understood to mean "a follower of Christ" even though, as we have seen in the early part of this chapter, the interpretation of what exactly that means can be varied, to say the least. Even the dictionary suggests a similar meaning:

**Christian**

*noun*

1. a person who believes in Jesus Christ
2. a person who exemplifies the teachings of Christ
3. a member of any of certain Protestant churches

005 · CHRISTIAN · REORIENT

*adjective*
1.  pertaining to, or derived from, Jesus Christ
2.  pertaining to, believing, or belonging to a religion based on teachings of Jesus Christ

This definition certainly seems consistent with the popular notion of the word and can appear rather obvious, since the word *Christian* appears, at first glance, to have "Christ" as its root word.

But is that so?

I am not suggesting that the dictionary is inaccurate. Remember, modern dictionaries update meanings regularly, based upon universally accepted definitions of words at a given time.

Many times, however, the dictionary definition doesn't accurately convey the historical connotation. And in this case, the modern definition of the word *Christian* has little in common with the original meaning of the word.

As flattering as the term *Christian* might sound today, the connotation in the context of this verse was meant to be anything but flattering.

The way the word *Christian* is defined today, we usually understand it as a term of endearment. But the etymology of the word is quite different. In fact, the original implication was mocking, unflattering, and even derogatory.

## TO BE A CHRISTIAN IN JESUS' TIME, YOU HAD TO BE STUPID, FOOLISH, LAZY, GLUTTONOUS, OR REALLY SUPER-ANOINTED

The word *Christian* is believed to have had two possible origins and, subsequently, two different meanings when initially applied to Jesus' disciples. The first asserts they were "stupid, foolish, evil, or lazy gluttons." The second suggested the disciples were actually like "little anointed ones" or "little messiahs," said with a mocking or belittling tone.

The implication that the disciples were stupid, foolish, evil, or lazy gluttons is based on the word *Christian* having origins in the Greek and later French word *cretin.*

Here's the dictionary definition:

**Cretin**
*noun*
1. a very stupid or foolish person
2. a person suffering from cretinism

*Origin(s):*
French crétin, dial. form of chrétien; lit., Christian, hence human being (in contrast to brutes) < LL(Ec) Christianus, Christian: sense development, as in silly

The word *cretin* apparently was a popular eighteenth-century French one, *chretien,* and became pronounced and subsequently associated with the word *Christian* or *Christianus,* meaning "silly."

Critics of this derivation of the word *Christian* point out – and rightfully so – that the word *cretin* refers to inhabitants of the Greek island of Crete, who were called Cretans.[29]

The Bible does use the word *Cretan* to describe a person from a physical place called Crete, which it mentions two or three times in the New Testament. But the description it gives of the inhabitants of Crete is consistent with the definition the dictionary provided above. For example, see how Cretans are described in the Bible when Paul sends Titus to Crete to deal with the people there:

> One of their [very] number, a prophet of their own, said,
> **Cretans ‹meaning a person from Crete› are always liars,**
> **hurtful beasts, idle and lazy gluttons.**
> ~ *Titus 1:12,* AMP, **emphasis added**

Cretans were also mentioned as being present when the disciples left the upper room on the day of Pentecost (fifty days from Passover) upon receiving the gift of the Holy Spirit and the miracle of speaking in other tongues:

*Cretans* and Arabians too – we all hear them speaking in our own native tongues [and telling of] the **mighty works ‹miracles, etc.›** of God!

~ Acts 2:11, AMP, **emphasis added**

In these two examples, it's clear the disciple knew who Cretans were and how they were viewed. It's also clear that being referred to as a *cretin* or *Christian* was meant to imply that, like the Cretans, the disciples were looked at as simple, stupid, or foolish people.

The bigger question, however, might be *why?* Why refer to them in such a derogatory manner?

The answer lies in what the disciples proclaimed and demonstrated as a result of their encounters with and mandate from Jesus.

Consider how these simple men of regular, working-class realms of influence suddenly emerged on the scene. After only a few years with Jesus, the disciples began announcing in a public square, for people of all different backgrounds to hear:

The establishment of a new kingdom is at hand,

The anointing of a new King has taken place,

The ability to speak in unknown tongues is now possible,

The power to make the blind see,

The power to make the lame walk,

The power to make the deaf hear,

The power to bring about freedom for the oppressed is now possible –

The same power is here for anyone who wants it and believes it!

Wouldn't you agree, this is some radical, crazy, and foolish-sounding stuff? That's not to even mention their just-as-crazy claim that this is was all made possible because of …

The miraculous virgin birth of a "Son of the living God,"

The same Son of God who then walked among us as a man,

The same man who did these same miracles as our example,

The same man who was brutally and publicly crucified,

The same man who was then miraculously resurrected from the dead,

The same man who then sent His Holy Spirit to empower us!

Imagine you had never heard such things before. What would be your impression of these men and their claims?

Even today, this kind of rhetoric seems to defy all logic and commonsense. It may find acceptance in a minority of religious or mystic Christian circles, but I'm not sure the majority of people who claim to be Christians would have much of an ear for someone standing up and making the same claims today.

Try it the next time you are hanging out with your Christian or non-Christian friends. Stand up, ask for their attenntion and declare:

The establishment of a new kingdom has taken place,

The anointing of a new King,

The ability to speak in unknown tongues is now possible,

The power to make the blind see,

The power to make the lame walk,

The power to make the deaf hear,

The power to set captives free,

The power to bring about freedom for the oppressed,

This is all possible now for anyone who wants and believes it!

Who's ready?

Now wait for a moment and gauge their response!

While these claims are every bit as valid as when Jesus and His first few disciples made them, these kinds of supernatural assertions are often an offense to the intellectual mind and impossible to believe for most people. It was the same during Jesus' time on Planet Earth – His message was only good news to those who had an ear to hear it and the courage to believe it. It was even better news to those who actually experienced its miraculous power directly.

The Bible says the whole premise of these claims was considered utter foolishness to those who weren't being saved by its power:

> For the message of the cross is foolishness to those who are perishing, but to us who are being saved it is the power of God.
>
> ~ 1 Corinthians 1:18

It's no different today. As noted in the "Religion" chapter, even for most so-called people of faith or believers, these things seem preposterous. Miracles like these are fine to talk about in the historical or future tense, but the minute someone starts to declare these kinds of things as a present-tense reality, skeptics abound and mockery is commonplace.

Some might equate such faith to believing in Santa Claus or the Easter Bunny. Others may even think you have completely lost your mind. Some may become downright hostile for what they might consider your intent to deceive, mislead, and exploit the simple-minded.

I have experienced all of these reactions, at times, from well-intentioned believers and non-believers alike – some of them my own friends and family members. Until I became convinced of this reality, I was in the corner with the mocking unbelievers myself, so I can understand where they're coming from. Who can blame them? Without demonstrable evidence, why should anyone believe it, anyway? Miracles, really?

In April 1996, Supreme Court Justice Antonin Scalia told a legal society's prayer breakfast, "Christians should assert their faith even if intellectuals dismiss them as

**REMEMBER**
Even Jesus said that if He didn't demonstrate this stuff, nobody should believe Him either, right? (John 10:37.)

simpleminded for believing in miracles. We are fools for Christ's sake," he said, adding that the word *cretin*, or *fool*, is derived from the French word for *Christian*.[30]

Whether you subscribe to the *cretin* origins of the word *Christian* or not, it's obvious from the biblical text, the followers of Christ understood the contempt their critics had for them:

> *We are [looked upon as] fools on account of Christ and for His sake, but you are [supposedly] so amazingly wise and prudent in Christ! We are weak, but you are [so very] strong! You are highly esteemed, but we are in disrepute and contempt!*
>
> ~ *1 Corinthians 4:10,* AMP

What about the other possible origins of Christian? Could it be that the disciples were being called "little anointed ones," but with a mocking or belittling undertone?

The Greek word *Christos* (*Christ* in English) means "Anointed." *Christos* is a popular New Testament Greek translation of the Hebrew word *Masiah* (*Messiah* in English), meaning "one who is anointed." As such, the Greek word *Christianoi* (*Christian* in English), believed to be derived from the same root word *Chresto*, literally means "anointed ones" or "messiah people."

**RECONSIDER**

This same root word *Christos* is thought to be derived from a much older Greek word, *Chrestos*. However, this word was not originally associated with Jesus, the Christ, or Christians. Early forms and symbols of the word *Chrestos* are believed to have predated the biblical use of *Christos,* and later *Christian,* by nearly four hundred years.

One pagan symbol, the ancient labarum as it's called, displayed the Greek symbols chi rho. This was later adopted by so-called Christians. Originally, this chi rho symbol, ☧, made by combining and superimposing two Greek letters that also form the word *Christ, P* and *X,* meant "good."

This symbol was used by pagan Greek scribes to mark in the margins of valuable, relevant, or otherwise good passages of a text. Because of its general resemblance to a cross, it was later used to form what then became known as a type of Christogram.

Much later, the same symbol was even adopted and modified slightly to become a monogram emblazoned on flags, armor, and shields of Christian soldiers during the life and time of Constantine.

Some contend a slight modification of the chi rho symbol later evolved into the symbol now recognized by pharmacists worldwide as the symbol for pharmacy or prescription. That's because the letters XP (chi rho) may also be interpolated and offset to form PX, creating the famous ℞ Greek *pharmakia* symbol.

This is intriguing for several reasons. When Greek symbols of this nature are reversed, generally the meaning is also. So, if the Greek letters chi rho (XP) later came to refer to the Christ, then reversing the letters to PX, or ℞, may indicate a return to the Chrestos, or possibly a reference to something as Antichrist or against Christ. Critics of this theory dismiss this idea as a fanciful extrapolation, asserting the symbol ℞ is simply representative of the letters R and X, an abbreviation of the Latin word for recipe.[31]

Like the critics, I might be easily persuaded to dismiss this one as pure legend or a kind of conspiracy theory if it weren't for another little bit of biblical irony.

The Greek word translated *witchcraft* in the New Testament is *pharmakia,* which is the same word *pharmacy, pharmaceutical,* and *pharmacology* derive from today.

Do you find that ironic? Remember that verse we covered way back in the "Sin" chapter about things that separate people from inheriting the kingdom of God? It turns out that one of the things in that list was practicing things considered witchcraft.

REMEMBER
The acts of the sinful ‹*cause people to miss the mark*› nature are obvious: sexual immorality, impurity and debauchery; idolatry and **witchcraft** ‹*pharmakia*›; hatred, discord, jealousy, fits of rage, selfish ambition, dissensions, factions and envy; drunkenness, orgies, and the like. I warn you, as I did before, that those who live like this will not inherit the kingdom of God.

~ Gal. 5:19–21,
*emphasis added*

267

The same word *pharmakia,* translated as *witchcraft* in this verse, is translated as *sorcery* in other verses (Rev. 9:21; 18:23, NKJV).

Now, before you think taking an aspirin makes you an accessory to the Antichrist or that I am suggesting medicine is of the devil, think of it this way.

The Bible equates witchcraft with a kind of rebellion or control.

> *Rebellion is as sinful as witchcraft, and stubbornness as bad as worshiping idols.*
>
> ~ *1 Samuel 15:23,* NLT

When you think about it, when used in the science of healing humans, control is really for medicinal purposes, right? Pharmaceuticals are simply a method or means of controlling a body process or function that is not working most excellently.

So, since one of the names for Jesus is Jehovah Rophe, meaning "God my healer," and the Word of God is called health and medicine for our bodies (Prov. 4:20–22), it makes sense that being set against these notions would be considered rebelling or choosing another method to control the healing process than God provided.

I want to stress, however, that nowhere in the Bible does it suggest – nor am I suggesting – that a person who chooses a medicinal method to obtain healing is evil or is in any way displeasing to God.

Healing is good, whether divinely or pharmacologically achieved. The latter is simply not the most cost-effective, efficient, or side-effect-free method to obtain the healing Christ came to provide. Divine healing is simply love's ideal for a person.

We will have plenty of opportunity to talk more about divine healing and other such miracles in later chapters. For now, my point is simply this: Symbols like these were not uncommon, but the majority of them developed well after Jesus' time on earth, and though they have meaning now, they were not likely used by people in Jesus' time to identify His followers as Christians.

Probably the most popular modern-day example is the familiar fish symbol, or *ikhthus,* . This Greek word for *fish* is often used as a Christian symbol today, but wasn't during Jesus' time.

Why is this important? Because these symbols and terms, and especially the ones associated with the Greek words *Christos* or *Christianos,* were not of Hebrew or Jewish origins, but rather were Greek and pagan in nature. Because of that, it's believed it was Gentiles or non-Jewish unbelievers who were the ones likely to first use these symbols to refer to the disciples in the book of Acts.

As David Stern suggests in the *Jewish New Testament Commentary,* if the assignment of the Greek word *Christianoi,* or Christian, literally meaning "anointed ones" or "messiah people" wasn't assigned to the followers of Jesus by believing Jewish people, then it was most likely a term used by non-believing Gentiles in the region.

They may have kept hearing about *Christos,* or Christ. Being familiar with the Jewish notion of messiah, in a somewhat derogatory way, they assigned the term "little *Christos*", little Christs, or anointed ones to the followers of Jesus. This would have been based on what they thought their leader was called: Jesus "the Christ" or Jesus the "Anointed One."

Theoretically, if a Jewish believer assigned a term to the followers of Jesus, they would have most likely used an Old Testament or Hebrew term they were already familiar with, not adopted a Greek term like Christian.

The term most familiar to Jewish people was "those belonging to the way." Unlike the term *Christian,* which Jesus or His followers never used to describe themselves, "the way" was a phrase Jesus, Paul, and others used a number of times.

In either case, the term *Christian,* whether derived from *cretin* or *Christos* and ascribed to the disciples by believers, unbelievers, Jews, or Gentiles, has the same implication. It was a term contemptuously applied to the followers of Jesus to mock, deride, and demean their assertions and activities.

**RECONSIDER**

This fish symbol was used by ancient Christians to mark meeting places and tombs and to distinguish friends from foes.

Jesus' disciples certainly understood the contemptuous connotation and implications of the word as it was applied to them. For example, consider this verse:

> But if [one is ill-treated and suffers] as a Christian [which he is contemptuously called], let him not be ashamed, but give glory to God that he is [deemed worthy to suffer] in this name.
>
> ~ 1 Peter 4:16, AMP

Notice first, the use of the phrase "as a Christian." By using this phrase, Peter was not calling himself a Christian, but was comparing the suffering he spoke of to be like that of a Christian. Also notice how the Amplified Version uses the phrase "which he is contemptuously called" in regard to being called a Christian. Apparently, being called a Christian was regarded as such a reproach, it was considered "suffering ill-treatment" for which a person had to be encouraged to "not be ashamed."

Would you consider yourself a Christian based on the definitions we have looked at so far? Does what the word *Christian,* as originally communicated, pose a problem for you, in terms of what it communicates today?

RECONSIDER
Any of this way
(Acts 9:2, NKJV)

Prepare the way
(Matt. 3:3, NKJV)

Difficult is the way
(Matt. 7:14, NKJV)

I am the way (John 14:6, NKJV)

The way of righteousness
(Matt. 21:32, NKJV)

The way of peace
(Luke 1:79, NKJV)

THE BIGGEST PROBLEM WITH THE TERM *CHRISTIAN* TODAY IS THAT IT COMMUNICATES SO MUCH AND YET COMMUNICATES NOTHING

In modern times, being identified as a Christian generally indicates that a person has:

Some relationship with Jesus,

Some level of spiritual awareness,

Some level of spiritual maturity,

Some God-like or moral standard.

Unfortunately, the term actually says nothing about any of these things. In other words, the term *Christian* is used today by people to communicate so much, but at the same time communicates nothing at all.

Think about it. When someone is identified or identifies themselves as Christian in our modern society, what is the hearer supposed to conclude? Does it mean:

The person was raised in church?

The person went to church at some point or goes now?

The church they attend is in one of the 38,000 denominations we listed?

The church they attend is in one of the hundreds of denominational subgroups?

Beyond the affiliation ...

What does it say about the person's individual level of commitment?

What does it say about how often they attend – regularly, on occasion, or hardly ever?

What does it say about what the person believes?

What does it say about their level of agreement or adherence to those beliefs?

What does it say about whether they actually practice what they believe?

What does it say about how mature they are in those beliefs?

And beyond their beliefs ...

Do they practice what they believe?

Do they pray?

Do they study the Bible?

Do they believe what it says?

Do they endeavor to emulate Jesus in any way?

Do they have any level of personal mastery in their beliefs or practice?

Do they have any fruit in their life to indicate their level of mastery?

We could go on with questions like these because using the term Christian seems to imply something about all these things. And yet, at the same time, it provides answers to none of them.

The absence of any kind of standard definition of what it means to be a Christian makes it a meaningless term that fails to communicate anything of real value.

When originally used to describe the disciples, though used in a derogatory way, the word at least referred to a kind of visible, definable activity and, hence, evidence of their beliefs and ability. The mighty works they did were themselves the sign and evidence that convinced people the disciples were Christians.

Today, however, labeling something Christian is often an attempt to convince people that a set of godly beliefs or activities are present. The visible evidence or activities that would warrant the term are rarely the yardstick used for the label.

This has resulted in countless disappointments, hurts, and conflicts between people – all supposedly in the name of God.

Have you ever heard of someone who has been hurt, wronged, disappointed, offended, or completely blindsided by so-called Christian behavior say something like:

But I thought they were supposed to be Christians,

But we went to church together for twenty years,

But we prayed together,

But we went to Bible study together,

But I thought I could trust them.

But I thought they were mature Christian people,

But how could they act like that and still call themselves Christians,

But that wasn't very Christ-like behavior for someone who claimed to be a Christian,

But they had that little Christian symbol on their business card or bumper of their car,

But, but, but ... ?

I have heard these statements and a hundred others like it too many times to recount. It's sad that anyone is ever hurt in the name of Christianity. The greater tragedy is, in most cases, it could have been easily avoided if another standard would have been used to evaluate the relationship.

That's because too often the Christian label is relied upon to communicate a God-like quality, standard of conduct, or level of spiritual maturity that may not really exist. But in actuality, to determine a God-like standard, another measurement is needed all together.

## GROWING OUT OF THE CHRISTIAN LABEL

At its very best, the term Christian – or *born-again* Christian, as it is sometimes called – can only communicate one thing: that a person was a baby once and may still be!

In fact, being "born again" or "born from above" is the terminology the Bible uses to describe a person's initial relationship with Christ and to mark the beginning of a person's spiritual maturity in the kingdom of God.

Here is how Jesus said it:

*... who came to Jesus at night and said to Him, Rabbi, we know and are certain that You have come from God [as] a Teacher; for no one can do these signs (these wonderworks, these miracles – and produce the proofs) that You do unless God is with him. Jesus answered him, **I assure you, most solemnly I tell you, that unless a person is born again (anew, from above), he cannot ever see (know, be acquainted with, and experience) the kingdom of God.** Nicodemus said to Him, How can a man be born when he is old? Can he enter his mother's womb again and be born? Jesus answered, I assure you, most solemnly I tell you, unless a man is born of water and [even] the Spirit, he cannot [ever] enter the kingdom of God ‹**Ezek. 36:25–27**›. **What is born of [from] the flesh is flesh [of the physical is physical]; and what is born of the Spirit is spirit.** Marvel not [do not be surprised, astonished] at My telling you, You must all be born anew (from above).*
~ John 3:2–7, AMP, ***emphasis added***

Without dissecting this verse in detail, I want to simply draw your attention to the notion that Jesus is saying someone's initial baptism, literally meaning "immersion into the things of God", is equated with being a newborn infant. Though the Bible never uses this term exactly as it relates to the term Christian, it's where the popular term or tradition of identifying someone as a "born-again Christian" comes from.

What's interesting is how Jesus doesn't use the term *Christian,* but parallels the spiritual development and maturity of a person to physical human development and maturity.

While it's a concept that is easy to relate, it can be equally problematic unless a few important distinctions are made between how a person's physical and spiritual development occur.

The number of stages and corresponding ages of human development varies depending on the scientific model used. It's generally accepted and universally observable, however, that under normal circumstances, that humans pass through at least five different stages of development between physical birth and death:

Birth,

Infancy stage (0–3),

Childhood stage (3–11),

Adolescence stage (11–19),

Adulthood stage (20+),

Senior adult stage (60+),

Death.

The same way the physical development of a person progresses through these stages, the Bible says that people spiritually progress through five spiritual stages of development between spiritual birth and death:

Birth,

Infants,

Children,

Young men or women,

Adults,

Mature ones or fully mature ones,

Perfect.

The physical development of a person is easily discernable, and age alone can be a simple indicator. For example, those who are zero to three years old look like babies; three- to eleven-year-olds look like children; those older than twenty look like young adults and adults; and those over sixty years of age look like senior adults.

Spiritual babies, children, young adults, and fully mature adults, however, can't be discerned by age alone. This is where things can be problematic and where an important distinction must be made be-tween physical and spiritual stages of development. Spiritual stages of development the Bible uses are more behavior-driven and not always age related.

In other words, everybody ages physically, but not everyone arrives at spiritual maturity. Someone who is seventy years old and looks like a mature senior adult physically can become born again and be a mere infant spiritually.

In contrast, someone who is twelve years of age physically can have more spiritual maturity and be more spiritually developed than some-one who is physically fifty years old.

Think about David. As a youth – some say twelve years of age – he killed the lion, the bear, and ultimately Goliath. This was a feat that men many times his age with more physical experience and strength could not muster the faith to achieve (1 Sam. 17:1–58).

How about Jesus? At twelve, He was found teaching in the temple with such spiritual wisdom and insight that He was confounding even the most astute and learned scholars of the time (Luke 2:39–52).

Under normal circumstances, humans can be born and, by getting basic food and shelter, automatically pass through the physical stages of development as they age chronologically. Progressing and identi-fying spiritual maturity, however, requires more than just being born again and is never an automatic outcome of simply progressing in age chronologically.

For this reason, identifying someone's stage of spiritual maturity is far more important than applying a one-size-fits-all label like born again or *Christian*. Can you imagine going into a job interview and having someone ask you about your qualifications for the job and then reply-ing, "Well, I was born once, and I have lived with other people who were born once, too, for more than twenty-five years now."?

If the employer assessed, qualified, and hired people like most Christians prequalify their relationships with other Christians, their reply would be something like, "Praise God! I am glad to hear that.

We have so much in common. I was born once, too, as was everyone else who works here. This is going to be great. You're hired!"

Would any employer assume someone is qualified or mature enough for a job based upon having been born once? Yet ironically, people – especially so-called Christians – do this very thing by assuming someone who says they are a Christian has matured in any way since they were born again!

So, what's the alternative? Wouldn't it be great if people just came with another kind of label altogether, a kind of warning label and rating system attached to their forehead? Something like:

**CAUTION: I'M A LEVEL-TWO SPIRITUAL INFANT**

I may exhibit the following BEHAVIORS:

+_____

+_____

+_____

WHICH may cause the following problems:

+_____

+_____

+_____

People with warning labels – it sounds funny, I know. But the Bible actually provides just such a warning system. It's not a physical label, true, but it can be just as easily observed if a person is trained.

## DROPPING THE CHRISTIAN LABEL FOR A BETTER WAY TO IDENTIFY THE MATURITY OF REAL DISCIPLES OF JESUS

Unlike physical stages of maturity, you can't determine or label spiritual maturity based upon age. That's because spiritual maturity is more situational than chronologically developed. Unlike physical stages of maturity, spiritual maturity can only be identified and labeled after it is observed. Additionally, the time it takes for a person to progress through the phases of spiritual maturity is different for everyone. And spiritual maturity is not the inevitable result of simply passing through a previous phase, as is the case with physical development.

Jesus said the only visible way to tell where a person is in their spiritual development or maturity is by observing behavior. He likened it to knowing what kind of tree you are observing by the kind of fruit it produces:

*Yes, just as you can identify a tree by its fruit, so you can identify people by their actions.*

*~ Matthew 7:20,* NLT

How a person behaves and acts in certain situations is the fruit and the evidence of what kind of tree they are and the sign of how mature they are in their development.

Just like certain behaviors and abilities are easily discernable at the various stages of physical development, there are certain behaviors (fruits) that, when observed from the outside over time, help reveal a person's level of spiritual maturity.

Let's briefly consider each stage, starting at infancy.

## THE INFANCY STAGE

The term *infant* is derived from the Latin word *infans*, meaning "unable to speak" or "speechless." The New Testament Bible uses the Greek word *nepios* (pronounced nay-pee-os) to identify people at the infant stage of development.

**Nepios**

*adjective*

1. an infant, little child
2. a minor, not of age
3. metaphor: *childish, untaught, unskilled*

This term is often applied to children between birth and twelve months old; however, definitions vary between birth and three years of age. *Infant* is also a legal term in most cultures referring to any child under the age of legal adulthood.

Peter describes a group of people as being "spiritual infants" this way:

> *Like newborn babies ‹nepios – infants› you should crave (thirst for, earnestly desire) the pure (unadulterated) spiritual milk, that by it you may be nurtured and grow unto [completed] salvation.*
>
> *~ 1 Peter 2:2,* AMP, ***emphasis added***

Notice how this compares their level of maturity to spiritual infants desiring spiritual milk to grow up. Just like a newborn baby needs physical milk to grow, when people first become born again, they need a steady diet of the unadulterated Word of God, what the Bible calls "milk of the Word," to begin to grow.

So, how would you know if someone is at this infancy stage of development spiritually? What behavior might they exhibit to give you a clue? Just like physical infants:

They are dependent,

They need lots of attention,

They often require others to feed, cover, and protect them spiritually,

They are not always aware they need to change and hence, rarely self-correct,

They often need help from others to know when and how to change,

They need lots of grace while cleaning up the messes they make,

They need constant reassurance to feel safe and stay at peace,

They lack good communication skills and most often get attention by crying or whining,

They are prone to throwing emotional fits to get what they want.


Given these descriptions, do you know any spiritual infants?

It's critical not to expect much from people at the infancy stage. Just like you would not expect a physical infant to understand much or to take up certain responsibilities around the house, you simply can't expect spiritual infants to contribute much until they begin to mature.

Just as there is no shame in being a physical infant, spiritual infancy is a necessary phase, and there should be no shame associated with being at this stage of spiritual development.

Even for the caregivers, overseers, or attendants of spiritual infants, it can be a joyful time of discovery and wonder. Spiritual infancy is a time of receiving love, not giving love – for receiving care, not giving care to others.

People at this stage need lots of grace and need to be fed accordingly until they exhibit the behavioral signs that they are moving to the next phase of spiritual development – childhood.

Listen to how Paul describes his inability to talk about more substantial matters with some of his brothers who were perceived as being spiritual infants long after the time they should have grown up:

> However, brethren, **I could not talk to you as to spiritual [men], but as to nonspiritual [men of the flesh, in whom the carnal nature predominates], as to mere infants [in the new life] in Christ [unable to talk yet!]** I fed you with milk, not solid food, for you were not yet strong enough [to be ready for it]; but even yet you are not strong enough [to be ready for it], for you are still [unspiritual, having the nature] of the flesh [under the control of ordinary impulses]. For as long as [there are] envying and jealousy and wran-

*gling and factions among you, are you not unspiritual and of the flesh, behaving yourselves after a human standard and like mere (unchanged) men?*
                    *~ 1 Corinthians 3:1–3,* AMP, **emphasis added**

Physically, the men Paul is talking to here are his adult peers, but spiritually, he is describing them as infants based upon their behavior – in this case, the "envying and jealousy and wrangling and factions" among them.

As cute as a physical newborn infant's behavior can be, the same behavior is anything but at age forty.

Can you imagine meeting a forty-year-old drinking coffee from a bottle? As odd as that would seem physically, it can be a very real phenomenon spiritually. That's why meeting someone identified as a "born-again" Christian can be so misleading; it's not clear whether that means they were born once as an infant, needing to be bottle-fed the things of God, or if they are still at the infant stage at age forty and desiring milk.

Regardless of a person's wisdom, fame, corporate achievements, acting skills, athletic prowess, or ability to obtain wealth, when they enter the kingdom of God, like everyone else, they are infants spiritually, and need to mature. A person can have everything intellectually, physically, and financially a human could desire, but spiritually they have to mature in the things of God, just like an infant matures to adulthood physically.

*Jesus answered him, I assure you, most solemnly I tell you, that unless a person is born again (anew, from above), he cannot ever see (know, be acquainted with, and experience) the kingdom of God.*
                    *~ John 3:3,* AMP

Everybody has to be born once. It's a glorious time and should be celebrated. But just like it's unrealistic to expect infants to become mature adults overnight, you can't hold a recently born-again person to the same standards of conduct as a more mature follower of God.

In Jesus' own words, infancy is a requirement and nothing to be ashamed of. But the goal is still to grow up.

# THE CHILDHOOD STAGE

The post-infancy phase of physical and spiritual development is called childhood and is generally accepted as occurring between ages three and eleven. The New Testament Bible uses the Greek word *paidion* (pronounced pahee-dee'-on) to identify people at this stage..

**Paidion**

*noun*

1.  a young child, a little boy, a little girl
    a.  children, little ones
    b.  an infant (implying recently born but more advanced or mature)
2.  children (like children) in intellect

Listen to how Paul describes his developmental progression from childhood:

> *When I was a child ‹paidion – simple minded, immature›, I talked like a child, I thought like a child, I reasoned like a child; now that I have become a man ‹a fellow, mature, husband-like, a sir›, I am done with childish ways and have put them aside. For now we are looking in a mirror that gives only a dim (blurred) reflection [of reality as in a riddle or enigma], but then [when perfection comes] we shall see in reality and face to face! Now I know in part (imperfectly), but then I shall know and understand fully and clearly, even in the same manner as I have been fully and clearly known and understood [by God]. And so faith, hope, love abide [faith – conviction and belief respecting man's relation to God and divine things; hope – joyful and confident expectation of eternal salvation; love – true affection for God and man, growing out of God's love for and in us], these three; but the greatest of these is love.*
> *~ 1 Corinthians 13:11–13, AMP, emphasis added*

Notice in verses eleven and twelve how Paul describes being simple-minded – talking, thinking, and reasoning like a child – before he became more mature. Also notice how he uses the idea of looking in a mirror that gives only a dim reflection of reality, allowing a person to only know in part.

As this verse suggests, people in the childhood stage of both physical and spiritual development are learning new ways to talk, think, and reason. They are also trying to see clearly how the world works around them and their relationship to it, which can be foggy at times. Like both the physical and spiritual stages of development, and as the following verses suggest, the ability to master language is a sign of maturity and an indication of what a person can be taught:

> For even though by this time you ought to be teaching others, you actually need someone to teach you over again the very first principles of God's Word. You have come to need milk, not solid food. **For everyone who continues to feed on milk is obviously inexperienced and unskilled in the doctrine of righteousness (of conformity to the divine will in purpose, thought, and action), for he is a mere infant [not able to talk yet]!**
>
> ~ Hebrews 5:12–13, AMP, **emphasis added**

So, how can you tell if someone is at this stage? They are like physical children:

They can be talkative,

They can be inquisitive,

They can lack poise,

They can be easily exasperated,

They can lack accuracy in communication,

They can be passionate, but lack elegance in getting their points across,

They can have the wisdom to communicate what things are, but lack the ability to communicate how things really work,

They can lack the restraint to act in a more measured way.

Have you ever heard a child rattle on, impassioned about something they are trying to express, but using words that are unintelligible to anyone except their immediate family? It's similar with spiritual children.

I remember my daughter telling me one day that she had the best "sense of human" of anyone in her third grade class. Of course, I knew she really meant "sense of humor" and tried to gently correct her. She was so passionate about it, however, she actually corrected me: "No, Dad, human!"

Had she said the same thing to someone outside our family, however, they may not have understood. They may have asked her to explain and maybe even insisted upon giving her the more correct words and meanings.

In the same way, spiritual children often say things that seem appropriate at the time and in the context of their experience. However, their language can lack meaning or relevance in everyday life and be largely unintelligible by people outside their immediate spiritual family.

For the most part, it's cute and not worth correcting at this stage, but if it continues into later stages, it can become a problem.

Using certain terms and labels that allude to deeper spiritual truths might make someone sound mature or spiritual among other people, but being able to communicate spiritual truth plainly and articulately with wisdom and meaning to others without the labels is a sign of much greater maturity.

You will also notice that children at this stage are emerging from whining to asking as the best method to obtain their heart's desires.

I can't help but think how many times I have to remind our two-and-a-half-year-old, for example, that he simply needs to ask and not cry when he needs something!

Spiritual children at this stage can seem similarly demanding. Repetition and modeling mature behavior is essential. This is a formidable time for both physical and spiritual children as they learn the most excellent ways to interact with the world around them. The training they get is crucial for how well and how quickly they make the transition to more mature phases. Like the famous proverb suggests:

> Train a **child** in the way he should go, and when he is old he will not turn from it.
>
> ~ Proverbs 22:6, **emphasis added**

Proper training and modeling at this stage is a vital component that determines how easily or quickly things progress later.

Progress needs to be celebrated, but responsibility needs to be given in measured amounts as children at this age demonstrate the ability to handle more of it.

Being too critical or harsh at this stage makes room for shame to dominate their development, which can devastate their will to continue and inevitably stunt growth. It's critical spiritual children get encouragement, not criticism. The Bible says it this way:

> Therefore, there is now **no condemnation ‹adverse sentence› for those who are in Christ Jesus.**
>
> ~ Romans 8:1, **emphasis added**

God will convict people when they miss it. It's certainly appropriate for people to correct children at this stage; however, God never condemns people. We should never burden physical or spiritual children with condemnation for missing the highest good. Just lovingly correct.

How can you tell the difference between conviction and condemnation? One is heavy and one is light. For example, condemnation says, "You failed and you're a failure," leaving a person with a heavy yoke around their neck. Conviction says, "Yes, you failed, and here is the way to be more excellent," leaving them feeling light again. At any stage of development, God's burden is always light:

> For my yoke is easy to bear, and the burden I give you is light.
>
> ~ Matthew 11:30, NLT

It's also important to know that physical and spiritual children don't always play well with others. They can be selfish and need to be reminded constantly to prefer others. They are learning the world doesn't revolve around them and that there are others to be considered with every action. Spiritual children have to be constantly reminded and shown how to allow love to rule even when they are hurt and don't agree with love's rules.

The good news is that under normal conditions, children at this stage are resilient; they learn new things at a rapid pace and seem to grow up quickly under healthy and consistent instruction.

Remember, however, even so, they will ask endless questions and are in constant pursuit to know the *why* of everything.

Physical and spiritual children are capable of grasping ideas and even some fairly complex thoughts. They have a tendency to be impulsive, have extremely short attention spans, and become easily distracted and enamored with simple things that have little or no real long-term value.

This can be a time of great wonderment as children explore the world around them. It can also be difficult and even dangerous, as both physical and spiritual children are easily fooled by counterfeits and relatively simple deceptive practices.

Think about how easy it is for a three- to five-year-old to fall for the "make the object disappear behind my back" trick. Convincing a seven- to ten-year-old of the same things is far more difficult.

**RECONSIDER**
But whoever causes one of these little ones who believe in and [a] acknowledge and cleave to Me to stumble and sin [that is, who entices him or hinders him in right conduct or thought], it would be better ([b]more expedient and profitable or advantageous) for him to have a great millstone fastened around his neck and to be sunk in the depth of the sea.

~ Matt. 18:6, AMP

Likewise, spiritual children can become easily discouraged when they discover they have been fooled or deceived. Jesus said causing a child to miss it would have serious consequences. (Matt. 18:6).

The problem is not that there are counterfeits. Every mature person knows there will always be things that aren't as they appear. The problem is that most people never mature to tell the difference. Many just quit and lose their resolve to continue growing.

But it's in this exact context that Paul says we need to mature and grow up in these things:

> So then, we may no longer be children, tossed [like ships] to and fro between chance gusts of teaching and wavering with every changing wind of doctrine, [the prey of] the cunning and cleverness of unscrupulous men, [gamblers engaged] in every shifting form of trickery in inventing errors to mislead.
>
> ~ Ephesians 4:14, AMP

If children are protected and have room to experiment and fail in a safe place, they will begin to reason well. Early on in life, they will develop a keen sense of discernment.

As they increase in discernment and learn to interact well with others, they can be trusted to handle more complex truths.

This is precisely why Jesus spoke to the majority of people in parables, but to the disciples, who were more experienced and mature followers, He spoke openly:

> Then the disciples came to Him and said, Why do You speak to them in parables? And He replied to them, To you it has been given to know the secrets and mysteries of the kingdom of heaven, but to them it has not been given. For whoever has [spiritual knowledge], to him will more be given and he will be furnished richly so that he will have abundance; but from him who has not, even what he has will be taken away.
>
> ~ Matthew 13:10–12, AMP

Children at this stage don't always draw the right conclusions, so you must pay close attention to how they handle and act on what they learn. While children can be easily overwhelmed and unstable at times, God rewards and treasures childlike hunger and enthusiasm; it's a precious thing that He never judges or condemns – nor should people who discern another person to be at this stage of development.

The key to training people at this stage of development is being steady, gracious, and always understanding that despite their enthusiasm and occasional flashes of brilliance, they are still at a childish stage of dependence.

Rebellion requires discipline, but ignorance is just a sign that more training is required. Patiently training children and pointing them to love's ideal as the end goal while refraining from being critical of their progress is essential. As they demonstrate the ability to respond to, choose, and contend wisely for love's ideal in the way they talk, think, and reason, they're ready for the next phase – what's called the adolescent or young adult stage!

## ADOLESCENT, YOUNG ADULT, AND ADULT STAGES

The New Testament Bible uses the Greek word *teknon* (pronounced tek'-non) to identify people at this stage of development.

### Teknon
*noun*
   a.  Offspring, children  child
   b.  pupils or disciples are called children of their teachers because the latter, by their instruction, nourishes the minds of their pupils and molds their characters.
   3.  citizens and inhabitants

In the Western world, the post-childhood phase of human development is frequently called the teenage, adolescent, or young adult years and is generally accepted as occurring between eleven and twenty years of age.

Where early childhood is often called the "age of dependence," developmental psychologists most often refer to the stage following childhood as the "age of independence," and for good reason. It can be a glorious, yet difficult, time marked by significant physical, mental, emotional, and attitudinal changes. Despite the challenges that can be common, it's a necessary and critical phase of growth where both physical and spiritual adolescents begin to develop their own identities and require greater levels of personal freedom and independence.

The way the world thinks and what the Bible says in terms of what constitutes a physical and spiritual infant or child are similar. However, in the next stages of development, there are some very clear differences.

One is the way modern human developmental models and the Bible use the terms *adolescent* or *adolescence*. Modern models think of adolescence as the transitional stage of physical and human development between childhood and legal adulthood.

Adolescence is considered synonymous with and referred to as *the teenage years* or sometimes *young adulthood.* In contrast, the Bible assigns adolescence to the childhood years, not the teenage years.

To see what I mean, consider the following verse:

> *Rejoice, O young man, in your* **adolescence ‹meaning child-hood›,** *and let your heart cheer you in the days of your [full-grown]* **youth ‹young adulthood›**. *And walk in the ways of your heart and in the sight of your eyes, but know that for all these things God will bring you into judgment.*
> *~ Ecclesiastes 11:9,* AMP, ***emphasis added***

The age range assigned to adolescence may seem trivial, but because it changes what others can and should expect from a person in terms of spiritual and behavioral maturity, the implications are significant.

The word *adolescence* is derived from the Latin word *adolescere*, meaning literally "to grow up." Assigning the term *adolescence* to the teen years instead of the childhood years delays the "growing up" phase by many years and significantly lowers the maturity standards that society considers acceptable.

By thinking of adolescence and young adulthood as synonymous, modern society essentially permits, condones, and accepts behavior that by biblical standards would be considered childish and unacceptable at the same age.

In Jesus' family and culture, boys of twelve years of age and girls of thirteen years of age were considered mature adults. For both boys and girls, the term *young adult* was the literal standard applied to them at this point. Still today, under Jewish law, when a child reaches twelve to thirteen years of age, they are considered responsible for themselves and have certain obligations and rights as adult citizens.

That's why, in addition to the Greek word *teknon*, the New Testament also uses the Greek word *neaniskos* (pronounced neh-an-is'kos) to identify people at this stage of development who are exhibiting more mature behavior.

**Neaniskos**
*noun*
1. a young man, youth
   a. used of a young attendant or servant
2. able (to bear the family name)

*Bar mitzvah* and *bat mitzvah* are used to refer to an event or celebration where Jewish people publicly acknowledge their children's coming of age and transition to adulthood.

Though they are still growing physically and intellectually, boys and girls at this age are expected to be grown up and spiritually mature. By Jewish law, they are considered:

To be capable of observing the laws of God,

To be capable of keeping the laws of God,

To be morally responsible for their own actions,

To be able to read the Bible publicly as an adult,

To be able to provide commentary on the Bible publicly as an adult,

To be able to participate in a minyan (as discussed in the "Church" chapter),

To be able to undertake responsibilities in a minyan,

To be able to purchase property,

To be able to sustain a livelihood,

To be able to become legally married,

To be able to enlist in the military,

To be able to perform military functions.[32]

As hard as it is for many people to expect this kind of maturity from what we consider an adolescent or teenager today, it is the biblical standard. You might say this is where experience should meet wisdom. It's the stage where someone should be transitioning from a stage of dependence to one of independence.

While people at this stage may still show some signs of immaturity, like ...

Being inattentive,

Being impatient,

Being fidgety,

Being pleasure-focused,

Being uncertain at times

... they should also be in a time of peak mental and physical strength and capable of greatness with minimal direction.

> In the last days, God says, I will pour out my Spirit on all people. Your sons ‹**huois**› and daughters ‹**thugater**› will prophesy, your young ‹**neaniskos**› men will see visions, your old men will dream dreams.
>
> ~ Acts 2:17

Though there is no verse that gives her exact age, Jesus' own mother, Mary, whom the Bible says was a virgin (meaning a young woman of marriageable age[33]), had amazing spiritual dreams and visions. She was not only entrusted with greatness and mightily used of God, but she did it with immense poise under unspeakable pressure. Mary was not only conceptually mature enough to "bear God's family name," she literally did. It is believed by many scholars that Mary would have been between thirteen and fourteen years of age at the time of her miraculous conception (Luke 1:27).

Being entrusted to raise the very Son of God would seem to require a level of spiritual maturity beyond what people expect from someone in their early teens today. Because of what we consider adolescence today, people aren't required or even expected to demonstrate this kind of maturity until past college age, which, in many cases, means their mid- to late twenties.

But what if we expected more? What if children are really capable of reaching young adult levels of maturity at thirteen instead of twenty or twenty-five? What if we quit thinking less of them and began training children earlier to conduct themselves in this way? Can you imagine the impact on families and society as a whole?

This is exactly what Paul was saying to Timothy (a youth) in the following verse:

> Let no one **despise or think less** of you because of your **youth,** but **be an example (pattern) for the believers in speech, in conduct, in love, in faith ‹confidence›, and in purity.**
>
> ~ *1 Timothy 4:12,* AMP, **emphasis added**

We should think more of young adults and fully respect their ability to be mature examples of God-like conduct, love (yes, the *agape* kind), faith, and purity for believers of any age.

Obviously, despite their age and potential for greatness, not everyone in what the world currently calls adolescence or the Bible calls the young-adult phase of physical development is a spiritually mature example of what's possible at this level. So, how do you know the level of spiritual maturity of a so-called Christian in the adolescent or young adult stage of their development?

Like infancy and childhood, the parallels to physical and spiritual behavior or maturity in young adulthood are similar.

What kind of behavior do people generally associate with someone in the teenage or young adult years?

How about youthful passion or zeal? In and of themselves, these are not a sign of immaturity. God wants us to be passionate (Matt. 11:17; Rev. 3:15–16) unless the passions are continually misplaced, focused on inferior pleasures, extreme to the point they are overbearing and show little regard or honor for others.

What about the impatience and attention deficits so often associated with adolescence today? This is a common sign of spiritual immaturity, too: someone's inability to keep their body, will, and emotions under submission or control or who is ruled only by their flesh (a word the Bible uses to describe a lower or immature spiritual nature).

Look at the example the Bible gives of this very thing, when a young adult who fell asleep during one of Paul's teachings literally fell to his death from a third-story window:

> And there was a young man ‹**youth or adolescent**› named Eutychus sitting in the window. He was borne down with deep sleep as Paul kept on talking still longer, and [finally] completely overcome by sleep, he fell down from the third story and was picked up dead.
>
> ~ Acts 20:9, AMP

This would be a tragic story had Paul not rushed to the boy, embraced him, and then raised him from the dead, as recorded in the very next verse.

Jesus had a similar instance with His own disciples who were still not spiritually mature enough to stay awake and recognize the importance of the hour, even after Jesus pleaded with them three times to stay awake:

> **All of you must keep awake (give strict attention, be cautious and active) and watch and pray, that you may not come into temptation. The spirit indeed is willing, but the flesh is weak.** Again a second time He went away and

*prayed, My Father, if this cannot pass by unless I drink it, Your will be done. **And again He came and found them sleeping,** for their eyes were weighed down with sleep. So, leaving them again, He went away and prayed for the third time, using the same words. **Then He returned to the disciples and said to them, Are you still sleeping and taking your rest?***

~ Matthew 26:41–45, AMP, **emphasis added**

Can you relate to Jesus' challenge? Have you ever known a teenager who wanted to sleep for hours on end? Or how about one who needed to be reminded again and again to stay focused, to pay attention, to stay alert, or to be cautious at a critical time?

How about an adolescent's almost incessant desire for entertainment or endless hours of social time to just chill with friends with no real purpose or agenda? Spiritual adolescents are similar and fill massive amounts of time with so-called Christian activities or hanging with Christian friends, doing things more for their entertainment value than for equipping value.

I am not advocating a prudish or rigid absence of fun activities, just a mature balance of them. It's appropriate for mature adults to enjoy equal amounts of work, recreation and entertainment.

But at the adolescent stage, it is important to learn to say no to play when it's time to work with intense focus.

Knowing the length, time, and season for things requires maturity (Eccl. 3:1). Mature people are ready to do both with equal passion and commitment, both in and out of season (2 Tim. 4:2).

Yes's and no's are not as firm in adolescence as they are when matured. As the following verse suggests, such is yet another sign of spiritual immaturity:

*Simply let your 'Yes' be 'Yes,' and your 'No,' 'No'; anything beyond this comes from the evil one.*

~ Matthew 5:37

Temperance is also a key spiritual fruit at this stage. The ability to show restraint, exercise self-moderation, and demonstrate self-control is one of the greatest indicators that someone is maturing both physically and spiritually.

> In a similar way, urge the younger men to be self-restrained and to behave prudently [taking life seriously].
>
> ~ Titus 2:6, AMP

Conversely, an ongoing lack of temperance is one of the most prominent indicators that someone is still in physical and spiritual childhood or adolescence. It's only small children and immature adolescents who consistently throw temper tantrums to get what they want or manipulate others to do their will.

God places such a high value on temperance that it's listed as one of the nine primary fruits of the Spirit of God Himself:

> But the fruit of the Spirit is love, joy, peace, patience, kindness, goodness, faithfulness, gentleness and self-control ‹temperance›.
>
> ~ Galatians 5:22–23

Despite a person's age, status in life, degrees of knowledge, or Christian titles, unless they can consistently exercise and demonstrate these fruits of the Spirit, they are not spiritually mature.

Unfortunately, like every phase of maturity we have discussed so far, these fruits are not the automatic result of simply being a born-again Christian, growing up in a Christian home, having Christian friends, or attending Christian events. It takes commitment and discipline to become mature in Christ.

> And in [exercising] **knowledge [develop] self-control ‹temperance›, and in [exercising] self-control [again temperance] [develop] steadfastness (patience, endurance), and in [exercising] steadfastness [develop] godliness (piety),** and in [exercising] godliness [develop] brotherly affection, and in [exercising] brotherly affection [develop] Christian love ‹**the agape kind discussed in the first chapter**›. For as these qualities are yours and increasingly abound in you,

*they will keep [you] from being idle or unfruitful unto the [full personal] knowledge of our Lord Jesus Christ (the Messiah, the Anointed One).* **For whoever lacks these qualities is blind, [spiritually] shortsighted, seeing only what is near to him, and has become oblivious [to the fact] that he was cleansed from his old sins ‹the typical qualification for being labeled a Christian today›.**

*~ 2 Peter 1:6–9,* AMP, ***emphasis added***

I like how this verse describes each fruit as being developed or added over time, contingent on the ability to exercise the previous: temperance precedes patience, which precedes steadfastness, which precedes godliness expressed in the form of brotherly affection, which ultimately precedes abounding in love's ideal.

## MATURE, FULLY MATURE, AND PERFECTED

Concerning post-adolescence, or what the Bible calls young adulthood, the Bible makes very little distinction about what is possible or can be expected from people regarding maturity in the things of God.

Not only can a person mature, but they can become fully mature and even perfected with God's help.

The New Testament uses the Greek word *huios* (pronounced hwee-os) to identify people at this stage of development and who exhibit more mature behavior.

**Huois**
*noun*
1. as child (son)
   a. a fully mature one
2. a descendant of one's own posterity
   a. dearly loved
   b. beloved

*And a voice from heaven said, "This is my dearly loved Son ‹**huios**›, who brings me great joy."*
~ *Matthew 3:17,* NLT

This should be the goal of every follower of Christ, regardless of age: to finally mature into what God says is a fully mature son or daughter. People should not just be content with being fully mature, but be constantly developing until they attain the same level of faith and understanding that Jesus Himself perfected:

*[That it might develop] until* ***we all attain oneness in the faith and in the comprehension of the [full and accurate] knowledge of the Son of God, that [we might arrive] at really mature manhood ‹teleios – perfect›*** *(the completeness of personality which is nothing less than the standard height of Christ's own perfection), the measure of the stature of the fullness of the Christ and the completeness found in Him.*
~ *Ephesians 4:13,* AMP, ***emphasis added***

Jesus is the standard we *all* are called to emulate – not just those in ministry or with special gifts. This is the hope of everyone's calling who has ever been born again (Eph. 1:18–23).

Everyone of a mature age should be ever-conforming to the exact image of Jesus. He is not only the ultimate model of perfection and of someone who is fully mature and perfected, but ...

He is the goal,

He is complete,

He is lacking nothing,

He is fully mature,

He is a finished work,

He is perfection,

He is our example.

He is what every man or woman should aspire to think like, behave like, and produce like. He is what the Greek New Testament calls *teleios*.

**Teleios**
*noun*
1. brought to its end, finished
2. wanting nothing necessary to complete
3. perfect
4. that which is perfect
   a. consummate human integrity and virtue
   b. full grown, adult, of full age, mature

As hard as it is for many people to believe that perfection is possible, everyone who is spiritually born again, regardless of age, gender, race, or social status, has the same seed of perfection and maturity deposited in them from the start (2 Cor. 5:17) – it's in the form of the actual Spirit of God Himself.

Growing up and becoming fully mature in God is simply the process of willfully choosing to conform the way you think, talk, and act to that image (Col. 1:27–29).

Consider the impact Jesus had on the world as a single individual who was willing to be perfected and become fully mature in God.

Can you imagine the impact if only a small portion of two billion people in the world who call themselves "born-again Christians" grew up in the things of God and became as spiritually mature and capable as Jesus?

They would be unstoppable!

The very same spirit that was present in Jesus is present in everyone who is born again (Rom. 8:11). The world simply needs everyone who is born again to grow up, to mature into full-grown sons and daughters of God who, just like Jesus, can do everything He did and equally as well.

One of the most dramatic passages in the entire New Testament says that all creation is waiting with what it calls "birth pains" for this very thing – for the fully mature sons and daughters of God to be manifested and to liberate it from the futility of not living under heaven's rule and love's ideal. (Rom. 8:1–38).

So, how do you go from being a young adult to a more fully mature one? Just like Jesus did. Every adolescent and young adult becomes fully mature and perfected by learning to be led by God to bring their own will and desires into agreement with love's ideal.

It was exactly the same for Jesus:

> *Although He was a Son, He learned [active, special] obedience through what He suffered* ‹**experienced, sensations, passion, felt**› *and, [**His completed experience**] making Him perfectly [equipped], He became the Author and Source of eternal salvation to all those who give heed and obey Him.*
> ~ Hebrews 5:8–9, AMP, **emphasis added**

The word *suffered* here is not talking about physical suffering, like going to the cross – Jesus already did that, so we don't have to. The word means "to experience a sensation or impression, to feel, to have passion, to suffer (sometimes painfully, but not always)." In the King James Version of the New Testament, the same Greek word translated *suffered* is sometimes translated *passion* or *felt*.

In the same way Jesus was made perfectly mature, a spiritually mature person learns from experience how to bring their own will into agreement with God's, regardless of the passions, sensations, or resistance they feel or experience to the contrary.

So, how do you know if someone is fully mature in this way? Like the other stages of development, there are some common behaviors that can be observed to give you a clue:

They are temperate in all things,

They are passionate, but not demanding,

They are resolved, but not arrogant,

They are focused, but not insensitive,

They consider God their source of all things, not people,

**RECONSIDER**
For all creation is waiting eagerly for that future day when God will reveal who his children ‹*huois*› really are.

~ Rom. 8:19, NLT

299

They are not ignorant as children and, therefore, not dependent on others,

They are focused on serving, not being served,

They are confident to act alone, but are still considerate of others,

They are experienced and wise, yet not arrogant,

They are skilled at making distinctions instead of judgments,

They are aware that if anyone thinks they're something, they're nothing (Gal. 6:3),

They are comfortable with being valued as the very image of God on earth (Col. 3:10),

They are comfortable being the righteousness of God to others (2 Cor. 5:21),

They are convinced that in and of themselves they know nothing (1 Cor. 8:2),

They are equally aware they're anointed by God to have all knowledge (1 John 2:20),

They are aware of themselves, that they've earned and have nothing (1 Cor. 4:7),

They are joyously content that God gives them richly all things to enjoy (1 Tim. 6:17),

They are convinced that apart from God they can do nothing (John 15:5),

They are convinced that with God nothing is impossible (Luke 1:37), and

They are convinced that in God they have the ability to do all things well (Phil. 4:13),

They love well.


Fully mature people are more practiced in all these things and have their senses trained to distinguish what is good and bad for them. Fully mature spiritual people are less prone to pursue things that promise little value or benefit.

> But solid food is for full-grown men ‹**teleios**› for those whose **senses and mental faculties are trained by practice** to discriminate and distinguish between what is morally good and noble and what is evil ‹**something of little value or benefit**› and contrary either to divine or human law.
> ~ Hebrews 5:14, AMP, **emphasis added**

For this reason, as the following verse suggests, mature adults will tend to come across more temperate, sensible, self-controlled, and sound in their faith and love:

> Urge the older men to be temperate, venerable (serious), sensible, self-controlled, and sound in the faith, in the love, and in the steadfastness and patience [of Christ].
> ~ Titus 2:2, AMP

To grow up and become a fully mature adult, they must master the ability to express truth in all things enfolded in love:

> Rather, let our lives lovingly express **truth [in all things, speaking truly, dealing truly, living truly]. Enfolded in love, let us grow up in every way and in all things into Him Who is the Head,** [even] Christ (the Messiah, the Anointed One).
> ~ Ephesians 4:15, AMP, **emphasis added**

You will also notice that spiritually mature adults are more Spirit-led in their motivations to do things. This is one of the biggest and most important attributes of a spiritually mature person.

> For all who are **led by the Spirit of God are sons of God.**
> ~ Romans 8:14, AMP, **emphasis added**

Being led by the Spirit of God can take several forms, all of which were common ways that Jesus and others were led: an audible voice, a physical vision, the written Word of God, a strong sense in a person's own spirit, or the counsel or giftings of others.

Being led by the Spirit of God means that a person is not led by money, opportunity, reason or intellect, feelings, emotions, or personal desire. They are not led by pressure from others, fear of loss, guilt, or any other thing that can often factor into the reasons why people do certain things.

Jesus didn't do His own will; He only did what He was directed by the Spirit of God to do (John 5:19, 30). Jesus' only desire was to do the Father's will, and so it must be with anyone who desires to become fully mature. Just like physical children who grow up by learning how to follow their own mother and father's example and instruction, spiritual children must do the same.

A physical parent knows their child has reached maturity when they can demonstrate the ability to do something as well as if the parent had done it. In the same way, God measures our maturity by our ability to do His will and administer His kingdom in the same manner He would do it Himself or, in the case of Jesus, did Himself.

It's not overcomplicated, but is a much overlooked attribute of spiritual maturity. It's not something learned overnight, but it is something that virtually every spiritual gift given to man by God was designed to achieve.

According to the following verse, it's really the whole purpose behind what has been traditionally called the fivefold ministry gifts – to help God's children become equally confident in the knowledge of God and to be fully mature like Jesus:

> It was He ‹**God**› who gave some to be apostles, some to be prophets, some to be evangelists, and some to be pastors and teachers, **to prepare God's people for works of service,** so that the body of Christ may be built up **until we all reach unity in the faith ‹assurance or confidence› in the knowledge of the Son of God and become mature, attaining to the whole measure of the fullness of Christ.**
> ~ Ephesians 4:11–13, **emphasis added**

We are going to look more at this verse, and especially the specific gifts, in a whole new way later. For now, however, I only want you to see that the purpose of these gifts (apostles, prophets, etc.) was to prepare people and build them up in their own maturity until they were all able to confidently do the work of administering the kingdom themselves, just like Jesus would.

These gifts were not designed to only do the work of administering the kingdom on behalf of others, but rather to equip people to do the work of administering the kingdom for themselves.

Mature people aren't looking for people to act on their behalf or looking to act on behalf of others. Mature people are looking to perfect the ability to act and administer the kingdom for themselves and demonstrate to others how to do the same.

It reminds me of an invaluable piece of parenting advice I once received from a very accomplished matriarchal mother after announcing to her the birth of our first child. She was a woman we respected on many levels. I asked what advice she might give to two young parents desiring to realize the same kind of success she had achieved as a parent of children who were now thriving both physically and spiritually. She said, "Kevin, the best advice I can give you is this: from the earliest ages, you must resolve it's not your job as a parent to meet your children's needs but to constantly and lovingly equip them to meet their own." The most spiritually mature people are less interested in impressing you with their amazing spiritual gifts and abilities and more interested in equipping you to function in yours. As spiritually mature people train and equip others by example, their actions and results will always speak louder than their words.

Maybe that's why it was in the book of "Acts" that the disciples were first called Christians. It was their "acts" that provoked the title, not just their words!

Think about the way you provide a signature or sign – something to indicate your approval, acknowledge your involvement, enter you into an agreement, or obligate yourself to perform in some manner. God does the same thing when He acknowledges His involvement in things with an accompanying "sign."

In that sense, a sign, which the Bible defines as a miracle, a token, or an indication, can be thought of as God's signature, indicating and validating His involvement in a matter or with a person:

*Then the disciples went out and preached everywhere, and the Lord worked with them and **confirmed his word by the signs** that accompanied it.*

*~ Mark 16:20, **emphasis added***

Certainly, the disciples were reproached and publicly ridiculed. This was evident by the new Christian label they had been assigned by others. Yet, God confirmed and approved their audacious and seemingly surreal claims with equally stunning and miraculous signs that followed them everywhere they went.

Regardless of what people thought of the disciples, you couldn't ignore the signs and wonders that followed them.

The way God confirmed and signed off on their words and actions gave the disciples a boldness that didn't exist just days before. It was the signs and wonders that confirmed the disciples were the real deal, and it should be no less with anyone who desires to be a so-called Christian today.

It's only someone's actions, the fruit of their life over time, and the miraculous signs that make others wonder if someone or something is really of God – not the Christian label.

# CHRISTIAN_RELATE

So, how do you relate to the term *Christian* now?

Will it be something you call yourself or, like the disciples, will it be just how others describe you?

How closely do the reasons why you or others use the term compare to the reasons the disciples were called Christians?

To find out, try a four-part exercise.

The first two parts involve using the following development grid. Consider each behavior (fruits of the spirit) listed down the left side of the grid. Indicate your level of maturity exhibiting that specific fruit by circling a number in one of the maturity columns to the right. For example, if you feel you love well 30% of the time, circle 3% in the infant column. If you feel you are joyful 80% of the time, circle 8% in the adult column.

When you've completed this for each of the fruits of the spirit, write the number you circled in each column in the selection box at the end of each row. Upon completion, sum the numbers in the selection column to get a sense of your overall development level. An example of a finished grid would look like something like this.

## SAMPLE COMPLETED DEVELOPMENT GRID

| | Newborn | Infant | Child | Young Adult | Adult | Fully Mature | Selection |
|---|---|---|---|---|---|---|---|
| | 20% | 30% | 50% | 70% | 80% | 100% | |
| Love | 2% | 3% | (5%) | 7% | 8% | 10% | 5% |
| Joy | 2% | 3% | 5% | (7%) | 8% | 10% | 7% |
| Peace | 2% | 3% | 5% | (7%) | 8% | 10% | 7% |
| Patience | 2% | 3% | (5%) | 7% | 8% | 10% | 5% |
| Kindness | 2% | 3% | 5% | 7% | (8%) | 10% | 8% |
| Goodness | 2% | 3% | 5% | (7%) | 8% | 10% | 7% |
| Faithfulness | 2% | 3% | (5%) | 7% | 8% | 10% | 5% |
| Gentleness | 2% | 3% | (5%) | 7% | 8% | 10% | 5% |
| Temperence | 2% | 3% | 5% | (7%) | 8% | 10% | 7% |
| Power | 2% | 3% | 5% | 7% | (8%) | 10% | 8% |

Development Level ( 64% )

So now, let's do the exercise, shall we? First, use the grid to evaluate yourself. Second, give the same grid to someone close to you and ask them to do the same for you (i.e., a family member, spouse, significant other, or friend).

## PART ONE

Complete the following grid by asking yourself, where do I think I am?

| | Newborn | Infant | Child | Young Adult | Adult | Fully Mature | Selection |
|---|---|---|---|---|---|---|---|
| | 20% | 30% | 50% | 70% | 80% | 100% | |
| Love | 2% | 3% | 5% | 7% | 8% | 10% | |
| Joy | 2% | 3% | 5% | 7% | 8% | 10% | |
| Peace | 2% | 3% | 5% | 7% | 8% | 10% | |
| Patience | 2% | 3% | 5% | 7% | 8% | 10% | |
| Kindness | 2% | 3% | 5% | 7% | 8% | 10% | |
| Goodness | 2% | 3% | 5% | 7% | 8% | 10% | |
| Faithfulness | 2% | 3% | 5% | 7% | 8% | 10% | |
| Gentleness | 2% | 3% | 5% | 7% | 8% | 10% | |
| Temperence | 2% | 3% | 5% | 7% | 8% | 10% | |
| Power | 2% | 3% | 5% | 7% | 8% | 10% | |

Development Level ( )

# PART TWO

Complete the following grid by asking _____, where do you think I am?

| | Newborn | Infant | Child | Young Adult | Adult | Fully Mature | Selection |
|---|---|---|---|---|---|---|---|
| | 20% | 30% | 50% | 70% | 80% | 100% | |
| Love | 2% | 3% | 5% | 7% | 8% | 10% | |
| Joy | 2% | 3% | 5% | 7% | 8% | 10% | |
| Peace | 2% | 3% | 5% | 7% | 8% | 10% | |
| Patience | 2% | 3% | 5% | 7% | 8% | 10% | |
| Kindness | 2% | 3% | 5% | 7% | 8% | 10% | |
| Goodness | 2% | 3% | 5% | 7% | 8% | 10% | |
| Faithfulness | 2% | 3% | 5% | 7% | 8% | 10% | |
| Gentleness | 2% | 3% | 5% | 7% | 8% | 10% | |
| Temperence | 2% | 3% | 5% | 7% | 8% | 10% | |
| Power | 2% | 3% | 5% | 7% | 8% | 10% | |

Development Level ( )

Compare the results. How consistent are they? Use these responses to begin focusing on areas in which you need to mature. You can also use the following generic grid to consider any ten behaviors (beyond just the fruits of the spirit) as listed earlier in this chapter. Remember, don't be ashamed – everyone starts somewhere and grows up from there!

# PART THREE

For the third part of our exercise, consider sending a short e-mail to ten or twenty people you interact with from different areas of your life and realms of influence – family, friends, work or church associates. It should read something like:

> Hello (insert person's name), I am doing a personal research project to help me become more excellent. Would you consider taking sixty seconds to thoughtfully answer the following two questions about me? A single word answer or short paragraph of 500 characters or less will do.

Whenever I think of (insert your name), I think of

_____.

I consider (insert your name) the go-to person for

_____.

You might also consider asking a third question:

I know (insert your name) is a Christian because

_____.

When you receive the responses, consider them in total and then ask yourself some questions:

What I am most known for?

How consistent are the responses I received with how I see myself?

How consistent are the responses across my various realms of influence – in other words, do the people at work think of me the same way people at church think of me, etc.?

How do my responses compare to what Jesus or one of His first followers might have received if the people who knew them were asked the same questions?

If you used question three, were the responses to this question related more to your affiliations or actions?

## PART FOUR

For the last and probably most difficult part of all, ask yourself:

If I sent the same questions to my adversaries, how would they respond? How would they label or describe me?

That last part of this initial exercise might sound intimidating, but remember, it was the disciples' adversaries who labeled them as Christians, not their friends and family!

I am not suggesting that knowing what others think should be an all-consuming desire or a definitive description of who you are or will become. To the contrary, many times it takes time for you to fully develop the courage to act on God's leading despite what others might think – especially your adversaries.

I am suggesting, however, that in terms of how well you are doing as a so-called Christian, what others can observe about you matters. Jesus Himself said that other people, or specifically "they," referring to people in the world, would know His followers by His followers' acts. Jesus never suggested people would know His followers by what His followers thought of or called themselves.

Jesus had a strong internal scoreboard by which He measured His own success. He was more concerned with what God the Father thought of Him and how well He was maturing into the Son He knew His Father desired Him to be. It should be the same for anyone who desires to be like Jesus.

To go beyond relating to the term *Christian* as an outward title or label based solely on what others can perceive or observe about our identity in God, let's do a second exercise. The following exercise will help you develop and maintain a more internal scoreboard to determine how well you are doing in your relationship with God and others.

Answer the following questions related to the descriptions we provided in the Reorient section.

> Where am I in my spiritual development?
>
> In what areas do I most need to mature?
>
> Would others agree with my assessment?

When compared to Jesus as our example of what fully developed maturity looks and acts like, where did you place yourself in your spiritual development?

Are you a born-again spiritual infant? Do you relate more to the adolescent or young-adult stage, or would you consider yourself a more mature one spiritually? And finally, would others agree with your assessment if you chose to share it with them?

The stage where you begin or the areas you most need to grow in is irrelevant, in terms of how quickly God can mature you. Remember, no shame! We all had to start somewhere – even Jesus.

Just identify the areas where you need to grow up to become more mature and ultimately more like Jesus in the way you think, talk, and act or in the mighty works you demonstrate – and go after it.

All that is ever required of us is to be willing to agree with the Holy Spirit, follow His leading, and resolve to do whatever it takes to conform to the image of Jesus He shows us. This is truly how a person becomes a follower of Jesus – which is a far more important distinction than being identified as a Christian.

Not everyone, who identifies themselves as a Christian, is a follower of Christ to this level – but, most everyone who follows the Holy Spirit in this way will almost always be identified as a Christian.

> So too the [Holy] Spirit comes to our aid and bears us up in our weakness; for we do not know what prayer to offer nor how to offer it worthily as we ought, but the Spirit Himself goes to meet our supplication and pleads in our behalf with unspeakable yearnings and groanings too deep for utterance. And He Who searches the hearts of men knows what is in the mind of the [Holy] Spirit [what His intent is], because the Spirit intercedes and pleads [before God] in behalf of the saints according to and in harmony with God's will [Ps. 139:1–2]. We are assured and know that [God being a partner in their labor] all things work together and are [fitting into a plan] for good to and for those who love God and are called according to [His] design and purpose. For those whom He foreknew [of whom He was aware and loved beforehand], He also destined from the beginning [foreordaining them] to be molded into the image of His Son [and share inwardly His likeness], that He might become the firstborn among many brethren.
>
> ~ Romans 8:26–29, AMP

**RESOURCE**
You can learn more about our family's process and our annual lists of skills we are honing at www.iamkevinweaver.com.

# CHRISTIAN__REACT

Top three things you are taking away from this chapter:

.......................................................................................................................................

.......................................................................................................................................

.......................................................................................................................................

.......................................................................................................................................

.......................................................................................................................................

.......................................................................................................................................

.......................................................................................................................................

What action can you take now on what you've learned?

.......................................................................................................................................

.......................................................................................................................................

.......................................................................................................................................

.......................................................................................................................................

.......................................................................................................................................

.......................................................................................................................................

.......................................................................................................................................

Our righteousness is in You

Our authority is in You

Our power is in You

Our hope is in You

– IN YOU –

*Lyrics by Kevin Weaver It's Feasible Publishing, LLC*

Download the complete lyrics and an .mp3 version of this
song in its entirety at www.thereorientbook.com.

# DISCIPLE

# What's your REACTION to the word?

⊕ Positive

⊖ Negative

◎ Neutral

# What does the word MEAN TO YOU?

_____

_____

_____

_____

_____

_____

_____

_____

_____

Now let's see what others say. ▶

The way people surveyed
reacted to the word DISCIPLE.

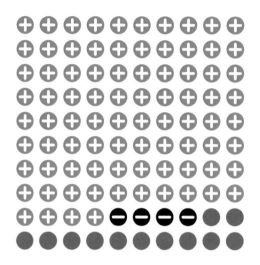

84.23%
Positive

03.58%
Negative

12.19%
Neutral

See a video of respondants in the Resource section for this chapter at www.reorientbook.com.

Common words people surveyed associated with the word DISCIPLE.

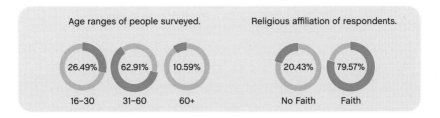

Age ranges of people surveyed.

26.49% 62.91% 10.59%

16–30 31–60 60+

Religious affiliation of respondents.

20.43% 79.57%

No Faith Faith

# DISCIPLE__REDISCOVER

## OLD TESTAMENT HEBREW WORDS FOR DISCIPLE

USED  *6 times*

WORDS  LIMMUWD */lim-mood/*

DEFINITION  *Instructed, learned, or taught*

## NEW TESTAMENT GREEK WORDS FOR DISCIPLE

USED  *More than 260 times*

WORDS  MATHETES */math-ay-tes/*

DEFINITION  *A learner, a pupil, or a follower*

# DISCIPLE_RECOUNT

# DISCIPLE

OLD TESTAMENT VERSES
USING THE HEBREW WORD

# 5

NEW TESTAMENT VERSES
USING THE GREEK WORD

# 252

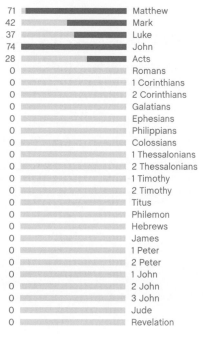

| Genesis | 0 |
| Exodus | 0 |
| Leviticus | 0 |
| Numbers | 0 |
| Deuteronomy | 0 |
| Joshua | 0 |
| Judges | 0 |
| Ruth | 0 |
| 1 Samuel | 0 |
| 2 Samuel | 0 |
| 1 Kings | 0 |
| 2 Kings | 0 |
| 1 Chronicles | 0 |
| 2 Chronicles | 0 |
| Ezra | 0 |
| Nehemiah | 0 |
| Esther | 0 |
| Job | 0 |
| Psalm | 0 |
| Proverbs | 0 |
| Ecclesiastes | 0 |
| Song of Songs | 0 |
| Isaiah | 3 |
| Jeremiah | 2 |
| Lamentations | 0 |
| Ezekiel | 0 |
| Daniel | 0 |
| Hosea | 0 |
| Joel | 0 |
| Amos | 0 |
| Obadiah | 0 |
| Jonah | 0 |
| Micah | 0 |
| Nahum | 0 |
| Habakkuk | 0 |
| Zephaniah | 0 |
| Haggai | 0 |
| Zechariah | 0 |
| Malachi | 0 |

| 71 | Matthew |
| 42 | Mark |
| 37 | Luke |
| 74 | John |
| 28 | Acts |
| 0 | Romans |
| 0 | 1 Corinthians |
| 0 | 2 Corinthians |
| 0 | Galatians |
| 0 | Ephesians |
| 0 | Philippians |
| 0 | Colossians |
| 0 | 1 Thessalonians |
| 0 | 2 Thessalonians |
| 0 | 1 Timothy |
| 0 | 2 Timothy |
| 0 | Titus |
| 0 | Philemon |
| 0 | Hebrews |
| 0 | James |
| 0 | 1 Peter |
| 0 | 2 Peter |
| 0 | 1 John |
| 0 | 2 John |
| 0 | 3 John |
| 0 | Jude |
| 0 | Revelation |

*Graph is based on the highest
verse use and shown visually as
a percentage of the highest value.

# DISCIPLE__REORIENT

For those involved in the discipleship or shepherding movement of the 1970s and early 1980s, the words *disciple* or *discipleship* can evoke painful emotions.[34] For everyone else, not much thought is given to the word *disciple* or what it actually means to be one.

However, understanding what it means to be a disciple and what it actually takes to become one is vitally important. It's essential understanding:

God's plan for mankind,

God's chosen method to transform all of creation,

God's description of the kind of people it takes to bring it about.

For me, reorienting to the word *disciple* was like pulling a small thread on the hem of a garment. While this word initially appeared small and insignificant, a continued pull on the thread toward its origin unraveled the very fabric of a tightly woven veil of tradition. Not knowing the real significance of this word had obscured my vision about my role in the kingdom of God and the real hope of my calling as a committed follower of Jesus.

**RECONSIDER**

Fun with *disciple* word usages:[35]

Word frequency usage from 1539–2007 in occurrences per 100,000 words per year

Phone Digits: (..3) 472-4753

Synonym: adherent

Rhymes: archetypal

Scrabble Score: 13

Reorienting to what it means to be a disciple changed me and it challenged my theology in many areas. Among other things, it profoundly altered any ideas about:

The real cost of mastery,

The real mind-set required to do what Jesus did,

The real way God intended an *ekklesia* to function,

The real role leadership plays in equipping people,

The real work of administering the kingdom of God on earth,

The real relationship God intended disciples to have with each other.

Here is how the dictionary defines the word *disciple:*

**Disciple**
*noun*
1. one of the twelve personal followers of Christ
2. one of the seventy followers sent forth by Christ
3. any other professed follower of Christ in His lifetime
4. any follower of Christ
5. a member of the Disciples of Christ denomination
6. a person who is a pupil or adherent of the doctrines of another; follower: *a disciple of Freud*

*verb*
1. (archaic) to convert into a disciple
2. (obsolete) to teach; train

This definition is consistent with how the majority of the modern world thinks of the term. Among people we surveyed, common definitions were:

A believer

A Christian

A follower

An observer

A servant

A student

Additionally, some listed a few of the names of Jesus' first twelve disciples:

| Matthew | Luke | James |
|---------|------|-------|
| Mark | Peter | John |

How do these responses compare to yours? And how consistent do you think the dictionary's definition of a disciple is with how Jesus and His followers used the term?

The implied connotation of the word is actually a far cry from the emphasis Jesus and His early followers placed on the word. This is especially evident when compared to the minimal emphasis they placed on the word *Christian.*

Unlike the term *Christian,* which is used approximately three times in the entire biblical text and never by Jesus or His followers, *disciple* is used more than 250 times in the King James Version and more than 280 times in the Amplified Version of the Bible. The term *disciple* was without question the preferred way Jesus and His followers chose to describe themselves.

But what did the term mean to them?

In the Old Testament, the Hebrew word *limmuwd* (pronounced lim-mood), translated *disciple,* was used just five times and meant "to be instructed; accustomed; to learn; to be taught or used" (Isa. 8:16; 50:4; 54:13; Jer. 2:24; 13:23). In the New Testament, the Greek word *mathetes* is used more than 250 times and translated to English as *disciple.* Here is what it means:

**Disciple *(mathetes)***
*noun*
1. a learner or a pupil

*verb*
1. to learn, be appraised
2. to increase one's knowledge, to be increased in knowledge
3. to hear, be informed
4. to learn by use and practice

5. to be in the habit of, accustomed to doing

At first glance, the meanings of the Hebrew or Greek words appear similar to the commonly accepted notions we have of the word *disciple* today; however, a closer look at the context and use of the word in the biblical text reveals a profound difference.

This is not with the translation of the word, which is accurate, but in the cultural difference and application of the word. Specifically, how a learner or pupil in a Greek or Western cultural model is defined and viewed is very different from how a learner is defined in the Hebrew or Eastern model.

This is a critical distinction because remember Jesus and His followers were from the Middle East, not the Middle West. Jesus and His disciples' schools of thought were based on Hebrew and Jewish traditions, not Greek and Roman traditions.

The differences between the two cultures and schools of thought are in many ways diametrically opposed to each other. In fact, the differences between them is considered by many experts to be responsible for much of the confusion between how biblical precepts (which were written from a Hebrew and Eastern perspective) get interpreted and lived out in modern Western life (which is largely influenced by Greek-Western thought).

Few concepts in the Bible highlight these differences more than in the meaning and application of the word *disciple.*

In the same way *assembly* as the English translation of the word *ekklesia* becomes confusing because it evokes the same imagery as church in the mind of a modern hearer, the English translation of *mathetes* as *disciple,* meaning "pupil, follower, or learner," is similarly confusing and problematic.

We need to do four things to reorient to the word *disciple* and begin relating to the word as Jesus and His first followers intended.

To reorient to the meaning of the word *disciple,* we must highlight a few of the major differences between Greek-Western and Hebrew-Eastern thought.

006 · DISCIPLE · REORIENT

To reorient to what it means to live as a disciple, we need to eliminate cultural bias and consider the term strictly from a Hebrew-Eastern viewpoint.

To reorient to what it takes to become a disciple, we must learn the mind-set of special-forces soldiers, Olympic athletes, and successful entrepreneurs.

To reorient to the real power of a disciple to rise up and change the world, we must reorient to the role in the context of an *ekklesia* and not in that of a traditional church leadership paradigm only.

## THE MAIN DIFFERENCES BETWEEN GREEK AND HEBREW THOUGHT AND THE REAL MEANING OF A DISCIPLE OF JESUS

In the book *Irrational Man: A Study in Existential Philosophy,* William Barrett suggests that the fundamental difference between the Western mind and the Hebrew mind is in the area of knowing versus doing. He says, in summary:


Hebrew is concerned with practice,

The Greek with knowledge.


Hebrew is concerned with right conduct,

The Greek with right thinking.


Hebrew is concerned with duty and strictness of conscience,

The Greek with spontaneous and luminous play of the intelligence.


Hebrew is concerned with moral virtues as the substance and meaning of life;

The Greek subordinates them to the intellectual virtues.

Hebrew extols practice,

The Greek, theory.

Hebrew extols the moral man;

The Greek extols the theoretical or intellectual man.

---

RECONSIDER

The key aspects of Greek-Western versus Hebrew-Eastern thought

| Greek-Western Thought | Hebrew-Eastern Thought |
|---|---|
| Knowledge-based | Practice-based |
| Right thinking | Right conduct |
| Linear logic* | Contextual logic |
| Categorical | Relational |
| Hierarchical lists | Functional positions |
| Individualistic* | Community-oriented |
| Competitive* | Cooperative |
| Man-centered* | God-tribe-family-centered |
| Rules by logic and science* | Rules by stewardship |
| Intellectual virtues* | Moral virtues |
| Linear time and events* | Cyclical time and events |
| Chronological history | Relational history |
| Achievement-oriented* | Blessing-oriented |
| Blind and mystical faith* | Knowledge-based faith |

*Examples added from a more extensive table of comparisons in an article by Brian Knowles titled "The Hebrew Mind vs. the Western Mind."[36]

These distinctions may explain why so many churches and individual Christians in the West today, whose practices have been knowingly or unknowingly shaped largely by Greek patterns of thought, focus on issues of doctrine and knowledge. Often their daily practices exclude actually living out what they believe.

Truly understanding the Hebrew and Eastern idea of discipleship requires overcoming Greek paradigms that emphasize...

Mastering knowledge,

Mastering concepts,

Mastering principles,

Mastering classroom or university-style methods of learning

... in favor of the Hebrew kind of learning that emphasizes the wisdom, experience, and personal mastery that results from actually doing something in practice.

When Jesus or His followers used the word *disciple,* they didn't think of a pupil, learner, or follower in a classroom or university-style setting gaining knowledge. They thought of the kind of learning an athlete, soldier, or aspiring craftsman working in direct apprenticeship with a single master teacher might obtain.

It's hard for some people to relate to Jesus this way. From a cultural viewpoint, Jesus was more Chinese in His discipleship methodologies than He was American. So to truly reorient to Jesus' methodologies, we need a more Eastern viewpoint.

## GETTING AN EASTERN VIEWPOINT ON WHAT IT MEANS TO BE A DISCIPLE

Imagine you were born early in the first century into a middle-class family and lived in a small fishing village in the Far East.

The only life your family has known for generations is that of fishing. You have none of the modern communication, education, or transportation options we have today.

Your whole family is skilled and accomplished at the craft of fishing. However, they know little or nothing about training you to succeed at other trades.

Though nobody in your family or circles of relationships has direct experience as a soldier, athlete, or farmer, you develop a burning desire to learn and obtain a level of mastery in one or all of these disciplines. To learn the skills and master the ability to succeed, you need someone willing to teach you.

You will need a master teacher.

Assuming you were able to find a master teacher, you would most likely choose that teacher based upon their own personal level of mastery in each discipline. Further, a competent master teacher would most likely choose to teach you based on your passion, willingness to seriously commit, and ability to learn to master the discipline.

The information transfer and the practice of mastering the new skill would be costly to both the master and the student and would need to be considered soberly.

To ensure a complete transfer of both understanding and experiential mastery, living life together for extended periods of time would almost certainly be required.

Your time as a direct understudy of the master teacher would be generally open-ended. The time learning would only be considered complete when you had fully demonstrated the ability to perform at least as well as your master teacher.

For a more modern pop-culture image, consider the relationships ...

Between Caine ("Grasshopper") and Master Po in the TV series *Kung Fu*,[37]

Between Daniel ("Danielson") and Mr. Miyagi in the movie *Karate Kid*,[38]

Between Obi Wan Kenobi and Luke Skywalker in the *Star Wars* films,[39]

Between Neo and Morpheus in the movie *The Matrix*.[40]

The relationships between these fictional characters resemble the Eastern kind of teacher-pupil, instructor-learner, leader-follower, or master-disciple model that Jesus and His followers had.

As common as university-style learning is today, granting certificates to individuals based on their "degrees of knowledge" versus their "personal areas of mastery" in practice is a relatively modern Greek approach.

This type of learning wasn't formalized until around AD 600 and popularized in Western Europe until around 1080. England's University of Oxford, for example, was founded in 1167 and represented a significant departure from the discipleship model of learning that was commonplace for thousands of years before.[41]

Interestingly, the word *university* is derived from a Latin phrase – *universitas magistrorum et scholarium* – roughly meaning "community of teachers and scholars."

This very definition hints at one of the primary differences between the Greek-Western university model of education, where a person learns from a community of teachers, versus Jesus' Hebrew-Eastern model of learning from a single master teacher.

These different approaches to learning affect many areas of so-called modern Christian life, but none more dramatically than how the success of successful learners or pupils (disciples) is measured.

In the Greek-Western university model and system of learning, for example, a student, pupil, or learner can succeed in obtaining a master's degree in business by learning the principles of running a business from a community of scholars while having never actually run a business. By contrast, in the Hebrew-Eastern model, students, pupils, or learners are only considered successful by their ability to follow a single master teacher's example and the degree to which they mastered running an actual business.

Or consider the difference between how a university student earns a master's degree in liberal arts versus how a person earns a master's degree in martial arts. Both types of learning take time and commitment, but the approach to demonstrating degrees of success is measured in very different ways. This is why in many modern practice-based educational disciplines, like the field of medicine, internships are necessary.

If a student wants to study medicine with the intent to give actual patient care, a practice-based internship with other accomplished physicians is required before they are licensed to do so. This is not a requirement to just teach medicine.

In summary, the Greek model of learning defines success based on a person's ability to master knowledge, but the Hebrew model defines success based on a person's knowledge to master ability.

Paul said it this way:

> *Jews demand miraculous signs and Greeks look for wisdom.*
> ~ *1 Corinthians 1:22*

Greek scholars desire a pupil to imitate their methods of study in order to perfect knowing what they know the way they know it. Jesus preferred His followers imitate His ways in order to perfect doing what He did the way He did it!

This is why I say that the way Jesus invited His individual disciples to follow Him was more like that of a Jedi Knight and a star pupil than a Greek scholar and his students. Jesus' method of teaching was more like Obi Wan Kenobi than Socrates.

And this is what God the Father in the Old Testament and Jesus the Son in the New

**REMEMBER**
It was in this context that Jewish people described Jesus' followers as those "belonging to the way," not those "believing in or knowing the way."

And I persecuted the followers of the Way,
~ Acts 22:4, NLT

But I admit that I follow the Way, which they call a cult.
~ Acts 24:14, NLT

At that point Felix, who was quite familiar with the Way...
~ Acts 24:22, NLT

Jesus answered, "I am the way and the truth and the life."
~ John 14:6

329

Testament had in mind when they called people to follow them as disciples. They wanted "doers," not just "knowers."

## REORIENTING TO WHAT THE BIBLE ACTUALLY SAYS ABOUT BECOMING A DISCIPLE WITH A NEW PERSPECTIVE

The only way to become spiritually mature children of God is to commit to being taught by God to become a disciple.

> *And all your [spiritual] children shall be disciples [taught by the Lord and obedient to His will], and great shall be the peace and undisturbed composure of your children.*
> *~ Isaiah 54:13,* AMP

Notice how this Old Testament verse says that "all your spiritual children shall be disciples," implying, as we discussed in the "Christian" chapter, that the two are independent of each other.

Spiritual children who are taught by God to be obedient to the will of God shall be disciples, not children who are knowledgeable of His will only. I also like how this verse says that peace and undisturbed composure are the fruit of a child who has been taught by God to be a disciple. It reminds me of the fruit of temperance we discussed in the "Christian" chapter as indicative of a more mature follower of Christ.

Now let's consider a disciple verse from the New Testament:

> *And He said to them, Come after Me [as disciples – letting Me be your Guide], follow Me, and I will make you fishers of men!*
> *~ Matthew 4:19,* AMP

Notice how Jesus proposes Himself as their guide to make them fishers of men, not just to teach them to think like or behave like fishers of men.

And one more example:

> *As Jesus passed on from there, He saw a man named Matthew sitting at the tax collector's office; and He said*

*to him, Be My disciple [side with My party and follow Me].*
*And he rose and followed Him.*

*~ Matthew 9:9,* AMP

I like how the Amplified Version of this verse adds the notion of "siding with My party" to the idea of following Jesus.

In modern terms, what comes to mind when thinking of joining or siding with a party? For most people in the United States, that would be considered a uniquely political act, such as joining the Democratic, Republican, or Independent party.

Remember that in the church chapter, we learned that Jesus' ultimate aim was to build an *ekklesia* – a kind of political uprising. So, when you think about Jesus' plans to establish His governmental rule on earth as it is in heaven, the idea of a disciple being one who sides with His party becomes extremely relevant.

With our Eastern viewpoint in mind, look at the implications in a few other example verses where Jesus called disciples to follow Him:

*And he who does not take up his cross and follow Me **[cleave steadfastly to Me, conforming wholly to My example in living and, if need be, in dying also]** is not worthy of Me.*
*~ Matthew 10:38,* AMP, ***emphasis added***

*Jesus answered him, If you would be perfect **[that is, have that spiritual maturity which accompanies self-sacrificing character]**, go and sell what you have and give to the poor, and you will have riches in heaven; and come, **be My disciple [side with My party and follow Me].***
*~ Matthew 19:21,* AMP, ***emphasis added***

*And as He was passing by, He saw Levi (Matthew) son of Alphaeus sitting at the tax office, and He said to him, Follow Me! [Be joined to Me as a disciple, side with My party!] **And he arose and joined Him as His disciple and sided with His party and accompanied Him.***
*~ Mark 2:14,* AMP, ***emphasis added***

*The next day Jesus desired and decided to go into Galilee; and He found Philip and said to him, Join Me as My **attendant and follow Me.***

*~ John 1:43, AMP, **emphasis added***

*The sheep that are My own hear and are listening to My voice; and I know them, **and they follow Me.***

*~ John 10:27, AMP, **emphasis added***

Notice how Jesus repeatedly asked disciples to follow Him and to join Him ...

By siding with His party,

By being His attendant,

By listening to His voice and following,

By cleaving to Him,

By adhering to Him,

By conforming fully to His example,

By being followers in the sense of imitating Him.

Over and over in hundreds of examples where the word *disciple* is used, Jesus' disciples are encouraged to be followers. They are literally asked to be "imitators" of Jesus' ways, not only knowledgeable of them.

The Greek word used many times in the New Testament for follower or imitator, *mimetes,* is the same one used interchangeably to describe what it means to be a disciple.

*Mimetes* is the Greek word we get the modern English word *mimic* from. It's in this very

## RECONSIDER

So I urge and implore you, be imitators of me.
~ 1 Cor 4:16, AMP

Be imitators of God [copy Him and follow His example], as well-beloved children [imitate their father].
~ Eph 5:1, AMP

Brothers, join in imitating me, and keep your eyes on those who walk according to the example you have in us.
~ Phil 3:17, ESV

In order that you may not grow disinterested and become [spiritual] sluggards, but imitators, behaving as do those who through faith (by their leaning of the entire personality on God in Christ in absolute trust and confidence in His power, wisdom, and goodness) and by practice of patient endurance and waiting are [now] inheriting the promises.
~ Heb. 6:12, AMP

context that the popular method evolved of referring to members of various religious groups as adherents.

It's said that Christianity has approximately 2.1 billion adherents world-wide.[42] The term *adherent* implies someone who adheres to or sticks to a particular belief or practice like an adhesive.

Regardless of what the religious practice is or how its adherents are classified ...

Actually imitating Jesus,

Actually mimicking Jesus,

Actually following Jesus,

Actually adhering to Jesus' ways,

Actually conforming to the image of Jesus, the Master Teacher

...should be the ultimate aim of any true disciple of Jesus!

While every single person on earth is welcomed and called to follow Jesus and perform at His level of mastery, few historically have chosen to do so. It is simply easier for most people to take the traditional approach to discipleship, which only involves ...

Learning to pray about matters of salvation versus working out your salvation,

Learning about heaven versus bringing heaven about on earth,

Learning to pray to God versus learning to listen to God,

Learning about God versus acting like God,

**REMEMBER**

For those whom He foreknew [of whom He was aware and loved beforehand], He also destined from the beginning [foreordaining them] to be molded into the image of His Son [and share inwardly His likeness], that He might become the firstborn among many brethren.

~ Rom. 8:29, AMP

333

Learning about the faith of God versus having the faith of God,

Learning to fast for God to do something versus doing what you know God would do,

Learning about what Jesus did versus doing what Jesus did,

Learning what the image of God is like versus conforming yourself to that image.

Becoming a disciple from an Eastern standpoint requires much more than verbal confessions or acknowledgments that Jesus was special, the application of a Christian label, or gaining biblical knowledge at a religious seminary.

Like becoming great at anything, becoming a master-level disciple requires a serious commitment of both time and energy. It requires enduring certain kinds of hardness.

## HOW MUCH TIME IT TAKES TO BECOME A MASTER AND THE SCIENCE BEHIND THE IMMERSION-STYLE LEARNING OF JESUS' DISCIPLES

How long does mastery take? It's the question neurologist Daniel Levitin, who studied the formula for success mastery and who was highlighted in Malcolm Gladwell's bestselling book *Outliers,* sought to answer:

> The emerging picture from studies is that ten thousand hours of practice is required to achieve the level of mastery associated with being a world-class expert in anything. In study after study of composers, basketball players, fiction writers, ice skaters, concert pianists, chess players, master criminals, and what have you, the number comes up again and again. Of course, this doesn't address why some people get more out of their practice sessions than others do. But no one has yet found a case in which true world-class expertise was accomplished in less time.

It seems it takes the brain this long to assimilate all that it needs to know to achieve true mastery.[43]

How long is ten thousand hours? It's roughly equivalent to practicing three hours a day, twenty hours a week, for ten years.

That can sound like a lot. But according to a 2009 Nielsen study called the *Three Screen Report*,[44] American adults spend more than three hours per day watching a television, computer, or phone screen consuming some form of video entertainment. The same study reported that young adults spend more than four hours and adolescents often exceed five hours per day.

What if the same people dedicated only half that time to what I like to call *discipling up* instead?

In one of my favorite commentaries on this subject, Jane McGonigal, a video game designer, offers a clue. She spoke at the annual TED conference about her goal to make it as compelling to solve problems in real life as it is in virtual life.[45] What if the world, which is currently collectively spending three billion hours weekly playing online video games, dedicated the same kind of time and energy to solving real-world problems?

Why would anyone invest so much time and energy developing virtual skills to solve virtual problems in a virtual world for virtual rewards that have little or no application in real life?

Jane's insightful answer to that question is both simple and profound. The answer, she says, is the enjoyment and pursuit of what she calls the "epic win."

That's the exact same reason I believe anyone would ever do what it takes to become a disciple of Jesus.

Unlike virtual gaming, the resulting benefits of immersion and commitment to developing the skills of a disciple of Jesus have real-world benefits and result in real-world wins of epic consequence for both the individual disciple and those around them.

RESOURCE
To watch the video of Jane McGonigal's TED presentation, visit the resource section for this chapter at www.thereorientbook.com.

Imagine enjoying the same kind of daily intimacy with the God of all creation that Jesus Himself did. Imagine becoming equipped to function just like Jesus (the original superhero) functioned and going about doing the same kind of things Jesus did – even doing, producing, and enjoying the same epic wins Jesus did:

Having victory over blind eyes,

Having victory over deaf ears,

Having victory over every kind of sickness,

Having victory over every kind of disease,

Having victory over of all manner of disease,

Having victory over hunger,

Having victory over poverty,

Having victory over all lack,

Having victory over every kind of evil in all its various forms!

These are the daily recreational activities and achievable "epic wins" for every person who will dedicate themselves to becoming a mature disciple of Jesus.

Just like Jesus, disciples use the skills they perfect to become master-level virtuosos, merging what, to some, is only the virtual reality of heaven with the present-tense reality of life on earth. Now that's an epic win worth contending for! Bringing about love's ideal is the most epic of wins!

**REMEMBER**
But thanks be to God! He gives us the victory through our Lord Jesus Christ.

~ 1 Cor. 15:57

And just think: Assuming you can agree with the ten-thousand-hours mastery theory, this level of ability and these types of epic wins are possible to anyone who would dedicate just ten years of part-time effort to the mastery of them.

Devoting at least forty hours per week of practice could reduce the number of years by half, to approximately five. It seems reasonable, considering it takes between five and six years of full-time study to get a master's degree at a university or to obtain the master's level in certain forms of martial arts.

But even more exciting for me personally is this: If someone will adopt a complete immersive style of learning, like the disciples had with Jesus, it can accelerate the learning process even more and still yield equally impressive results.

What is immersion-style learning? Think about how Jesus' first twelve disciples lived with Him twenty-four hours a day, seven days a week, for roughly three years. They were completely "immersed" in the discipleship process with Jesus as He taught them directly, in an intimate one-on-one and small-group environment.

In just thirty-six months, these twelve men of relatively simple means, ability, educational experience, and social status were utterly transformed. They became "superhuman."

They apparently matured so quickly under this model of learning that in just three short years, they were considered qualified enough by Jesus to be sent out two by two to represent Him (the Master Teacher) and expected to perform equally well.

> And He called to Him the Twelve [apostles] and began to send them out [as His ambassadors] two by two and gave them authority and power over the unclean spirits.
>
> ~ Mark 6:7, AMP

Sure, learning in this way wasn't always easy. At times it required them to make massive and somewhat abrupt changes to their ways of thinking, believing, and acting, not to mention their life priorities. The disciples' mistakes were frequent, but it's hard to deny how quickly they matured.

**RECONSIDER**
Do you find it interesting that the Greek word for "baptized" in the New Testament, *baptizo,* means "to immerse, to completely submerge, to make whelmed"?

Based on the historical account we have in the New Testament writings, the results of this immersive style of learning speak for themselves.

The same is true for anyone choosing to become a direct disciple of Jesus today. It can require making significant lifestyle adjustments and a reordering of priorities to renew our minds and to become immersed in His ways.

But if a person is simply willing to ask, God will supernaturally give them the necessary understanding, training, and ability to conform to Jesus' exact image.

God never says you have to be extraordinary, superhuman, or uniquely gifted or qualified to become a disciple. You just have to be willing to learn to follow Jesus' example, for He was, in and of Himself, all of these things and much more.

Remember, everyone is called to be a disciple.

God doesn't call qualified people, but He qualifies everyone He calls,

God doesn't qualify perfect people, but He always perfects those He qualifies,

God doesn't require people be strong,

God doesn't require people to have already overcome all of life's challenges,

God does, however, make every disciple strong,

God does make every disciple more than an overcomer if they are willing to immerse themselves in life with Him.

People often say to me, "But Kevin, the disciples lived with Jesus for three years. I will never have the opportunity to be with Him every day and be taught directly by Him like they were."

My reply usually surprises them: "Right. You have something even better, something far greater than having Jesus walk with you every day like the first disciples did. If you have been born again, you have Jesus 'in you' every day!"

*For God wanted them to know that the riches and glory of Christ are for you Gentiles, too. And this is the secret: Christ lives in you. This gives you assurance of **sharing** his glory.*
*~ Colossians 1:27, NLT*

Jesus actually said it was better this way:

*But in fact, it is best for you that I go away, because if I don't, the Advocate ‹**the Holy Spirit**› won't come. If I do go away, then I will send him to you.*
*~ John 16:7, NLT*

For every person who is born again and is committed to becoming a disciple, the Holy Spirit, whom God the Father sent in Jesus' name, will teach them all things and bring to their mind everything that Jesus said or did during His time on earth:

*But the Comforter (Counselor, Helper, Intercessor, Advocate, Strengthener, Standby), the Holy Spirit, Whom the Father will send in My name [in My place, to represent Me and act on My behalf], He will teach you all things. And He will cause you to recall (will remind you of, bring to your remembrance) everything I have told you.*
*~ John 14:26, AMP*

Stunningly, even after Jesus' death and resurrection, and as recorded in the book of Acts, every instruction from God that the disciples received came from the Holy Spirit, not Jesus Himself in the flesh as we think of it.

Every inspired word the disciples spoke and every mighty work they did – the original twelve, the next seventy, and every true disciple that has followed since – was empowered by the same Holy Spirit that we have available to us today.

As we discussed in the Christian chapter, it should go without saying: to become a spiritually mature disciple, a person has to learn how to be Spirit-led.

**REMEMBER**
It's worth noting the obvious here: the book of Acts in the New Testament is so named because it records the "acts" of the disciples, not just their beliefs.

339

Jesus was the Master Teacher of the original twelve disciples when He was with them physically. In the same way, more than fifty times in the book of Acts alone, the Holy Spirit is referenced as the Master Teacher of Jesus' disciples.

The book of Acts records how, just like Jesus did previously ...

The Holy Spirit instructed the disciples,

The Holy Spirit showed the disciples how to speak,

The Holy Spirit influenced the way the disciples thought,

The Holy Spirit led the disciples where to go,

The Holy Spirit showed the disciples who to interact with,

The Holy Spirit gave the disciples divine wisdom,

The Holy Spirit comforted the disciples,

The Holy Spirit consoled the disciples,

The Holy Spirit exhorted the disciples when they needed it,

The Holy Spirit gave the disciples confidence,

The Holy Spirit gave the disciples boldness,

The Holy Spirit infused the disciples with supernatural power and ability,

The Holy Spirit caused the disciples to triumph over every kind of evil.

The Holy Spirit, in other words, made them just like Jesus.

And why not? Jesus was instructed, led, and empowered by the exact same Spirit. He just taught His disciples to be led as He was.

Everything Jesus did for the disciples as their Master Teacher while He was with them in person, the Holy Spirit did for them and others in Jesus' physical absence.

Consider Paul, who only met Jesus spiritually one time, on the road to Damascus (Acts 9:1–30). Paul, who was not even one of the original twelve disciples of Jesus, is credited with authoring thirteen of the twenty-seven books – or more than 30 percent of the entire New Testament.

After an initial encounter, it has been by learning to be led by the Holy Spirit that Paul and every disciple that has followed since has learned to mimic Jesus.

He was not interested in only amassing followers who attended His sermons, agreed with His theology, and spread His teachings. Jesus was interested in making disciples. And to Jesus, a disciple meant someone who could and would choose to imitate Him, as the Master Teacher, in every way.

---

RECONSIDER

Until the day when He ascended, after He through the Holy Spirit had instructed and commanded the apostles (special messengers) whom He had chosen.

~ Acts 1:2, AMP

But you shall receive power (ability, efficiency, and might) when the Holy Spirit has come upon you, and you shall be My witnesses in Jerusalem and all Judea and Samaria and to the ends (the very bounds) of the earth.

~ Acts 1:8, AMP

And while Peter was earnestly revolving the vision in his mind and meditating on it, the [Holy] Spirit said to him, Behold, three men are looking for you!

~ Acts 10:19, AMP

Then Peter, [because he was] filled with [and controlled by] the Holy Spirit, said to them, Rulers of the people and members of the council (the Sanhedrin) . . .

~ Acts 4:8, AMP

For the promise [of the Holy Spirit] is to and for you and your children, and to and for all that are far away, [even] to and for as many as the Lord our God invites and bids to come to Himself.

~ Acts 2:39, AMP

So the church ‹**ekklesia**› throughout the whole of Judea and Galilee and Samaria had peace and was edified [growing in wisdom, virtue, and piety] and walking in the respect and reverential fear of the Lord and in the consolation and exhortation of the Holy Spirit, continued to increase and was multiplied.

~ Act 9:31, AMP

In Jesus' time and even now, acknowledging that Jesus was extraordinary and benefiting from His teachings and ministry is fairly easy. Choosing to follow the Holy Spirit and learning to do what it takes to imitate Jesus requires a much greater commitment and determination.

It's why in the New Testament, the word *disciple* carried the idea of:

> " *Someone willing to endure hardness, like a first class soldier, athlete, or farmer, to become just like the master.* "

In fact, it's this definition and implication of what it means to be a disciple that caused the writers of the New Testament to most often liken the life of a disciple of Jesus to becoming an Olympic athlete, a special-forces soldier, or a successful farmer (we might say entrepreneur today).

Paul used the same imagery while describing the life of a disciple of Christ to one of his own "spiritual sons," Timothy:

> *So you, my son, be strong (strengthened inwardly) in the grace (spiritual blessing) that is [to be found only] in Christ Jesus. And the [instructions] which you have heard from me along with many witnesses, transmit and entrust [as a deposit] to reliable and faithful men who will be competent and qualified to teach others also. **Take [with me] your share of the hardships and suffering ‹endure hardness› [which you are called to endure] as a good (first-class) soldier of Christ Jesus. No soldier when in service gets entangled in the enterprises of [civilian] life; his aim is to satisfy and please the one who enlisted him. And if anyone enters competitive games, he is not crowned unless he competes lawfully (fairly, according to the rules laid down). [It is] the hard-working farmer***

**RECONSIDER**
You therefore must endure harship as a good soldier of Jesus Christ.

~ 2 Tim. 2:3, NKJV

*[who labors to produce] who must be the first partaker of the fruits. Think over these things I am saying [understand them and grasp their application], for the Lord will grant you full insight and understanding in everything. Constantly keep in mind Jesus Christ (the Messiah) [as] risen from the dead, [as the prophesied King] descended from David, according to the good news (the Gospel) that I preach. For that [Gospel] I am suffering affliction and even wearing chains like a criminal. But the Word of God is not chained or imprisoned! Therefore I [am ready to] persevere and stand my ground with patience and endure everything for the sake of the elect [God's chosen], so that they too may obtain [the] salvation which is in Christ Jesus, with [the reward of] eternal glory.*

~ *2 Timothy 2:1–10,* AMP, ***emphasis added***

Notice how Paul says nothing of being:

A good scholar,

A proficient Bible student,

An avid consumer of godly knowledge,

A master of theoretical principles.

Instead, Timothy is instructed to understand things with the intent of grasping them in application. Notice how Paul uses the ideas of . . .

Suffering or enduring as a first-class soldier,

Competing and being crowned as a top-level athlete,

The rewards of a hard-working farmer who labors to produce fruit

343

...while explaining to Timothy what it takes to be a disciple.

Paul wasn't the only one in the New Testament to use the soldier, athlete, or farmer metaphors to describe what it takes to become a disciple. Jesus used the same themes in many of His parables, as did other writers of the New Testament.

## A DISCIPLE AS A SPECIAL-FORCES SOLDIER

Today, most people would consider it a stretch to think of a call to ministry or enlisting to become a disciple of Jesus as equivalentto answering a call to arms and signing up to be a special-forces soldier.

Where I grew up, a prevailing but unspoken ideology was that strong men went off to fight wars as soldiers or became accomplished athletes, hard-working farmers, or captains of enterprise. By default, it was implied that weaker, more sensitive, and philosophical men stayed back, took care of their families, and ministered to the women and children at church.

You only had to be standing in a local coffee shop among the "real men" when the local preacher walked in. "Morning, preacher" was the usual welcome. It was often preceded by or quickly followed by a few tongue-in-cheek comments or jokes at his expense. They all liked him well enough and apparently didn't mean any disrespect. Yet, jokes about supporting ministers perceived to have cozy lives and no real means of income other than the money of hard-working people were frequent. Even though I knew they were joking, through the eyes of a child I could discern elements of truth they intended to convey. Among the "real men," this kind of second-handing was considered anything but honorable.

In contrast, I recall a young man returning from overseas military deployment who came in for morning coffee. I distinctly remember the honor and respect – and rightfully so – given to him. I don't recall anyone chiding him about not holding down a job while engaged in military training. I don't recall anyone joking about their tax dollars being used to finance his military deployment. I don't recall – and again rightfully so – that anyone thought he was less of a man because he wasn't earning a living and providing real value while serving. I don't recall anyone implying this soldier was a second-hander.

Clearly, most people didn't and still don't equate the life of a disciple to a special-forces soldier engaged in warfare. But the Bible did and still does! It calls ministry "a call to service."

In fact, in verses like the following, Paul again uses the soldier analogy and even equates being what he called an apostle and the expense and support needed to be one as the exact same as a soldier going off to fight:

> Who goes to **war** at his own expense? Who plants a vineyard and does not eat any of its grapes? Or who takes care of a flock and does not drink any of its milk?
> ~ 1 Corinthians 9:7, ISV, **emphasis added**

Ironically, the Greek word for *war* that Paul used in the verse above literally means:

1. to serve, as in military service
2. to lead soldiers to battle
3. to be in active service
4. to fight
5. figuratively, the apostolic career (with its arduous duties and functions)

So, why is there such a difference between how the world sees the life of a soldier and a disciple today? There are at least two reasons.

First, many people in ministry have historically failed to approach the role of being a disciple of Christ with the same mind-set and precision required of a highly skilled and capable soldier and, therefore, have not earned the same kind of respect.

Second, most people think of ministry as a purely philosophical or emotional exercise. They don't equate the rigors of administering the reality of the kingdom with that of a highly skilled special-forces soldier in an advancing army engaged in an epic conflict!

So, what is a special-forces soldier, and how would having the mind-set of one, as Paul suggests, make someone a better disciple?

Consider the following description taken from a popular military website:

> [A special-forces soldier is] a breed apart, a cut above the rest. Another kind of soldier. Mature. Highly skilled. Superbly trained. Unquestionably the world's finest unconventional warfare expert. A teacher first, and fighter of uncommon physical and mental caliber. Ready to serve anywhere at any time.
>
> ... [They are expected to deal] with special combat situations you won't find in most textbooks. The mission: unconventional warfare operations and counter-insurgency.
>
> You have to be resolute, resourceful and resilient ... . Each team member is a highly-skilled specialist – and cross-training ensures the multiple utility of each soldier on the team ... .
>
> Special Forces involves the most rigorous, intensive and challenging training you'll ever tackle ... .
>
> Special Forces requires raw guts, unwavering determination and dedication to duty ... .
>
> Special Forces is not just a challenge, it's a way of life. As a highly skilled, superbly trained professional the word "impossible" isn't in your vocabulary.[46]

### RESOURCE

For a more thorough understanding of a soldier's life, one of my favorite books on the topic is called *Never Surrender: A Soldier's Journey to the Crossroads of Faith and Freedom* by LTG (Ret.) Jerry Boykin.[48] Gen. Boykin was one of the founding members of the world's premier Special Operations unit Delta Force and commander of US special forces around the world for more than twenty years. He is also a friend and a disciple.[48]

What kind of mind-set and training does it take be this kind of soldier and, subsequently, a disciple?

Both begin with volunteering or enlisting and beginning basic training. Let's imagine for a moment you've just enlisted in the US military and are beginning the six to twelve weeks of basic training. If that's hard to imagine because, like me, you have never been in the armed forces, Google the phrase *military basic training* and read a few articles that describe the regimen.[47]

Most every resource makes clear that a primary goal of US military basic training is to teach soldiers to obey orders at all times while continuing to press on and endure hardness, even when their mind and body feel like quitting.

Even basic military training likely surpasses anything civilian life demands, in terms of physical and *psychological* rigor, unless you're a professional athlete. And, of course, initial basic training hardly compares to the rigors of advanced special-forces training.

In any respect, like most new recruits, three days into basic training and you are already at the breaking point from the near-constant physical and psychological training you receive from sun-up to sun-down.

As you adjust to a whole new way of life and daily routine – starting each day with a 5:00 a.m. roll call and grueling workout where your mind screams, *Quit! This isn't worth it!* and your muscles rebel in weakness – your thoughts drift to simpler times!

Just when you think you can't go any further, the commanding officer is in your ear, pushing you and stretching you beyond what you ever thought was possible. Again, your thoughts betray you: *Why would I voluntarily enlist for this? What was I thinking?* You have to constantly remind yourself, *This is for my benefit. It will make me stronger. I will not quit!*

The ability to press on despite your mind and body's near-constant objection will

**RESOURCE**
Interested in learning more about what it takes to become a disciple, as likened to a special-forces soldier in the United States military? Consider watching the Discovery Channel's documentary *Two Weeks in Hell,* which is an overview of the Special Forces Assessment and Selection (SFAS) course at Camp Mackall, North Carolina. Links to a nine-part YouTube version of the broadcast are provided in the resource section for this chapter at www.thereorientbook.com. Warning: Due to the graphic nature of the material and language used, viewer discretion is advised.

be the only thing that separates you from the large number of other enlistees who will quit before they reach the end of basic training.

Though it feels like punishment, by the end of twelve weeks of training, your ability to endure hardness and continue has made you stronger. It's made you confident you can do the impossible. It's made you a soldier. It's made you a disciple.

Then the greater reality hits you. This was basic training – what's next? Though rigorous, these were only the basic things you had to learn and overcome to give you the proper mind-set required to continue to more advance training – even special-forces training.

Believe it or not, this is the same kind of mind-set that every disciple needs to be great and the basic requirement needed to move up and handle greater things as a soldier in the army of God.

Without a proven, hardened resolve and will to continue, it's simply impossible to survive the rigors and demands of real-life warfare – the spiritual warfare – a disciple of Jesus will endure.

The warfare a disciple of Jesus wages is against spiritual opponents, of course, and our weapons are designed to destroy a different kind of enemy altogether: anything and everything that exalts itself against the love of God and His will to establish His kingdom on earth as it is in heaven.

> For though we walk (live) in the flesh, we are not carrying on our warfare according to the flesh and using mere human weapons. For the weapons of our warfare are not physical [weapons of flesh and blood], but they are mighty before God for the overthrow and destruction of strongholds, [inasmuch as we] refute arguments and theories and reasonings and every proud and lofty thing that sets itself up against the [true] knowledge of God; and we lead every thought and purpose away captive into the obedience of Christ (the Messiah, the Anointed One), being in readiness to punish every [insubordinate for his] disobedience, when your own

> *submission and obedience [as a church]* ‹*ekklesia*› *are*
> *fully secured and complete.*
>
> *~ 2 Corinthians 10:3–6,* AMP

The military imagery Paul uses here is so appropriate. He refers to the idea of overthrowing strongholds, by which he means "fortified or vigorously defended thoughts and arguments that have set themselves against the true knowledge of God."

The way Paul expresses the need to take every thought captive and bring it into obedience – meaning "to make agree with" – of Christ, the anointed Master, and the willingness to punish any thought that doesn't want to agree or submit to love's ideal is so practical.

Like a soldier in basic training who must punish his body to make it obedient to his will to continue despite the hardness, a disciple must bring his mind, will, and emotions into agreement to God's will – love's will – and this takes serious discipline.

And that's just the basics.

As in traditional military service, to obtain more advanced training, be schooled to function in a specific capacity, and be deployed to accomplish a greater mission, each soldier must apply the disciplines they have acquired in basic training to gain competency in the next area of mastery: basic weapons training.

It's in this context that Paul describes the weapons that a disciple must master, likening them to the standard accoutrements of a first-century soldier arrayed in battle armor:

> *In conclusion, be strong in the Lord [be empowered through*
> *your union with Him]; draw your strength from Him [that*
> *strength which His boundless might provides]. Put on God's*
> *whole armor [the armor of a heavy-armed soldier which*
> *God supplies], that you may be able successfully to stand*
> *up against [all] the strategies and the deceits of the devil*
> ‹*the adversary or enemy*›*. For we are not wrestling with*
> *flesh and blood [contending only with physical opponents],*
> *but against the despotisms, against the powers, against*
> *[the master spirits who are] the world rulers of this present*

*darkness, against the spirit forces of wickedness in the heavenly (supernatural) sphere. Therefore put on God's complete armor, that you may be able to resist and stand your ground on the evil day [of danger], and, having done all [the crisis demands], to stand [firmly in your place]. Stand therefore [hold your ground], having tightened the belt of truth around your loins and having put on the breastplate of integrity and of moral rectitude and right standing with God, and having shod your feet in preparation [to face the enemy with the firm-footed stability, the promptness, and the readiness produced by the good news] of the Gospel of peace. Lift up over all the [covering] shield of saving faith, upon which you can quench all the flaming missiles of the wicked [one]. And take the helmet of salvation and the sword that the Spirit wields, which is the Word of God.*
*~ Ephesians 6:10–17,* AMP

As Paul makes clear, not only does being both an effective soldier and disciple require massive commitment and good basic training, it requires effective armor and weaponry.

The kind of armor and weaponry that Paul describes in this verse are the minimum requirements for mastery in the basic training of a disciple and for initial deployment into the more public realms of life.

The kind of armor and weaponry Paul lists also seems to hint at the specific categories of opposition that every disciple faces as they exit basic training and begin to engage in conflicts of even greater consequence.

## EMERGING DISCIPLES NEED TO GET A FEW WINS UNDER THEIR BELT

Being girded with a belt of truth suggests that every disciple will be challenged to discern truth and overcome lies, especially concerning the nature of God. In fact, the enemy himself is called the father of lies and of all that is false (John 8:44). The idea of tightening or girding a belt around you, as some translations say, is akin to saying, "Fasten your seat belts, people." We are about to have a collision with lies so significant that if you are not buckled in, you could be easily unseated.

This is a formative stage in the development of any disciple and one, sadly, that many are ill-equipped to handle. Some surveys suggest as many as 30 percent of people quit pursuing a relationship with God because they become disillusioned or lose their faith through what they called hypocrisy. This is another way of saying, "I felt deceived." This can be especially common among younger disciples who, like young children, are more easily deceived and discouraged than more mature and experienced ones.

However, if a disciple is well-equipped at this stage and gets a few "wins" under their belt, so to speak, their chances of failure at later stages are substantially reduced. It reminds me of how during World War II, young fighter pilots who had just completed training and were sent into combat had more than a seventy percent chance of being shot down during their first encounter with the enemy. By their tenth mission, however, the chance of their being eliminated dropped to less than one percent.[49]

## EMERGING DISCIPLES NEED GOOD BODY ARMOR

What about being equipped with a breastplate of righteousness? In Greek, the word translated to English as *breastplate* was a type of corslet or thorax, the heaviest and most defensive piece of bronze armor that a soldier wore.[50]

The breastplate was designed and hinged in such a way as to go around the soldier's entire front and back to protect their heart and vital organs and withstand the most substantial blows from an enemy's weapon. Today, we might call this body armor. As we have already discussed, the word *righteous* implies right standing. Being equipped with a breastplate of righteousness suggests the enemy will likely hurl his mightiest weapons at the very heart or core of every disciple in an effort to destroy their right standing with God. It's why the traditional concepts around sin can be such powerful weapons in the hands of the enemy. He uses them to erode mankind's confidence and make them second-guess their collective right standing with God.

It's the very tactic the enemy used when trying to tempt Jesus Himself, as described in His encounter with the enemy in the wilderness (Matt. 4:1–11). By asking Jesus repeatedly, "If you are the Son of God, then …," the enemy was attacking Jesus' very right standing with His Father. The strategy the enemy used against Jesus and every disciple since to keep them separate from God and to get them to abort their mission is to challenge their identity and confidence as true sons and daughters of God.

## EMERGING DISCIPLES NEED GOOD COMBAT BOOTS

Paul goes on to say that every disciple must have their feet "shod … in preparation … of the Gospel of peace." It's interesting to note that the Greek word translated *Gospel* is generally accepted to mean "a good message," and the Greek word Paul chooses here that is translated *peace* literally means "prosperity."

If we implemented our replace-and-read-again-with-the-original-meaning strategy here, this verse would read: "Have your feet shod with the preparation of a good message of prosperity."

This seems to indicate that virtually everywhere a true disciple will walk, the enemies of God will try to create strife by challenging God's message of goodness and willingness to prosper us with a contrary and dominant message of bad news and lack.

If you are not sure what I mean, just try consistently proclaiming a message that God is always good and that He wants you and others to be healthy and rich. See if it stirs up any strife. I have seen people threaten violence over perpetuating just such a message – what they call the "health, wealth, and prosperity gospel."

I am certainly aware of people harmed by charlatans who have shamefully exploited a prosperity-type gospel premise for personal gain. However, I am not sure I understand much of the opposition to it theologically.

After all, if you don't believe God wants disciples healthy, wealthy, and prospering, what's the alternative? Does God prefer them to be sick, impoverished, and lacking? That certainly doesn't sound like good news to me – let alone a strategy for a strong army.

When Jesus and His disciples walked the earth, all sickness, disease, poverty, and lack came from the enemy. In many religious circles today, however, a disciple of Jesus who makes such a theological stand in their "gospel boots" would cause some people to say they are of the enemy! This may be why Paul suggests that a few additional pieces of armor may be required to successfully mature as a disciple of Jesus.

## ABOVE ALL ELSE, EMERGING DISCIPLES NEED A DECENT SET OF SHIELDS, SWORDS, AND HELMENTS

In the conclusion of our focus verse, Paul suggests that above all, a disciple needs a shield of faith to quench the fiery darts of the wicked one, a helmet of salvation, and a sword of the Spirit, the Word of God.

Paul reinforces the need for a shield of faith, even when a disciple has the courage to stand, having their feet shod with the good news of the gospel of peace. It suggests the enemy may endeavor to extinguish a disciple's passion by undermining their faith in God – their conviction, confidence, and assurance – to actually manifest this kind of gospel in a person's life.

Being equipped with a helmet of salvation suggests that the adversary will bombard the mind of a disciple to challenge and strip them of the benefits of salvation. By definition, these benefits include the same kind of healing, deliverance, and provision they are charged to bring about for others.

And having a sword of the Spirit suggests that the enemy will do everything in his power to minimize a disciple's ability to wield God's Word effectively.

From these verses, it's clear that Paul understood that the mind-set and weaponry of a highly skilled soldier was required to be a competent disciple.

Anyone who has endeavored to live as a disciple, more than a casual consumer or advocate for the things of God, can relate to these soldier and equipping metaphors. The nature of the great co-mission to go into every part of the world, which is many times hostile towards the good news of the kingdom, and see it transformed by love's ideal requires hardened and highly trained combatants. Being skilled only in rhetoric and good scholastics is insufficient.

Even among loved ones, contending for love's ideal can be hard – let alone going into more hostile parts of the world, where the enemy is more formidable and less merciful than friends and family might be.

## A DISCIPLE AS COMPARED TO AN OLYMPIC ATHLETE

Though people of Hebrew-Eastern origins were not big into competitive sports, the people of Greek-Western culture to whom Paul was often required to relate were. The Greeks invented our modern-day Olympic Games. The first competitive games of this nature are believed to have been held almost eight hundred years before Jesus' birth in Olympia, Greece . Such Olympic-type games were a prominent part of Greek life until nearly four hundred years after Jesus' time.[51]

To the ancient Greeks, the Olympic Games were as much religious festivals as they were athletic events. To understand the Greek reverence for sport, one only needs to look at their poetry, architecture, art, and statues. The intricately chiseled human physique they offered through sculpture resemble only the most fit and powerfully sculpted athletic bodies in our modern age.

It was in this context that Paul made reference to the life of an athlete. He compared an Olympic-type athlete, competing to do well in competitive games, to that of running the race of life and receiving a prize as a disciple of Christ:

> And if anyone enters competitive games, he is not crowned unless he competes lawfully (fairly, according to the rules laid down).
>
> ~ 2 Timothy 2:5, AMP

To understand discipleship as it relates to Olympic athletics, let's consider the following description about what it takes to be an Olympic athlete from the most decorated athlete in the history of the Olympic games: Michael Phelps.

In 2008, the world watched in awe as the twenty-three-year-old American swimmer won his eleventh gold medal, the most ever in a single Olympic tournament. With an additional four medals to his name from the 2004 games in Athens, Greece, and thirty-eight world records and counting to his credit, Michael Phelps is a great example of an accomplished athlete at the top of his game.[52] But what qualifies him for such greatness? Many people cite ...

His unique physical makeup, which provides an unfair advantage over others in the water,

His size fourteen, double-jointed feet, which rotate 15 degrees more than average,

His 6'7" arm span, which is three inches longer than his height,

His abnormally long torso,

His short legs,

His heart that pumps thirty liters of blood per second, double that of the average person.

While these are all great physical attributes, I am not convinced that they alone make Michael the most decorated Olympian of all time.

While these attributes doubtless help Michael compete well, they would be irrelevant without his willingness to endure the physical hardness of daily training and adherence to his coaches' relentless pursuit of swimming perfection.

I'm sure even Michael Phelps himself would agree that training and conditioning six hours per day, six days per week, three-hundred-plus days per year had more to do with standing on the winner's podium at the end of the race, than did his natural abilities alone. I am in awe of the focus and dedication this must have taken.

There must be mornings when his body doesn't want to play along. There must be days when he would prefer to stay in bed instead of making the cold 6:00 a.m. walk to the pool. There must times when he questions the necessity of adhering to an eight-miles-per-day or fifty-miles-per-week swimming regimen for a defining event that is years away. There must be days he doesn't feel up to consuming the staggering 12,000 calories each day just to get enough fuel to support the physical demands placed on his body from that much training. (By the way, the average person only needs 2,000 calories, and professional power-lifters need around 8,000 calories per day.)

How much is 12,000 calories per day? According to Michael, it's:

A breakfast consisting of three fried-egg sandwiches,

A topping of cheese, lettuce, tomatoes, fried onions, and mayonnaise,

A portion of toast,

A large omelet,

A bowl of oatmeal,

A serving of three pancakes, and

A serving of two cups of coffee.

It's also:

A lunch consisting of a pound of pasta,

A side of two ham-and-cheese sandwiches, and

A chaser of approximately 1000 calories of energy drinks.

As well as:

A dinner consisting of another pound of pasta,

A pizza, and

A few more energy drinks.

This, of course, doesn't include the daily regimen of nutritional supplements required to feed his muscles in between each of these meals.[53] I don't know about you, but for me, it would be an accomplishment of Olympic proportions to even prepare and eat that much food per day!

When asked how he maintains and manages this kind of regimen when training for the Olympics, Michael responded: "It's simple; I sleep, I eat, I swim."

For a kid reportedly raised by a single mom and diagnosed with severe attention-deficit hyperactivity disorder (ADHD), that's a lot of focus.

Asked how he maintains this kind of intense focus for such long periods of time, he said in one interview:

"Every day, I visualize myself standing on the podium, getting the gold medal. I let the feeling of achievement motivate me. The training is simply what will be required for me to make that vision a reality. On the days when that vision alone isn't enough, I remind myself that every day I am not in the pool training, my opponent is!"

What a great visualization. Ironically, that's the exact way Paul describes the one thing he and other mature disciples do:

> Not that I have already obtained all this, or have already been made perfect, but I press on to take hold of that for which Christ Jesus took hold of me. Brothers, I do not consider myself yet to have taken hold of it. But one thing I do: Forgetting what is behind and straining toward what is ahead, I press on toward the goal to win the prize for which God has called ‹invited› me heavenward in Christ Jesus.

*All of us who are mature should take such a view of things. And if on some point you think differently, that too God will make clear to you. Only let us live up to what we have already attained. Join with others in following my example, brothers, and take note of those who live according to the pattern we gave you.*

*~ Philippians 3:12–17*

Paul uses the same kind of athletic imagery in these famous verses:

*And I do this for the sake of the good news (the Gospel), in order that I may become a participator in it and share in its [blessings along with you]. Do you not know that in a race all the runners compete, but [only] one receives the prize? So run [your race] that you may lay hold [of the prize] and make it yours. Now every athlete who goes into training conducts himself temperately and restricts himself in all things. They do it to win a wreath that will soon wither, but we [do it to receive a crown of eternal blessedness] that cannot wither. Therefore I do not run uncertainly (without definite aim). I do not box like one beating the air and striking without an adversary. But [like a boxer] I buffet my body [handle it roughly, discipline it by hardships] and subdue it, for fear that after proclaiming to others the Gospel and things pertaining to it, I myself should become unfit [not stand the test, be unapproved and rejected as a counterfeit].*

*~ 1 Corinthians 9:23–27,* AMP

What if every person in the world who identified themselves as a Christian committed themselves to being a disciple with the same kind of vigor, focus, and determination?

What if they were willing to endure the same kind of hardness as a special-forces soldier or an Olympic athlete in their pursuit of Jesus-like perfection, in order to be conformed to the very image of the Author and Finisher of their faith?

What if a single vision of the gospel having its full effect and of obtaining the prize of a more eternally abundant life for themselves and everyone they knew was at the forefront of their mind and motivating every action?

What if every person in the world who identified themselves as a Christian and committed themselves to be a disciple lived with constant awareness that the God of all creation was willing to take them in any condition and lovingly train them?

What if God would personally train them to become perfect, strong, and courageous, able to withstand and overcome anything an adversary presented as an obstacle, to finish the race with excellence?

What if all it took was a willingness to commit, to follow God's instructions, to be trained, and to then commit with a holy, violent enmity against the slightest thought of failure until we could do everything He does equally well?

What if the prize was both temporal and eternal and every private triumph would one day be rewarded openly on the largest stage imaginable in front of all creation?

Would you be willing to "disciple up"? If so, you might consider the following verses as your daily mantra:

> Therefore then, since we are surrounded by so great a cloud of witnesses [who have borne testimony to the Truth], let us strip off and throw aside every encumbrance (unnecessary weight) and that sin which so readily (deftly and cleverly) clings to and entangles us, and let us run with patient endurance and steady and active persistence the appointed course of the race that is set before us, looking away [from all that will distract] to Jesus, Who is the Leader and the Source of our faith [giving the first incentive for our belief] and is also its Finisher [bringing it to maturity and perfection]. He, for the joy [of obtaining the prize] that was set before Him, endured the cross, despising and ignoring the shame, and is now seated at the right hand of the throne of God. [See Psalm 110:1.] Just think of Him Who endured from sinners such grievous opposition and bitter hostility against Himself [reckon up and consider it all in comparison with

*your trials], so that you may not grow weary or exhausted, losing heart and relaxing and fainting in your minds. You have not yet struggled and fought agonizingly against sin, nor have you yet resisted and withstood to the point of pouring out your [own] blood. And have you [completely] forgotten the divine word of appeal and encouragement in which you are reasoned with and addressed as sons? My son, do not think lightly or scorn to submit to the correction and discipline of the Lord, nor lose courage and give up and faint when you are reproved or corrected by Him; for the Lord corrects and disciplines everyone whom He loves, and He punishes, even scourges, every son whom He accepts and welcomes to His heart and cherishes. You must submit to and endure [correction] for discipline; God is dealing with you as with sons. For what son is there whom his father does not [thus] train and correct and discipline? Now if you are exempt from correction and left without discipline in which all [of God's children] share, then you are illegitimate offspring and not true sons [at all]. [See Proverbs 3:11–12.] Moreover, we have had earthly fathers who disciplined us and we yielded [to them] and respected [them for training us]. Shall we not much more cheerfully submit to the Father of spirits and so [truly] live? For [our earthly fathers] disciplined us for only a short period of time and chastised us as seemed proper and good to them; but He disciplines us for our certain good, that we may become sharers in His own holiness. For the time being no discipline brings joy, but seems grievous and painful; but afterwards it yields a peaceable fruit of righteousness to those who have been trained by it [a harvest of fruit which consists in righteousness – in conformity to God's will in purpose, thought, and action, resulting in right living and right standing with God]. So then, brace up and reinvigorate and set right your slackened and weakened and drooping hands and strengthen your feeble and palsied and tottering knees [Isaiah 35:3], and cut through and make firm and plain and smooth, straight paths for your feet [yes, make them safe*

*and upright and happy paths that go in the right direction],
so that the lame and halting [limbs] may not be put out of
joint, but rather may be cured. Strive to live in peace with
everybody and pursue that consecration and holiness without which no one will [ever] see the Lord. Exercise foresight
and be on the watch to look [after one another], to see that
no one falls back from and fails to secure God's grace (His
unmerited favor and spiritual blessing), in order that no
root of resentment (rancor, bitterness, or hatred) shoots
forth and causes trouble and bitter torment, and the many
become contaminated and defiled by it.*

*~ Hebrews 12:1–15,* AMP

And with this mindset – like that of a good soldier or athlete – if a
disciple does not become weary in doing good, in proper time, like a
good farmer, they will reap just such a harvest (Gal. 6:9).

In fact, let's look at Paul's description of what it means to be a disciple
through the eyes of a diligent farmer or laborer. The Bible often uses
the word *laborer* interchangeably with *farmer* because the word *farmer*
means "one who labors.":

> **[It is] the hard-working farmer [who labors to produce]
> who must be the first partaker of the fruits.** *Think over
> these things I am saying* **[understand them and grasp
> their application],** *for the Lord will grant you full insight
> and understanding in everything.*
>
> *~ 2 Timothy 2:6–7,* AMP, **emphasis added**

## A DISCIPLE AS COMPARED TO A FARMER

Like Paul, Jesus often used aspects of the life of a farmer, laborer, or
manager of a business to explain what the kingdom of God was like
and what it meant to be a disciple. By most accounts, Jesus used at
least fifty-seven different analogies, or what the Bible calls parables
(a word derived from a Greek word meaning "to set side by side for
comparison"), more than half of which dealt with aspects of farming
or laboring.

Jesus spoke in these terms so often because He primarily interacted with people immersed in these areas of everyday life. Even more, it was exactly these aspects of everyday life that Jesus most desired to see His kingdom invade.

It's really just practical. If your aim is to equip people to rise up in the public arenas of life and be effective, it makes sense to start your uprising by calling out disciples to accomplish this mission who are already immersed in these areas.

But what was it about the life of a farmer that uniquely qualified them to make a good disciple or better relate to how the kingdom of God operates?

For one thing, like becoming a soldier or an athlete, farming isn't easy. To succeed takes resolve and a willful determination. It also takes a lot of faith in a principle God established called seedtime and harvest. (Gen. 8:22).

Today in the Western world, most farming is done with the assistance of modern machinery and technology. In an industrialized world and an information age, very little work is done entirely by hand or with animal assistance.

**RESOURCE**
A full 100 percent of Jesus' parables dealt with aspects observable in the everyday life and things a common person could relate to. With some overlap, 40 percent dealt with money, 30 percent dealt with various aspects of business or labor, and 26 percent dealt specifically with farming. A complete list of Jesus' parables can be found in the resource section for this chapter on our website at www.thereorientbook.com.

This was not the case, of course, for the majority of people in Jesus' time. Work for the average person was hard. It began at sun-up, ended at sun-down, and often rewarded the laborer with barely enough to sustain his own family, let alone enough excess to sustain others.

The terrain and climate in the Middle East was equally unrelenting. The ground was hard, rocky, and sandy, and rain was an essential but scarce resource. Long-term storage of goods and produce was difficult – refrigeration was non-existent. Famines were commonplace.

Only the best stewards of available resources and observers of the times and seasons survived in this environment. If you were impaired and unable to work or provide for yourself or your family for any reason, life could be near impossible without the generosity of others or divine intervention.

Needless to say, success in Jesus' time for the majority of people, especially farmers, was called survival.

If you were a successful farmer or businessman in Jesus' time, just like a soldier or an athlete, you had most likely developed a kind of resolve, focus, and determination that few others were willing to exercise.

The philosophy of farming is fairly easy to grasp, but you're hardly qualified to call yourself a farmer until you actually find a suitable field, plant something, and produce a harvest.

Even in the midwestern United States, where I grew up and where the conditions are more ideal for farming, I can assure you that consuming the produce a farmer produces is much easier than actually producing it!

The work of a farmer or laborer is hard, and those willing to do it are increasingly rare. But for those prepared to put their hand to the plow, not look back, and do the work, when the harvest is ripe – just like being a disciple – they are rewarded richly.

Consider Jesus' words in this context:

> Now after this the Lord chose and appointed seventy others ‹**more disciples**› and sent them out ahead of Him, two by two, into every town and place where He Himself was about to come (visit). And He said to them, The harvest indeed is abundant [there is much ripe grain], but the farmhands are few. Pray therefore the Lord of the harvest to send out laborers ‹**farmers**› into His harvest.
>
> ~ Luke 10:1–2, AMP

In one of the greatest, most all-encompassing parables ever told, look at how Jesus master-

**REMEMBER**

Jesus wasn't trying to build a religious church movement in the traditional sense, but rather a social *ekklesia* movement.

fully lays out how the kingdom operates. He describes the disciple's role in manifesting it and the amazing rewards for perfecting the metaphorical craft of a disciple who cultivates kingdom fruit like a successful farmer.

Here is the parable in its entirety, followed by Jesus' explanation of its meaning. It is twenty verses long, but easy to read, easy to understand, and well worth it.

*Again Jesus began to teach beside the lake. And a very great crowd gathered about Him, so that He got into a ship in order to sit in it on the sea, and the whole crowd was at the lakeside on the shore. And He taught them many things in parables (illustrations or comparisons put beside truths to explain them), and in His teaching He said to them: Give attention to this! Behold, a sower went out to sow. And as he was sowing, some seed fell along the path, and the birds came and ate it up. Other seed [of the same kind] fell on ground full of rocks, where it had not much soil; and at once it sprang up, because it had no depth of soil; and when the sun came up, it was scorched, and because it had not taken root, it withered away. Other seed [of the same kind] fell among thorn plants, and the thistles grew and pressed together and utterly choked and suffocated it, and it yielded no grain. And other seed [of the same kind] fell into good (well-adapted) soil and brought forth grain, growing up and increasing, and yielded up to thirty times as much, and sixty times as much, and even a hundred times as much as had been sown. And He said, He who has ears to hear, let him be hearing [and let him consider, and comprehend].*

*And as soon as He was alone, those who were around Him, with the Twelve [apostles], began to ask Him about the parables. And He said to them, To you has been entrusted the mystery of the kingdom of God [that is, the secret counsels of God which are hidden from the ungodly]; but for those outside [of our circle] everything becomes a par-*

### RECONSIDER
Jesus said to him, No one who puts his hand to the plow and looks back [to the things behind] is fit for the kingdom of God.

~ Luke 9:62, AMP

*able, in order that they may [indeed] look and look but not see and perceive, and may hear and hear but not grasp and comprehend, lest haply they should turn again, and it [their willful rejection of the truth] should be forgiven them. [See Isaiah 6:9–10 and Matthew 13:13–15.]*

*And He said to them, Do you not discern and understand this parable? How then is it possible for you to discern and understand all the parables? The sower sows the Word. The ones along the path are those who have the Word sown [in their hearts], but when they hear, Satan comes at once and [by force] takes away the message which is sown in them. And in the same way the ones sown upon stony ground are those who, when they hear the Word, at once receive and accept and welcome it with joy; and they have no real root in themselves, and so they endure for a little while; then when trouble or persecution arises on account of the Word, they immediately are offended (become displeased, indignant, resentful) and they stumble and fall away. And the ones sown among the thorns are others who hear the Word; then the cares and anxieties of the world and distractions of the age, and the pleasure and delight and false glamour and deceitfulness of riches, and the craving and passionate desire for other things creep in and choke and suffocate the Word, and it becomes fruitless. And those sown on the good (well-adapted) soil are the ones who hear the Word and receive and accept and welcome it and bear fruit – some thirty times as much as was sown, some sixty times as much, and some [even] a hundred times as much.*

*~ Mark 4:1–20,* AMP

## THOUGHTS ON THE MYSTERY, JOY, AND REWARDS OF DISCIPLING UP LIKE A SOLDIER, ATHLETE, OR FARMER

The parable of the sower is so rich in insight and implication, we could dedicate an entire chapter to it and not exhaust all the revelation it contains. We don't have room to do that, but let me draw your attention to a few aspects.

Can you imagine God openly disclosing to you the mysteries of His kingdom, how it works, and, most importantly, His thoughts and intents behind creating everything in the first place?

This is one of the great privileges of anyone willing to become more than a casual observer of the things of God. It's one of the great rewards of being a disciple – being considered a friend of God and knowing the Master's business:

> *You are my friends if you do what I command* ‹**the instructions He gives**›. *I no longer call you servants, because a servant does not know his master's business. Instead, I have called you friends, for everything that I learned from my Father I have made known to you.*
>
> ~ John 15:14–15

This kind of intimacy, disclosure, and complete openness between God and His disciples distinguishes the relationship from all others.

For example, consider how Jesus spoke to the disciples versus how He spoke to the crowd, starting in verse 10 of the parable we just visited. Jesus always spoke with the disciples openly, but to others he spoke in parables. Consider how everything Jesus spoke from verse 10 forward, the crowd did not hear.

In fact, had the Bible not given us the unique perspective we have today, previously reserved only for Jesus' closest disciples or friends, we wouldn't have the benefit of knowing Jesus' thoughts and intents behind the parable, either.

The crowd was in the same meeting, heard the same message, and saw the same supernatural demonstrations as the disciples did, but the crowd didn't get the benefit of hearing Jesus' private thoughts and intents behind what He spoke and did.

This was not an isolated incident, either. Private disclosures like this were frequent between Jesus and His disciples.

It's the same way today. This kind of intimate training and full disclosure is reserved only for those who are fully committed and willing to follow the Master Teacher as a disciple.

This is also another important aspect of the "greatness of smallness" found in an *ekklesia* versus a larger congregational approach to equipping individual people. There are things you just cannot share with a crowd of people who are all at various stages of interest, commitment, maturity, and qualification in the kingdom that you can share with an individual or small group with whom you are in the trenches of life.

The kind of intimacy, training, and disclosure of the greatest mysteries of the kingdom is always reserved for and entrusted to individuals and small groups of disciples, not crowds. Jesus said it this way:

> And He said to them ‹**the disciples**›, To you has been entrusted the mystery of the kingdom of God [that is, the secret counsels of God which are hidden from the ungodly]; but for those outside [of our circle] everything becomes a parable.
>
> ~ Mark 4:11, AMP

According to one resource, the Greek word *musterion,* translated in English as *mystery,* means "a kind of secret information revealed on a need-to-know basis." The word was often used in the context of a commanding officer communicating to a soldier in the field.

I can't think of a better description for the kind of communication and disclosure Jesus offers His disciples than comparing it to that of a commanding officer with his soldiers in the field.

In addition, I can think of few incentives greater than the ability to talk openly and be mentored directly by the King of kings, Lord of lords, and Father of all creation.

How awesome to be the benefactor of every bit of insider information you will ever need to know, exactly when you need it, in order to equip you to achieve the highest good as an ambassador of the kingdom of God on earth!

It's only the disciple God allows to steward such greatest mysteries (1 Cor. 4:1–2). As exciting as that is, it's equally true that, like anyone in any area of life entrusted with high levels of non-public information, it requires us to be mature and capable of handling it.

The very nature of being a disciple in this context requires that someone prove themselves capable of administering the things of God in tough situations. Can you imagine giving someone access to the most top-secret information on US national security, who has never so much as held an administrative position of trust? Of course not. That kind of disclosure is usually reserved for military veterans who have proven themselves in battle conditions and have increased in rank over time.

In the same way, Jesus shared more and more information with His disciples as they increased in their ability to handle it.

As glorious as the disciples' relationship with Jesus was, it was difficult at times, and they all suffered because of the trust they put in Him.

**RECONSIDER**

Do your best to present yourself to God as one approved, a workman who does not need to be ashamed and who correctly handles the word of truth.
~ 2 Tim. 2:15

For to this end we both labor and suffer reproach, because we trust in the living God, who is the Savior of all men, specially of those who believe.
~ 1 Tim. 4:10, NKJV

Because he preferred to share the oppression [suffer the hardships] and bear the shame of the people of God rather than to have the fleeting enjoyment of a sinful ‹*separated, missing the mark*› life.
~ Heb. 11:25, AMP

This suffering is something they willfully chose to endure and, in many cases, considered it a joy to choose such suffering above other pleasures (Col. 1:11, 24; Heb. 11:25; 2 Cor. 7:4).

But why?

Soldiers, athletes, and farmers, like disciples, are not expected to endure suffering or hardness for its own sake. Like boot camp, going to the gym, or the difficulty of initially plowing a field, the hardness or resistance is always temporary. The benefits, however, are long-lasting – even eternal – though it doesn't always feel like it at the time.

For me, being willing to set aside my own personal desires to follow and obey the Holy Spirit's leading can at times seem like suffering, both physically and emotionally. But just like a well-trained and disciplined soldier, athlete, or farmer, I have found the rewards of winning always outweigh the rigors of the training.

Jesus Himself was not even immune to this kind of suffering:

*Although He was a Son, He learned [active, special] obedience through what He suffered [resistance or hardness] and, [His completed experience] making Him perfectly [equipped], He became the Author and Source of eternal salvation to all those who give heed and obey Him [Isaiah 45:17], being designated and recognized and saluted by God as High Priest after the order (with the rank) of Melchizedek [Psalm 110:4]. Concerning this we have much to say which is hard to explain, since you have become dull in your [spiritual] hearing and sluggish [even slothful in achieving spiritual insight]. For even though by this time you ought to be teaching others, you actually need someone to teach you over again the very first principles of God's Word. You have come to need milk, not solid food. For everyone who continues to feed on milk is obviously inexperienced and unskilled in the doctrine of righteousness (of conformity to the divine will in purpose, thought, and action), for he is a mere infant [not able to talk yet]! But solid food is for full-grown men, for those whose senses and mental faculties are trained by practice to discriminate and distinguish between what is morally good and noble and what is evil and contrary either to divine or human law.*

*~ Hebrews 5:8–14,* AMP

Notice how Jesus was made perfect and increased in rank by suffering and enduring hardness. In this sense, He was our example, and if we want to be conformed to His image, we must willfully submit to the same kind of training.

I'm not talking about going to the cross – that was a different kind of suffering altogether and uniquely required of Jesus. It was not required of His disciples.

As a result, when you think of the kind of suffering or hardness required to become a disciple, you must think in terms of going to the gym, not going to a hospital or a torture chamber.

What if everyone who called themselves a Christian in the world today committed to being trained and qualified as a disciple with the same determination and commitment required of special-forces soldiers, Olympic athletes, or successful farmers? What if everyone who called themselves a Christian maintained this kind of Christlike resolve to obtain His level of mastery? What if they exercised this level of mastery in their everyday lives and realms of influence to carry out the mission of the *ekklesia*?

What if committing to this kind of discipleship was the key to reproduce the miraculous results that Jesus and His first disciples did? Would you do it? If your answer is yes, the rest of this chapter is for you, and I promise, despite the training requirements, it's a joy!

## MATURE DISCIPLES DO IT FOR THE PURE JOY OF IT

Did you know Jesus did everything He did, even enduring the hardness of the cross, for the joy set before Him?

> *Let us fix our eyes on Jesus, the author and perfecter of our faith, who for the joy set before him endured the cross, scorning its shame, and sat down at the right hand of the throne of God.*
>
> ~ Hebrews 12:2

In the same way, anyone who is seriously committed to following Jesus as a disciple and performing at His level of mastery will need to find the same kind of intrinsic joy to motivate them. Like an Olympic athlete, they must keep their eyes fixed on the ultimate prize. They must be motivated by the same joy of high achievement to maintain the strength to continue and to endure the rigors of training to Christlike perfection.

Not only is joy one of the primary fruits of the Holy Spirit and a key indicator God is involved in a matter, the Bible actually says the joy of the Lord is our strength (Neh. 8:10). When someone has lost their joy, they are in a weakened condition and susceptible to losing their will to continue, burning out, and quitting. You simply can't sustain the kind of resolve needed to "disciple up" over time without joy.

The same kind of joy Jesus had was evident when the seventy disciples returned from being sent out on their first mission by Jesus:

> The seventy returned with **joy**, saying, Lord, even the demons are subject to us in Your name! And He said to them, I saw Satan ‹**the adversary**› falling like a lightning [flash] from heaven. Behold! I have given you authority and power to trample upon serpents and scorpions, and [physical and mental strength and ability] over all the power that the enemy [possesses]; and nothing shall in any way harm you.
>
> ~ Luke 10:17–19, AMP

What is so exciting about this verse is how these seventy disciples – not even the original twelve disciples – after being trained by Jesus for only a short time, go out and do the very same things Jesus did.

Can you imagine their delight to hear Jesus say, "You did it. I watched you bring down the adversary in a flash. And oh, by the way, you did it so well that I'm going to give you even more power and authority – so much so that nothing will in any way ever harm you!"

These seventy were executing the exact same mission Jesus came to accomplish:

> The reason the Son of God was made manifest (visible) was to undo (destroy, loosen, and dissolve) the works the devil [has done].
>
> ~ 1 John 3:8, AMP

Every gift God has ever given to mankind was designed to accomplish the same mission: equip disciples of Jesus to imitate Him as the Master Teacher, in order to maintain a holy, violent enmity against evil wherever it exists and to bring about freedom for the pure joy of seeing everyone liberated to enjoy love's ideal.

The disciples who are most likely to realize the joy of being rewarded as more than overcomers in all these things are disciples who succeed in mastering obedience as a first-class soldier, faithfulness like a skilled athlete, and stewardship like a diligent farmer to bring them about.

# DISCIPLE__RELATE

Before incorporating what we have learned to empower you as a disciple to rise up and change the world with the gospel in the next chapter, I want to recommend a two-part exercise.

## PART ONE

For the first part of this exercise, thoughtfully answer the following six questions. As you do, write things down in order of their personal priority to you.

Especially as it pertains to questions five and six, I strongly encourage you to write down the desires of your heart in these areas and the things that most delight you and make your joy complete. Resist the temptation to write what you think the desire of God's heart is for you or what you think He or others might prefer you to say.

Remember, God said He wants you to delight yourself in Him and that He would give you the "desires of your heart" – not only the desire of His heart for you (Ps. 37:4).

Of course, I am not saying God's desires are unimportant, but for the purpose of this exercise, I want you to consider your heart's desires and your personal delights. Here are the questions:

In terms of how we have defined the term, are you a disciple?

------------------------------------------------------------

------------------------------------------------------------

------------------------------------------------------------

------------------------------------------------------------

If not, what adjustments do you need to make in your life to become a disciple?

........................................................................

........................................................................

........................................................................

........................................................................

With respect to what it means to be and become a disciple, where do you see yourself at this stage in your own life and your relationship with Jesus as His follower: as a soldier mastering obedience, as an athlete mastering faithfulness, or as a farmer mastering stewardship?

........................................................................

........................................................................

........................................................................

........................................................................

If you already consider yourself a disciple, are there areas where you could "disciple up" with even greater resolve and determination? What are those areas?

........................................................................

........................................................................

........................................................................

........................................................................

What aspects of Jesus and His nature most excite and inspire you and make you want to emulate Him and aspire to His level of mastery?

........................................................................

........................................................................

........................................................................

........................................................................

When you think of those aspects, what specifically would you want Him to teach you if, for example, you had the benefit of having Him personally train you for the next three years like He did the original disciples?

........................................................................................................

........................................................................................................

........................................................................................................

........................................................................................................

Are you comfortable with your answers to all the above questions? If not, go back and take your time; there is no rush. The answers to your questions are important for the second part of the exercise.

To set up the second part of our exercise, I want to ask you to consider the following scenario.

Imagine I could arrange for Jesus to personally come train you, one on one, as a private instructor for the next three years. Jesus would literally become your private personal coach or tutor, like one you might hire if you went to an exclusive gym or boot camp. Unlike going to a costly gym or boot camp, however, if you were willing, He would just come and live with you full-time like a trainer would live with an elite celebrity or athletic superstar, but at no charge to you.

Now imagine, in addition to providing you with an extensive training manual, which contains a written version of all He will instruct you in, Jesus agrees to personally interpret it for you and offer His personal commentary.

To help you integrate His written instruction into every area of your own life, He also agrees to accompany you as you go about your daily life. He agrees to be with you on every errand, at every meeting, while you drive, eat, talk, and interact with others, or as you do mundane household activities. In every scenario, He is there to offer His private thoughts and perspective on everything you hear, see, and do in real time.

He also agrees to use the most advanced communication technology ever developed to enable you to be in constant contact with Him at all times, even when it's not appropriate for Him to be physically present.

This allows you to go about your daily life like a special-forces operative on a top-secret mission in constant contact with central command.

This technology allows Jesus' communications to operate like a wireless signal in your ear which, once you are dialed into it, constantly plays in the background of your mind, instructing you which way to go, what to say, how to act, and how to interpret every situation. You hear what He hears!

In addition to being able to hear His constant audible instructions, there is more. He deploys technology to project His thoughts like a television signal onto the back of your retina, giving you His perspective on everything – kind of like a heads-up display on the window to your own world. You see what He sees!

Having both an audio and visual feed allows you to navigate your own way, yet benefit from His perspective at the same time without it being overly distracting.

The overall combination of written, audible, and visual instruction, along with just having Jesus present with you every minute of every day creates a kind of immersion-style learning that accelerates your development. As you begin to adhere to Jesus' leading, others begin to notice you're different – even Christlike.

Eventually, you become so familiar with how Jesus talks, acts, and thinks that, nearing the end of the three-year period, you begin to anticipate what His instructions will be. You are now so familiar with His ways that they have become your own.

As Jesus watches you emulate Him and bring your own will into agreement with His with the need for less and less prompting, Jesus begins sending you out on your own.

You begin to notice that even without His physical presence, you perform equally well and produce results as stunning as Jesus Himself did.

The many private and public victories pale in comparison, however, to the joy of hearing Him laugh with you and say, "Well done!"

At this stage, you realize that the learning portion of your time with Jesus, though never ending, is changing as He begins to encourage you to go and make disciples and to encourage others to learn from Him in the same manner.

Now, what if this was not a hypothetical scenario at all but, in fact, reality and is possible for you to begin now?

Of course, everything I just described is the call of discipleship.

Isn't this scenario the exact same one the first twelve disciples, the next seventy disciples, and everyone who followed after them experienced? Why, then, don't more people experience this kind of scenario today or, in most cases, even think it's possible?

I believe the answer is the same today as it was in Jesus' time. Jesus said people simply did not have eyes open to see, ears open to hear, or minds renewed to comprehend the kingdom of God in a present-tense way.

As we discovered in the sin chapter exercise, it's sometimes hard for people to realize God is with them – right now.

Which brings me to the second portion of our exercise. The goal of the final part of our exercise is to help you develop spiritual eyes to see, spiritual ears to hear, and a renewal of your mind to comprehend the very present-tense reality of God leading you in your everyday life. After all, how can you truly become a disciple of Jesus and be taught personally by Him without that ability?

I know many people argue that all you need for that is a Bible, but I am not sure I agree. Jesus didn't just give His disciples the Torah and say, "Here, read this. It's all you'll ever need." In fact, they didn't even have a Bible as we know it today. The written Word of God is very important, but having a relationship directly with the Author is what gives the written Word context and meaning – it makes it come alive, literally making it the living Word.

So, to begin our exercise, I want to suggest a kind of survey. However, unlike the external survey we did in the "Christian" chapter, this one is internal – just between you and God.

Find a place to be alone with God where you have nothing to stimulate you externally for at least an hour. No people, no phones, no computers, and no audible or visual stimulation of any kind, except maybe some simple lighting or instrumental background music to eliminate any potential white noise.

Though our goal is to begin experientially reconnecting with God and sharpening our ability to hear, see, and interact with Him, I want to stress a couple of things before we start. For the purpose of this exercise, we are not going to be praying, *per se,* in terms of how prayer is traditionally taught. And though it's entirely possible, we are not going to be focused on trying to hear an audible voice with our natural ears or looking for a physical vision with our natural eyes. I am also not going to be asking you to meditate in the traditional sense of the word, where the goal is to empty your mind of all conscious thought. Instead, I am going to invite you to do something the Bible calls *learning to imagine.*

## PART TWO: IMAGINATION

Once you are settled into a comfortable seated or lying down position, I want you to be still for a few minutes.

With your eyes closed, begin paying attention to any images you see in your mind's eye, so to speak. No matter how trivial they appear, I want you to notice the images.

Depending on how naturally imaginative you are or how your mind was stimulated before this exercise, you may see a lot of fairly random images or what may seem like nothing at all except dots of fleeting light. Both are normal. Just be still and, with your eyes closed, continue to note the images for a few minutes, even if the only image you see is the back of your eyelids.

Once you are comfortable in your surroundings and are focused on seeing images in your mind, with your eyes still closed, simply ask Jesus out loud to manifest Himself to you and to come meet with you. That's it; nothing more. Just ask and then continue to note the images.

Now, as you continue with your eyes closed, begin to imagine Jesus approaching you in your mind's eye.

Imagine Him reaching out to you and inviting you to take His hand to walk with Him somewhere. Take your time and let the image develop.

Once you can see Jesus clearly, begin to imagine walking alongside Him and talking with Him in whatever setting that comes to your mind. It could be a beach, along a stream, in the woods, in the mountains, or in your own home or neighborhood. It doesn't matter where you begin; the possibilities are literally infinite.

If for any reason you get distracted and lose your ability to see, don't worry. Just go back to where you left off and begin again.

As you continue to imagine Jesus walking with you, begin taking notice of where you are and where you are going with Him. Notice what He is doing. What is He saying to you, if anything?

If you don't see an image or a setting clearly at first, don't be alarmed. This is called an exercise for a reason. Just keep at it.

As you develop the ability to imagine in more detail and your ability to see and hear increases, begin to take notice of the perspective or viewpoint from which you are interacting with Jesus.

For example, are you seeing yourself interacting with Him from a third-person perspective, like watching yourself in a movie? Or are you imagining yourself interacting with Him more in the first person, as if you were looking at Him out of your own two eyes? The answer can provide insight to the level of intimacy with which you are beginning your interaction.

I have done this exercise almost daily for several years, and I have noticed that my perspective or viewpoint, in terms of how I see and interact with God, has changed slightly. When I first began this exercise, I almost always imagined myself interacting with Him from a third-person perspective. Over time, however, I noticed my perspective changed to be more face to face. More recently, I noticed my perspective has shifted, and it's as though I am looking at images through His eyes at times, as opposed to only my own.

I am amazed how God has used this simple imagination exercise as the starting place to teach me how to see and hear Him in a much more clear way. What started only as an exercise before bed became a regular part of my day and the model for how I learned to see, hear, and discern God's leading and instruction in every aspect of my life. We have since taught countless others to do the same thing.

I recall how we used the same method to teach our seven- and eight-year-old children when they asked how to hear and see God when they pray. I asked them to close their eyes and think of a physical place they have been in the last few days. I suggested they think of a place where they had the most fun and then tell me what it was. They immediately thought of an outdoor skate park near our home.

With their eyes still closed, I asked them to describe it to me in as much detail as they could remember. Of course, they went on for five minutes, describing every ramp and each person they encountered as if reliving it again in intricate detail.

I asked them if the skate park was a real, physical place, to which, of course, they replied emphatically, "Yes, Dad."

I then asked, "But are you physically there right now, guys, as you sit on our couch in our living room?" Of course, the answer was no.

So my next question was, "How did you get to the skate park and see those people from here, then?" They answered, "We just imagined it, Dad!"

I finished with explaining that heaven is a real place and Jesus is a real person, and to initially begin to see them both, you do the exact same thing – you first begin to imagine it. They immediately got the correlation and have been growing in their ability to see and hear God since – and with amazing accuracy, I might add.

I recall one instance when at an Outback Steakhouse, the imagination we had was that Jesus was explaining He loved our waitress and that she had just received unexpected news today and was no longer expecting. When our waitress came to the table, in the course of a normal conversation, we asked her if, in fact, she had gotten any unexpected news today and was no longer expecting.

To everyone's amazement, her mouth dropped open and she burst into tears. She later explained that while she was driving into work, she had learned that her mother was diagnosed with a terminal form of cancer. We immediately agreed to pray for her mother's healing.

I then asked if she was no longer expecting, but she acted as if she had no idea what I was talking about.

Given her response, we just left it at that and assumed we had missed it and that, unlike the first part, maybe that part was only our vain imagination.

A few minutes later, after returning to the table from a quick trip to the kitchen, the waitress was even more visibly moved and now shaking. When I asked her what was wrong, she said she was just overwhelmed that we would know that kind of information and that God would reach out to her in that way.

We encouraged her to keep contending for her mom's healing and simply reaffirmed God's love for her. We then laughed and explained to her how we really only got half the information right anyway and were still growing in our ability to hear God.

At that moment, she looked faint and asked to sit down at our table. She then said, "No. You didn't. I am also no longer expecting. I recently had an abortion, and nobody except the people at the clinic who performed the procedure knows about it."

This is just one example of hundreds I could share where taking the time to first imagine what God would think, say, or do in a situation turned out to be a literal vision of what God did do and say.

To some people, the idea of using your imagination doesn't seem like a biblical concept. The term conjures up thoughts (which, of course, are in and of themselves an imagination) of leading someone off into a kind of new-age trance.

However, despite how the term has been hijacked by inferior forms of meditation, imagining is a very sound biblical notion.

How would a person ever recognize the "immeasurably more than they can ask or imagine" (Eph. 3:20) if they never imagined in the first place? Or, as we discussed in the disciple-as-soldier section of this chapter, how could you be expected to "cast down every vain imagination that exalts itself against the knowledge of God" if you never had an imagination in the first place? The answer to both of these questions is, of course, you can't.

In an attempt to demystify the concept, the word *imagine* as used in this verse, and found many other places in the Bible, simply means "to revolve something around in your mind."

The same Greek word translated *imagine* is also translated several times as *meditate* (1 Tim. 4:15, NKJV) and sometimes *premeditate* (Mark 13:11, NKJV).

Certainly, nobody would argue that Jesus didn't pray or meditate on the things of God. When Jesus was physically on earth and said He only did what He saw His Father do and only said what He heard His Father say (John 5:19), how did He do that? How did He hear, exactly? How was it that He could close His eyes and see into heaven?

Said another way, how did Jesus train the eyes of His heart to see what the Father was doing in heaven while He was on earth? How exactly did He learn to distinguish between what the Bible says was His own will, literally meaning His own internal inclinations or imaginations, and the will of his Father (John 6:38)? Remember, the Bible is clear: Jesus didn't have any advantage over us in this regard.

It seems strange to people to think Jesus had an imagination or that He had to revolve things around

> **REMEMBER**
> Now to him who is able to do immeasurably *more than all we ask or imagine, according to his power that is at work within us, to him be glory in the church ‹ekklesia› and in Christ Jesus throughout all generations, for ever and ever!* Amen.
>
> ~ Eph. 3:20–21,

381

in His mind to learn to distinguish His own thoughts and desires from God's, but He did.

Jesus was not all-knowing at birth. To the contrary, He grew up in these things and had to learn how to walk in obedience and agreement with God, just like His disciples did and just like we have to today.

Now, to be clear, I am not suggesting that conversations between God and Jesus were or are a figment of a person's imagination. What I am saying is that the process of a disciple learning to be led by the Holy Spirit and the ability to see and hear God directly is the same as having an imagination.

I don't think of my imagination as the goal but as the bridge that extends my ability to experience the reality of God and His kingdom beyond what I can see with my natural eyes. My imagination is a low-level vision that sets the stage for God to do exceedingly above what I can imagine. A properly developed imagination is a powerful tool and can play a critical role in connecting a person's heart to their head.

Sure, there are vain imaginations (Acts 4:25), but one part of growing up as a disciple is learning to tell the difference and keeping your mind fixed on what is God, ignoring what is not. If the imagination was not important, why do enemies of God spend so much time, money, and energy trying to capture the imagination of people?

Think about how all different forms of media – advertisements, movies, videos, music, games, and so much of life – compete for people's attention and use the imagination to pull us deeper into a relationship with their product, offering, or agenda. In the same way the enemy can use a person's imagination to pull a person into an inferior relationship, God can use the imagination to draw a person into a deeper relationship with Him!

Learning to properly use your imagination, or, as the Bible says it, meditate on the things of God, is an essential starting place for learning how to see God, hear God, and follow God's leading to mature as a disciple.

Learning to be taught by God to align your thoughts, will, emotions, and actions with His using the precision of the most disciplined soldier or highly skilled athlete is the key to completing the first phase of training as a disciple.

RECONSIDER
Finally, brothers,
whatever is true,
whatever is noble,
whatever is right,
whatever is pure,
whatever is lovely,
whatever is admirable –
if anything is excellent
or praiseworthy – think
about such things.
Whatever you have
learned or received
or heard from me, or
seen in me – put it into
practice. And the God of
peace will be with you.

~ Phil. 4:8–9

# DISCIPLE__REACT

Top three things you are taking away from this chapter:

........................................................................................................

........................................................................................................

........................................................................................................

........................................................................................................

........................................................................................................

........................................................................................................

........................................................................................................

........................................................................................................

What action can you take now using what you've learned?

........................................................................................................

........................................................................................................

........................................................................................................

........................................................................................................

........................................................................................................

........................................................................................................

........................................................................................................

........................................................................................................

........................................................................................................

........................................................................................................

The battle plan's a mystery

You give it on the need to know

You draw nearer to me saying

Perfect love is what this ground was

meant to grow, oh, oh,

It seems half together

There's broken pieces all around

Your love is the anchor

That keeps me tied to higher ground

You keep me tied to higher ground

– BATTLEGROUND –

*Lyrics by Kevin Weaver It's Feasible Publishing, LLC*

Download the complete lyrics and an .mp3 version of this
song in its entirety at www.thereorientbook.com.

# GOSPEL

# What's your REACTION to the word?

⊕ Positive

⊖ Negative

◎ Neutral

# What does the word MEAN TO YOU?

_____

_____

_____

_____

_____

_____

_____

_____

_____

_____

Now let's see what others say. ▶

The way people surveyed
reacted to the word GOSPEL.

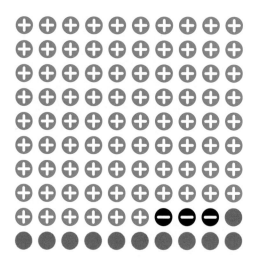

85.51%
Positive

03.18%
Negative

11.31%
Neutral

See a video of respondants in the Resource section for this chapter at www.reorientbook.com.

Common words people surveyed
associated with the word GOSPEL.

WORD OF GOD
TRUTH
STORY OF JESUS
HOPE MISSION
NEW TESTAMENT
GOOD
MATTHEW
MARK
LUKE &
JOHN
PROPAGANDA
NEWS
BIBLE
OUTDATED
MUSIC
JESUS
NOT ASHAMED
TEACHING
SALVATION
WAY TO
HEAVEN

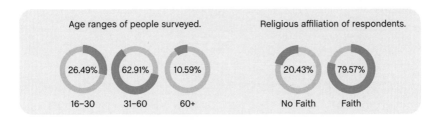

Age ranges of people surveyed.

26.49%   62.91%   10.59%

16–30   31–60   60+

Religious affiliation of respondents.

20.43%   79.57%

No Faith   Faith

# GOSPEL__REDISCOVER

## OLD TESTAMENT HEBREW WORDS FOR GOSPEL

USED   *24 times*

WORD   BASAR */baw´-sar/*

DEFINITION   *To announce glad news, preach, publish, show forth, bear, bring, carry, tell good tidings, be a messenger*

---

## NEW TESTAMENT GREEK WORDS FOR GOSPEL

USED   *More than 75 times*

WORD   EUAGGELION */yoo-ang-ghel´-ee-on/*

DEFINITION   *Good spell or message*

# GOSPEL__RECOUNT

# GOSPEL

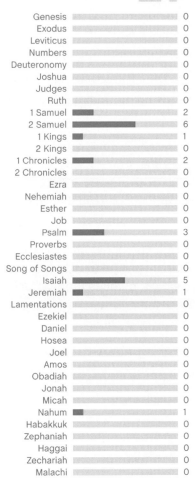

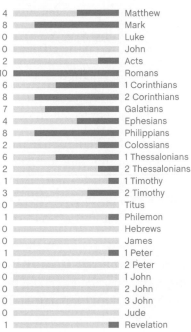

OLD TESTAMENT VERSES
USING THE HEBREW WORD

**21**

NEW TESTAMENT VERSES
USING THE GREEK WORD

**74**

|  |  |
|---|---|
| Genesis | 0 |
| Exodus | 0 |
| Leviticus | 0 |
| Numbers | 0 |
| Deuteronomy | 0 |
| Joshua | 0 |
| Judges | 0 |
| Ruth | 0 |
| 1 Samuel | 2 |
| 2 Samuel | 6 |
| 1 Kings | 1 |
| 2 Kings | 0 |
| 1 Chronicles | 2 |
| 2 Chronicles | 0 |
| Ezra | 0 |
| Nehemiah | 0 |
| Esther | 0 |
| Job | 0 |
| Psalm | 3 |
| Proverbs | 0 |
| Ecclesiastes | 0 |
| Song of Songs | 0 |
| Isaiah | 5 |
| Jeremiah | 1 |
| Lamentations | 0 |
| Ezekiel | 0 |
| Daniel | 0 |
| Hosea | 0 |
| Joel | 0 |
| Amos | 0 |
| Obadiah | 0 |
| Jonah | 0 |
| Micah | 0 |
| Nahum | 1 |
| Habakkuk | 0 |
| Zephaniah | 0 |
| Haggai | 0 |
| Zechariah | 0 |
| Malachi | 0 |

| Count | New Testament |
|---|---|
| 4 | Matthew |
| 8 | Mark |
| 0 | Luke |
| 0 | John |
| 2 | Acts |
| 10 | Romans |
| 6 | 1 Corinthians |
| 8 | 2 Corinthians |
| 7 | Galatians |
| 4 | Ephesians |
| 8 | Philippians |
| 2 | Colossians |
| 6 | 1 Thessalonians |
| 2 | 2 Thessalonians |
| 1 | 1 Timothy |
| 3 | 2 Timothy |
| 0 | Titus |
| 1 | Philemon |
| 0 | Hebrews |
| 0 | James |
| 1 | 1 Peter |
| 0 | 2 Peter |
| 0 | 1 John |
| 0 | 2 John |
| 0 | 3 John |
| 0 | Jude |
| 1 | Revelation |

*Graph is based on the highest
verse use and shown visually as
a percentage of the highest value.

# GOSPEL__REORIENT

It was July 4, and I was seated along a picturesque main street in a small midwestern town with my family and a few friends. Waiting for the start of the Independence Day parade, there was joy and excitement in the air. Fire engines were beginning to sound their sirens and the symbolic sounds of marching bands and the smell of kettle corn and smoked turkey legs filled the small downtown area.

Kids were perched like cheetahs on their haunches, ready to pounce at the first sign of candy being tossed from the oncoming floats. The rest of us waited to see the familiar hand-waving captains of floats featuring local politicians, businesses, and nonprofit organizations that had chosen this day to celebrate America's independence – and, of course, not so subtly advertise their reason for existing.

Since the population of the town we were visiting was only about 1,300 people, the parade was by no means on par with a Macy's Day spectacular, but to our three young children, it was just as exciting.

As the floats began streaming by, I couldn't help noticing that something about the parade seemed different this year. The parade was abnormally short – the down economy causing local schools and businesses to cut their budgets and consequent participation in local festivities. But that wasn't the main difference I noticed.

The main difference was the unusually high number of churches with floats in the parade. Maybe it was the absence of other businesses and organizations that amplified their presence or perhaps there actually were more than I remembered from past years. Either way, this year it seemed that nearly every other float was by a church.

Of course, in and of itself, that wasn't troubling. Actually, I was excited that so many churches had made such an intentional effort to make themselves known.

As I began to compare their individual slogans and themes, I noticed that though each church expressed it in a slightly different way, each one seemed to herald the same basic message:

"We fulfill the Great Commission by going into all the world and preaching the gospel to save the lost and reach the city, nation, and world for Christ."

Each message was underscored by an invitation to join the church in their efforts and be part of their local gathering. Of course, this was all reinforced by the obligatory four-fingered parade wave from those atop the float, a handshake by a person on the ground, and a smattering of candy to keep the kids engaged.

As I watched church after church pass by, I began to wonder about the goal they had for participating in the parade.

Was it to advertise their existence?

Was it to make people aware of their mission?

Was it fulfilling the church's Great Commission?

Was it the "go preach the gospel" part of that commission?

Was it simply a way for church members to participate in the festivities?

Was it celebrating what the church's mission efforts had accomplished that year?

Was there no point at all?

These questions opened the floodgates of my mind. I remember thinking, *If the goal is to make themselves known, how is the casual observer supposed to distinguish one church from another?* After all, they each had the same basic mission statement.

If participating in the parade was a way of fulfilling the Great Commission, what gospel message were they communicating to the Independence Day revelers?

And who was the gospel preaching intended to reach among the crowd? Was it the lost people in the crowd, as so many of the banners indicated? If so, and if the gospel message successfully found its intended mark, what would be the resulting fruit of the effort? How would the church know their decision to invest time and effort into this parade had paid off?

If someone was lost among the crowd, would they know it? How would they know? If someone did know it, would the lost person call the church and say, "Hey, I saw your float and I realized I am lost. Can you help me get saved?" Once they got saved, what would be next for them? Would they be on the float next year, celebrating their salvation and fulfilling the same gospel mission to help others get saved?

I wondered how long it would take each local church body to know when their mission was complete and they had successfully reached their city, the nation, and the world with their gospel. Assuming the goal of the Great Commission is to get people saved, what would a city, nation, or world of saved people look like? Is there a saved city on the planet we could look to as the model?

I then wondered about the small town itself. What had been the impact of the gospel message preached by the ninety-plus churches listed in the local directory of this county of less than forty thousand?

I knew that I needed to be careful to avoid the subtle trap of judgment and bitterness that can so easily mask itself as divine revelation.

In this particular instance, that was easy: I was acquainted with people who both oversaw and attended many of those same churches, and I considered them to be sincere, good, honorable, and well-intentioned people.

But from that point forward, however, whenever I heard the term *gospel* in any context, similar questions surfaced. They prompted study and reflection that led me to:

A better perspective of what I now believe was really wrong with the July 4 picture,

A reoriented view of the real meaning and implications of the word *gospel,*

A reoriented view of the rarely communicated gospel Jesus actually preached,

A reoriented view of the role mankind plays in causing the gospel to have its full effect,

A reoriented view of the gospel's role in the so-called Great Commission,

A discovery about the implications of the real gospel that convinced me most people in the world have never heard the gospel,

A revelation about the traditional way the gospel is presented, revealing that its presentation may be one of the biggest sins of all time!

Are you ready to reorient to the gospel?

## THE PROBLEM WITH THE GOSPEL AS WE KNOW IT

In retrospect, the most unsettling thing about that July 4 parade for me was the obvious disparity between the promises of the gospel as presented, compared with the reality it appeared to be producing in the individual lives of people and the community as a whole.

The primary promise of the gospel, in the most basic and elementary terms and as traditionally presented, is essentially this: people are eternally lost, meaning because of sin they are estranged from God. The gospel, or good news, then, is a message about how Jesus loves them, died on a cross for them, and made a way for them to be "saved," meaning they go to heaven when they die.

An added implied bonus which, depending on your denominational view, may not always be clearly explained in quantifiable terms – is that a better life now will also result.

The implied social outcome of this approach to the gospel is that as more people in a city, a nation, and the world hear the gospel, get saved, and begin experiencing a better life, the cities, nations, and the world we live in become a better place.

But does it? There were more than ninety churches in that small mid-western area preaching some version of what they called the gospel. And yet, by most observable metrics, you would be hard-pressed to say the community or the surrounding area was measurably better off than most any other city of comparable size in the United States.

So, what is wrong with this picture?

That question was the title of the first chapter of *An Introduction to the Old Testament Template*, written by Landa Cope.[54] In it, she tells of happening across a television program hosted by a British journalist about the most Christianized city in America. As Landa explains, she tuned in at the exact moment the commentator was saying:

> "Christians believe that many of their members being in a community will affect that community for good. The greater the Christian presence, then the greater the benefit to the society at large."

As Landa writes, the commentator went on to propose they look at the most Christianized city in the United States – meaning "the city with the largest percentage of believers that attended church regularly" – to see how this influence works out practically.

To my surprise, that city was Dallas, Texas, where apparently more people go to church on any given Sunday per capita than in any other city in America.

In an attempt to determine the practical impact the gospel was having on the community, the program makers proposed comparing demographic data from Dallas with that of less Christianized cities. The kind of data considered included:

| | | |
|---|---|---|
| Crime rate statistics | Healthcare statistics | Income level statistics |
| Education statistics | Homelessness statistics | Infant mortality rates |
| Emergency room records | Hospital admission statistics | Infectious disease statistics |
| Graduation statistics | | |

| Job market statistics | Public safety statistics | Test scores |
|---|---|---|
| Law enforcement statistics | Racial equality statistics | Unemployment statistics |
| Other general economic indicators | School safety statistics | And so on |

According to the statistics, Dallas, the most Christianized city in the United States and what many locals call *the buckle of the Bible belt,* did not fare well. Dallas was one of the lowest-ranking cities in the nation providing core services to its residents, and it appeared that Christians and the gospel were having little positive impact on the condition of the city as a whole.

The journalist concluded the program by asking a group of Dallas-area pastors, who were known to be leaders with integrity and of some status in the community, what they thought of the data. In various ways, they all replied, "Those things do not concern us; we are spiritual leaders."

In her book, Landa expressed how this obvious disconnect produced the same kind of unsettling and head-scratching feelings in her that I had experienced during my Independence Day observations.

I wasn't armed with the same kind of statistical data used in the Dallas study that Landa responded to. I did grow up in the community I observed, however, and having firsthand experience with the demographic realities of that area, I intuitively knew the details to be equally dismal, if not worse.

Since joining Youth With A Mission (YWAM) in 1971, Landa has become a recognized expert on world missions, having spoken and worked in more than 110 nations.[55] She is the founding international dean of the College of Communication for YWAM's University of the Nations and is the founder of the Template Institute.

Her work in the global mission field allowed her to apply the same criteria used in the Dallas study to observe the practical effects of the gospel as we know it in other nations of the world.

She chronicles one trip in particular, which included traversing the western, eastern, and southern parts of Africa, visiting many of the most "Christianized" nations, which included Togo, Ghana, Nigeria, Kenya, Uganda, and South Africa.

She recounts the conflict she endured while reconciling her dwindling belief that it takes only twenty percent of a society believing anything to influence, even lead, the other eighty percent in a given direction and how encouraging that made the mission statistics she often quoted:

"Africa, 80 percent Christian south of the Sahara by the end of the twentieth century."

"Africa, the most evangelized continent in the world."

"Africa, the most churched continent by the end of this century."

But her sobering conclusion was:

> in each nation, the story was the same: poverty, disease, violence, corruption, injustice and chaos met me at every turn. I found myself asking: "Is this Thy Kingdom come, Thy will be done on earth as it is in heaven"? Is this what the blessing of the gospel brought into a community looks like? Is this what a nation looks like when it is "reached"? In this southern part of Africa, we have nearly reached every person. Churches are planted and full. African evangelists abound and continue the work. Is this what it looks like when our work as Christians is finished in a nation? God forbid! My anguish increased ...
>
> My heart was heavy as I traveled Africa, as I thought about my own nation. My prayer became, "Lord, what has gone wrong?" Nearly two hundred years of concentrated mission effort on this continent – how could it result in this? With a dawning revelation that that would change my understanding of missions and my life calling, God

spoke simply, fundamentally, and permanently. "The devastation you see is the fruit of preaching salvation alone [the gospel of salvation], without the rest of the biblical message."[56]

What could possibly be wrong with the gospel of salvation? To borrow a phrase from Steven Covey, the answer is "simple but on the far side of complex." Why? Because in the simplest terms, there is technically nothing wrong with the gospel or salvation, at least in the ways they were originally defined. The problem, as with the other words we have looked at so far, is with the meaning and implication that tradition has ascribed to them.

## THE REAL MEANING OF THE GOSPEL AND THE GOOD NEWS THAT IT WAS ORIGINALLY MEANT TO COMMUNICATE

Have you ever been given a gospel tract? When you hear the word *gospel,* do you think of the Bible, the cross, and the sinner's prayer? Do you think of a type of religious music or envision someone preaching a fiery gospel sermon to get people saved so they go to heaven when they die?

Would it surprise you to learn that neither Jesus nor His disciples would have such associations with the gospel? To begin to reorient to the associations they would've had, let's look at the meaning of word *gospel* itself.

The modern dictionary defines it this way:

**Gospel**
*noun*
1. the teachings of Jesus and the apostles
2. the story of Christ's life and teachings, especially as contained in the first four books of the New Testament, namely Matthew, Mark, Luke, and John: collectively the Gospels
3. something regarded as true and implicitly believed: *the gospel truth*
4. a doctrine regarded as of prime importance: *political gospel*

5. glad tidings, especially concerning salvation and the kingdom of God as announced to the world by Christ

6. gospel music

*adjective*

1. of, pertaining to, or proclaiming the gospel or its teachings: *a gospel preacher*

2. in accordance with the gospel; evangelical

3. of or pertaining to gospel music: *a gospel singer.*

*Origin(s):*

before 950; ME *go(d)spell,* OE *gōdspell* (see good, spell); trans. of Gk *euangélion* good news; see *evangel*

When we asked people to share the first thing that came to mind upon hearing or seeing the word *gospel,* they told us:

| | | |
|---|---|---|
| Choir | One of the New Testament books of Matthew, Mark, Luke, or John | The Great Commission |
| Evangelism | | |
| Going to heaven | | The message of Jesus |
| Good | Preaching | The story of Jesus' life |
| Good message | Sermon | |
| Good news | The Bible | Truth |
| Music | The good news of salvation | Word of God |

## RECONSIDER

Fun with *gospel* word usages:[57]

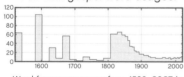

Word frequency usage from 1539–2007 in occurrences per 100,000 words per year

Phone Digits: (...) .46-7735

Crossword puzzle clues: God's honest truth, Grammy category

Scrabble Score: 9

As expected, our respondents' impressions of the word *gospel* were fairly consistent with how the modern dictionary defines the term.

The most frequent association with the word *gospel* was the title given to the four accounts of Jesus' life as recorded by Matthew, Mark, Luke, and John in the New Testament Bible – collectively, the Gospels.

When asked about the meaning of the gospel, the most frequent response was *good news* or a *good message.* It was most often associated with telling others about Jesus dying to save them from sin.

As we begin to reorient to the real meaning and implications of the gospel and then reassociate it with the real mission of an *ekklesia,* you will see why the author James Rutz said:

> ❝ *If Disney were going to make a movie about the modern church, they would call it* Honey, I Shrunk the Gospel! ❞

Knowing what I do now, I couldn't agree more. Limiting the gospel to the traditional notions of getting people saved to go to heaven alone has minimized the impact of the real gospel which is Jesus. Shrinking the gospel to the traditional notion of salvation alone has prevented it from having its full effect in the world. This one-dimensional approach is responsible for much, if not all, the grim statistical realities that most Christianized places on earth are experiencing.

The really good news (pun intended), however, is that if people will reorient to the original meaning of the gospel, it can unleash the supernatural power of God to reverse these same statistics.

To see what I mean, we need to go back and consider the origins of the word *gospel* and then separate the word from its traditional context.

According to the dictionary, the modern English word *gospel* is derived from an Old English word *gōd-spell,* sometimes spelled *gōd-spel,* and means "good news" or "glad tidings."

The Old English word was actually *good-spell,* but because of the long *o* sound and subsequent rendering of *gōd-spel* in English, it's believed *gōd,* which should be pronounced *good,* was mistakenly associated with *god,* and hence the evolution of the word *god-spell* over the original and more accurate rendering *good-spell.* The Old English translation *gōd-spel* was known as a calque – a word-for-word or verbatim translation of a word or phrase from one language to another.

Good-spell is a word-for-word translation in the New Testament of the Greek word *euaggelion* (pronounced yoo-ang-ghel'-ee-on) – *eu,* literally meaning "good," and *angelion,* meaning "spell" or "message." When combined, the two words, *eu-aggelion,* should read *good-spell* or *good-message,* not *God-spell* or *God-message.*

This may appear to be a slight distinction, but it's actually quite significant. Why? Because like the word *Christian,* which appears to most people today to be obviously derived from the word *Christ* when, in reality, it may have little or nothing in common with the word, the historical rendering of *god-spel,* minus the long o, has contributed to the word *gospel* being given a religious meaning and connotation that the evolutionary history – the context of its original meaning – doesn't support.

In its original context, the word *gospel* – and more specifically, the Greek word *euaggelion,* from which we derive our English word for *gospel* – had no such religious connotation and did not refer to the preaching of a specific message or even the message itself.

According to the first definition listed in the New Testament Greek lexicon, the Greek term interpreted in English as *gospel* was defined as "the reward of a good tiding or good message."

At first glance, this definition may not appear substantially different from the modern use of the word *gospel* taken to mean "a good message." To fully grasp the subtle but profound differences between the original definition of *euaggelion* and the traditional translation of the word, a different context is needed.

The Greek word *euaggelion,* translated as *gospel,* was used by the New Testament writers more than seventy-five times and was rarely found in writings outside the biblical text. However, its origins predate the biblical use.

In the same way the people in Jesus' day would not have thought of a modern-day church upon hearing the word *ekklesia,* but a kind of political, social, or military uprising or call to battle, people in Jesus' day did not have a religious context for the word we know now as gospel, let alone an immediate association with Jesus dying on a cross to make a way for them to go to heaven when they died.

That's because, like the word *ekklesia,* a *euaggelion,* or gospel message in the classical context most often pertained to matters of political or military significance and, occasionally, important wedding or birth announcements.

In its original classic context, the Greek word *euaggelion* would have conjured up images of an approaching runner, or what was called a *euaggelistes,* the Greek word for someone who brings or announces good news. In English, the same Greek word is translated *evangelist.*

As the runner (evangelist) approached and prepared to deliver or announce a gospel message, those preparing to receive it often referred to these messengers as *aggelos,* the Greek word for an envoy, messenger, or someone who announces, proclaims, or bears a message. In English, the same Greek word is translated *angel.*

The act of delivering a message of this nature was called *proeuaggelizomai,* (pronounced pro-yoo-ang-ghel-id'-zom), the Greek word used to describe speaking a message of gladness, proclaiming good news, or promising something. In English, the same Greek word is translated *evangelizing!*

Especially in the military, runners or evangelists of this nature were routinely authorized and ordained by higher-ranking political or military officers to deliver gospel messages to soldiers in the field or on the frontlines.

It's harder to image such a scenario today, as more modern means of communication have made this practice obsolete.

It's probably less difficult to imagine that being a military runner or evangelist of this kind was a dangerous job and not for immature or inexperienced soldiers. It almost always required leaving the safety of a headquarters, trench, bunker, or any other kind of shelter in order to move from one battlefront to another, many times through enemy territory.

When you think about the demands of the job, it is easy to see why military runners, as a unique combination of supreme athlete and elite warrior, were highly regarded as a special breed of soldier. You're probably already seeing why disciples, who were entrusted to deliver the gospel of the kingdom, have been likened to special-forces soldiers and Olympic-level athletes.

Just like Jesus' first disciples, military runners were often entrusted with delivering top-secret information of great social, political, and military importance. In many cases, it would dictate the outcome of a conflict. Gospel runners were often required to run great distances through difficult and dangerous terrain. In addition to the athletic demands of the job, they were required to push through enemy resistance, and subdue adversaries.

Upon arrival, they were expected to quickly compose themselves and deliver the gospel message exactly as instructed and consistent with how the commanding officers themselves would have delivered it.

For examples of these types of runners from more recent history, you might think of someone like Paul Revere.[58] Though he was not delivering a gospel message, *per se,* those familiar with early American history will recognize Paul Revere as a patriot from the American Revolution and a type of military runner. He was celebrated for his role as a messenger in the battles of Lexington and Concord, and he became most famous for his midnight ride that warned people of British troop movements and prepared Americans to rise up for battle.

You might also consider the role of military runners in World War I. The boots-on-the-ground, trench-style warfare needed to win this historic conflict required lots of runners.

Of course, at any time in history, the sight of an approaching runner (evangelist) with a gospel message was considered good news and welcome respite for soldiers still engaged in conflict, In many cases, the message pertained to a significant victory or ultimate triumph, indicating to soldiers in the field that the battle had already been won.

But as good as the sight of an approaching messenger was in this context or regardless of how good the announcement he carried promised to be, believe it or not, his message was not considered the best news. That's because even though the term *gospel* eventually became associated with the message itself, the term was never meant to refer to the message or its declaration of good news only.

The best part of the gospel that an evangelist was meant to deliver was the "reward" of the message the runner had been given the authority to deliver.

See, in addition to being a runner, or evangelist charged with delivering a gospel message, the gospel runner also carried the political and military authority and power to deliver the "spoils of war" from any preceding victory to those still fighting on the frontlines.

The delivery of the spoils of war was called the *promise* or *reward* of the message.

The present-tense reality of being able to receive the reward or promise contained in the gospel message meant that the gospel message carried not just good news but, in the words of Andrew Wommack, a well known Bible teacher, "nearly-too-good-to-be-true news."[59]

That is why the original definition of the Greek word *euaggelion,* or gospel, was "the reward of a good tiding or good message."


Are you catching this?


The gospel is not the message!

The gospel is the reward!

The gospel is not a message about victory!

The gospel delivers the spoils of war resulting from victory!

The good news of the gospel is the reward it carried and should never be limited to only the message. This means the reward of the real gospel is present tense and future tense and should never be limited only to a future promise. In other words, the gospel doesn't just promise something good – it actually brings it about in reality now!

To use a common English figure of speech, receiving the real gospel is like having one's cake and eating it, too. The implication is that you not only have been promised something good in the future, but you can have it and enjoy it fully now.

To a soldier in the field who is war-torn and battle-fatigued, it's good news to know a larger victory has been won and that you will receive some relief and potential rewards at a future time. It's even better news, though – *even nearly-too-good-to-be-true news* – to be rewarded and to benefit, partake, and enjoy those rewards now, in the present tense!

## A BIBLICAL VIEW OF THE CLASSIC NEARLY-TOO-GOOD-TO-BE-TRUE SOCIAL, POLITICAL, AND MILITARY GOSPEL

When I first began reorienting to this historical (some might say classical) version of the word *gospel* outside the traditional religious view of the word, I was filled with excitement to see how consistent it would be with how the Bible uses the term.

Did Jesus and His initial disciples think of the term in this way? Did they draw upon this classically understood meaning of the word *gospel* when communicating to people in their day?

After all, this classical version of the word *gospel* from the perspective of a runner delivering nearly-too-good-to-be-true news to soldiers in the field with rewards of social, political, and military consequence seems amazingly consistent with our discoveries so far about an *ekklesia* and what we learned it means to be a disciple, doesn't it?

When you think about love's ideal and how Jesus was trying to build an *ekklesia* (which, in and of itself, we've learned is an uprising – a call to battle of social, political, and military importance), and when you think about how Jesus' disciples were compared to Olympic runners and special-forces soldiers charged to bring about love's ideal for people who had not yet heard it was possible, doesn't it only make sense that the gospel message they were charged to deliver to the world would have a similar context?

The short answer is yes. The biblical use of the term *gospel* is consistent with the classical use of the term, and the implications are far-reaching.

Reorienting to the biblical meaning of the gospel in this classical context affects how;

You'll see the term and relate to it in daily life,

You'll understand the real goal of the so-called Great Commission,

You'll know who was charged with declaring the gospel to the world,

You'll expect the rewards given to those who receive it,

You'll see the nearly-too-good-to-be-true news the gospel was to deliver.

The first thing you notice as you research the term *gospel* in the biblical text is that it was not exclusively a New Testament concept.

In the Old Testament, the Hebrew word *basar* (pronounced baw-sar) was used more than twenty times and means "to announce glad news, preach, publish, show forth, bear, bring, carry, tell good tidings, be a messenger." The Hebrew word *basar* is most often translated *good news* or *good tidings*. It is used in identical context to the classical definition of *gospel* and is considered by scholars to be the Hebrew counterpart to the Greek word translated *gospel* in the New Testament.

For example, while speaking on the topic of the gospel in the New Testament book of Romans, the Apostle Paul said:

> *And how can they preach unless they are sent? As it is writ-*
> *ten, "How beautiful are the feet of those who bring **good***
> ***news ‹euaggelizo, or gospel›!"***
>
> ~ Romans 10:15, **emphasis added**

Paul's statement in this verse is a direct quote from the following Old
Testament verse, taken from the book of Isaiah:

> *How beautiful on the mountains are the feet of those who*
> *bring **good news ‹basar›**, who proclaim peace, who bring*
> ***good tidings ‹basar›,** who proclaim salvation, who say to*
> *Zion, "Your God reigns!"*
>
> ~ Isaiah 52:7, **emphasis added**

One prominent American Theologian, Dr. R. C. Sproul, provided this
commentary on these two verses:

> The reference to beautiful feet reflects the joyous an-
> ticipation of the watchman who is posted as a look-out
> for an approaching messenger. Without the benefit of
> (CNN), ancient people relied on the reception of reports
> by runners. The experienced watchman could discern
> the outcome of the message by the distant sight of the
> movement of the messenger's feet. If the runner appeared
> to be sluggard or plodding, it indicated the footsteps of
> despair – bad news. If the messenger's feet were flying,
> an obvious excitement and eagerness to complete the run,
> it signaled good news. Hence, the sight of the feet of the
> runner who brought good news was deemed "beautiful."[60]

I share this commentary for two reasons:

1.  It reflects and reinforces the kind of imagery the classical or origi-
    nal meaning of the gospel message was supposed to invoke in
    the hearer.

2.  In the same article, Dr. Sproul indicates that his preceding com-
    mentary was in response to a reference found in *Kittel's Theological
    Dictionary of The New Testament,* which described the Greek term
    translated *gospel* as being employed in antiquity for almost any

kind of good message or good tiding, such as the report of the outcome of a battle delivered by a "marathon runner."

Even the word *marathon* originated from a legend about a Greek messenger – a military runner named Pheidippides.[61] It's believed he was sent from the Battle of Marathon on a mission to deliver a message to the citizens of Athens regarding the Persian defeat around 490 BC. Legend holds that Pheidippides ran the entire distance without stopping and burst into the local assembly exclaiming, "We have won, we have won!" before he collapsed and died from exhaustion.

The route Pheidippides is believed to have taken matches the modern-day route of the Marathon to Athens highway, which is approximately 42 kilometers, or 26.2 miles – the current distance standard for an Olympic marathon. In honor of Pheidippides' legendary example of superhuman endurance and sacrifice to deliver a gospel message, in the classic sense, it has become the tradition of the modern Olympics to end the games with the men's marathon and a triumphant finish inside the Olympic stadium.

Given that the legend of Pheidippides was prominent in Greek culture for nearly five hundred years before, during, and after Jesus' time on earth, it's probable that the New Testament writers, especially Paul, drew upon the classical meaning of the term *gospel* when delivering the gospel message of the kingdom.

This classical context for the gospel not only adds a profound level of continuity to all the words we have covered so far – love, sin, religion, church, Christian, and disciple – but it also adds a richness, power, and practicality to so many verses in the New Testament.

Consider the classical context and implications of the gospel while reading the following two passages where Paul describes the gospel he was appointed to deliver to those who had not yet heard the good news and to whom the whole matter was a foreign concept:

> For [the proclaiming of] this [Gospel] ‹**the reward of good news**› I was appointed a herald (preacher) and an apostle (special messenger) and a teacher of the Gentiles ‹**a**

*foreign race or tribe, sometimes simply meaning a non-Jewish group of people*›.

~ 2 Timothy 1:11, AMP

Notice how Paul describes himself as being appointed to deliver the reward of good news as a special messenger to those who were foreigners – or, in other words, those who were unaware of it.

Or what about this reference:

*And I do this for the sake of the good news (the Gospel)* ‹**the reward of good news**›, *in order that I may become a participator in it and share in its [blessings along with you]. Do you not know that in a race all the runners compete, but [only] one receives the prize? So run [your race] that you may lay hold [of the prize] and make it yours.*

~ 1 Corinthians 9:23–24, AMP

Notice how Paul not only brings the reward of good news, but he also expresses his intent to share in its blessings and then encourages his readers to each become runners, to compete in order to lay hold of the prize and make it theirs.

A friend, Sam Soleyn, tells a story about a time he traveled in Greece and saw a mail truck with the word *Apostolos* written on the side. When Sam asked his Greek interpreter about the meaning of the word Apostolos, she smiled and said, "Oh, that's the mailman."

How amazing is that? Even in Greece today, the one who is sent to bring the mail or deliver messages to people is called the *apostolos,* or *apostle* in English.

## THE REAL GOSPEL MESSAGE JESUS AND HIS FOLLOWERS WERE SENT TO DELIVER THE REWARDS OF

Given the original context of the gospel, exactly what was the gospel message Jesus and His disciples evangelized the world with?

As we've already alluded, it was not the gospel of salvation, in terms of converting others to Christianity or getting people saved in order for them to go to heaven when they die.

Amazingly, especially given the emphasis on it in modern times, the phrase *gospel of salvation* is not even in the Bible, nor is the traditional notion of associating the gospel only with Jesus' death and resurrection to make a way for people to go to heaven.

This traditional understanding has historically and tragically reduced the gospel and the idea of getting saved in our modern age to a one-dimensional reward and benefit God never intended.

As the actual definition of the term implies, gospel can conceivably be applied to any kind of good message or good tiding in reference to or as an announcement of a reward or benefit to a hearer.

Even the New Testament writers were sometimes varied in their use of the term *gospel* and used several different qualifiers to the word, depending on the context of the message and the specific benefit of the gospel message they were trying to communicate.

Jesus and other New Testament writers used some nineteen unique qualifiers for the word *gospel:*

1. Gospel of the kingdom (Mark 1:14).

2. Gospel of Jesus Christ (Mark 1:1).

3. Gospel of the grace of God (Acts 20:24).

4. Gospel of His Son (Rom. 1:9).

5. Gospel of God (Rom. 15:16).

6. Gospel of your salvation (Eph. 1:13).

7. Gospel of uncircumcision (Gal. 2:7).

8. Gospel of peace (Eph. 6:15).

9. Gospel of our Lord Jesus Christ (2 Thess. 1:8).

10. Christ's gospel (2 Cor. 2:12).

11. Word of the gospel (Acts 15:7).

12. Mystery of the gospel (Eph. 6:19).

13. Faith of the gospel (Phil. 1:27).

14. Word of the truth of the gospel (Col. 1:5).

15. Hope of the gospel (Col. 1:23).

16. Glorious gospel of the blessed God (1 Tim. 1:11).

17. Afflictions of the gospel (2 Tim. 1:8).

18. Bonds of the gospel (Philem. 1:13).

19. Everlasting gospel (Rev. 14:6).

When considering this list, it surprises most people to discover that the New Testament writers used the word *salvation* only one time in connection with the word *gospel*. More surprising is discovering that the singular reference is to something called "the gospel of your salvation" and not "the gospel of salvation," as traditionally emphasized in modern culture.

Here's the verse from the Amplified Version of Bible:

> *In Him you also who have heard the Word of Truth, the glad tidings (Gospel) ‹**the promise or reward of a message**› of your salvation ‹**literally, in this context, of being rescued to safety**›, and have believed in and adhered to and relied on Him, were stamped with the seal of the long-promised Holy Spirit. That [Spirit] is the guarantee of our inheritance [the firstfruits, the pledge and foretaste, the down payment on our heritage], in anticipation of its full redemption and our acquiring [complete] possession of it – to the praise of His glory.*
>
> *~ Ephesians 1:13–14,* AMP

414

While this verse obviously uses the word *salvation* in reference to the gospel, it's not in the context of being saved to go to heaven when you die, though it could potentially include that.

Instead, the word *saved* in this verse actually means "being rescued" and "receiving a long-promised gift" – in this case, the Holy Spirit. Consistent with the classical definition of the gospel as being the reward of a good message, the Holy Spirit is the reward being given or promised in this verse, "the guarantee of our inheritance."

But there is even better news. The verse goes on to say that this initial reward of the gospel is only "the firstfruits, the pledge and foretaste, the down payment" until we acquire complete possession of it. The implication is that you not only get a reward now, but even more of a reward later.

Now, that's a good reward and certainly qualifies as good news, even nearly-too-good-to-be-true news. But that still was not the primary gospel Jesus or His followers declared to the world. That's because the gospel Jesus most often spoke about and charged others with preaching to the world was called the *gospel of the kingdom.*

Consider the following two verses where Jesus uses the phrase:

> And **Jesus went about all Galilee,** *teaching in their synagogues, and preaching* **the gospel of the kingdom,** *and healing all manner of sickness and all manner of disease among the people.*
> ~ Matthew 4:23, KJV, **emphasis added**

And again in this verse:

> And **Jesus went about all the cities and villages,** *teaching in their synagogues, and preaching the* **gospel of the kingdom,** *and healing every sickness and every disease among the people.*
> ~ Matthew 9:35, KJV, **emphasis added**

The phrase *gospel of the kingdom* used in these two verses and many others throughout the New Testament is the one Jesus most often used in conjunction with the gospel message He preached.

With the exception of the gospel according to Matthew, which primarily uses the phrase *kingdom of heaven,* it is also the primary phrase Jesus' first disciples used, as recorded in the gospels of Mark, Luke, and John.

So, what is the gospel of the kingdom, specifically? And how does the promise of receiving the gospel of the kingdom differ from the traditional notion of the gospel of salvation?

The *kingdom of God* and the *kingdom of heaven* are considered big concepts, theologically speaking. To some theologians, what I am about to share may seem oversimplified and even unorthodox. Regardless, I am confident that as you search these matters out for yourself and endeavor to validate the following conclusions, you will discover they are biblical and need not be more complicated.

In most commentaries, and in the minds of most people, the terms *kingdom of God* and *kingdom of heaven* are simply different ways of saying the same thing. The precedent for their interchangeability most often stems from the way the New Testament book of Matthew primarily uses the phrase *kingdom of heaven,* whereas the other three gospels of Mark, Luke, and John primarily use the phrase *kingdom of God.*

Those espousing this idea do so for good reason. Matthew used the word *heaven* in the phrase *kingdom of heaven* in virtually the same way the other writers used the term *God* in the phrase *kingdom of God.*[62] In fact, unlike the other gospel writers, Matthew references the kingdom by a variety of terms some fifty times:

31 times as the kingdom of heaven,

5 times as the kingdom of God,

4 times as the Father's kingdom,

2 times as the kingdom of the Son of Man,

7 times as the kingdom without any other designation.

Sometimes Matthew even varies the use of the phrases within the same text. To illustrate, in one verse – also a key indicator to most people that the terms *kingdom of heaven* and the *kingdom of God* are synonymous – notice how Matthew accredits Jesus with using both of the phrases interchangeably:

> Then Jesus said to his disciples, "I tell you the truth, it is hard for a rich man to enter the **kingdom of heaven.** Again I tell you, it is easier for a camel to go through the eye of a needle than for a rich man to enter the **kingdom of God.**"
> ~ Matthew 19:23–24, **emphasis added**

The exact same account is recorded in the gospels of Mark and Luke, but neither writer accredits Jesus with using the term *kingdom of heaven,* only the *kingdom of God.* (See Mark 10:25 and Luke 18:25.)

While Matthew's interchangeable use of the phrases *kingdom of heaven* and *kingdom of God* contributes to debate, most scholars believe he had valid reasons for choosing this approach and was not implying the two terms were synonymous.

In Matthew's time, among Jewish people, the act of speaking the name of God was considered an extreme act of piety. Out of respect and reverence, it is still a common practice among Jewish people today to represent the name of God in writing as *G-d* or sometimes *YHWH* and when speaking as *Adonai* (Hebrew for Lord) to avoid uttering the name of God when in prayer, worship, or other public discussions.

We don't know for sure if Matthew's interchangeable use of these terms was an attempt to honor his Jewish audience or whether he actually believed and meant to imply the kingdom of God and the kingdom of heaven were the same thing.

Regardless of Matthew's interchangeable use of the phrases, they are his accounts of the events of Jesus' life, and I am sure he had valid reasons for how he chose to relate them to his audience.

For the same reason, we should distinguish between the terms *kingdom of God* and the *kingdom of heaven* and change the way we relate them to a modern audience.

Unless we adjust the way we communicate these kingdom concepts, we risk miscommunicating the implications and causing an entire generation to live life without experiencing the real power of the gospel Jesus preached while they are on earth.

By making only a few simple distinctions, however, between the gospel of the kingdom of God and the kingdom of heaven, it's immediately clear to people why the gospel is not only really good news for an eternity in heaven, but is also really good news now, in the present tense.

The first and most basic distinction is to begin thinking of the terms *kingdom of God* and *kingdom of heaven* as closely related but, at the same time, completely separate and distinct. To do that, all that's required is to simply consider the actual meanings of the individual words that make up each phrase and, subsequently, the implied meanings when combined.

Since the phrases *kingdom of God* and *kingdom of heaven* have the word *kingdom* in common, let's consider its meaning first.

## KINGDOM

By most counts, the word *kingdom* appears over 160 times in the New Testament as the English translation of the Greek word *basileia*. In the Old Testament, it's the English translation of the Hebrew word *malkuwth*. This also represents a rare case when the Greek and Hebrew root words mean and imply exactly the same things when translated into English. In this case, both mean "a realm, rule, or measure of rule, reign, or dominion of a sovereign, as in a king."

Regardless of the translation you prefer, the majority of all scholars see the concept of the kingdom as the main emphasis of Jesus' message.

So, what about the meanings of the two words that distinguish the phrases *kingdom of heaven* and *kingdom of*

**RECONSIDER** One group of scholars has lobbied to have the word *basileia* translated in the biblical context as *love's domain* or *love's rule* because the kingdom of God is where God, who is love, rules.[63]

*God* from each other – heaven and God, respectively? Let's consider them both individually, looking first at the word *heaven.*

## HEAVEN

The Bible uses three words that are translated into English as *heaven.* One word, the Hebrew word *shamayim* is used to refer to what we might call the cosmos, atmosphere, or observable expanse or arch of the sky just above the earth's surface. It is sometimes called the firmament, the cosmos, or the first heaven (Gen. 1:14).

A second word translated heaven is the Greek one *epouranios,* meaning "above." This word for heaven is most often used to refer to the solar system of stars, planets, and other celestial bodies. It is sometimes called the celestial heaven or second heaven above the earth (1 Cor. 15:40).

A third word translated *heaven* is the Greek one *ouranous,* meaning "sky" and by extension implying the abode, home, or dwelling place of God Himself. It is sometimes referred to as the "third heaven" above the earth's surface (2 Cor. 12:4).

This third word, *ouranous,* is the one most often used in the context of the phrase *kingdom of heaven.*

By definition, then, since the word *kingdom* means a realm or a place of rule and the word *heaven* means God's abode, the phrase *kingdom of heaven* could be rendered:

**Kingdom + Heaven = Realm of God's Abode**

Now let's consider the Greek word translated *God* in the phrase *kingdom of God.*

## GOD

The Greek word *theos translated "God"* simply means "a supreme deity or magistrate" or literally "a god." You might recognize *theos* as the obvious root of our English word for *theology* (which is the study of God).

So, using the same approach as with the kingdom of heaven, by definition the word *kingdom* implies a realm or rule and the word *God* means a deity or magistrate (or in this case, actually means God).

The phrase *kingdom of God* could then be rendered:

**Kingdom + God = Rule of God**

So, by definition, the phrase *kingdom of heaven,* or the realm of God's abode, could be thought of as related but different and distinct from the *kingdom of God,* or the rule of God.

The kingdom of heaven can be meant to refer to and describe the physical location or eternal dwelling place for God Himself existing dimensionally above or beyond the earth and the solar system (the third heaven).

The kingdom of God can be meant to refer to the rule of God, or any place where the domain or rule of God's kingdom in heaven is extended beyond its physical dwelling place into another realm.

Of course, there can be overlap between these two kingdoms, as in the way Matthew used the terms, but it is not necessary to abandon the mutually exclusive meanings and implications of the individual phrases.

For example, nobody would argue that in the primary realm of God's abode (the kingdom of heaven), the presence of God is fully manifested while, at the same time, the rule of God (the kingdom of God) is in full effect.

It's equally true, however, that in other places – like on earth, for example – the realm of God's abode (the kingdom of heaven) remains in full effect in heaven while the rule of God (the kingdom of God) is not in full effect, nor is His Spirit manifested to the same degree everywhere on earth.

That's because even though the place where God dwells and is fully manifested is in one place (the kingdom of heaven), the rule of that place (the kingdom of God) needs to be extended into other realms by representatives of that kingdom.

For a modern application of the same concept, you might think of a sovereign king or leader – for example, Queen Elizabeth II of the United Kingdom. The queen and her royal family currently reign over sixteen independent sovereign states, known as commonwealths or realms (Canada, Australia, New Zealand, Jamaica, Barbados, etc.).

Though the royal family's physical dwelling place or abode (a parallel to the kingdom of heaven) is primarily considered to be Windsor Castle and is physically located in England, the rule of the queen and her kingdom (a parallel to the kingdom of God) is administered in both her immediate realm and fifteen other realms.

The queen's rule in other realms is not administered directly by the queen herself, but rather she confers the rule of her kingdom to those who are often called prime ministers. Each prime minister is appointed and authorized by the sovereign queen herself with sufficient power and authority to be an extension of her rule in these realms, speaking and acting for her as though she was physically present.

An identical parallel can be observed by looking at how Jesus conferred the kingdom on others just as His Father conferred one on Him:

> *And I confer on you a kingdom, just as my Father conferred one on me.*
>
> *~ Luke 22:29*

This is just one of many ways the administration of the kingdoms of this world can be likened to, or paralleled, as below, to how the Bible talks about the administration of the kingdom of God that Jesus came to confer on those who would choose to submit to His leadership and embrace His mission.

**The Kingdoms of Man**
King
Heir(s)
Royal residence

**The Kingdom of God**
God the Father
Jesus the Son, mankind
Heaven

421

| | |
|---|---|
| Territory or realm | Earth |
| Opposing kingdom | Enemy's kingdom |
| Constitution | Covenant |
| Citizens | Children of God |
| Laws | Commandments |
| Privileges | Birthright by adoption |
| Army | Angels and men |
| Health system | Divine healing |
| Educational system | Holy Spirit, discipleship |
| Taxation system | Tithing |
| Communication system | Gifts of Holy Spirit |
| Economic system | Seedtime, harvest |
| Administrative system | *Ekklesias* |
| Ambassadors | Apostles |
| Foreign ministers | Ministers |

As you begin to see God and His plans for mankind through the lens of the gospel of the kingdom, you begin to see that the entire Bible is really a book about advancing the kingdom of God on earth and not about simply getting people to gain the kingdom of heaven when they die.

Seeing the eternal kingdom of heaven established on earth under man's joint rule with God is precisely what God has been trying to do since He put Adam and Eve in the garden:

RESOURCE
For a more in-depth study on this topic, I recommend beginning with a book from which this list was adapted called *Rediscovering the Kingdom* by Myles Munroe. You can find a link to this book in the resource section for this chapter on our website at www. thereorientbook.com.

*Then God said, "Let Us make man in Our image, according to our likeness; let them have dominion ‹**same root as kingdom and literally meaning rule**› ..."*
~ Genesis 1:27, NKJV

The problem has been that even though God manages His kingdom in heaven perfectly, He delegated the task of advancing His kingdom on earth and the management of it to man:

*The highest heavens belong to the Lord, but the earth he has given to man.*
~ Psalm 115:16

Sadly, up until now mankind has done a fairly poor job of completing the mission. Mankind's collective failure to advance God's kingdom and extend its rule on the earth hasn't caused the inhabitants of heaven to suffer; however, the opposition to His kingdom rule on earth has caused its inhabitants to suffer violently.

The good news of the gospel about an advancing kingdom has been replaced with a message of a retreating kingdom more concerned with getting people saved to go to heaven when they die than equipping them with heaven's rewards now, in order to rise up and live fully alive under God's rule on earth.

Adam and Eve never lost their eternal access to God or to heaven in the first place, but rather were deceived by an adversary about their power and ability to continue extending that rule and to administer the reality of heaven on earth now.

As a result, Jesus (whom the Bible calls the Second Adam) didn't come to earth on a search-and-rescue mission in order to save people for heaven's sake. Jesus came from heaven bearing the good news about His ability to confer all the benefits of the kingdom of heaven to the inhabitants of earth and to give them sufficient power and authority to rise up with a holy, violent love and take back this planet for His kingdom now (Matt. 11:12).

Like a sovereign king in modern times who sends ambassadors and foreign ministers to oversee the advancement of his kingdom's interest in other realms, God's plan and ultimately Jesus' mission is about advancing His kingdom (the kingdom of heaven) and equipping man to extend the rule of that kingdom (the kingdom of God) to every realm on earth.

Similarly, Jesus and His followers were also considered ministers of the gospel of the kingdom of God. Not surprisingly, it's in this very context, in what's famously known as the Lord's Prayer, that Jesus said:

> "Our Father in heaven ‹**Greek word ouranous, meaning the third heaven above the earth, the dwelling place, or the abode of God**›, hallowed be your name, your kingdom come, your will be done on earth as it is in heaven ‹**Greek**

423

*word ouranous, again meaning the third heaven above*
*the earth, the dwelling place, or the abode of God›.*

*~ Matthew 6:9–10*

It should be obvious that Jesus was not suggesting that God relocate heaven to earth in this verse but rather saying that the focus of our prayer and intercession (which, interestingly, means "to entreat or intervene") should be to extend the rule of heaven to earth so the will of God would be done on earth as it is in heaven.

Jesus is not suggesting that the primary focus of our intercession should be getting people only to go to heaven when they die but rather to get heaven to earth now.

By extending the rule of the kingdom of heaven on earth, Jesus came to deliver the gospel and its rewards to people while they are still alive. The rewards of Jesus' gospel were a down payment for the fullness of what would be fully realized when heaven is realized in all its fullness.

Jesus Himself said it was one of the primary reasons He came to the earth:

> *But He said to them, **I must preach the good news (the Gospel) of the kingdom of God to the other cities [and towns] also, for I was sent for this [purpose].***
>
> *~ Luke 4:43,* AMP, *emphasis added*

He also said that the job will not be done, the mission will not be complete, and the end will not come until this gospel of the kingdom is preached throughout all the earth:

> *And this **gospel of the kingdom** will be preached in the whole world **as a testimony to all nations,** and **then the end will come.***
>
> *~ Matthew 24:14, **emphasis added***

In this context, the book of Revelation provides a glimpse into what the final outcome of this mission will look like:

> *The seventh angel sounded his trumpet, and there were loud **voices in heaven ‹God's abode›,** which said: **"The***

> *kingdom of the world has become the kingdom of our*
> **Lord** *and of his Christ,* **and he will reign** *for ever and ever."*
> *~ Revelation 11:15,* ***emphasis added***

This is the gospel of the kingdom that Jesus went about declaring, and it did more in three years to revolutionize the world than the relatively modern version of the gospel of salvation has done in more than 150 years of concentrated mission efforts.

As the final verse I want to share in this section makes clear, for those that heard this gospel, believed it, and thought differently afterward, the gospel of the kingdom that Jesus preached put all of the realities and rewards of the kingdom of heaven within their reach now:

> *And saying, The time is fulfilled, and the kingdom of God is at hand: repent* ‹**think differently after**› *ye, and believe the gospel* ‹**the reward of a good message**›.
> *~ Mark 1:15,* KJV

I want to draw your attention to three aspects of this verse, each having profound implications.

1. See how Jesus says, "The time is fulfilled"? In other words, He is saying there is no more waiting for a future-tense reality; the time is now.

2. See how Jesus says, "The kingdom of God is at hand"? In other words, Jesus is saying it is within arm's reach – grab it!

3. See how Jesus says, "Repent and believe the gospel"? The word *repent* simply means to "think differently afterward."

When you combine all this with the notion of believing the gospel or the rewards of a good message, using modern vernacular Jesus is literally saying:

There is no more waiting. All that heaven has to offer is within arm's reach. Believe it, receive its rewards now, and think differently.

Does all this sound nearly too good to be true? It did to most people in Jesus' day!

Unlike the traditional promises associated with the gospel of salvation today, which largely delegate the best rewards of the kingdom to a future time, Jesus' gospel of the kingdom not only promised rewards but had the requisite authority and power to bring them about and deliver them now and in the future.

And even better news is this: What's required to receive the rewards of the gospel of the kingdom then and now is exactly the same – simply believe and think differently afterward!

## THE REAL REWARDS OF THE GOSPEL

So, what was the good news and the reward of the gospel of the kingdom? Who is qualified to deliver these rewards, and how exactly does a person receive them now?

The answers are actually quite simple and fairly obvious. But like most things we've reoriented to so far, it often requires us to think differently to fully grasp their implications.

Martin Luther once said, "A gospel that does not deal with the issues of the day is not the gospel at all."

I think Jesus would concur. So, what were the issues of the day in Jesus' time, and what are the primary issues most people deal with today that the good news of the gospel is meant to address?

Let's start with the obvious and ask ...

What is good news to someone who is blind?

What is good news to someone who is deaf?

What is good news to someone who is lame?

What is good news to someone who is sick?

What is good news to someone who is poor?

What is good news to someone who is lonely?

What is good news to someone who is oppressed?

What is good news to someone who is demonized?

You get the idea. The list could go on and on. The answer to any and all of these questions was and still is the good news of the gospel of the kingdom that Jesus preached.

If you were blind, the good news of the gospel was and still is that you can see.

If you were deaf, the good news of the gospel was and still is that you can hear.

If you were lame or sick, the good news of the gospel was and still is that you can be healed.

The magnitude of the problem was irrelevant if you were ...

Poor,

Lonely,

Oppressed,

Demonized,

Afflicted,

Divorced,

Abandoned,

Beaten down,

Brokenhearted,

Undervalued,

Unfulfilled in life,

Or just feeling a little bruised.

The good news of the gospel that Jesus was anointed and sent to announce was – and still is – that if you will believe and let God rule in that realm of your life, the answer is within arm's reach!

In case you think I'm overstating this, consider this quote from Jesus Himself that began His public ministry and declaration of the gospel of the kingdom:

> The Spirit of the Lord [is] upon Me, because He has anointed Me [the Anointed One, the Messiah] to preach the good news (the Gospel) to the poor; He has sent Me to announce release to the captives and recovery of sight to the blind, to send forth as delivered those who are oppressed [who are downtrodden, bruised, crushed, and broken down by calamity].
>
> ~ Luke 4:18, AMP

This is exactly what Jesus did. Everywhere Jesus went for the next three years, it seemed He was announcing the good news of the gospel of the kingdom, teaching about its realities and delivering its rewards to anyone open to receiving them.

Think about how many times in the New Testament Jesus was found telling people about the gospel of the kingdom, and what the kingdom of God or the kingdom of heaven was like.

> For the kingdom of heaven is like the owner of an estate who went out in the morning along with the dawn to hire workmen for his vineyard.
>
> ~ Matthew 20:1, AMP

In parable after parable, Jesus was endeavoring to get people to see and to understand what the kingdom was like in order to receive the rewards of gospel He was declaring.

Jesus wasn't teaching people about the kingdom so they could fantasize about its benefits in some future-tense utopia like most of the scribes in His day. Jesus taught about the gospel of the kingdom as one having the authority to bring its rewards and realities about now, and it astonished the people who heard it:

*And they were **completely astonished at His teaching, for
He was teaching as One Who possessed authority, and
not as the scribes.***

~ *Mark 1:22,* AMP, ***emphasis added***

It's important we remember that Jesus didn't just announce the good
news or teach people about it. He actually used His authority as a
kingdom ambassador to deliver the goods to them.

The New Testament is filled with verses like these where Jesus went
about all of Galilee, His physical realm of influence, preaching the
good news of the gospel of the kingdom and healing every disease
and every weakness and every infirmity:

*And He went about all Galilee, teaching in their synagogues
and preaching the good news (Gospel) of the kingdom, and
healing every disease and every weakness and infirmity
among the people. So the report of Him spread throughout
all Syria, and they brought Him all who were sick, those
afflicted with various diseases and torments, those under
the power of demons, and epileptics, and paralyzed people,
and He healed them.*

~ *Matthew 4:23–24,* AMP

The good news was that people could be healed, and the even better
news – the nearly-too-good-to-be-true news – was they actually were!

Why did this happen? Jesus said that it was because the kingdom of
God (the rule of God) had come upon them!

*But if I drive out demons by the Spirit of God, then the
kingdom of God has come ‹**been superimposed**› upon you.*

– *Matthew 12:28*

Jesus came from heaven bearing the good news about His God-given
ability to confer all the benefits of the kingdom of heaven upon the
inhabitants of earth.

How and why does this practically happen?

Since none of the maladies we listed earlier exist in the kingdom of
heaven (the realm of God's abode) or where God's Spirit is fully mani-

fested, they simply can't exist where the kingdom of God (the rule of God) is genuinely extended into other realms, either, or where the Spirit of God is made present. Where the Spirit of the Lord is, there is always complete and total freedom (2 Cor. 3:17)!

This is a profound and simple concept that most any child can grasp, though even the wise in Jesus' day seemed to stumble over it.

But it shouldn't be difficult to believe. In fact, you almost have to be conditioned – taught – not to believe it.

For example, ask most anybody the following questions, assuming they believe heaven exists at all:

Is there any blindness in heaven?

Is there any deafness in heaven?

Is there any poverty in heaven?

Is there any sickness in heaven?

Is there any disease in heaven?

And so on, for any of the maladies we listed earlier.

Without even thinking about it, most people, especially children, will immediately answer with an emphatic, "Of course not!"

So why is it so hard for people to grasp the notion that the same is true of the kingdom of God here on earth? It's not that it's complicated and doesn't make good sense. Even children get this concept easily. But as people age and are taught differently, they begin to lower their expectations to match their reality. Maybe that's why Jesus said:

> *"I tell you the truth, **anyone who will not receive the kingdom of God like a little child will never enter it.**"*
> *~ Mark 10:15, **emphasis added***

Beginning to reorient and receive the gospel of the kingdom of God is simply a matter of being willing to think differently after you hear the truth and the good news about it. This explains why John the Baptist and Jesus spent so much time trying to get people to repent (think differently after) to receive the rewards of the gospel of the kingdom they were preaching.

We desperately need to reorient! There are rewards of the gospel that Jesus preached that should be contended for now.

It is also worth mentioning that Jesus delivered to people this same gospel of the kingdom years before His atonement, or what is traditionally viewed as His saving work on the cross. Even though the Bible says this heroic act by Jesus defeated the last enemy of death, making a way for those who believe in Him to inherit heaven, the rewards of the gospel should by no means ever be limited to that alone. The very act of doing so might qualify as one of the biggest sins mankind has ever committed, Why a sin? Think about the definition of sin again:

> *To be separated, to miss the mark, or to be estranged and/or mistaken in such a way as to not have a share in the prize or reward.*

If we limit the gospel only to heaven, we miss the mark by limiting the gospel to only one aspect of its intended purpose, and, as a result, people never share in the full prize or reward it was intended to bring about. Wouldn't that technically be considered a sin?

For most people, the full implications of this may never be realized until they get to heaven and hear the real gospel – that everything heaven has to reward was available for them to enjoy all along. All they needed was a real messenger of the gospel to tell them good news about it, a messenger with sufficient authority to actually hand-deliver its rewards and faith so they could actually receive them.

# THE REAL MESSENGERS GOD SENT TO HAND-DELIVER THE REWARDS OF THE GOSPEL TO THE WORLD

For many people, the real rewards of the gospel described in the last section seem like the stuff of religious legend and childlike fantasy.

For others, it seems plausible that Jesus could deliver these kind of gospel promises but inconceivable and maybe heretical that others would even claim to walk in such divine authority and advance the kingdom of God with such power.

For others still, these kind of things are relegated to the realm of the religious fringe and reserved only for a small group of mysteriously gifted people, spiritual gurus, or those in professional ministry.

But these very same rewards of the gospel were and still are available to anyone willing to receive them. And, just as exciting, the mandate and supernatural ability to be a messenger of the gospel and advance the kingdom of God on earth just as it is in heaven is available to anyone willing to "disciple up" and master the ability to administer it (be a "minister" of it).

Let's take a quick look at the gospel messengers of the Bible and see if you can relate to being one of them.

The first gospel message was technically delivered to mankind by angels, who were aptly named since, as pointed out previously, the English word *angel* comes from the Greek word for *gospel* – *aggelion* – and means "a messenger."

Here is an example where the *euaggelion,* or gospel, was first proclaimed to mankind by angels:

> *And the angel said unto them, Fear not: for, behold, I bring you good tidings ‹**euaggelizo, which shares the same root as gospel**› of great joy, which shall be to all people.*
>
> *~ Luke 2:10,* KJV

In this context, God is even referred to in the Old Testament as the Lord of Hosts, which means "the commander of the angel armies," or you might say "army of gospel messengers."

Similar to the military runners described in an earlier section, the Bible makes clear that God consistently uses angels as both warriors and messengers to assist mankind in advancing His kingdom on earth:

> Are not all angels ministering spirits sent to serve those who will inherit salvation ‹**that's all of us**›?
>
> ~ Hebrews 1:14

Both angels and mankind are described as warriors and messengers commissioned by God to announce the gospel of the kingdom, deliver its rewards, and extend the realm of the kingdom in every part of the world. Because we share this mission, angels (spiritual messengers) are sent forth to assist and serve mankind until the mission is complete and the inhabitants of earth inherit salvation.

I realize it's easier for some people to think of angels having supernatural ability to advance the kingdom in this way but find it harder to think of an earthborn man operating as a messenger in this capacity. But remember, Jesus operated as a man on the earth, not as an angel. The Bible makes it clear that, like the rest of mankind, Jesus was made lower than angels, yet while on earth He was gifted and crowned by God with glory and honor to walk with a kinglike dominion on earth to extend the kingdom of heaven's rule into this realm (Ps. 8:1–9).

Not only were angels and Jesus given special endowments or gifts by God to be messengers of the gospel of the kingdom and demonstrate a supernatural ability to bring about the kingdom on earth, but so are you and I and every other person who desires to be.

Do you think of yourself that way? Would you like to go about spreading the gospel of the kingdom and delivering its supernatural rewards to those who have not yet heard it, and would you like to be able to do this in every aspect of your life with the same master-level competence that Jesus and the disciples did? Well, you can! It's just another one of the many rewards and benefits of the gospel of the kingdom.

For those who were unaware of this epic news, what we are about cover will be incredibly empowering. For those leading or sitting under traditional ministries who teach that such abilities are reserved for select groups of mysteriously gifted people, spiritual gurus, or only those in upper levels of professional ministry this may require massive reorientation.

Regardless of what tradition has taught, every person must resolve that God is no respecter of persons (Acts 10:34; Rom. 2:11) and shows no favoritism. Every person on the planet was called by God and given the opportunity and grace to operate in the same level of giftedness that Jesus operated in during His time on earth.

This doesn't mean every person will operate at this level. Unfortunately, most people live their entire lives ignorant, misinformed, or underequipped to operate in these gifts, let alone at a master's level.

But it is the mission of everyone who calls themselves a disciple, and the Bible is full of examples where the disciples were the first to do just that. Check out this verse:

> Then Jesus called together the Twelve [apostles] and gave them power ‹**literally miracle-working power**› and authority ‹**the capacity to rule like a magistrate, legal jurisdiction**› over all demons, and to cure diseases, and He sent them out to announce and preach the kingdom of God and to bring healing.
>
> ~ *Luke 9:1–2*, AMP

Look how Matthew records Jesus' words to the disciples:

> And as you go, preach, saying, The kingdom of heaven is at hand! Cure the sick, raise the dead, cleanse the lepers, drive out demons. Freely (without pay) you have received, freely (without charge) give.
>
> ~ *Matthew 10:7–8*, AMP

And later, when John asked the disciples for proof that Jesus was the real deal, Jesus instructed them to tell John:

> *Go and report to John what you hear and see: The blind receive their sight and the lame walk, lepers are cleansed (by healing) and the deaf hear, the dead are raised up and the poor have good news (the Gospel) preached to them [Isaiah 35:5–6; 61:1).*
>
> ~ Matthew 11:4–5, AMP

This supernatural ability and gifting to deliver the rewards of the gospel was not limited to Jesus and the disciples. The other gospel accounts, the book of Acts, and the rest of the New Testament provide account after account of the disciples and many others doing the same things.

Here is just one instance:

> *Now after this the Lord chose and appointed ‹**called to exhibit**› seventy others and sent them out ahead of Him, two by two, into every town and place where He Himself was about to come (visit). And He said to them, The harvest indeed is abundant [there is much ripe grain], but the farmhands are few. Pray therefore the Lord of the harvest to send out laborers into His harvest.*
>
> ~ Luke 10:1–2, AMP

I like how Jesus says, "The harvest indeed is abundant but the farmhands, [some translations say the workers or laborers] are few." In other words, the problem is not with the timing or the season to produce such results; in fact, the rewards of the harvest are available now. The limitation is in the number of people capable of bringing them about – disciples.

What exactly did Jesus send these seventy into every town and place to do and tell them to pray for more laborers (disciples) to do? The answer is provided just a few verses later:

> *And **heal the sick in it and say to them, The kingdom of God has come close to you.***
>
> ~ Luke 10:9, AMP, **emphasis added**

And just like Jesus and the original twelve disciples before them, that's exactly what these seventy people did:

*The **seventy returned with joy, saying, Lord, even the demons are subject to us in Your name! And He said to them, I saw Satan falling like a lightning [flash] from heaven. Behold! I have given you authority and power to trample upon serpents and scorpions, and [physical and mental strength and ability] over all the power that the enemy [possesses];** and nothing shall in any way harm you.*

~ Luke 10:17, AMP, **emphasis added**

I am not suggesting that everyone is required to operate in the same kind of supernatural gifting and authority as Jesus, the original twelve disciples, or the next seventy. It's important that people know God will never love them more or less either way. But for those who desire to do this stuff, it's equally important that they know they can and have God's blessing to do so. God has made these extraordinary powers and abilities available to everyone who desires to come to Him and receive it, and He doesn't want anyone to be ignorant of them.

It's critical that we get this because these spiritual endowments of supernatural energy (spiritual gifts) are just as much a reward of the gospel of the kingdom as the others we listed. They are essential for every messenger who doesn't want to just tell people about the rewards of the gospel but actually bring them about.

I can't stress enough that it's not a requirement of God that you operate in these spiritual gifts for God to love you. If you lack in ability or understanding about these gifts, there is no reproach in that. Just ask and God will help you and give you understanding and disciple you to grow in these abilities (James 1:5). While God will never love you any more or less because of your maturity in these areas, it's equally true He doesn't withhold these gifts and abilities from anyone who loves Him and desires to grow in them.

It's also important to make clear that it's quite possible for the Spirit of God to be with a person in some measure who doesn't operate in these gifts. It's equally impossible, however, for any person or small group to bring about the rewards of gospel fully without operating in these spiritual gifts and endowments.

Paul even said himself that he didn't consider the gospel fully preached until these kinds of supernatural signs and wonders were demonstrated:

> *[Even as my preaching has been accompanied] with the power of signs and wonders, [and all of it] by the power of the Holy Spirit.* [The result is] that starting from Jerusalem and as far round as Illyricum, *I have fully preached the Gospel [faithfully executing, accomplishing, carrying out to the full the good news] of Christ (the Messiah) in its entirety.*
>
> ~ Romans 15:19, AMP, **emphasis added**

The greatest power of the gospel to fully execute God's kingdom-expanding mission on earth is contained in the gospel messengers' ability to demonstrate the supernatural power of God.

For this reason, the gospel was never intended to be limited to a message delivered with persuasive words about a future benefit but demonstrated with the Spirit's power to bring about love's ideal in people's daily lives:

> *My message and my preaching were not with wise and persuasive words, but with a demonstration of the Spirit's power.*
>
> ~ 1 Corinthians 2:4

Without these accompanying signs, Jesus said many will never believe the gospel:

> *"Unless you people see miraculous signs and wonders,"* Jesus told him, *"you will never believe."*
>
> ~ John 4:48

And as Paul would indicate later, the presence of these spiritual gifts is the sign, indication, or mark that someone is actually an apostle from God to begin with:

> *The things that mark an apostle – signs, wonders and miracles – were done among you with great perseverance.*
>
> ~ 2 Corinthians 12:12

## UNFOLDING THE FIVEFOLD MINSTRY GIFTS
## AND REORIENTING THE WAY PEOPLE RELATE
## TO HOW THE GOSPEL IS DELIVERED

Based on what we have covered in this chapter so far about the real gospel Jesus preached, can you relate?

Have you ever heard the gospel before within the context of the supernatural and present-tense rewards it was actually meant to deliver? Or, more importantly, have you received the rewards of the gospel in your own life, and can you relate to delivering them to others just like Jesus and His first disciples did?

Sadly, most people have trouble relating to the real rewards of the gospel of the kingdom this way and are equally challenged to relate to God entrusting the delivery of the gospel to anyone but professional ministers or clergy.

That's because those commissioned by God to preach the gospel are most often thought of as uniquely gifted individuals, operating within one of five specific capacities, or what is traditionally referred to in modern times as the fivefold ministry giftings of:

Apostles,

Prophets,

Evangelists,

Pastors,

Teachers.

These giftings most often get relegated to people appointed to specific offices or positions within a local church structure. In this capacity, each person is considered to have limited authority to operate within these gifts and only under the covering of those with higher-ranking giftings or offices. Traditionally, then, people within this framework are given commensurate responsibilities to administer the things of God to masses of people, who are not thought of as called to professional ministry within the context of the local church.

Non-professional ministers, or people who don't hold specific offices or positions within a local church, are then thought of and referred to as Christian workers, laymen, or laypeople.

But is this how Jesus intended the rewards of the gospel to be received and how He envisioned the giftings He gave mankind to be administered? Is this how Jesus expected people to relate to being a "minister" of the gospel?

The short answer is an emphatic *no!*

The gospel of the kingdom and the supernatural endowments of grace (spiritual giftings) Jesus gave to mankind to bring it about were never meant to be confined only to an office or position within a church. Likewise, they were never intended to be thought of as *only* the exclusive right of a few professional ministers.

While these gifts can operate and should freely operate within a church, thinking of them *only* in that context may be the reason we don't see more real gospel messengers and may be the greatest limiting factor preventing the real gospel from having its full effect in the world.

God didn't give these supernatural endowments of grace with a warning label, cautioning people:

> " *These gifts are only for professionals; don't try to administer these gifts at home or without supervision.* "

So, why do we predominately relate to these terms this way? Like many things we have reoriented to, the answer is in the tradition itself.

Frank Viola, the author of many books on first-century followers of Jesus, points out that what are traditionally known as the five-fold ministry gifts were not framed in that context until 1842, when a Presbyterian pastor in Scotland, Edward Irving, began teaching what he said were called the five-fold ministry gifts that had disappeared from the church and needed to be restored.[64]

Irving's *five-fold* term was a specific reference to a list of five spiritual gifts listed in two verses in the New Testament, and this framework has dominated the way most people discuss and relate to these gifts ever since.

But how does the Bible frame these gifts? Let's look at the two verses that use the terms and see.

> *And the same one who descended is the one who ascended higher than all the heavens, so that he might fill the entire universe with himself. Now these are the gifts Christ ‹**the anointed**› gave to the church ‹**ekklesia**›: the **apostles,** the **prophets,** the **evangelists,** and the **pastors** and **teachers.** Their responsibility is to equip ‹**recover wholeness in or perfect**› God's people to do his work and build up ‹**architect**› the church ‹**ekklesia**›, the body of Christ. This will continue until we all come to such unity in our faith and knowledge of God's Son that we will be mature in the Lord, measuring up to the full and complete standard of Christ ‹**the anointed**›.*
>
> ~ Ephesians 4:10–13, NLT, **emphasis added**

The traditional implications of this verse are far-reaching, and to the extent it's possible to summarize centuries of religious tradition into a few paragraphs, they are these:

After Jesus (who is the called Head of the church) ascended to heaven, He appointed and gifted certain people with authority to operate under Him. He appointed ...

Apostles,

Prophets,

Evangelists,

Pastors,

Teachers

... which are, by most people, considered the leaders of the church.


The most gifted and higher-ranking leaders are responsible ...


For operating in specific capacities to advance the gospel,

For planting churches,

For overseeing churches,

For administering local church affairs,

For ordaining and setting in place more leaders to do the same (usually thought of as the traditional role of an apostle).


Apostles and prophets are largely thought of as interpreting the divine will of God for the local and global church and are often appointed as the overseers and covering for local church leaders. Local church leaders typically, then, are people serving in the capacity of a pastor or teacher. Most people then relate to pastors or teachers as full- or part-time paid ministers or clergy with the task of doing the day-to-day work of the local church ministry.

These official giftings and, subsequently, this hierarchical approach of relating to them are the typical framework most ministries work within to oversee and teach varying numbers of laymen or people (collectively, the body of Christ).

The work of local church ministry is then primarily focused on evangelizing (through the work of evangelists) people in the local area and getting people saved to go to heaven. Saved people are then invited to become active in the local church and equipped by a local church pastor or teacher to live a life that measures up to God's standard.

Within the corporate structure of the church, the official rank and interweaving of the gifts of the apostle, prophet, evangelist, pastor, or teacher are frequently thought of in descending order of rank and oversight of the core church government.

The first and highest rank is the apostle, followed by the prophet, evangelist, pastor, and teacher, some of which are sometimes considered equivalent to each other but above the less sacred office of the Christian worker, layman, or layperson.

But is this the kind of structure Jesus had in mind?

This specific ranking seems to be supported by the way the terms apostle, prophet, evangelist, pastor, and teacher are used in the following verse:

> And God has put some in the church, **first, Apostles; second, prophets; third, teachers;** then those with wonder-working powers, then those with the power of taking away disease, helpers, wise guides, users of strange tongues.
> ~ 1 Corinthians 12:28, BBE, **emphasis added**

If most people were to illustrate the traditional view and rank of these five ministry gifts and their relationship to each other and the body of Christ, it might look something like the following:

**Traditional Five-Fold Ministry Hierarchy**

Father
God

Christ
Apostles
Prophets
Evangelists
Pastors or Teachers
Laymen

The Church
(Collective Body of Christ)

Most anyone who has ever been involved in a traditional ministry, or most any organization for that matter, can probably relate to this kind of top-down approach to rank, authority, administration, and communication flow.

This kind of leadership model has been around for centuries. It's consistent with the leadership framework for most companies and organizations in the Western world and, at first glance, appears to be the logical and even obvious implication of the two verses we just read.

The problem with this structure, however, is twofold. First, this framework and approach to leadership is largely a Greek and Western construct, and is in stark contrast to the more Eastern-Hebrew way Jesus championed and His first followers modeled in the New Testament.

As we discussed in the "Disciple" chapter, a Greek-Western-influenced mind tends to automatically define and organize things in ...

Logical,

Categorical,

Hierarchical,

Individualistic,

Competitive,

Achievement-oriented ways

... whereas a Hebrew-Eastern viewpoint tends to define and organize things in more ...

Contextual,

Relational,

Functional,

Communal,

**REMEMBER**
Jesus didn't come to build a church as we know it today, but rather an *ekklesia,* an uprising and call to battle of political, military, and social consequence.

Cooperative,

Fruit-based ways.

To relate differently to these terms, you have to make this distinction and adjust for this bias.

The second problem with the traditional framework is that it assumes the church is the center of God's universe and, therefore, that the expression of the gifts He gave to man and the administration of them are primarily limited to church life. Again, that idea couldn't be in more stark contrast to the way Jesus modeled and taught and which His first followers emulated.

Remember, the modern concept of what we call church didn't even exist for nearly sixteen hundred years after Jesus came, and there is no evidence He ever intended these gifts to be expressed or administered only in the context of synagogue or temple life (the equivalent to our modern-day church).

To the contrary, the center of God's universe has always been the individual human life, whose heart and giftings are ideally formed and nurtured in the context of a loving family. While gifted individuals can and should also masterfully express and administer these same giftings equally well within a church or temple structure, they were never intended by God to be limited to or related in only that context.

After all, some statistics say the typical seventy-five-year-old American has spent ...

9 percent of their life in church,

39 percent of their life at work,

28 percent of their life engaged in leisure activity,

12 percent of their life in school,

18 percent of their life in retirement.[65]

To see a global uprising, to see these gifts on public display, and to see these giftings administered with power to bring about the full rewards of the gospel in every place on earth, we need more than just a few talented people doing this stuff 9 percent of the time.

We need an ever-expanding army of individuals operating with the Master's level of competence in the five giftings of apostle, prophet, evangelist, pastor, and teacher, along with the sixteen other gifts God gave to mankind, which are equally important but rarely emphasized.

## REORIENTING TO WHAT IT REALLY MEANS TO BE AN APOSTLE, PROPHET, EVANGELIST, PASTOR, AND TEACHER

To relate differently to the well-known ministry gifts of apostle, prophet, evangelist, pastor, and teacher and to provide a different framework for how people can function in them to deliver the rewards of the gospel in everyday life, we first need to reorient to the meanings tradition has assigned them. Here is a quick summary.

1. *Apostle* is derived from the Greek word *apostolos* and generally means anyone who is sent forth like a messenger or a delegate, specifically as an ambassador of the gospel, a sent one with miraculous powers.

2. *Prophet* is derived from the Greek word *prophētēs* and simply means "to speak forth an inspired truth."

3. *Evangelist* is derived from the Greek word *euaggelistēs* and simply means someone who announces good news.

4. *Pastor* is derived from the Greek word *poimēn* and simply means someone who literally or figuratively shepherds.

5. *Teacher* is derived from the Greek word *didaskalos* and simply means "an instructor" and generally or specifically implies a master teacher.

When you consider these definitions in light of the real meaning of the gospel, relating to these terms and how they function in everyday life becomes intuitive and practical.

For example, in the context of the gospel as the reward of a good message delivered, it's easy to relate to an apostle as simply someone who is sent to deliver that message.

This is the reason each of the twelve disciples Jesus sent into the world as messengers of the gospel were called apostles. They were simply ones who were sent.

Despite the actual definition of the word and contrary to how it is used by the New Testament writers, religious tradition often assigns more weight, rank, and authority to the gift of the apostle than to those that appear to operate in what are considered lower-ranking gifts.

For example, have you ever noticed that the original twelve apostles are never referred to as prophets, evangelists, pastors, or teachers and yet, by definition, they clearly functioned in those gifts also? Are we supposed to conclude that Jesus intentionally and exclusively picked twelve followers to become His disciples who were capable of receiving only the highest rank, to the complete exclusion of those people He perceived more suited for only lower-ranking gifts like prophet, evangelist, pastor, or teacher?

Not only would that seem contrary to the very spirit of Jesus' message, it's in complete contrast to the way He and others functioned in these gifts as recorded in the New Testament.

Jesus never called the disciples apostles, and the disciples didn't refer to themselves as apostles as a formal title – not even once. Like the term *Christian,* only in a more positive sense, *apostle* was simply the description given to the disciples by others because they were sent by Jesus into the world to deliver a gospel message. And it's only when the term *apostle* is used in the context of the gospel that it takes on the added meaning of "one who is sent as a messenger with miraculous signs following."

**REMEMBER**
Even in Greece today, the *apostolos* (apostle) refers to the person sent to deliver the mail (messages).

Jesus never makes distinctions between sacred or non-sacred work and noble or less noble callings. He also makes no distinction between classes of workers among His disciples. In Jesus' model, there are no unimportant people or inferior jobs or giftings in the kingdom of God.

The New Testament record bears that out. Jesus' first twelve disciples, or apostles, appeared to be anything but extraordinary, supernatural, uniquely gifted, or qualified by noble birthrights or sacred professions to become His representatives on the earth and fulfill His Great Commission when He met them.

As you'll see as you consider the background of each of the first disciples, they were not qualified by ...

Their distinguished bloodline,

Their elite education,

Their unique talent,

Their religious affiliation,

Their political affiliation,

Their notable accomplishments,

Their ordination by another person with any of the above.

I don't know about you, but for an ordinary guy like me from a microdot on the midwestern map of the United States, that's really good news.

We must reorient to the way we see these first disciples and how they functioned in the gifts God gave them.

The term *prophet* or *evangelist* can refer to anyone who speaks an inspired truth or announces a good message. For example, the word *evan-*

**RESOURCE**
For a snapshot of the background of the first disciples' birthplaces, occupations, and relationship to each other, consider the Background of the First Disciples document included in the resource section for this chapter at www.thereorientbook.com.

*gelist* is the title I have used for years as the founder and president of my business. My business card says *Kevin Weaver, President and Chief Idea Evangelist, It's Feasible LLC.*

These same words used in connection with the gospel, however, give them additional meaning. A prophet, then, is not just someone who speaks forth an inspired truth, but someone who speaks forth an inspired truth *about the divine will of God.* An evangelist doesn't just announce any kind of good news; in the context of the gospel, they announce good news *about the present-tense rewards of the gospel.*

Likewise, a pastor can describe anyone who shepherds. In the context of the gospel, however, the term means the same thing but takes on the added meaning of someone who leads and shepherds people to possess the rewards of gospel of the kingdom.

Finally, the term *teacher* can technically be used to describe anyone who instructs people at a master level. In the context of the gospel, however, a teacher implies someone who instructs others *to mature to a level beyond just receiving the gospel, but also administering it for themselves and others at a master's level.*

## AN ALTERNATIVE WAY TO RELATE TO THESE FIVE AND THE SIXTEEN OTHER MINISTRY GIFTS GOD GAVE TO BRING ABOUT THE TREASURES OF THE KINGDOM TO A WORLD THAT DESPERATELY NEEDS IT

With these definitions in mind, minus the traditional church context and with our added Hebrew-Eastern viewpoint, let's consider segments of our core verses again, and let's consider some additional bullet-pointed commentary to set the stage for us to consider an alternative framework for relating to these gifts and others.

Here is the first portion of our core verse:

> *Now these are the gifts Christ ‹**the anointed**›*
> *gave to the church ‹**ekklesia**› ...*
> ~ *Ephesians 4:11,* NLT

Remember, the word *gifts* used in this verse is consistent with how the term *spiritual gifts* is used in other places in Scripture.

The term *spiritual gifts* is derived from the Greek word *charismata* and is literally meant to imply:

A spiritual gift of extraordinary powers,

A divine grace,

A special ability,

A manifestation of supernatural power,

An endowment of supernatural energy.

It's also important to note that the Bible never refers to these kind of spiritual gifts as offices, ranks, or leadership positions that were confined to a church. They were designed to be expressed individually and publicly in the context of an *ekklesia*.

With that in mind, let's read the next part of the verse with the actual definitions of these five specific spiritual gifts inserted:

> ... the apostles ‹**sent ones with miraculous signs following**›, the prophets ‹**those who speak forth divine truth**›, *the* evangelists ‹**those who announce good news**›, *and the* pastors ‹**those who shepherd**› *and* teachers ‹**those who can instruct at a master's level**›.
>
> ~ verse 11

As you read that portion of the verse a second time and consider the definition of each spiritual gift in the order of its listing, can you see the obvious practicality these gifts offer in the context of a gospel messenger who is sent to deliver the rewards of the gospel?

It's also fairly obvious that a single person could most certainly operate in more than one of these spiritual gifts. Each spiritual gift need not be limited to a single

**RECONSIDER**
Note the Greek word for grace means: The divine influence on the human heart to give it a miraculous capability

449

individual who has been appointed to an office or given the sole authority to express it on behalf of others who don't possess that gift.

For example, some who are sent and have miraculous signs following them wherever they go function in the grace of an apostle. It is also possible for that same person to be capable of speaking forth an inspired truth when required, announcing good news, helping lead others, and instructing others on how to possess fully the rewards of the gospel. In fact, the delivery of the real gospel often follows that exact path:[66]

They are sent,

They speak,

They announce,

They instruct,

They help others obtain.

While it's true some people can and do frequently appear more spiritually gifted and graced in some gift more than another, it's equally true God never withholds any spiritual gift from anyone genuinely desiring to function in it. Remember, God gave all the spiritual gifts for the benefit of all (1 Cor. 12).

And what are people to do with these spiritual gifts who desire them? The answer is provided in the next portion of our core verse:

> Their responsibility is to equip ‹**recover wholeness in or perfect**› God's people to do his work and build up ‹**architect**› the church ‹**ekklesia**›: the body of Christ ‹**the anointed**›.
> ~ verse 12

As indicated above, the purpose of these spiritual gifts is to equip, which literally means to recover wholeness or to perfect, God's people so they can do His work and then build up *ekklesias* (not churches), which are, according to this verse, the body of Christ, or literally "the body of anointed" people.

And apparently, according to the next and last portion of our core verse ...

> This will continue until we all come to such unity in our faith and knowledge of God's Son that we will be mature in the Lord, measuring up to the full and complete standard of Christy ‹**the anointed**›.
>
> ~ verse 13

I like how this verse says these spiritual gifts will continue to function this way *until we all* come into the unity of *faith,* which in this verse means "to become fully confident, have full assurance, or be completely convinced in our own faith and knowledge of Jesus, completely mature and measuring up to His standard and abilities."

Notice it doesn't say these gifts are needed until we are all saved to go to heaven or agree to be unified around doctrine. No, it says until we are unified in our own faith or confident in our experience with God and His grace in our lives, which empowers us to emulate Him at Jesus' own standard of performance, which is not only love's ideal but:

The fruit of any real Christian,

The real power of an *ekklesia,*

The greatest reward of the gospel,

The primary goal of any true disciple,

The only way all parts of the body of Christ will ever function at their full capacity.

The power behind these five spiritual gifts, or any of the other sixteen we will list, was never meant to be concentrated into an office or position of a single leader or institution that is given authority to rule over and do the work of ministry for God's people. To the contrary, Jesus instructed His disciples to think differently about their leadership structure after receiving the rewards of the gospel.

> Jesus said to them, "The kings of the Gentiles lord it over them; and those who exercise authority over them call themselves benefactors. **But you are not to be like that.** Instead, the greatest among you should be like the youngest, and the one who rules like the one who serves ‹**attends to**›. For who is greater, the one who is at the table or the one who serves ‹**attends to**›? Is it not the one who is at the table? But I am among you as one who serves.
> ~ Luke 22:25–27, **emphasis added**

Jesus is not speaking about oppressive leaders in this verse but a type of hierarchical or top-down leadership structure that was commonplace then and now among the kingdoms of the world but was in contrast to the way He intended for kingdom of God.

In Jesus' Hebrew-Eastern model of kingdom authority and how it functions, those who are most experienced in administering spiritual gifts are not thought of as leaders or called to rule over others from the top down. Instead, as in the previous verse, the greatest, most gifted, and experienced among God's people are called to be servants.

The English word *servant,* or "one who serves," as used in the previous verse, comes from the Greek word *diakonos* (pronounced dee-ak-on-eh'-o) and means "to be an attendant," that is, to wait upon menially as a host, friend, or, figuratively, teacher.

You might recognize this same Greek word as the obvious root of the English word *deacon.* Ironically, even though Jesus called it the greatest attribute of a leader in the kingdom of God, being a deacon is often given much lower rank and measures of authority in traditional church leadership structures when compared to apostles, prophets, evangelists, pastors, and teachers.

The implications of the term *servant* or *deacon* are also similar to another familiar term in traditional religious circles – b*ishop,* which is derived from the Greek word *episkopē,* meaning "to superintend" or "to be a superintendent."

In any case, the implications of the roles of servants, deacons, and bishops are the same: to attend to or superintend others who were doing the work of the ministry – not doing the work of ministry for others.

Those most experienced in functioning in spiritual gifts are not called out by God to be leaders over less gifted people but to attend to and serve others until they can function, at the very least, at their same level of mastery.

And in the context of the *ekklesia,* they are not called to be the singular apostle, prophet, evangelist, pastor, or teacher, but to encourage, incite, and disciple others to exercise these gifts, to love, and to do mighty works (Heb. 10:25).

The Bible calls those who are most experienced and seasoned at equipping others to do the work of the ministry *elders,* a term derived from the Greek word *presbyteros* and meaning "one who is older, senior, or more experienced."

Of course, elders are not exempt from doing the work of the ministry, but they are most valuable when they are equipping others to do it also. I liken elder disciples to the most elite Unites States special-forces soldiers today, sometimes called cadres[67]; while they are the most highly trained, skilled, equipped, and disciplined soldiers in the world, they are often used as *force multipliers* to train other troops to function at equivalent levels. One high-ranking military general told me that special forces units of twelve men are used to effectively train groups of hundreds and thousands in very short timeframes.

That same general indicated this force multiplication strategy is frequently and covertly used to facilitate many of the "uprisings" we see in countries where small groups of revolutions become equipped and capable of overthrowing oppressive and dictatorial regimes.

It's always been God's heart and Jesus' mission that every person in the kingdom of God and the body of Christ function fully together in all the spiritual gifts He provided.

The analogy of many members and functions of the human body is the exact metaphor Paul uses to describe the diversity of spiritual gifts God gave mankind and their function in relationship to one another under the direction, leadership, and inspiration of the head, which He calls the Holy Spirit of God Himself (1 Cor. 2:12–31).

In these verses, Paul explains how a diversity of gifts, including ...

Words of wisdom,

Words of knowledge,

Gifts of faith,

Prophecy,

Healing,

Discerning of spirits,

Miracles,

Tongues,

Interpretation of tongues,

Helps,

Administration,

Service,

Exhortation,

Giving,

Mercy, and mostly

Love

... should work together like many parts of the same body.

For thirty-one verses, Paul gives an impassioned plea that none of whom he called his brethren be ignorant of any of these spiritual gifts and how *all* the gifts should function in *all* members of the body of Christ for the benefit of all the body.

Despite this emphasis, the most-often-cited portion of the entire chapter is the verse we provided at the beginning of our second core text at the beginning of this section:

> And in the church ‹ekklesia› God has appointed ‹set, or-dained, placed› first of all apostles, second prophets, third teachers, then workers of miracles, also those having gifts of healing, those able to help others, those with gifts of administration ‹governments›, and those speaking in different kinds of tongues.
>
> ~ verse 28, emphasis added

Sadly, the only portion of this verse most people are familiar with is the first portion – "God has appointed first of all apostles, second prophets, third teachers." But as you can see, it doesn't stop there. The verse goes on to list six other gifts in this verse that are rarely ever mentioned alongside the first five, let alone given an office at a local church.

Have you ever been introduced to anyone in the context of a traditional church leadership model as being …

The senior miracle-worker,

The staff healer,

The associate governmentalist,

The head of tongue-speaking?

It may sound funny, but why not? These gifts are listed in the exact same verse and context as the others. The only reason it sounds funny is because we've had centuries of tradition that have taught us to relate to five specific gifts in different ways than others.

Consider how familiar and accepted it is to think of a person with a pastoral gifting as functioning as the head of a local church. Yet the word pastor is not even listed in the verse we just read, and the Bible knows nothing of the notion of elevating a person who operates in a pastoral grace or gifting as the head of a church *(ekklesia)*.

As always, I am not being critical of anyone functioning in that capacity. I have deep respect and honor for anyone who can do that job well. Given the traditional dynamics and requirements of being a pastor and doing it well, they may well qualify for one of the toughest jobs in the world.

Nonetheless, the undeniable fact remains: The Bible simply does not emphasize this one gifting in the same way traditional leadership models do. The word *pastor* is used only once in the entire Bible and never in the context of heading or leading a church or especially an *ekklesia* (Eph. 4:11). The Greek word translated *pastor* in this single instance is used twenty-nine other times in the New Testament but translated *shepherd* and is used in the context of Jesus as the *Good Shepherd.*

So, what does our second core verse mean when it says, "And in the *[ekklesia]* God has appointed first of all apostles, second prophets, third teachers"? It simply implies the order in which these are typically administered while delivering the rewards of the gospel – not hierarchically but functionally.

To see what I mean, let's consider this statement in light of the following:

> For, "Everyone who calls on the name of the Lord will be saved." How, then, can they call on the one they have not believed in? And how can they believe in the one of whom they have not heard? And how can they hear without someone preaching to them? And how can they preach unless they are sent? As it is written, "How beautiful are the feet of those who bring good news!"
>
> ~ Romans 10:13–15

The obvious answers to the rhetorical questions posed in this verse provide solid, practical, and logical reference points for the alternative way we are considering the implications of our core verse.

In other words:

007 · GOSPEL · REORIENT

1.  There are no beautiful feet bringing the gospel unless someone is first sent (the apostolic gift).

2.  The nearly-too-good-to-be-true news of the gospel is never heard until someone then declares an inspired truth about it (the prophetic gift).

3.  It's impossible for those who hear the gospel to know how to fully possess its rewards and walk in the fullness of the gospel at a master level until they are instructed (the teaching gifts).

4.  People never learn to rise up, operate, and administer these gifts for themselves and others in order to see the power of the gospel penetrate every realm of society until more experienced people begin to superintend them functioning publicly in these gifts in the body of Christ and the *ekklesia*.

Listing the gifts of an apostle, prophet, and teacher in the order they are found is simply a practical, orderly, and natural expression of how these gifts function in real life and is not intended to imply they should be given superior priority, hierarchical ranking, or more authority than other gifts.

In the chapters before, including, and after our second core text and spanning more than eighty verses (1 Cor. 12:1–31; 13:1–13; 14:1–40), Paul goes into great detail about:


How we should all desire and pursue the best gifts,

How the greatest of these supernatural gifts is love,

How he desires that nobody be ignorant of any of these gifts,

How everyone should learn to function in them as one body.


In a beautifully crafted analogy, Paul likens the way we should relate to the diversity and function of the spiritual gifts God gave to the body to the way we can observe the human body functioning.

The human body is made up of many individual members that are designed to provide different functions but are controlled by the same head to benefit the whole. Likewise, many members of the body of Christ have been given the ability to operate in a variety of gifts and functions in order to benefit the whole body.

To reorient, you have to see that, in the same way ...

There's no unimportant body part,

There's no unimportant member of the body of Christ,

There's no unimportant function that a member of the body performs,

There's no unimportant gift a member of the body performs,

There's only one head of the human body,

There's only one head of the body of Christ,

There's only one head to communicate to all parts of the human body,

There's only one head to communicate to every member of the body,

There's only one head to activate a body's functions for the benefit of the whole body,

There's only one head activating the body of Christ's functions to benefit that body,

There's only one head to orchestrate the expression and timing of certain actions,

There's only one head to orchestrate the expression and timing of certain gifts.

And just as every part of the human body needs the same care and attention to allow the body to function optimally, the body of Christ needs every member functioning in these gifts to their full capacity to ever see it perform optimally.

The human body was never designed to be split into separate divisions (what are called *schisms* in 1 Corinthians 12:25, KJV) that rule over smaller parts of the body. The Bible doesn't promote a body of Christ that involved God speaking to a denomination that rules over many smaller churches and then communicates His will through a chain of command. An ecclesiastical hierarchy of apostles, prophets, evangelists, pastors, and teachers who then administer things God wants done in the kingdom on behalf of those who never become equipped to do it for themselves is not His plan. Frank Viola, the author *Who Is Your Covering? A Fresh Look at Leadership, Authority, and Accountability* says:

> Using Paul's body metaphor as support for a hierarchical form of leadership, where God sends messages to higher-ranking heads of denominations to lower-ranking heads of churches who then relay the message down a lower-ranking chain of command and ultimately arrive at the individual members of the body, ignores even the most the basic functions of human anatomy. Everyone knows the head or the brain sends direct messages to the body parts it seeks to influence and therefore controls all the body parts immediately and directly. In other words, the head doesn't tell the hand to tell the feet what to do, which then relay the message to the toes. The head is connected and communicates directly to all parts of the body![68]

It is also easy to see how Paul and others endeavored to model and reinforce this functional body approach to ministry of the gospel and leadership in the kingdom of God by the way they consistently addressed communications to the members of the church body *(ekklesia)* as a whole and never to a single leader or head of the assembly. Consider how:

Paul was with the church *(ekklesia)* in the wilderness (Acts 7:38).

Paul was with the whole church *(ekklesia)* (Acts 15:22).

Paul embraced the whole church *(ekklesia)* at Antioch (Acts 18:22).

Paul called all elders of the church *(ekklesia)* at Ephesus (Acts 20:17).

Paul wrote to the church *(ekklesia)* at Corinth (1 Cor. 1:2).

Paul wrote the church *(ekklesia)* in the house (Philem. 1:2).

The writer of Hebrews wrote concerning the general assembly and church *(ekklesia)* of the firstborn (Heb. 12:23).

John wrote to the church *(ekklesia)* (3 John 1:9).

Jesus spoke to the angel of the church *(ekklesia)* of Ephesus (Rev. 2:1).

Jesus spoke again to the angel of the church *(ekklesia)* in Philadelphia (Rev. 3:7).

What is surprisingly absent from these communications and all others in the New Testament is a single communication directed to a pastor, leader, teacher, master, or single individual as the head of a local assembly or responsible for doing the work of the ministry on behalf of others.

To the contrary, and in keeping with Jesus' admonishment to them, the writers of the New Testament never call each other rabbi or teacher (Matt. 23:8), father (Matt. 23:9), master (Matt. 23:10), or priest. Even Paul said that people shouldn't follow or revere him but should:

> *Follow my example, as I follow the example of Christ.*
> *~ 1 Corinthians 11:1*

In the same spirit, Jesus' followers as individuals and members of the *ekklesia* chose other terms to relate to one another. They called each other ...

The elect,

The citizens,

The general assembly,

The household,

The temple of the Holy Spirit,

The local assembly,

The regional assemblies,

The brethren.

Notice how there are no terms of distinction reserved for individuals on this list.

As Frank Viola accurately points out in *Who is Your Covering?* the word *brethren* is the preferred term Jesus and others used in the New Testament. Viola goes on to say that while the term *elder* is only used five times and *pastor* only once in the entire New Testament, the word *brethren* is used 346 times in the context of those who exercise spiritual gifts and do the work of the ministry.

And what kind of work did the brethren do? The Bible says ...

They organized their own affairs (1 Cor. 11:33–34; 14:39–40; 16:2–3),

They disciplined one another (1 Cor. 5:3–5; 6:1–6),

They warned one another (1 Thess. 5:14),

They comforted one another (1 Thess. 5:14),

They supported one another (1 Thess. 5:14),

They abounded in the work of ministry with one another (1 Cor. 15:58),

They admonished one another (Rom. 15:14),

They taught one another (Col. 3:16),

They prophesied to one another (1 Cor. 14:31),

They bore one another's burdens (Gal. 5:13),

They cared for one another (1 Cor. 12:25),

461

They loved one another (Rom. 13:8; 1 Thess. 4:9),

They were devoted to one another (Rom. 12:10),

They showed kindness and compassion to one another (Eph. 4:32),

They edified one another (Rom. 14:19; 1 Thess. 5:11),

They exhorted one another (Heb. 3:13; Col. 3:16),

They incited one another to love and mighty works (Heb. 10:24),

They encouraged one another (1 Thess. 5:11),

They prayed for one another (Jas. 5:16),

They showed hospitality to one another (1 Pet. 4:9),

They fellowshipped with one another (1 John 1:7),

They confessed sins to one another (Jas. 5:16).

In other words, they delivered the rewards of the gospel to each other!

Despite the pervasive notion in modern times that this work of the ministry is solely the work of pastors, elders, and other so-called leaders of local churches and religious organizations, delegating this kind of work to a single leader or small group of individuals is unrealistic and unbiblical. It's also ineffective on many levels for the leader and those being ministered to. To consolidate all this work into the responsibility of a single person or a few leaders is unhealthy. The sheer responsibly and activity of it all would wear down and burn out even the most committed disciple – and it does!

An August 1, 2010, article in the *New York Times* suggests studies now show that members of the traditional clergy suffer from obesity, hypertension, and depression at rates higher than most Americans. In the last decade, their use of antidepressants has risen while their life expectancy has fallen dramatically. Many clergy say they are burned out and would change jobs if they could avoid what they call "a sense of a duty to God to answer every call for help from anybody" and being called upon 24/7 to meet every need.[69]

One website among many dedicated to the sole topic of pastor burnout compiling statistics from a variety of sources says professional pastors have the second-highest divorce rate among all professions and are the third-highest-ranking profession to have problems with drug abuse, alcoholism, and suicide.[70] (Only doctors and lawyers ranked higher.) The same study suggests that among pastors surveyed:

90 percent feel unqualified,

50 percent feel unable to meet the demands of the job,

52 percent say being a pastor is downright hazardous to a family,

70 percent say they have no close friends,

75 percent report severe stress.

The same pastors said the following stresses occurred regularly enough to make them to consider leaving the pastoral profession for more secular work:

Alienation from others,

Anger,

Anguish,

Bewilderment,

Depression,

Fear,

Worry.

According to the Barna Group, in 2001 more than half a million paid pastors (half with fewer than one hundred active members in the congregation they were leading) were serving in this capacity in Protestant churches alone.[71]

These statistics shouldn't be surprising. After all, we would never expect a single body part, like the head, to do all the work of the other parts of the body, since the head is simply not designed to function that way. Doing so would put an unrealistic demand on the head and would hinder the other body parts from functioning at their peak capacity. Likewise, expecting a single person (or head) of a church to do all the work of ministering to the figurative body of Christ would not only be hazardous to their own family and physical well-being, but it would also hamper the body from ever functioning at its full capacity.

If we ever hope to see the rewards of the gospel administered on a more pervasive scale and the kingdom of God extended into every realm of society, we have to relate differently to these gifts and their function within the body.

It's essential that every member relate to their responsibility to administer these gifts and do the work of the ministry in every aspect of life and not relegate this work to a few gifted people at the top of a church's organizational chart.

I like how a commentary I found in the *Word in Life Study Bible* uses examples from the book of Acts to provide an overview of the eclectic, untidy collection of people that initially became disciples of Jesus after observing the supernatural acts of the initial twelve.[72]

Jesus' initial disciples ranged from the wealthy and privileged individuals to destitute beggars, slaves, and even criminals.

They were multicultural:

African,

Arab,

Greek,

Hebrew,

Roman.

They had different political allegiances:

Civil,

Government,

Military,

Reactionary,

Refugee,

Revolutionary.

They were male, female, young, old, and practiced every manner of religious tradition before coming to Christ:

Greek,

Idol worship,

Judaism,

Mystery cults,

Pagan,

Roman mythology,

Sorcery.

They were from every manner of profession:

Landowners,

Healthcare workers,

Therapists,

Lecturers,

Teachers,

Government officials,

Government workers,

Civic leaders,

Garment industry professionals,

Tailors,

Tentmakers,

Importers and exporters of all kinds,

Hotel and hospitality industry workers,

Woodsmen.

As this list demonstrates, Jesus' first disciples and those that followed had little in common. They were united only by their hunger for more, their decision to follow Jesus, and their willingness to initially endure failure, doubt, and resistance to become conformed to the very likeness of Jesus Himself – to become His disciple.

Nothing in Jesus' time prequalified or disqualified a person from becoming a true disciple and that is still true today. But in order to see more people rise up to master the ability to administer this reality and model for others, there are a few absolutes.

We must cease relating to …

The gospel as only a future-tense reality,

The present-tense rewards of the gospel as less important,

The real rewards of the gospel as only religious legend,

The messengers of the gospel as only professional clergy,

The sacred and non-sacred aspects of our work as mutually exclusive,

The distinctions between gods, kings, and priests as mutually exclusive,

The administration of the gospel as only for professional ministers and not laypeople,

The people who hold no specific office or position in a church as inferior,

The spiritual gifts God gave to all mankind to advance His kingdom on earth as being limited to ecclesiastical offices or positions of specific hierarchical rank and authority.

If we ever hope to reverse the grim gospel statistics cited at the beginning of this chapter, we must adopt a more functional framework for how the gospel rewards are delivered to the world, how gospel messengers are equipped, and how the supernatural fruit the real gospel was intended to produce is measured.

To help the reorientation process, I would like to provide an illustration for an alternative and more functional ministry framework. I believe it is more consistent with Jesus' New Testament model than the traditional hierarchical, top-down chain of command.

My hope is that this simple illustration will help us relate differently to the absolutely critical role we each play as:

Individuals in the kingdom of God,

Individuals connecting to God,

Individuals receiving the rewards of the gospel,

Individuals becoming Jesus' disciples,

Individuals rising up to be messengers of the gospel,

Individuals functioning in all the special graces Jesus made available,

Individuals helping others receive the same rewards of the gospel.

## A New Ministry Framework

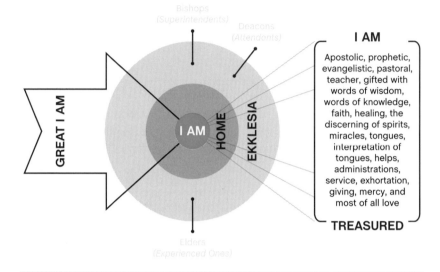

Let's walk through the illustration together and a bit of the reasoning behind it.

Notice "I AM" is in the center of this illustration and not the church. This doesn't pertain to me literally, but the first-person, present-tense way each of us as God's children should see ourselves in terms of our central importance to God and His plans for all creation.

Now notice how I AM is connected to, receives, and communicates directly with the GREAT I AM. I specifically chose the term GREAT I AM to collectively refer to both Jesus and God for a couple reasons:

1.  I AM is a term God Himself used when first instructing His children to relate to Him:

    *God said to Moses, "I AM WHO I AM. This is what you are to say to the Israelites: 'I AM has sent me to you.'"*

    *~ Exodus 3:14*

    And since Jesus instructed us to relate to Him and the Father as one and the same, it's certainly an appropriate term for Jesus also:

    *"I and the Father are one."*

    *~ John 10:30*

2. I wanted to represent God as the GREAT I AM and us as I AM to help us relate to being created in the exact image of God (Gen. 1:27) and predestined to be conformed to Jesus' own image (Rom. 8:29) but not equal to God.

You may also notice this diagram is missing the traditional framework of God sitting atop a fivefold ministry hierarchy of appointed leaders who act as the figurative heads of the collective churches, mediators through a descending chain of command between God and man and responsible for doing the primary work of the ministry and proclaiming the gospel to the lost.

Instead, I AM is in direct connection with the GREAT I AM with no mediator between them except Jesus Himself:

> For there is one God and one mediator ‹*a go-between*› between God and men, the man Christ Jesus.
>
> ~ 1 Timothy 2:5

I'm not suggesting there is no place for anyone to serve in the traditional fivefold ministry capacity or to administer the things of God through a traditional church structure.

To the contrary, it's important that each person, even those in traditional positions of leadership, see themselves as I AM, but it's equally important to see that I AM is not a substitute for others doing the work of the ministry. All of us are important to the kingdom of God, and everyone should be given the same honor and respect:

> For there is no partiality with God.
>
> ~ Romans 2:11, NKJV

First and foremost, I AM responsible to connect with and personally receive the rewards of the gospel from the GREAT I AM. By practice, I AM then to learn to receive and operate in all the spiritual gifts He gives every disciple to administer well the kingdom of God in my own home first and then in the public assembly – the public *ekklesia*.

*(For if a man doesn't know how to rule ‹**to stand in rank, preside, or practice**› his own house, how will he take care of the church ‹**ekklesia**› of God?)*

~ 1 Timothy 3:5, NKJV

As I AM more experienced in functioning in these special graces, as evidenced by their fruit and manifestation in my own home first and then in the public *ekklesia,* I AM naturally going to cause others to relate to me as an elder (a more experienced one) and called upon to bishop (attend to) or deacon (superintend) others.

These attributes are not titles I AM assigned by someone in higher positional authority but rather are descriptions of how I AM to function based on experience and fruit.

As I AM maturing in these gifts and functioning equally well as more experienced ones, both in the home and in the *ekklesia,* mutual subjection is required so as to never lord over each other with these gifts or to put them on display as a banner of an individual's worth.

In the context of a home or public assembly that is made up of many members, we must see our individual gifts and graces operating in concert and to the benefit of all.

Bringing about specific rewards of the gospel and to allow the Spirit of God to rule in every public realm of life on Planet Earth often requires the giftings of many members, and people who operate in these gifts in the public assembly must be humbly subjected to one another in love to function effectively (Eph. 5:21 and 1 Pet. 5:5).

A mature and temperate disciple never lords over others their gifts but exercises a keen sense of preference as to which gift God needs each person to function in at any given time to bring about the highest good (See 1 Cor. 12).

As an individual who at any given time is outside the context of the assembly, however, wherever I go in the world it's critical that I know:

I AM the express image of God,

I AM a messenger of the gospel of the kingdom,

I AM gifted to function in all the special graces God has provided,

I AM able to bring about the rewards of the gospel in every realm of life,

I AM a messenger sent to administer the rewards of the gospel,

I AM someone to whom God wants to provide the treasures of heaven,

I AM someone God has sent to treasure others,

I AM someone God can equip to help equip others to do the same,

I AM treasured!

This is all possible because once we each receive the gospel, the Spirit of God is given to us as the reward. The GREATER ONE then lives in each of us, and the GREATER ONE who is the GREAT I AM is greater than anything is in the world and greater than I AM alone.

> But you belong to God, my dear children. You have already won a victory ‹**the good news**› over those people, because the Spirit who lives in you is greater than the spirit who lives in the world.
>
> ~ 1 John 4:4, NLT

Wherever I am sent by God, it's critical that I see, just like Jesus was and is the GREAT I AM and the master at administering all the gifts of the Spirit of God, that …

I AM an apostle (sent as an ambassador with miraculous signs following),

I AM a prophet (one who speaks forth inspired truths),

I AM an evangelist (one who announces good news),

I AM a pastor (one who can shepherd others to receive the rewards of the kingdom),

I AM a teacher (one who can teach others to operate at the master's level),

I AM graced with every supernatural endowment by THE GREAT I AM and to the extent I desire to operate in them,

I AM capable of functioning in all the gifts of His Spirit.

I AM able to deliver the gospel and bring about its rewards to anyone who wants them and is ready to receive and believe the nearly-too-good-to-be-true news.

I AM treasured and worthy along with them to inherit all the benefits of salvation!

In fact, that's the name of the website we set up for you and others to track and share how you have been treasured by other messengers of the gospel of the kingdom that are rising up all around the world.

---

**RESOURCE**
Visit online at
www.iamtreasured.com.

# GOSPEL__RELATE

As a closing exercise, individually and collectively as an I AM group if you have one, consider the following questions.

Have I heard the gospel as we've reoriented to it?

........................................................................................................................

........................................................................................................................

........................................................................................................................

How have the implications of the gospel changed for me?

........................................................................................................................

........................................................................................................................

........................................................................................................................

When I consider the rewards of the gospel, have I personally received them?

........................................................................................................................

........................................................................................................................

........................................................................................................................

When I consider the rewards of the gospel, am I a messenger of them?

........................................................................................................................

........................................................................................................................

........................................................................................................................

When it comes to operating in the twenty-one supernatural endowments of grace (tools) God gave to bring about the rewards of the gospel, which bring me the most joy when I consider operating in them (on a scale of 1 to 5, with 1 being the least joy and 5 being the most joy)?

| Tool | Joy Level | | | | |
|------|---|---|---|---|---|
| Apostle | 1 | 2 | 3 | 4 | 5 |
| Prophet | 1 | 2 | 3 | 4 | 5 |
| Evangelist | 1 | 2 | 3 | 4 | 5 |
| Pastor | 1 | 2 | 3 | 4 | 5 |
| Teacher | 1 | 2 | 3 | 4 | 5 |
| Words of Wisdom | 1 | 2 | 3 | 4 | 5 |
| Words of Knowledge | 1 | 2 | 3 | 4 | 5 |
| Gifts of Faith | 1 | 2 | 3 | 4 | 5 |
| Prophecy | 1 | 2 | 3 | 4 | 5 |
| Healing | 1 | 2 | 3 | 4 | 5 |
| Discerning of Spirits | 1 | 2 | 3 | 4 | 5 |
| Miracles | 1 | 2 | 3 | 4 | 5 |
| Tongues | 1 | 2 | 3 | 4 | 5 |
| Interpretation of Tongues | 1 | 2 | 3 | 4 | 5 |
| Helps | 1 | 2 | 3 | 4 | 5 |
| Administration | 1 | 2 | 3 | 4 | 5 |
| Service | 1 | 2 | 3 | 4 | 5 |
| Exhortation | 1 | 2 | 3 | 4 | 5 |
| Giving | 1 | 2 | 3 | 4 | 5 |
| Mercy | 1 | 2 | 3 | 4 | 5 |
| Love | 1 | 2 | 3 | 4 | 5 |

When it comes to operating in the twenty-one supernatural endowments of grace (tools) God gave to bring about the rewards of the gospel, which are you most experienced in and capable of superintending or eldering others in (on a scale of 1 to 5, with 1 being the least experienced and 5 being most experienced)?

| Tool | Experience Level | | | | |
|---|---|---|---|---|---|
| Apostle | 1 | 2 | 3 | 4 | 5 |
| Prophet | 1 | 2 | 3 | 4 | 5 |
| Evangelist | 1 | 2 | 3 | 4 | 5 |
| Pastor | 1 | 2 | 3 | 4 | 5 |
| Teacher | 1 | 2 | 3 | 4 | 5 |
| Words of Wisdom | 1 | 2 | 3 | 4 | 5 |
| Words of Knowledge | 1 | 2 | 3 | 4 | 5 |
| Gifts of Faith | 1 | 2 | 3 | 4 | 5 |
| Prophecy | 1 | 2 | 3 | 4 | 5 |
| Healing | 1 | 2 | 3 | 4 | 5 |
| Discerning of Spirits | 1 | 2 | 3 | 4 | 5 |
| Miracles | 1 | 2 | 3 | 4 | 5 |
| Tongues | 1 | 2 | 3 | 4 | 5 |
| Interpretation of Tongues | 1 | 2 | 3 | 4 | 5 |
| Helps | 1 | 2 | 3 | 4 | 5 |
| Administration | 1 | 2 | 3 | 4 | 5 |
| Service | 1 | 2 | 3 | 4 | 5 |
| Exhortation | 1 | 2 | 3 | 4 | 5 |
| Giving | 1 | 2 | 3 | 4 | 5 |
| Mercy | 1 | 2 | 3 | 4 | 5 |
| Love | 1 | 2 | 3 | 4 | 5 |

In order of priority to you, of the twenty-one supernatural endowments of grace that you are least experienced in, which ones would you like to disciple up in first?

..........................................................................................................

..........................................................................................................

..........................................................................................................

..........................................................................................................

Based on your answers to the above questions, connect with God and begin to ask, receive, and then exercise what He is imparting to you by beginning to treasure others with these gifts! Write down what He shows you.

..........................................................................................................

..........................................................................................................

..........................................................................................................

..........................................................................................................

..........................................................................................................

Track the fruit!

..........................................................................................................

..........................................................................................................

..........................................................................................................

..........................................................................................................

..........................................................................................................

# GOSPEL__REACT

What are the top three things you are taking away from this chapter?

What action can you take now on what you've learned?

Lord, you say

The kingdom of heaven's at hand

It's wherever I am

Wherever I stand

With ears to hear and eyes to see

Its power is present

Within arm's reach ...


- KINGDOM OF HEAVEN -

*Lyrics by Kevin Weaver It's Feasible Publishing, LLC*

Download the complete lyrics and an .mp3 version of this
song in its entirety at www.thereorientbook.com.

# SAVED

# What's your REACTION to the word?

⊕ Positive

⊖ Negative

◉ Neutral

## What does the word MEAN TO YOU?

Now let's see what others say. ▶

The way people surveyed
reacted to the word SAVED.

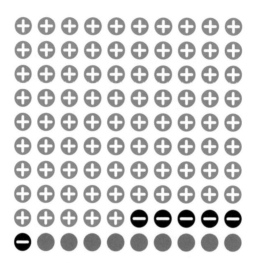

# 85.26%
Positive

# 05.61%
Negative

# 09.12%
Neutral

See a video of respondants in the Resource section for this chapter at www.reorientbook.com.

Common words people surveyed
associated with the word SAVED.

SET FREE
THANKFUL
NARROW-MINDED
FREEDOM
RIGHTEOUS
REDEEMED
JOY
SAVED BY GRACE
BORN AGAIN
ETERNAL LIFE
HEAVEN
FORGIVEN
FANATICAL CHRISTIAN
HEALED
BELIEVER
MYSTERY
HOPE
RECONCILED
LIFE
NEW

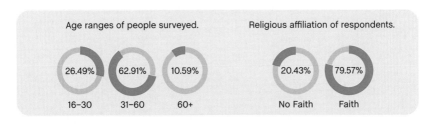

Age ranges of people surveyed.

26.49% — 16–30
62.91% — 31–60
10.59% — 60+

Religious affiliation of respondents.

20.43% — No Faith
79.57% — Faith

# SAVED__REDISCOVER

## OLD TESTAMENT HEBREW WORDS FOR SAVED

USED *More than 450 times*

WORDS YASHA */yaw-shah/*
CHAYAH */kwaw-yaw/*

DEFINITIONS **Yasha:** *to be liberated, delivered, and victorious in battle*
**Cheyah:** *to live, have life, remain alive, live prosperously, live eternally, be quickened, or be restored to life or health*

---

## NEW TESTAMENT GREEK WORDS FOR SAVED

USED *About 110 times*

WORD SOZO */sode ´zo/*

DEFINITION *To keep safe and sound or to rescue from destruction, injury, or peril; to save from suffering from disease, i.e., to make well, heal, restore to health; to save from the penalties of judgment or evil*

# SAVED__RECOUNT

# SAVED

| OLD TESTAMENT VERSES USING THE HEBREW WORDS | NEW TESTAMENT VERSES USING THE GREEK WORD |
|---|---|
| **553** | **103** |

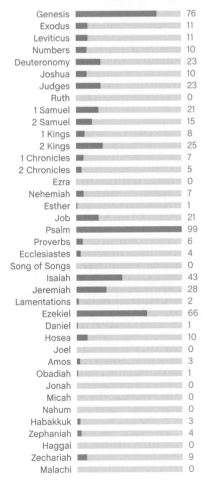

|  |  |
|---|---|
| Genesis | 76 |
| Exodus | 11 |
| Leviticus | 11 |
| Numbers | 10 |
| Deuteronomy | 23 |
| Joshua | 10 |
| Judges | 23 |
| Ruth | 0 |
| 1 Samuel | 21 |
| 2 Samuel | 15 |
| 1 Kings | 8 |
| 2 Kings | 25 |
| 1 Chronicles | 7 |
| 2 Chronicles | 5 |
| Ezra | 0 |
| Nehemiah | 7 |
| Esther | 1 |
| Job | 21 |
| Psalm | 99 |
| Proverbs | 6 |
| Ecclesiastes | 4 |
| Song of Songs | 0 |
| Isaiah | 43 |
| Jeremiah | 28 |
| Lamentations | 2 |
| Ezekiel | 66 |
| Daniel | 1 |
| Hosea | 10 |
| Joel | 0 |
| Amos | 3 |
| Obadiah | 1 |
| Jonah | 0 |
| Micah | 0 |
| Nahum | 0 |
| Habakkuk | 3 |
| Zephaniah | 4 |
| Haggai | 0 |
| Zechariah | 9 |
| Malachi | 0 |

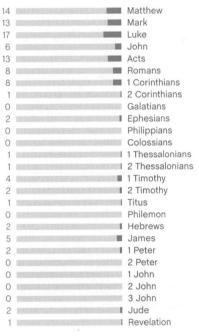

|  |  |
|---|---|
| 14 | Matthew |
| 13 | Mark |
| 17 | Luke |
| 6 | John |
| 13 | Acts |
| 8 | Romans |
| 8 | 1 Corinthians |
| 1 | 2 Corinthians |
| 0 | Galatians |
| 2 | Ephesians |
| 0 | Philippians |
| 0 | Colossians |
| 1 | 1 Thessalonians |
| 1 | 2 Thessalonians |
| 4 | 1 Timothy |
| 2 | 2 Timothy |
| 1 | Titus |
| 0 | Philemon |
| 2 | Hebrews |
| 5 | James |
| 2 | 1 Peter |
| 0 | 2 Peter |
| 0 | 1 John |
| 0 | 2 John |
| 0 | 3 John |
| 2 | Jude |
| 1 | Revelation |

*Graph is based on the highest verse use and shown visually as a percentage of the highest value.

# SAVED__REORIENT

It was 8:00 a.m. on a Friday. We had just finished breakfast, and I was discussing our family plan for the day while enjoying a cup of coffee with Michelle and the kids.

Since committing to spending Monday through Thursday each week writing this book, Fridays were now reserved for defragmenting, taking care of business matters, and doing fun things with the family. This Friday, however, was going to be the rare exception. That's because the day before, I had almost finished writing the "Gospel" chapter and was excited to bring it to conclusion.

According to my calendar, I had no scheduled meetings, and to the best of my knowledge no pressing matters to tend to that day. To say that was rare would be an understatement. Despite my delight in having free time to hang with Michelle and the kids, they shared my sense of urgency to finish the "Gospel" chapter and were gracious enough to let me spend yet another day immersed in *Re_Orient*.

As I was leaving our living room and walking to my office, I received this text from someone I will call Angelo:

> Kevin, I am so sorry! I am running late for our 8:00 a.m. meeting, and it's already 8:25 a.m. I've been driving for an hour, but according to my GPS, I'll be there in 15 minutes, but according to my gut, I may be lost. ;-( If you need to reschedule, I completely understand!

So much for my best laid plans! This meeting had obviously failed to make my schedule. It appeared the free day wasn't going to be completely free after all.

Angelo and I met about two years prior, through a mutual friend. Angelo was a great guy, and we enjoyed connecting around our similar passion for the things of God. However, our paths hadn't crossed much since our initial meetings. I was looking forward to reconnecting, but since failing to recall the meeting in the first place, remembering the exact reason for our meeting proved equally elusive.

As I was contemplating my reply to Angelo's text, I teetered between accepting his offer to reschedule to focus on the "Gospel" writing and honoring my apparent previous commitment to meet. Given that he had already driven more than an hour for the meeting, I was conflicted.

I entered my office and hesitatingly approached my computer with phone in hand and simply asked, "Lord, what do you want me to do today – finish the "Gospel" chapter or meet with Angelo?"

Immediately, it came up in my spirit. I don't mean an audible voice, but inside me I sensed God saying: "Kevin, do you want to write about the rewards of the gospel today or meet with Angelo and actually deliver them?"

Before I had a chance to reply to God or Angelo, the doorbell rang. It was Angelo. He was closer than he had thought. Michelle and the kids greeted him at our front door and were already showing him to my office as I pushed myself away from the computer and stood to say hello.

As Angelo descended the steps to my office, I was taken aback. As my eyes met his, I could still see the vibrant guy in his early thirties with a glowing smile and resolute constitution, but it was impossible not to notice how frail his body had become.

He was at least eighty pounds lighter than I remembered and struggled to keep balanced as he gripped the stair rails with shaking hands. He walked with equally unstable footing.

As we hugged, I could feel Angelo's body tremor slightly as he bravely shouldered what I would learn a few minutes later were the devastating effects of what he called advanced, untreatable, and incurable Primary Progressive Multiple Sclerosis (MS).

Since being diagnosed shortly after our last meeting, like many who have this heinous disease, Angelo had struggled with a cascading barrage of symptoms. He had loss of nerve sensitivity, complete paralysis in some areas of his body, especially the bottoms of his feet, and obvious difficulty with coordination and balance.

He was experiencing extreme weakness in his musculoskeletal system, having sporadic muscle spasms, and his speech and ability to swallow were deteriorating fast. Angelo's bladder and bowel functions were also severely and adversely affected. Extreme fatigue following even the smallest of activities was common, and struggling against and defeating deep depression was a daily battle. Among other things, Angelo's inability to function had cost him his job, decimated his financial ability to provide for his family, made intimacy with his wife virtually nonexistent, and now threatened to sever their already weakened marriage.

To say I had a holy, violent enmity against what this disease had stolen from my friend and his family would be an extreme understatement!

As Angelo told me of his recent plans to take his own life in a last-ditch effort to provide for his family through insurance proceeds, I could feel an unrelenting, holy, violent love rise in me for him. I could hardly contain my eagerness to share what I had just discovered about the real rewards of the gospel while I listened to Angelo share his story and specifically what led him to reconnect with me.

As I would soon learn, if it hadn't been for the way God used another mutual friend of ours – who at the time had no idea Angelo and I even knew each other – he would not be sitting in front of me this day or telling me his story.

Apparently, at one of the lowest moments in Angelo's struggle against MS, he had traveled to another city and made all the requisite plans to end his life. The location involved a small hotel, which ironically was being shared by our mutual friend and some of Angelo's work associates.

As Angelo sat outside the hotel on the tailgate of his truck, talking on his cell phone and attempting to consume enough alcohol to numb his mind to the painful decision points that lay ahead, our mutual friend overheard Angelo's conversation while talking with me on a separate call.

Of course, both of us were completely unaware of the unfolding drama happening nearby and the life that hung in the balance. But the topic of our conversation was how to follow God's leading to treasure others – in other words, doing the stuff we have been discussing in this book.

At the end of our call, God directed my friend to "treasure" Angelo, of all people, and to specifically affirm his future calling in God. What my friend failed to realize at the time was how his simple yet timely affirmation of Angelo apparently gave him reason enough to pause, reconsider his decision, and ultimately reach out to some old friends for help.

One of those old friends was me.

Thank God he did, because just a few minutes later in my house, while Angelo heard about the real rewards of the real gospel, he mustered up enough faith to receive one of them and was healed that day in my office! Well, he was at least eighty percent healed and left with a steady step, reduced paralysis in his feet, and a renewed passion for life. He is still improving today, and when I called him several weeks later to ask his permission to use his story, he was interviewing and had some promising job prospects.

I share his story with you because even though Angelo loved God, had confessed Jesus as his Lord many years prior, was confident of his place in heaven, was Spirit-filled, attended a great church, had many Christian friends who loved him, and had even seen God do miracles, Angelo came to appreciate and reorient – just as we are about to in the remainder of this chapter – to a whole new aspect of what it means to be saved in my office that day.

As Angelo will attest, being saved in terms of going to heaven when he died and, among other things, being free from MS when he got there was good news, but it was even better news – even nearly-too-good-to-be-true news – to learn that his battle with MS could be over now and that he could enjoy some of heaven's rewards in this life.

**RESOURCE**
Would you like to meet Angelo? With his permission, we've posted a segment of a video taken from my phone just moments after he started receiving the healing rewards of the gospel that day in my office. Visit the resource section for this chapter at www.thereorientbook.com.

You could say that even though Angelo had been saved many years prior, he was even more saved that day in my office and is still contending to be fully saved now as he learns to administer the power of God in his own life to revive and fully recover all that MS has stolen from him and his family.

What Angelo discovered is the same focus of our reorientation in this chapter:

*The mission of getting people saved is not all it's been traditionally presented to be – it's actually much, much more!*

## IS GETTING PEOPLE SAVED REALLY THE AIM OF THE GREAT COMMISSION, AND WHAT DOES IT REALLY MEAN TO BE SAVED ANYWAY?

These questions seem strange because, as we discussed in the "Gospel" chapter, getting saved is so often interchangeably linked to the gospel and the so-called Great Commission. It's become the understood and stated aim of most every church, Christian organization, and missionary.

But have you ever considered what the Great Commission actually says about getting people saved? Have you ever wondered what's so *great* about the so-called *Great Commission* anyway?

That was the question I asked in preparation for writing this chapter and upon waking one morning to hearing this phrase:

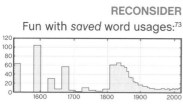

> *There is nothing great about what you call the Great Commission, and it has little to do with what people have traditionally called salvation!*

That statement was as radical to me as the first time I heard, "Kevin, you know it really is about religion, and relationship is a poor substitute," prompting me to begin reorienting to the word *religion.*

The thought of reorienting anyone to a new meaning of religion seemed daunting enough, but redefining something as sacred as what it means to be saved – and the so-called Great Commission – seemed a sure path to public scorn, excommunication, and martyrdom.

But despite the treacherous theological terrain I knew could lie ahead, I couldn't shake the phrase from my mind. The journey and immersion into the subject of being saved is the ultimate destination of all religious pursuits and the end goal of the so-called Great Commission. It is like traveling a well-worn, centuries-old dirt road to a mystical destination – a utopia, if you will – a place where a person is fully saved and not lacking for any good thing. In other words, perfection!

Since I was young, I've sensed in my gut it existed, but over the years I've simply lacked sufficient evidence to say with certainty that complete salvation is really possible, or at least attainable in this life. It seemed with age I had subconsciously given up on the pursuit of the fullness of salvation's promise, relegating it to a destiny only reachable in the utopian reality of the age to come – heaven!.

Even with a renewed and reoriented perspective, navigating the sometimes hostile theological terrain and vigorously defended belief systems centuries of traditional dogma have erected around the topic of salvation can make reorienting difficult.

The way Jesus modeled and illuminated for us to arrive at being saved is easily obscured by a preconditioned mind's ability to look right past it, even when it should otherwise be obvious and in plain sight.

491

As I began reorienting to what it really means to be saved, common platitudes, all-too-familiar interpretations of verses of Scripture, and exposure to centuries-old religious traditions betrayed my heart and mind's desire to follow the Holy Spirit's leading and rediscover what it means and to approach the Great Commission from a new perspective.

At times, I felt like a driver attempting to steer a car in one direction while wrestling against well-worn grooves in a heavily-traveled path that led in an entirely different direction.

I share this because, like me, you may feel a similar pull as we begin to look at these concepts from a fresh perspective.

But I want to encourage you to stay the course. Keep an open mind, and stay on the path until we arrive at the end. Reorienting to the real aim of the so-called Great Commission holds more promise to save the world in three years than the traditional approach has done in more than two thousand.

I want to start by reorienting to what most people traditionally consider the primary aim of the gospel – getting people saved – and why doing so is often considered the fulfillment of the so-called Great Commission given by Jesus.

We have already shown in the last chapter that the gospel was not interchangeably linked to the traditional notions of salvation, but what about the Great Commission? What does it have to do with getting people saved? Is going into the world, getting people saved, and converting them to Christianity really the goal?

Like the gospel, however, it's not that the traditional notion or mission of getting someone saved is in and of itself wrong. The problem, as usual, is with the meanings and implications tradition has assigned to both. It cages the very supernatural realities salvation and the so-called Great Commission were intended to bring about.

# REORIENTING TO THE GREAT COMMISSION

The Great Commission, as the majority of the Western world has come to know it, is the name traditionally given to an instruction from Jesus to His disciples near the end of His time with them on earth.

The Great Commission is also referred to as:

The Apostolic Commission,

The Christian Imperative,

The Divine Commission,

The Final Commission,

The Great Command,

The Great Evangelistic Command,

The Last Commission,

The Missionary Commission,

The Original Commission,

The Universal Commission

... just to name a few of the more than thirty I found.[74]

Biblical references to what is called the Great Commission are said to be found in all four of the Gospel accounts of Jesus' life and once in the book of Acts:

Matthew 28:18–20     Luke 24:46–49     Acts 1:8

Mark 16:15–20        John 20:21

The most famous version of what's called the Great Commission is found in the book of Matthew:

> And when they saw Him they ‹**disciples**› fell down and worshipped Him; but some doubted. Jesus approached and, breaking the silence, said to them, All authority (all power of rule) in heaven and on earth has been given to Me. Go ‹**as you go**› then and make disciples of all the nations ‹**races, tribes, and heathens**›, baptizing ‹**making whelmed**› them into the name of the Father and of the Son and of the Holy Spirit, teaching them to observe ‹**watch or keep an eye on**› everything that I have commanded you, and behold ‹**see**›, I am with you all the days (perpetually, uniformly, and on every occasion), to the [very] close and consummation of the age. Amen (so let it be).
>
> ~ Matthew 28:17–20, AMP

Here is Luke's version:

> And that repentance [with a view to and as the condition of] forgiveness of sins should be preached ‹**heralded as a divine truth**› in His name to all nations ‹**races, tribes, and heathens**›, beginning from Jerusalem. You are witnesses ‹**judicially provide evidence**› of these things.
>
> ~ Luke 24:47–48, AMP

Though I understand a few early manuscripts do not contain it, here is the version of the same Great Commission found in modern translations of the gospel according to Mark:

> He said to them, "Go into all the world and preach ‹**declare and herald a divine truth**› the good news to all creation. Whoever believes and is baptized ‹**made whelmed**› will be saved, but whoever does not believe will be condemned. And these signs will accompany those who believe: In my name they will drive out demons; they will speak in new tongues; they will pick up snakes with their hands; and when they drink deadly poison, it will not hurt them at all; they will place their hands on sick people, and they will get well." After the Lord Jesus had spoken to them, he was

*taken up into heaven and he sat at the right hand of God.*
*Then the disciples went out and preached everywhere, and*
*the Lord worked with them and confirmed his word by the*
*signs that accompanied it.*

*~ Mark 16:15–20*

John's account of Jesus' words is simply:

*Then Jesus said to them again, Peace to you! [Just] as the*
*Father has sent Me forth, so I am sending you. And having*
*said this, He breathed on them and said to them, Receive*
*the Holy Spirit! [Now having received the Holy Spirit, and*
*being led and directed by Him] if you forgive the sins of*
*anyone, they are forgiven; if you retain the sins of anyone,*
*they are retained ‹**to be used as strength**›.*

*~ John 20:21–23,* AMP

And lastly, here is the reference to the same general instruction as recounted by Luke in the book of Acts:

*And while being in their company and eating with them, He*
*commanded ‹**transmitted a message**› them not to leave*
*Jerusalem but to wait for what the Father had promised ‹**the***
***gospel**›, Of which [He said] you have heard Me speak. [See*
*John 14:16, 26; 15:26.] For John baptized ‹**made whelmed**›*
*with water, but not many days from now you shall be bap-*
*tized with (placed in, introduced into) the Holy Spirit. So*
*when they were assembled, they asked Him, Lord, is this*
*the time when You will reestablish the kingdom and restore*
*it to Israel? He said to them, It is not for you to become*
*acquainted with and know what time brings [the things*
*and events of time and their definite periods] or fixed years*
*and seasons [their critical niche in time], which the Father*
*has appointed (fixed and reserved) by His own choice and*
*authority and personal power. But you shall receive power*
*(ability, efficiency, and might) ‹**the gifts of the Spirit**› when*
*the Holy Spirit has come upon you, and you shall be My*

*witnesses in Jerusalem and all Judea and Samaria and to*
*the ends (the very bounds) of the earth.*

*~ Acts 1:4–8,* AMP

The basic and combined directives contained in these verses are re-garded by most evangelicals as primary tenets of their faith, the key mandate of the so-called church, and the primary mission of those who call themselves Christians.

In modern times, these verses and the so-called Great Commission have been reduced to mean the work of churches sending mission-aries into the world to witness or proselytize to lost people with the good news of the gospel.

And as previously discussed, the gospel is then traditionally under-stood to mean that Jesus died on a cross for the remission of people's sins in order to save them from going to hell when they die and enable them instead to inherit eternal life. All of this is said to be obtained by publicly proclaiming you're a sinner, praying a prayer of repentance, and then accepting Jesus as your personal Lord and Savior.

But given what we've covered in this book so far, are you already being alerted to the rather obvious disconnect between these traditional practices and what the verses we just read actually said? Are you noticing some familiar themes?

For example, did you notice how Matthew quotes Jesus as saying that "all authority or all power of rule in heaven and now on earth was given to Him"?

Also, did you notice how Matthew quotes Jesus as saying He is now sending His initial disciples to extend that same measure of rule into every part of the world?

And finally, did you see how Jesus instructed His disciples to go about it – by using the same method He used to equip them: making more disciples by baptism, or immersion, in the ways of the kingdom and providing evidence that they were the real deal by delivering the rewards of the gospel to the world now?

When you consider Matthew's version, Jesus' directive was simple and straightforward, at least to those disciples who didn't still doubt. Jesus basically said to go and extend the rule of heaven on earth as it is in heaven (Matt. 28:16–20).

So to begin reconciling this simple charge with the traditional approach used to bring about salvation and fulfill the Great Commission ...

Let's look more closely at these verses,

Let's look at the common ideas about their implications,

Let's look at the obvious goal of the so-called Great Commission they contain,

Let's start with Jesus' charge:

> *And that charge is to 'Go make disciples of nations by baptizing them into the name of the Father, Son, and Holy Spirit.'*

## REORIENTING TO WHAT IT MEANS TO BAPTIZE A NATION VERSUS THE TRADITIONAL NOTION OF TRYING TO SAVE ONE

Did you notice that in the verse we just read, Jesus didn't send the disciples into the world to save people but rather to disciple nations? What it means to disciple a nation? Or what about baptizing a nation – how does that work?

Based on this verse in Matthew and a few others, traditional theology reduces Jesus' charge to "baptize" to a doctrine of physical water baptism for individuals. To some denominations this is the primary

008 · SAVED · REORIENT

required rite of passage to be saved or, at the very least, a symbol of someone's individual conversion to the Christian faith.

But is that what Jesus had in mind? Is baptizing describing the literal act of water baptism, like when someone is immersed in water and then verbally blessed "in the name of the Father, Son, and Holy Spirit"?

After all, as discussed in the "Disciple" chapter, baptism (immersion) can also be used to describe a type of teaching or learning. In this context, immersion into a name can take on a different meaning – especially considering that in the Bible, a name is most often meant to stand for the authority and full nature of the person behind it, not just a title to identify the person.[75]

To baptize or immerse someone into the name of the Father, Son, and Holy Spirit can imply immersion into the full nature of God Himself and, by default, extend the authority and rule of the very nature of God to anyone and anything immersed in it.

The goal of being baptized was never meant to be reduced to the ritual act of physical immersion in water and then, when combined with a spoken blessing, designed to save someone.

To the contrary, the doctrine of physical water baptism at best can only ever be symbolic. It's only representative of the kind of full immersion into the things of God, which is required to bring about the very nature of the Father, Son, and Holy Spirit on earth as it is in heaven.

**RECONSIDER**
Consider how an ambassador of a government or kingdom comes "in the name of" the king or ruler of that nation and is thought to represent the full nature of that ruler and their kingdom for those willing to acknowledge it.

At best, a doctrine or ritual represents something. The goal is to experientially receive that which the doctrine or ritual represents! When Jesus is quoted by Matthew as saying ...

All authority (all power of rule) in heaven and on earth has been given to Me. Go ‹*as you go*› then and make disciples of all the nations ‹*races, tribes, and heathens*›, baptizing ‹*making whelmed*› them into the name of the Father and of the Son and of the Holy Spirit, teaching

> them to observe ‹*watch or keep an eye on*› everything
> that I have commanded you

… He is saying that disciples were to immerse nations into the full nature of God in order for them to connect with God – love's ideal – experientially and then teach them at a master's level to do the same. The goal was, among other things, that they might behold (which means "to see or provide evidence") that He was with the disciples.

So, in this context, the disciples were simply instructed by Jesus to do exactly what they saw Jesus, the Master Teacher, model and do every day.

This directive is as true today for any real disciple of Jesus as when He first gave it.

## THERE IS NOTHING GREAT ABOUT WHAT TRADITION CALLS THE GREAT COMMISSION, AND REORIENTING TO WHAT JESUS SAID IS EVEN GREATER

In reading the verses traditionally associated with what is called the Great Commission, did you notice there is no mention of Jesus using the words *great, greater,* or *greatest* to describe His directives?

Did that surprise you?

Did it make you wonder why that is?

Did it make you wonder where the phrase originated? In no place did Jesus or His disciples call these directives *great,* let alone use the phrase "the Great Commission" when referring to them?

Not once did they ever imply these verses should take any greater precedence over anything else Jesus taught or instructed His disciples to emulate.

To the contrary, at least in Matthew's version, Jesus actually says the disciples should not teach people to think of what He taught in these verses as being greater but rather that they should teach people to observe *all* He taught and instructed them.

Even more mind blowing than the way tradition labels these specific directives as the Great Commission when Jesus Himself never did is this: Jesus was actually asked about the "greatest commandment" and He did not reference these verses when He answered!

What did He say when asked what is the greatest or most important commandment? This:

> Teacher ‹**Master Teacher**› which kind of commandment is great and important (the principal kind) in the Law? [Some commandments are light – which are heavy?] And He replied to him, You shall love the Lord your God with all your heart and with all your soul and with all your mind (intellect). ‹**See Deuteronomy 6:5**› This is the great (most important, principal) and first commandment. And a second is like it: You shall love your neighbor as [you do] yourself. ‹**See Leviticus 19:18**› These two commandments sum up and upon them depend all the Law and the Prophets ‹**those who speak forth inspired truths**›.
>
> ~ Matthew 22:36–40, AMP

According to Jesus, the act of loving (the *agape* kind we discussed in the first chapter) God, other people, and yourself is the greatest of all commandments. According to Jesus, this should be thought of as the Great Commission, not the verses we read earlier.

So, why don't we associate this commandment by Jesus to love with the Great Commission?

Some sources[76] credit a Lutheran missionary, Justinian Von Welz[77], with initially coining the term the Great Commission during his lifetime between 1621 and 1668 (which is approximately twenty or so years after the word *church* first appeared in an English translation of the Bible). The same sources suggest the term was later popularized by Hudson Taylor[78] more than eighteen hundred years after Jesus' time on earth.

The phrase *the Great Commission* was essentially a marketing slogan crafted to cultivate interest in and support for foreign missions work.

It was obviously effective: We are still using it today. The phrase has become so deeply ingrained in culture and so synonymous with the brand of Christianity, it's rarely ever questioned as anything but the gospel itself.

The way so-called Western Christianity associates the Great Commission label with Jesus' instruction in the verses we read is analogous to how the Western world associates certain labels and brands with the thing itself. Like these iconic labels:

Coke,

Google,

Jacuzzi,

Kleenex,

Levis,

Pepsi,

Xerox.

The term *the Great Commission* was simply a clever, albeit effective, man-made label which over several hundred years of use has achieved such iconic awareness and acceptance that it's become synonymous with the thing itself – people associate it with the primary mission and brand of Christianity.

The term is so pervasive and has become so deeply ingrained in Western Christian culture, just saying or hearing the phrase *the Great Commission* can create a sense of awe-inspiring reverence in the minds of people.

It can evoke images of valiant church-planting missionaries forsaking all they have to be sent to far-off and foreign nations to evangelize the lost while making converts to the Christian faith and getting people saved through heartfelt prayers of repentance.

I am not making light of this, I am inspired by the unimaginable sacrifices of people, many I personally know and respect, who've dedicated their lives to these very things.

But it's important to point out that as fond as people are of the term and as effective as it has been to stir up interest in foreign missions, Jesus never said there was anything great about what is traditionally called the Great Commission.

Not to mention – and maybe even more importantly – the verses most often associated with the so-called Great Commission make ...

No mention of planting churches,

No mention of witnessing,

No mention of converting others to Christianity,

No mention of praying to get nations saved,

No mention of even getting individuals saved at all, for that matter – at least directly.

Despite the historical emphasis placed on it, the traditional notion of bringing individuals to salvation in the traditional sense is not even the understood aim of any of the verses tradition associates with the Great Commission.

Reconsider, for example, this small portion of Matthew's version about the so-called Great Commission:

> Go ‹*as you go*› then and make disciples of all the nations ‹*races, tribes, and heathens*›, baptizing ‹*making whelmed, immersing*› them into the name of the Father and of the Son and of the Holy Spirit, teaching them to observe everything that I have commanded you, and behold ‹**see**›, I am with you all the days (perpetually, uniformly, and on every occasion) ...
>
> ~ Matthew 28:19–20, AMP

Notice how the focus in this verse is on extending heaven's rule by making disciples of nations, baptizing or immersing them into the full nature of God and then teaching them to observe all that Jesus taught, so they (the nations) can see or be provided evidence that God is with them.

There is no mention in this verse of church-planting, making converts to the Christian faith, or getting people saved through prayers of repentance.

Meditate on these ideas for a minute.

Let this sink deep into your spirit.

Now reconsider this verse in light of what we covered in earlier chapters about what it really means to be a disciple, what it means to teach in the context of the ministry gifts we discussed in the "Gospel" chapter, and what it means to provide evidence sufficient to warrant being called a Christian in the "Christian" chapter.

While the real meaning of this verse is completely inconsistent with what is normally thought of as the Great Commission, this verse is surprisingly consistent with Jesus' unrelenting focus on extending His kingdom rule (heaven's rule) on earth – not just getting people saved to go to heaven when they die later.

It's clear even the disciples understood Jesus' directives in these verses to have present-tense, kingdom-establishing, and nation-changing implications, as evidenced by their question to Jesus in the version of the so-called Great Commission we read in Acts:

> So when they were **assembled,** they asked Him, Lord, is this the time when You will **reestablish the kingdom** and restore it to Israel?
>
> ~ Acts 1:6, AMP, **emphasis added**

503

Notice how the disciples didn't ask Jesus if it was time for everyone to be saved and restored to right standing with God.

Pause here. Don't rush past this important point.

To some people, making disciples of nations can sound impersonal, and making disciples of rulers or heads of nations can sound elitist or too social or political in its aim.

I understand the sentiment, especially given the emphasis Western Christianity and the traditional view of the Great Commission places on ministering to the tail of society – those deemed as the least or most oppressed among us – and staying out of the political and social realms of life.

But both are equally important. God loves the head and the tail just the same and wants every realm of society transformed by His kingdom. All people are valuable and treasured by God, whether the heads of nations or the homeless and destitute; the commission to go disciple all of them is equally great. You might say He is an equal opportunity distributor of the rewards of the gospel.

It's also true that everyone is capable of becoming a disciple and delivering the same rewards of the gospel to both the head and the tail of a nation. You don't have to be a politician to have an audience with and administer the rewards of a gospel to a head of a nation or system of government, and you don't have to be the head of a nation or system of government to administer the rewards of the gospel to an entire nation of people.

A person who is skilled in administering the things of the kingdom of God at a master's level of excellence will always be brought before kings and rulers of every realm of society and not just unknown men (Prov. 22:29).

Remember, Jesus never called His commission in these verses greater than any other, but the theme of transforming nations and the leaders of nations by making disciples is the theme and no less great. Indeed, transforming nations by effecting change in the social, commercial, governmental, and educational realms of society is a dominant theme in much of the biblical narrative.

Remember, Jesus called Himself King of a government without end – a holy nation. He intended to build *ekklesias* – uprisings of social, political, or military consequence. He likened disciples who assemble in these *ekklesias* to governmental ambassadors and special-forces soldiers with supernatural giftings and the authority to deliver the rewards of His gospel of the kingdom to the nations.

In the Old Testament alone, the topic of nations was referenced directly ninety-eight times. Abraham was promised by God that his descendants would become a great nation and be a blessing to all the nations of the earth (Gen. 18:18). In fact, the people of God were often called a holy nation (Ex. 19:6).

In the New Testament, the topic is mentioned more than thirty-three times. Paul was sent by God first to the nations, then to the kings or heads of those same nations, and then to the people of Israel –

in that order:

> And the Lord said to him, Go, for this [man] ‹**Paul**› is an elect vessel to me, to bear my name before both nations and kings and [the] sons of Israel.
>
> ~ *Acts 9:15,* DARBY

## SO, HOW DO YOU DISCIPLE A NATION, LET ALONE SAVE ONE?

What does it mean to baptize a nation, teach a nation, or disciple a nation, and how does it differ from making a disciple of an individual?

To answer these questions, let's start with an even more basic question: *What is a nation?*

The word as used in these verses is derived from the Greek word *ethnos*. This Greek word is used more than 150 times in the New Testament, and in addition to being translated *nation(s)* is also translated as the word *Gentile(s), people(s),* and even *heathen(s).* The Greek word *ethnos* literally means "a race" and refers to those having the same collective habits or what we might call today the same culture.

You may also recognize this same Greek word as the obvious root of the English words:

1. *Ethnic,* used to describe a common ancestry.

2. *Ethic,* used to describe a guiding philosophy or virtue.

3. *Ethos,* used to describe a set of collective beliefs or ideals.

I point out these three words because all of them are easily discernible as having a part in making up what people think when they think of a nation. In modern English vernacular, a nation is defined similarly but may also include the idea of having ...

A sovereign territory,

A physical boundary,

A sovereign head of state,

A collection of rulers who govern it,

A governing body

... who set the course for and administer ...

The political,

The social,

The military,

The judicial,

The monetary,

The economic,

The educational systems

... of a group of people.

As a result, it is easy to hear the word *nation* and primarily think of the term only in the context of the more than 190-plus sovereign nations around the globe. But the term could conceivably be and has been historically applied to much smaller groups of people. Even collections of families or tribes without a definable border or formal government were called nations.

For example, God called the Israelites a holy nation long before they had ever possessed a physical territory. In more recent Western history, native Indian tribes are nations (i.e., the Cherokee Nation).

In any respect, it should go without saying that just as in an individual family how the chief leaders or heads of a nation (sometimes called the firsts or royal families) are discipled can be a guiding force behind how the governmental systems of a nation are ultimately established and administered to all the families that make up that nation.

Guiding forces behind individual leaders or heads of nations can serve to influence ...

The identity,

The ethnic (collective ancestral makeup),

The ethos (collective character and dominant behaviors),

The ethic (collective moral virtues and philosophies)

... of the entire nation.

And sometimes this is true regardless of an individual citizen's adherence to an individual leader's beliefs or systems of administration.

An individual leader's influences, though sometimes subtle, are powerful forces that can serve to shape a society, especially when a collective or generally accepted ethic and ethos is reinforced over time. The end result is what we might call *tradition* which, for better or worse, can directly and indirectly control or at least permeate or influence virtually every aspect of a nation's culture and social realms.

That is why I believe God cares so much about sending disciples to disciple nations and the leaders of nations. It's because God cares and loves the people of every nation, whose individual lives are many times controlled or at the very least influenced by the individual leaders and collective ethos of that nation.

Let's face it. When you consider the most evil and dark places on earth, where people are the most oppressed and deprived of the benefits and rewards of the gospel, there is one thing they nearly all have in common: inept, oppressive, and corrupt governments.

In light of these observations, let me highlight one other subtle but important aspect of the word *nation* I believe helps bring clarity.

It's the way the Bible translates the Greek *ethnos* as *nation* in these verses, while in many other places translates the very same the word as *heathen.*

What comes to mind when you hear the word *heathen?* The word is important for two reasons: one, the nuances help to clarify Jesus' directive to "go to the nations," and two, it's a word we will discuss later in this chapter in the context of how to be saved.

Though *heathen* is thought of today as primarily referring to an unconverted, irreligious, uncultured, or uncivilized person, the translators of the Bible used the word differently.

**RECONSIDER**
To illustrate the subtle power of an ethos, consider that Greeks predominantly used the word to describe the subliminal power of music to influence an individual's emotions, behaviors, and ethics..

Biblically, the word *heathen* is used to describe "anyone not yet fully convinced or immersed in the things of God" and is the antonym (direct opposite) of the word *faith,* which means "fully convinced, completely persuaded, or having full assurance."

This is why, for example, the word *heathen* was often used by ancient Hebrews and Jewish people to refer to anyone who was non-Hebrew or non-Jewish in terms of their faith. A heathen was anyone who could not be or was unwilling to be fully convinced or immersed in Jewish ways of life.

A heathen nation, by definition then, at least in relationship to the gospel, could be any country or even small group of people who, for whatever reason, ...

Be it ignorance,

Be it lack of experience,

Be it deception,

Be it oppression,

Be it basic unwillingness to receive it

... is not yet fully convinced, persuaded, or assured the rewards of the gospel hold any real, present-tense promise or power to improve or influence their nation or culture for a higher kind of good.

This is why, while Matthew's version of Jesus' instruction and what is traditionally called the Great Commission emphasized making disciples, teaching by immersion, and being a witness to nations or heathens, Luke's version added the additional aspects of going about it by "preaching the repentance and forgiveness of sins in Jesus' name" to all nations or heathens – right where you are! Here is the verse again from Luke's version:

> And that repentance [with a view to and as a condition of] forgiveness of sins should be preached ‹**heralded as a divine truth**› in His name to all nations ‹**races, tribes, and heathens**›, beginning from Jerusalem. You are witnesses ‹**judicially provide evidence**› of these things.
>
> ~ Luke 24:47–48, AMP

**RECONSIDER**
Based on our reoriented meaning, a "heathen" could be anyone who is not a disciple!

509

## REORIENTING TO WHAT IT MEANS TO DISCIPLE A NATION IN YOUR OWN NEIGHBORHOOD AND A FRESH LOOK AT PREACHING REPENTANCE AND FORGIVENESS OF SINS

Reorienting to what Luke meant by repentance, forgiveness of sin, and being a witness has far-reaching implications, but first I want to highlight one other aspect of these verses from Luke's gospel.

Notice how Luke recounts how Jesus instructed His disciples to begin this nation-changing mission right where they were, in Jerusalem, and then to go from there to all nations.

Notice Jesus didn't send His disciples first to far-off foreign lands to begin their work, but instead told them to disciple the ethnos – heathen – nations in their immediate realm of influence, which was in Jerusalem. We might say today: *Begin first by making disciples of your own neighbors or neighborhoods, and then move out from there!*

This is a simple but significant distinction, especially when compared to the modern approach to missions, which traditionally and primarily emphasizes sending missionaries only to reach unreached people groups in the uttermost parts of the earth.

While it's right to take the rewards of the gospel to unreached people in all parts of the world, the all-consuming focus on and support for only going to foreign nations in the traditional sense is not. The Great Commission as we have come to know it unfortunately often takes precedence over people groups in our immediate vicinity who desperately need to receive the same rewards of the gospel being exported to foreign lands.

In addition to being consistent with what Jesus actually called the great commandment, to love your neighbor as yourself (Matt. 22:39), the direct approach of beginning to deliver the rewards of the gospel in your immediate realms of influence just makes practical sense.

Where and how did Luke say Jesus told them to begin doing that?

*Beginning from Jerusalem. You are witnesses ‹judically provide evidence› of these things.*

> ~ Luke 24:47–48, AMP

They were to begin right where they were, in their own city, Jerusalem, by declaring repentance, which means "to think differently afterward." In this case, the implication is to think differently after or upon hearing the nearly-too-good-to-be-true news about being forgiven of sin.

If anyone was still unsure about this message upon hearing it, the disciples were instructed to be prepared to be a witness, meaning they were to provide judicial evidence with miraculous signs following about the present-tense reality of the rewards of the gospel about which they spoke.

Do you see how these directives differ significantly from the traditional approach to the Great Commission but are so consistent with much of what we have reoriented to so far about the *real* Great Commission?

Jesus' disciples were not directed to go to all nations or people groups with a gospel message about everyone being sinners and needing to repent of sin to be forgiven. Just the opposite was true.

Jesus' disciples were sent to tell the world the divine truth: that sin was no longer a problem (because their Master Teacher, Jesus, took away the sin of the world) and they were forgiven, which was intended to bring about repentance (thinking differently afterwards) in order to receive the rewards of the gospel of the kingdom.

**Disciples were never instructed by Jesus to go into the world on a mission to convict others of their innate sinfulness, lead them through a prayer to get saved, and convert them to Christianity in order for them to go to heaven when they died. In fact, as we will discuss later, nowhere in the Bible does it even say that a person should even pray to be saved.**

Disciples were called to be witnesses (or to provide evidence) of these things in order that they might cause others to repent (think differently afterward) and become disciples, too.

This is such a huge distinction, I can't underscore it enough. Again, you really have to let this sink in. The disciples were instructed by Jesus to declare the good news about being forgiven of sin – *not* to declare someone's need to be forgiven because they were a sinner.

In John's version of the so-called Great Commission, he emphasizes this very aspect of Jesus' directive to His disciples:

> *Then Jesus said to them again, Peace to you! [Just] as the Father has sent Me forth, so I am sending you. And having said this, He breathed on them and said to them, Receive the Holy Spirit* ‹**according to the concordance and, by implication, to become superhuman**›*! [Now having received the Holy Spirit, and being led and directed by Him] if you forgive the sins of anyone, they are forgiven; if you retain the sins of anyone, they are retained* ‹**to be used as strength**›*.*
> ~ John 20:21–23, AMP

Notice John's emphasis on how Jesus instructed His disciples to go into the world with the power to forgive sin, so that it could not be used as a "strong force" against others to separate them from God any longer – just as He was sent to do.

Jesus literally says that if His disciples didn't forgive someone's sin, then their sins will be retained or continued to be used as strength against them and keep them from receiving the Holy Spirit of God designed to make them strong – even superhuman.

We are so accustomed to starting with the premise that people are in sin and that unless they do something, God will not forgive them and their sin will remain. But here Jesus is saying just the opposite. It's the *disciples'* job to tell people they are forgiven and that sin is not a problem that keeps their sin from remaining!

As strange as it sounds to hear it put this way, it's similar and consistent with how Jesus told His disciples that He was giving them the keys to the kingdom of heaven and that whatever they bound (disallowed) on earth would be bound in heaven and whatever they loosed (permitted or retained) on earth will be loosed in heaven, doesn't it? (Matt. 18:18).

The authority for the disciples to forgive sin is derived from the fact that sin is not a problem in heaven and, therefore, is not a problem wherever an ambassador of the kingdom of heaven is sent by God to extend heaven's rule on earth.

Being assured that you are forgiven and freed from sin or separation from God in this context is essential to receive the other rewards of the gospel Jesus' disciples were and still are empowered to deliver to a world separated from it.

Being a witness to the future- and present-tense rewards of the gospel, teaching people – or in the case of these verses, teaching nations – who are willing to receive them, and rising up with holy, violent love to contend for them is the primary job and mission of a disciple. Conviction or conversion of any other kind is the job of the Holy Spirit (John 16:8–11).

## DELIVERING THE REAL PROMISES AND REWARDS OF THE GOSPEL TO HEATHEN NATIONS AND THE POWER TO SAVE PEOPLE WHO BELIEVE AND RECEIVE IT

So, what are the other promises and rewards of the gospel of the kingdom of God for a heathen nation ...

That has not yet heard it,

That has been deceived about it,

That has rejected it,

That has not permitted people to receive it for whatever reason?

The answer is simple. It is the same nearly-too-good-to-be-true news and reward God has promised to every individual willing to receive it.

To a nation without hope, the nearly-too-good-to-be-true news of the gospel promise and the mission of those disciples who are equipped to bring it about is the earnest expectation that something good is about to happen.

To oppressed nations, the reward of the gospel and true disciples delivers and provides evidence of freedom.

To weak nations, the reward of the gospel and true disciples delivers and provides evidence of supernatural power.

To poor nations, the reward of the gospel and true disciples delivers and provides evidence of prosperity.

To corrupt nations, the reward of the gospel and true disciples delivers and provides evidence of divine truth and justice.

To nations ravaged by sickness and disease, the reward of the gospel and true disciples delivers and provides evidence of divine healing.

To nations in engaged constant strife and conflict, the reward of the gospel and true disciples delivers and provides evidence of supernatural peace.

To nations with seemingly insurmountable problems, the reward of the gospel and true disciples delivers and provides evidence of divine wisdom.

To nations who live with a constant fear of death, the reward of the gospel and true disciples delivers and provides evidence of eternal life.

To nations controlled by oppressive rulers who do evil for sport and to whom the gospel promises and rewards are utter foolishness, the reward of the gospel and true disciples delivers and provides evidence of the power of God to rise up and overthrow them and be saved (1 Cor. 1:18)!

To nations lacking a vision of what is possible and leaders capable of administering these realities, the reward of the gospel is a disciple of God to teach them how to inherit these promises.

As tempting as it is to water down this kind of rhetoric in fear of being mocked and shamed by those who consider it foolishness, we cannot be ashamed of this gospel.

Paul himself said it's this very gospel of the kingdom that needs to be proclaimed to all the nations of the world:

> I am not ashamed of the gospel, because it is the power of God for the salvation of everyone who believes: first for the Jew, then for the Gentile.
>
> ~ Romans 1:16

Remember, Mark's version of the so-called Great Commission even confirms these are the very signs or evidences that follow those who believed the gospel they preached:

> He said to them, "Go into all the world and preach ‹**declare and herald a divine truth**› the good news to all creation. Whoever believes and is baptized ‹**immersed, made whelmed**› will be saved, but whoever does not believe will be condemned. And these signs will accompany those who believe: In my name they will drive out demons; they will speak in new tongues; they will pick up snakes with

*their hands; and when they drink deadly poison, it will not*
*hurt them at all; they will place their hands on sick people,*
*and they will get well." After the Lord Jesus had spoken to*
*them, he was taken up into heaven and he sat at the right*
*hand of God. Then the disciples went out and preached*
*everywhere, and the Lord worked with them and confirmed*
*his word by the signs that accompanied it.*

~ Mark 16:15–20

Every spiritual gift or supernatural endowment of grace God made available to His disciples was and is designed with this purpose in mind: to bring about the present-tense rewards of the gospel in every area of life.

As Paul said in the verse we just read in Romans, it's the very administration of these gifts and subsequent rewards of the gospel that have the power to bring about true salvation.

## WHAT IT REALLY MEANS TO BE SAVED

So, if Jesus never called what is traditionally known as the Great Commission great, and if the verses we just looked at are more about making disciples of nations than getting individuals saved, what does it really mean to be saved, and how do you go about getting saved in all its fullness?

To answer, let's begin as usual with defining the word *saved.* Here is how the first few entries in the modern dictionary define the word:

**Saved**
*verb*
1. to rescue from danger or possible harm, injury, or loss: to save someone from drowning
2. to keep safe, intact, or unhurt; safeguard; preserve: God save the king
3. to keep from being lost
4. theology: to deliver from the power and consequences of sin.

*Origin(s):*
1175–1225; Middle English *sa(u)ven* < Old French *sauver* < Late Latin *salvāre,* to save; see *keep safe.*

As the modern dictionary suggests, the origins of our English word *saved* are thought to be the Latin word *salvāre.* Another online etymology dictionary cites the same Latin word *salvāre* as the original source of the words *saved* and *salvation* but adds the more modern so-called Christian implication of the word dating back to the early 1300s and in a non-Christian sense to the late 1400s.

How do these modern dictionary definitions and uses of the word *saved* compare with how the Bible defines the term?

The word *saved* appears more than 450 times in the Old Testament as the English translation of two Hebrew words. The first, *yasha* (pronounced yaw-shah), means:

To be liberated,

To be delivered,

To be victorious in battle.

In addition to being translated as *saved,* the same Hebrew word, *yasha,* is translated in English as meaning:

To avenge,

To defend,

To deliver,

To help,

To preserve,

To rescue,

**RECONSIDER**
The more modern implications of the word *saved* are thought to have given rise to phrases like *save our soul* in the Christian sense and *source of salvation* in the non-Christian sense. These phrases are believed by some to be the genesis of the SOS warning used to signal the need for help or rescue.

To be safe,

To make victorious.


The second Old Testament Hebrew word translated saved, *chayah* (pronounced kwaw-yaw), means:


To live,

To have life,

To remain alive,

To live prosperously,

To live eternally,

To be quickened,

To be restored to life or health.


In addition to being translated as *saved,* many times the same word *chayah* is also translated:


Alive,

Quicken,

Recover,

Revive,

Healed,

Kept alive.

In the New Testament, the word *saved* appears more than one hundred times as the English translation of the Greek word *sozo* (pronounced sode'zo), which literally means:

To keep safe,

To keep sound,

To rescue from destruction, injury, or peril,

To save from suffering from disease,

To make well,

To heal,

To restore to health,

To save from the penalties of judgment,

To save from evil.

In addition to being translated as *saved,* the same Greek word *sozo* is translated:

To make whole,

To make well,

To heal,

To restore,

To make safe,

To cure.

It is also translated as the word *recover.*

As you can see, the word *saved* represents a rare instance where the modern English dictionary and the biblical use of the Greek word – in this case, the word *sozo* – are essentially the same. Succinctly, the word *saved* simply means:

> ❝ *To heal, deliver, protect, prosper, and make whole and victorious.* ❞

In fact, this is the exact definition the Greek concordance of the New Testament gives for the biblical use of the word *saved*. It's also consistent with how Jesus and His disciples used the term.

Read this definition a few times before continuing on. Meditate on it for a moment and try to let it sink into your spirit.

Now, note the implications as you replace the word *saved* with its actual meaning in these two famous verses where the word is used:

> *For the Son of man is come to save ‹sozo – to heal, deliver, protect, prosper, and make whole and victorious› that which was lost ‹literally and figuratively, being ruined, losing, perishing, or destroyed›.*
>
> *~ Matthew 18:11, KJV*

And likewise in this verse:

> *For the Son of man is not come to destroy men's lives, but to save ‹sozo – to heal, deliver, protect, prosper, and make whole and victorious› them. And they went to another village.*
>
> *~ Luke 9:56, KJV*

As you read these verses with the actual definition of the word *saved* in mind, does it surprise you to see nothing that indicates Jesus only meant to save people from hell and provide entrance to heaven?

While certainly people will be saved – healed, delivered, protected, prosperous, and made whole and victorious – in heaven, there is nothing inherent in the definition of the word *saved* or in the way Jesus or

His followers used the word in these verses to indicate it was limited to the future-tense reality.

To the contrary, the majority of the benefits of being saved, as the definition of the word suggests, are obtainable both now and in heaven.

Not only is this evident in the definition of the word and in the two verses we just read, but it's also true for the way the word was used in the more than six hundred other instances in the Bible where the Hebrew words from the Old Testament and this Greek word from the New Testament are translated to English as some variation of the word *saved*.

I don't know about you, but had I known this to be true when I first got saved, I would have expected and contended for a whole lot more out of life this side of heaven!

Please be assured, I am not saying that being saved doesn't include going to heaven when you die. It most certainly can include that, too. However, I am saying we must reorient to the reality that in the same way the real rewards of the gospel were never meant to be only received in the future, salvation was never intended and should never be limited to the future-tense reality of heaven alone.

Limiting salvation to a future-tense reality minimizes the present-tense implications of what it means to be saved in the context of being *healed, delivered, protected, prospered, and made whole and victorious* that Jesus and His disciples emphasized the most.

## SAVED AND HEALED, DELIVERED, PROTECTED, PROSPERED, AND MADE WHOLE AND VICTORIOUS NOW, IN THIS LIFE

The following are just a few of the many examples in the New Testament where Jesus and His disciples used the Greek word *sozo* (the one we translate into English as *saved*) and meant instantly being healed, delivered, protected, prospered, and made whole and victorious.

For our first example, let's consider the dramatic account in the book of Luke about a man from the country of the Gerasenes (sometimes translated Gadarenes) who was possessed by devils, causing him to have an unsound mind and frequent seizures, was saved – meaning healed and delivered in the same instance:

> They sailed to the region of the Gerasenes, which is across the lake from Galilee. When Jesus stepped ashore, He was met by a demon-possessed man from the town. For a long time this man had not worn clothes or lived in a house, but had lived in the tombs.
>
> ~ Luke 8:26–27

And continuing a few verses later:

> For Jesus had commanded the evil spirit to come out of the man. Many times it had seized him, and though he was chained hand and foot and kept under guard, he had broken his chains and had been driven by the demon into solitary places. Jesus asked him, "What is your name?" "Legion," he replied, because many demons had gone into him.
>
> ~ verses 29–30

Again continuing a few verses later:

> And the people went out to see what had happened. When they came to Jesus, they found the man from whom the demons had gone out, sitting at Jesus' feet, dressed and in his right mind; and they were afraid. Those who had seen it told the people how the demon-possessed man had been cured ‹**sozo – to heal, deliver, protect, prosper, and make whole and victorious**›.
>
> ~ verses 35–36

Notice how Luke, himself a physician by trade, uses the technical term *sozo*, which the New International Version translates as cured in the verse we just read, to describe how Jesus delivered the man of the Gerasenes of demons, healed his seizures, and restored him to his right mind.

In several other modern translations of this verse, the same word *sozo* is translated healed, made well, or restored to health.

As another example, the passage in Matthew referring to the same physical, emotional, and spiritual healing of the man from Gerasenes says:

> *News about him spread all over Syria, and people brought to him all who were ill with various diseases, those suffering severe pain, the demon-possessed, those having seizures, and the paralyzed, and he healed them.*
>
> *~ Matthew 4:24*

In addition to specific examples where the word *sozo* is used to imply a specific kind of healing, deliverance, or freedom from a single infirmity or situation, in several instances *sozo* was used to imply that a person was made completely whole when they were saved.

## SAVED AND MADE WHOLE

Matthew recounts a story about a woman contending to simply touch Jesus' garment who, upon doing so, was saved or made whole:

> *For she said within herself, If I may but touch his garment, I shall be* **whole** *‹in this instance, sozo is translated made whole›. But Jesus turned him about, and when he saw her, he said, Daughter, be of good comfort; thy faith hath* **made thee whole** *‹sozo›. And the woman was made* **whole** *‹sozo› from that hour.*
>
> *~ Matthew 9:21–22,* KJV, ***emphasis added***

This story was also recorded by Mark and Luke, both of whom used the same word *sozo* to describe how the woman was made whole (Mark 5:28, 34; Luke 8:48).

The exact same language is used to describe how a blind man was made whole:

> *And Jesus said unto him, Go thy way; thy faith hath made thee whole* **‹sozo›.** *And immediately he received his sight, and followed Jesus in the way.*
>
> *~ Mark 10:52,* KJV

I especially like how this verse says the blind man was not only *made whole,* but then *immediately* received his sight and then followed Jesus *in the way.* Notice Jesus didn't only promise the man that one day in heaven he would be made whole if he repented of his sins and agreed Jesus was the way first.

## SAVED AND MADE PERFECTLY WHOLE

In other places, it says *all* were saved or made perfectly whole in the same manner as the two individuals we just read about. For example, look at this account where the benefits of salvation were delivered to *all* who were sick and saved by merely touching the fringe of Jesus' garment:

RECONSIDER
Other examples where *sozo* is used and what is implied:

Do well (John 11:12)

Healed and revived from death (Mark 5:23)

Healed from blindness (Luke 18:42)

Preserved and kept (Luke 17:33; 2 Tim. 4:18)

Rescued from drowning (Matt. 14:30; Jude 1:5, 23)

Revived, renewed, renovated, washed (Titus 3:5)

Set free or delivered from sin (Matt. 1:21)

Victorious overcoming (Matt. 24:13)

*And when the men of that place recognized Him, they sent around into all the surrounding country and brought to Him all who were sick and begged Him to let them merely touch the fringe of His garment; and as many as touched it were perfectly restored ‹**diasozo, meaning to save thoroughly**›.*
*~ Matthew 14:35–36, AMP*

Notice how this verse uses the wording *perfectly restored,* a phrase derived from the Greek word *diasozo,* which itself is a derivative of the word *sozo,* meaning "to save thoroughly."

Examples like these where Jesus saved people resulting in healing, deliverance, or immediate wholeness for the person being saved underscore why God, and specifically Jesus, is called the Savior in a third of the New Testament. In fact, savior is a title that often means healer (Eph. 5:23) and deliverer (Luke 2:11; John 4:42).

Even Jesus' atoning and saving work on the cross was not said to limit salvation only to the future-tense reality of heaven but included healing and wholeness now as one of the primary benefits.

To see what I mean, consider this famous verse:

> He personally carried our sins in his body on the cross so that we can be dead to sin and live for what is right. By his wounds you are healed ‹*sozo – made whole*›.
>
> ~ *1 Peter 2:24,* NLT

You may recognize this as a direct reference to an even more famous Old Testament verse from the book of Isaiah, which used the same language to describe what the writer foresaw Jesus would endure and accomplish on the cross:

> But he was pierced for our rebellion, crushed for our sins. He was beaten so we could be whole. He was whipped so we could be healed.
>
> ~ *Isaiah 53:5,* NLT

Again, notice these verses don't say Jesus carried our sins to the cross only to grant us entrance to heaven where we could live free of sin or be healed one day. Instead, it says He endured the cross so we can live for what is right now in this age and that by His wounds we "were healed and made whole," implying a past-, present-, and future-tense reality.

In other words, just like Angelo at the beginning of this chapter, a person ...

Can be saved,

Can be in the process of being saved,

Can be ultimately saved

... all at the same time.

**RECONSIDER**
God saved (past tense) (Rom. 8:24)

God is saving (present tense) (1 Cor. 1:18)

God shall save (future tense) (Rom. 10:9)

This is an important distinction that, because of the traditional way salvation is usually defined, doesn't get emphasized enough.

Jesus didn't do all that He did just so we could have a better life in an age to come. His accomplishments have the power to provide both a better life now in this age and in the age to come.

It's important to keep reinforcing this reality because there is a common tendency for people to relegate the most important and valuable aspects of what Jesus accomplished to the reward of eternal life, which is typically only thought of as existing in the age to come after a person dies.

But let's think about that.

What is eternal life? When does eternity actually start and end?

By its very definition, the word *eternal* implies something that is perpetual or exists in the past, present, and future. And if so, wouldn't the rewards of eternal life also have to have the same past, present, and future implications by default? Remember:

1.   God is eternal; He's the same yesterday, today, and forever.

2.   God's kingdom is eternal; it's the same yesterday, today, and forever.

3.   The gospel of the kingdom is eternal; it's the same yesterday, today, and forever.

4.   The gospel's rewards are eternal; they're the same yesterday, today, and forever.

Hence, the reason we must resolve that what Jesus did to save us by going to the cross is just as much about restoring our past- and present-tense life to wholeness as perfecting our future-tense life in heaven.

## GOD'S ONE-STEP PROGRAM TO SAVE THE WORLD

You might say, as the following verse suggests, that when it comes to getting people saved, God has a one-step program that delivers the past-tense, present-tense, and future-tense benefits of His kingdom:

> *But everyone* ‹**all, whosoever, any person**› *who calls on the name of the Lord will be saved* ‹**sozo – to heal, deliver, protect, prosper, and make whole and victorious**›.
> ~ *Acts 2:21,* NLT; *see also Romans 10:13 and Joel 2:32*

This one-step mandate and understanding of what it meant to be saved wasn't limited to the historical works of Jesus. Referring to how thousands were being saved and added to the *ekklesia* daily, Jesus' own disciples went about saving people in the exact same manner:

> *... praising God, and having favour with all the people, and the Lord was adding those being saved* ‹**sozo – to heal, deliver, protect, prosper, and make whole and victorious**› *every day to the assembly* ‹**ekklesia**›.
> ~ *Acts 2:47,* YLT

The disciples were so good at getting people saved in this manner that in one specific instance they were called into question by some religious leaders of the day and asked, "by what power or by what name" (Acts 4:7) they had saved a sick, feeble, and impotent man by "making him whole." They responded:

> *If we this day be examined of the good deed done to the impotent man* ‹**someone without strength, feeble, sick, or weak**› *by what means he is made whole* ‹**sozo**›.
> ~ *Acts 4:9,* KJV

Apparently, the disciples' success bringing about the present-tense benefits of salvation for people in their everyday lives was creating such undeniable impact that just a few verses later it says they were severely threatened with punishment by the powers that be if they didn't stop it (verses 13–18).

The disciples weren't saving people by witnessing to them about what Jesus did on the cross and then asking them to say a sinner's prayer to gain a better life in heaven when they died.

Instead, the disciples demonstrated many miraculous signs and wonders, including the power ...

To heal,

To deliver,

To protect,

To prosper,

To make people whole,

To save them now.

Contrary to the more modern approach of "witnessing" to people about the cross in order to get them saved to go to heaven, the disciples insisted it was the presence of the signs, miracles, and demonstrations of power that brought about salvation that were the "witness" of Jesus' resurrection and the future assurance of heaven's reality.

For example, in Paul's own words, he said:

> *For the word of the cross to those indeed perishing ‹**literally or figuratively losing, being destroyed, or dying**› is foolishness, and to us – those being saved ‹**sozo – to heal, deliver, protect, prosper, and make whole and victorious**› – it is the power ‹**the miracle-working power**› of God.*
> *~ 1 Corinthians 1:18,* YLT

And later he said:

> *I am not ashamed of the **gospel,** because it is the **power** ‹**again, the miracle-working power**› of God for **the salvation of everyone who believes:** first for the Jew, then for the Gentile.*
> *~ Romans 1:16, **emphasis added***

Can you see the way Paul, as a disciple of Jesus, said the gospel is the supernatural power of God to bring about salvation in this verse?

Think about this in the context of what we have learned so far. Think about the real meaning of a disciple. Think about their mandate to tell people about the gospel of the kingdom. Think about the spiritual gifts or supernatural endowments of grace that disciples were given by God in order to deliver the rewards of the gospel in the present tense to those still embattled who had not yet heard about it.

You might say the end result of someone being saved in all its fullness now and in the present tense is another way of saying *mission accomplished!*

For me, this helps explain the disparity we historically see between the promised rewards of the gospel of salvation, as traditionally presented, where someone only gains heaven when they die, versus the rewards of the gospel of the kingdom Jesus and His followers championed, designed to bring about the fullness of salvation by extending heaven's rule on earth now!

Success for the traditional approach of the gospel of salvation can be measured by the number of people who place their faith in Jesus to be saved when they die and go to heaven. And while this is a legitimate form of success, success for advancing the gospel of the kingdom is measured differently. Success for evangelizing this gospel of the kingdom can only be measured by the number of people receiving the rewards of the gospel and being saved – healed, delivered, protected, prospered, and made whole and victorious – on earth now.

Which leads to the questions:


Are you saved?

Are you saved in all the fullness of the word?

What must a person do to be saved in all the fullness of the word?


Once someone hears the rewards of the gospel are not just limited to heaven in the age to come, what must they do to receive those rewards now and be saved by their power?

## SO, WHAT MUST I DO TO BE SAVED IN ITS FULLNESS, NOW IN THIS LIFE AND IN THE AGE TO COME

When you think about the answer to the question, "What must I do to be saved – and by saved, I mean healed, delivered, protected, prospered, and made whole and victorious on earth, now and in the age to come?" what comes to your mind?

It's surprising for most people to discover that while they may do many good things, the answer the Bible gives to this question has nothing to do ...

With being a good person,

With observing the Ten Commandments,

With admitting you're a sinner,

With saying a prayer asking Jesus to forgive you,

With getting baptized,

With going to church,

With seeking out a spiritual guru with mystical powers to heal.

It's also surprising for most to discover there is no truth in the all-too-common belief among many theologians that there is *nothing we can do to be saved.* The implication is these types of present-tense miracles are solely dependent upon the mysterious and unknowable will of God who occasionally does them, but only when He decides and only for whom He chooses.

Hence the reason so many believe it's easier to simply relegate these things to a future-tense reality in heaven. But contrary to these commonly held beliefs, God has made His will plainly knowable, and it's not complicated or mysterious.

Remember, God wants *all men* to be saved:

*... who wants all men to be saved ‹sozo – to heal, deliver, protect, prosper, and make whole and victorious› and to come to a knowledge of the truth.*

*~ 1 Timothy 2:4*

If this verse and others like it that insist God is not slack concerning His promises and that it's never been His will that any would perish (2 Pet. 3:9) are true, why do people perish? Why is everyone not saved?

The answer should be obvious: It's not up to the will of God alone. People have a part to play in receiving everything God has promised.

God can love people,

God can take away the sin of the entire world,

God can provide supernatural endowments of grace to move heaven and earth,

God can long to give people heaven's reality,

God can do anything except make anybody get saved who doesn't have a will to be saved.

God leaves that part up to us.

If we don't do our part, as simple as it may be, even Jesus Himself said He was powerless to bring these things about on our behalf.

Are you ready to reorient to what God says we must do to be saved in all its fullness?

For the answer, I want to consider a verse from the book of Acts where this question was answered by Paul and his associate Silas after they were unjustly imprisoned and held in chains for freeing a slave girl from a demonic spirit.

"What must I do to be saved?" was the exact question asked by a stunned prison guard who apparently feared retribution from Paul and

Silas after a series of dramatic and miraculous signs and wonders facilitated their supernatural release from their chains and prison cell:

> After he had led them out of the jail, he asked, "What must I do to be saved ‹**sozo – to heal, deliver, protect, prosper, and make whole and victorious**›?" They replied, "Have faith in the Lord Jesus and you will be saved ‹**sozo – to heal, deliver, protect, prosper, and make whole and victorious**›! This is also true for everyone who lives in your home."
>
> ~ Acts 16:30–31, CEV

*Have faith in God!* That was Paul's and Silas' simple answer to the question of what someone must do to be saved.

Are you surprised?

Disappointed?

Deflated?

Most people I've encountered would say yes to all three.

Why? Because the phrase "just have faith" seems like a rather obvious and standard theological answer to a lot of tough questions. And if the usual blank looks I see on people's faces are any indication, it's a disappointing climax to what they were hoping might be a more insightful and dramatic revelation.

In my experience, the reason people feel this way is because the word *faith* is as equally overused and misunderstood as the other words to which we have reoriented so far.

Among the religious and unreligious alike, there are mountains of misinformation about faith and what it means to have it.

For many people, faith is a kind of nebulous and intangible platitude that is shrouded in as much superstition and mystery as the aforementioned will of God. Among the people we surveyed who considered themselves more intelligent, rational, logical, or scientifically minded, they often considered religious faith at odds with authentic reason.

In these social circles, religious faith is thought of as a crutch for mystics and weaker-minded people with lower intellectual standards. Phrases like "just have faith" are, for them, simply catch-alls to invoke unwavering commitment and blind allegiance by the simple-minded to something or someone without having any real assurance or convincing evidence.

As one celebrated scientist, Stephen Hawking, asserts, science is based upon what is observable and reasonable and that which "just works," whereas religious faith is unobservable, unreasonable, and therefore unable to be relied upon with any assurance or confidence it will work.[79]

These statements demonstrate an all-too-common presumption about what the Bible means when it says "have faith." Furthermore, they serve to inflame seemingly irreconcilable differences between religious faith and what people think of as science and reason.

Wrong presumptions like these have fueled the fires of heated debate for decades, putting scientists, who see scientific knowledge as superior to religious knowledge because it requires no faith, in direct opposition with people of faith, who are generally portrayed as perceiving scientists as being unwilling to acknowledge their faith as anything but pure fantasy.

Real biblical faith, however, was never meant to be mysterious and unpredictable and exercised in the absence of real evidence. To the contrary, by definition, biblical faith is substantive, observable, and real – something that someone should be able to be completely assured of and trust before putting their confidence in it.

For example, consider how Paul says: :

> Now faith is the substance ‹**the concrete support**› of things hoped for, the evidence ‹**proof**› of things not seen.
> ~ Hebrews 11:1, KJV

As this verse says, biblical faith is substantive and must be based upon the presence of real, observable evidence, or "proof," of things previously unseen or hoped for before someone is to be fully persuaded by it. That sounds more like a definition of the scientific method than how biblical faith is often portrayed!

But how, exactly, does the kind of biblical faith Paul describes here actually save a person?

## REORIENTING TO WHAT IT REALLY MEANS TO HAVE FAITH AND WHY IT'S REQUIRED TO SAVE YOU AND THE WORLD AS WE KNOW IT

There is no denying the emphasis the Old and New Testament writers placed on biblical faith. In addition to being referenced as a role in most every significant miracle or supernatural event in the Bible, real biblical faith is the central ingredient needed to literally save the world and every individual in it.

Consider taking a moment to read in your own Bible what Paul says in the verses following the one we just read in Hebrews 11:1 about the more than twenty of the most epic and legendary events and miracles of salvation God did through people like:

Abel,

Abraham,

Abraham's wife, Sarah,

David,

Enoch,

Isaac,

Jacob,

Joseph,

Moses,

Noah,

Samson,

Samuel

... all of which were said to be done "by faith" (Heb. 11:1–40).

Even in Jesus' own ministry, it's stunning to consider that of the twenty-one accounts of miracles of healing (a type of salvation) the Bible records that Jesus did, in seventeen of them He specifically mentions the person's individual faith as playing a dominant role in what they received from God – often saying things like "according to your *faith*, so be it" (Matt. 9:29), "your *faith* made you whole" (Mark 5:34), or "your *faith* has saved you" (Luke 7:50).

In fact, the Bible says:

> *For it is by grace ‹**divine spiritual influence on the human heart**› you have been saved ‹**sozo – to heal, deliver, pro-tect, prosper, and make whole and victorious**›, through faith – and this not from yourselves, it is the gift of God.*
> *~ Ephesians 2:8*

The Bible is clear that without this thing it calls faith, obtained through this thing it calls grace, a person cannot not be saved and fully receive what God has clearly made it His will to provide.

Consider how often Jesus said it was a lack of faith that prevented Him from doing the mighty works it was clearly the will of His Father in heaven for Him to do (Mark 6:1–5).

Not once did Jesus ever say it...

Was the enemy keeping Him from saving someone,

Was because it wasn't His Father's will to save someone,

Was because the timing wasn't right to save someone,

Was because a person was too bad or evil to be saved,

535

Was because His Father wasn't pleased enough to save someone.

That's because the only thing that God has ever required for a person to both receive and administer the rewards of the gospel and bring about all the benefits of salvation on earth now and in the age to come is simply faith.

Maybe that's why even Jesus' own apostles were found asking Jesus to increase their faith (Luke 17:5) and why, on the most difficult night of Jesus' life, hours before His crucifixion, Jesus was found praying for His disciples that their "faith" would not fail (Luke 22:32).

The fact that the Bible tells people to "fight the good fight of faith" (1 Tim. 6:12) to lay hold of the super-abundant life God has promised should be indication enough that some of the greatest battles are won and lost in the realm of a person's faith.

What the Bible calls faith is a really big deal in the kingdom of God and the necessary ingredient to bring about everything you have read about so far in this book.

> *Everything in heaven that God has made available by grace must be possessed by faith to become reality for us on earth.*

With what God calls faith, nothing is impossible. Jesus Himself said that even the tiniest amount of real biblical faith could move the largest mountain (Mark 11:23–24).

But what is real biblical faith, exactly, and why does our individual ability to get "in a place of faith" play such an important role?

The practical answer may surprise you. Not only that, but the ease with which you can operate in superhuman faith will not only delight you but make receiving all the benefits of salvation and doing the works that Jesus did everyday recreational activity.

The word translated *faith* in English appears more than two hundred times in the Bible but, amazingly, only twice in the Old Testament, making all the other applications of the word largely a New Testament phenomenon.

One of the two occasions the word *faith* appears in the Old Testament is found in the book of Habakkuk in a verse often quoted by New Testament writers:

> Behold, his soul which is lifted up is not upright in him: but **the just shall live by his faith.**
>
> *- Habakkuk 2:4,* KJV, **emphasis added***;*
> *quoted in Romans 1:17; Galatians 3:11; Hebrews 10:38*

In this verse, the word translated *faith* is derived from the Hebrew word *emuwnah* (pronounced em-oo-naw) and means:

> Something that is firmly, securely, or steadily established as being true.

So again, and contrary to the common way religious faith is too often framed, to live by faith, people are not asked by God to abandon all reason and place their hope in a mystical fantasy that can never be observed in the present tense. Real biblical faith, by definition and in this context, is just the opposite.

The Greek root of the word translated faith in the New Testament has three parts of speech and is used as a noun, adjective, and a verb.

## FAITH AS A NOUN

As a noun in the New Testament, the English word *faith* is most often derived from the Greek word *pistis* (pronounced pis'-tis') from the Greek root *peitho* (pronounced pi-tho) and means "to trust, be fully convinced, completely persuaded, and have full assurance in."

In fact, several times the same Greek word *pistis* is translated as *assurance* or *proof.*

## FAITH AS AN ADJECTIVE

As an adjective in the New Testament, the Greek word *pistos* (pronounced pis-tos') is most often translated to English as meaning "faithful, believer, or one who is sure."

## FAITH AS A VERB

When used as a verb, the Greek word *pistoo* (pronounced pis-to-o') is translated to English as meaning "to be fully assured of or completely convinced."

For one last point of reference and before we discuss the anatomy of how and why this kind of biblical faith is needed to be fully saved, let's consider one more New Testament word used in the context of faith.

The Greek word *oligopistos* (pronounced ol-ig-op'-is-tos) is translated to English as *little faith* and literally means "someone who is incredulous and who has no trust, is not fully convinced, completely persuaded, or any assurance." You may recognize this phrase from our earlier discussion about the Great Commission where we discussed the use of the word *heathen,* meaning a nation or group of people who are not yet fully convinced.

You might also recognize the phrase *little faith* from the way Jesus used it on several occasions to describe someone who consistently doubted and refused to believe, even after His many demonstrations of God's willingness to save people. The most famous example is when Peter began to doubt and sink after only moments of miraculously walking on the water:

> But when he saw the wind, he was afraid and, beginning to sink, cried out, **"Lord, save ‹sozo› me!"** Immediately Jesus reached out his hand and caught him. **"You of little faith ‹oligopistos›,"** he said, **"why did you doubt ‹waver›?"**
> ~ Matthew 14:31, **emphasis added**

Notice how this verse says Peter was doing exactly what Jesus did, to the point of even defying the natural laws of physics and walking on water. That is, until his faith began to diminish, causing him to sink and prompting him to cry out to be saved (rescued) by Jesus.

This is remarkable when you think about it, not only because Peter miraculously walks on water but because his faith was apparently the dominant factor in his ability to do this impossible task – not simply Jesus' will for him to do it!

But what happened within Peter? What caused such a drastic and almost instantaneous change in his faith and his subsequent ability to do exactly what Jesus was doing? More importantly, is there something we can glean from what Jesus said to Peter that provides a window into what real biblical faith is?

The answer is yes, and recent scientific breakthroughs in understanding the interoperability of human anatomy and physiology support it.

One key to understanding how this kind of faith works can be seen in how Jesus describes Peter as one of "little faith." Jesus' question to Peter about His doubt led me to an interesting discovery about how Jesus and others throughout the New Testament often alluded to the interdependence of something the writers called:

Doubt,

Unbelief,

Little faith.

Or conversely, as in the famous verse taken from the story of the fig tree, where Jesus tells His disciples if they would ...

Not doubt,

Believe,

Have faith

... they could do the impossible, just like He did.

Here is the story:

> On the day following, when they had come away from Bethany, He ‹**Jesus**› was hungry. And seeing in the distance a fig tree [covered] with leaves, He went to see if He could find any [fruit] on it [for in the fig tree the fruit appears at the same time as the leaves]. But when He came up to it, He found nothing but leaves, for the fig season had not yet come. And He said to it, No one ever again shall eat fruit from you. And His disciples were listening [to what He said].
>
> ~ Mark 11:12–14, AMP

A few verses later the story concludes:

> And when evening came on, He ‹**Jesus**› and His disciples, as accustomed, went out of the city. In the morning, when they were passing along, they noticed that the fig tree was withered [completely] away to its roots. And Peter remembered and said to Him, Master, look! The fig tree which You doomed has withered away! And Jesus, replying, said to them, Have faith ‹**trust, be fully convinced, completely persuaded, and have full assurance**› in God [constantly]. Truly I tell you, whoever says to this mountain, Be lifted up and thrown into the sea! and does not doubt ‹**waver, stagger in indecision**› at all in his heart but believes that what he says will take place, it will be done for him. For this reason I am telling you, whatever you ask for in prayer, believe (trust and be confident) that it is granted to you, and you will [get it].
>
> ~ verses 19–24

Note Jesus' response to Peter's astonishment and apparent disbelief about His ability to speak to the fig tree and determine its fate. See how Jesus tells Peter to have faith in God. See how he says if Peter would not doubt but believe in his heart, he could do the exact same thing, even to the extent of moving a literal or figurative mountain.

Jesus didn't just tell Peter to have faith. Rather, He told Peter to have faith without doubting, believing in his heart!

Though these things are often thought of as different ways of saying the same thing, when you search out what it means to not doubt, what it means to believe, and what it means to have faith, you discover that not only are they very different, they can be thought of as occurring in different areas of the human anatomy, but with a stunning level of interoperability and dependence.

Almost without exception, whenever the Bible talks about doubt, it refers to doubt as something that happens in the mind of a person. When the Bible talks about belief, it almost exclusively refers to an action of the human heart. And finally, when faith is mentioned, it most often associates faith with the human spirit.

In other words, as in the following diagram, you could say:

1. A person's mind has doubts.

2. A person's heart believes.

3. A person's spirit has faith.

For illustration purposes only, it's easy to think of the mind of a person as being in the head, the heart as being the literal organ in the chest, and the spirit as being in the belly of person.

**Anatomy of Doubt, Belief, and Faith**

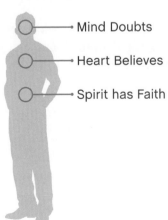

Mind Doubts

Heart Believes

Spirit has Faith

So, with this illustration in mind, I want to consider one more verse that not only provides additional confirmation as to the interoperability of these three things, it provides additional insight into the actual definition of what doubt is.

It also sets the stage for understanding the physiological science behind why doubting in the mind affects the way a person believes in their heart and ultimately their ability to have faith in their spirit for what the Bible calls "the fullness of salvation now."

> Now if any of you lacks wisdom, he should ask God, who gives to everyone generously without a rebuke, and it will be given to him. But he must ask in faith ‹**trust, be fully convinced, completely persuaded, and have full assurance**›, without any doubts ‹**wavering, staggering in indecision**›, for the one who has doubts ‹**wavers, staggers in indecision**› is like a wave of the sea that is driven and tossed by the wind. Such a person should not expect to receive anything from the Lord. He is a double-minded man, unstable in all he undertakes.
>
> ~ James 1:5–8, ISV

While this verse reinforces the relationship between doubt and faith we have been highlighting, that's not what I want to draw to your attention. Instead, I want you to see the way James describes a person who doubts as one who is like a wave of the sea, tossed by the wind, and one who is double-minded and unstable in all he undertakes.

James' description, while poetic, is much more than that. It's actually describing or alluding to the very definition of doubt itself and the anatomy of how it operates in a person.

The word translated in English as *doubt* in this verse is the Greek word *diakrinō,* (pronounced dee-ak-ree-no), which literally means "to separate two things, to discriminate, to have opposing thoughts, to waver or stagger between them (by implication to decide)."

This same Greek word is synonymous with the Greek word translated *double-minded,* which James uses just one verse later and which means "to vacillate in opinion or waver back and forth between two thoughts, to be of two minds, or to stand in two ways at the same time."

Even as you consider the spelling of both words, in English you can see the obvious correlation between the words *doubt* and *double-minded,* which share the root word *dou,* associated with the word *two* in English.

Are you starting to get the picture? When a person doubts, it means they:

Are wavering back and forth,

Are vacillating between two thoughts,

Are "dou'ing" in their mind,

Are standing in two ways in their mind,

Are being double-minded,

Are trying to decide in their mind.

But what are they trying to decide? When a person is trying to decide something in their mind, aren't they trying to decide what they believe? In fact, a belief is what we call it when a person finally makes up his or her mind on something.

The Bible likens the decisions we make about what we ultimately believe to strongholds in a person's heart. When vigorously defended and fortified, they are like physical castles – hard to penetrate from the outside.

It goes on to say that in order for a person to change or pull down strongholds of this nature, they must learn to cast down imaginations, thoughts, and perceptions that exalt themselves higher or against the knowledge of God by taking every thought captive and making it agree with Christ (2 Cor. 10:4).

To reinforce what is happening here, let's refer again to the anatomy illustration of doubt, unbelief, and faith. When a person has doubts, they are wavering back and forth between thoughts in their mind, until the point they make a final decision.

Once a decision is made, it becomes a belief in their heart, which will ultimately determine the state of their faith or, by definition, that which they are persuaded by, have confidence in, or are fully assured by.

In other words, what we think and the decisions we make about what we think determine what we believe. What we believe determines what we have faith to receive from God. And since God never forces His will on anyone who has not made the decision to believe Him for it, a person's faith can determine more about what they receive from God than God's will to provide it.

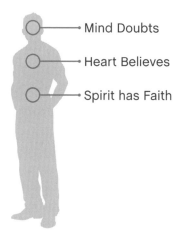

Mind Doubts

Heart Believes

Spirit has Faith

This is why what we decide to believe has so much to do with what we have the faith to receive and why James says someone who is still wavering in doubt and unbelief can't fully expect to receive from God.

Our decisions about what we believe can cut us off from the will of God, especially when it comes to receiving the fullness of salvation.

Even the English word *decision,* which means the "act of choosing between two constants," is rooted in the Latin word *decisioun* and means "to cut or make an incision in such a way as to murder the alternative."

Decisions we make and defend about what we believe determine what we are able to have faith in. The same decisions have the ability to murder the alternative of that belief from becoming a living reality in our lives!

This is equally true for the things we still have doubts about. When we still doubt something and have yet to make a decision, it's simply impossible to have sufficient faith to receive it or, for that matter, contend for it until it's a present-tense reality.

Don't rush past this insight. Let it sink in.

This basic relationship between our decision and the anatomy of doubt, unbelief, and faith is vitally important. This concept is the foundation for why faith matters when co-laboring with God to expand heaven on earth. It's also the foundation for understanding how real biblical faith actually comes about and how to have the faith of God to become superhuman.

## RECEIVING THE FAITH OF GOD TO BECOME SUPERHUMAN AND SAVE YOURSELF AND THE WORLD AS WE KNOW IT

Let's see how to apply what we've learned and reorient to faith sufficient to actually save a person and why even medical science confirms that not doubting can make you superhuman.

First, to understand how real biblical faith for salvation actually comes about, let's look at the answer the Bible gives:

> But they have not all heeded ‹**obeyed or agreed with**› the Gospel; for Isaiah says, Lord, who has believed (had faith in) what he has heard from us? ‹**See Isaiah 53:1**› So faith ‹**trust, being fully convinced, completely persuaded, and having full assurance**› comes ‹**originates**› by hearing [what is told], and what is heard comes by the preaching ‹**words or the utterance**› [of the message that came from the lips] of Christ (the Messiah Himself).
>
> ~ Romans 10:16–17, AMP

545

Paul is describing his struggle to get a certain people group (in this case, Israel) to have faith in or agree to receive the present-tense rewards of the gospel in order to be saved.

As Paul describes in the first portion of this verse, the limitation is not in God's willingness or in His ability to deliver these rewards to save them, but in the fact that not everyone believed or had faith in the rewards of the gospel they heard Paul speak about. Paul adds this very helpful insight when he says the kind of faith needed to save people comes about or originates at the point a person hears the literal "words or utterances" directly from the Messiah or Christ Himself.

Did you see that?

Paul is not referring to faith that comes about by simply hearing a person like himself speak or preach inspired words about salvation. Faith actually comes by hearing God speak about it!

And how exactly does the Bible imply God speaks these anointed words to a person? Where does this dialogue between God and a person take place?

Does God speak to a person's mind?

Does God speak to a person's heart?

Does God speak to a person's spirit?

The Bible is clear that God is a Spirit, and when He speaks to a person, He speaks directly to their spirit. And when He speaks, He speaks with the intent of writing what He speaks, His laws and precepts, on a person's heart (Jer. 31:33; Heb. 10:16).

The Bible goes on to say, in fact, that all things pertaining to the kingdom of God must be spiritually discerned or decided in the spirit of a person, as opposed to the mind or heart of a person (John 4:24; 1 Cor. 2:14). This is where we get the notion of someone being *spirit-led.*

In contrast, the Bible is also clear that there's an enemy to what God calls His heirs of salvation (Heb. 1:14). It is also clear this enemy speaks to the same heirs – in other words, us.

This enemy, whom the Bible calls Satan (which simply means "one who is adversarial" in the Old Testament and "an accuser" in the New Testament) is also a spirit. But where does that spirit speak to a person?

Does he speak to a person's mind?

Does he speak to a person's heart?

Does he speak to a person's spirit?

Unlike God, the Bible says this adversary has been given no access to the human spirit. However, this adversary does have the ability to lead and influence a person with vain imaginations by speaking to their mind. And not surprisingly, he speaks in order that he might find a dwelling place in the human heart (Eph. 2:2–3).

If we add these additional concepts to our illustration, it might look like this.

**Faith Comes by Hearing God Speak to Your Spirit**

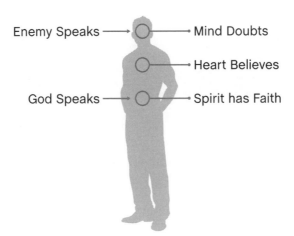

Enemy Speaks ⟶ Mind Doubts

Heart Believes

God Speaks ⟶ Spirit has Faith

In summary, God "gracefully" speaks to a person's spirit in order that He might divinely influence what they choose to believe in their hearts so they have faith to receive Him unto salvation (Rom. 1:16). The enemy, on the other hand, speaks to a person's mind in order to create doubt and keep people from believing in their heart so they won't have faith to be saved (2 Cor. 4:3).

As Paul suggests in this famous exhortation, the greatest weapons we have and the key to becoming fully alive or fully saved is the power to decide ...

What we will receive,

What we agree to believe,

What we ultimately have faith in, with respect to

What God speaks to our spirits.

And this is at the same time that ...

We ignore,

We disagree,

We take captive

... any thoughts in our minds that create doubts about it!

> (For the weapons of our warfare are not carnal, but mighty through God to the pulling down of strongholds ‹**strongly held beliefs**›;) casting down imaginations, and every high thing that exalteth itself against the knowledge of God, and bringing into captivity every thought to the obedience ‹**meaning to hear and make it agree**› of Christ.
> ~ 2 Corinthians 10:4–5, KJV

To illustrate this in simple terms and in a manner consistent with how we started this section, the biblical key to being saved in all its fullness is simply having faith (becoming fully convinced, completely persuaded, and having full assurance) in your spirit, believing in your heart, and then not doubting in your head the will of God for it and His desire to bring it about for you and others now and in the present tense!

Applying the same notion to our illustration, it might look like this.

**Don't Doubt, Have Faith, and Believe What God Speaks**

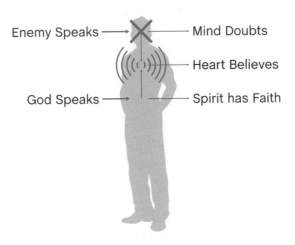

Wherever I teach these concepts, I ask people to stand and, by putting their hands on the appropriate part of their anatomy, provide answers to these simple questions. Regardless of age or experience with the things of God, people everywhere seem to unanimously answer the same way.

When I ask:

Where is your mind? They place their hands on their head.

Where is your heart? They place their hands on their chest.

Where is your spirit? They place their hands on their stomach.

When I ask:

Where does God speak – your head or spirit? They place their hands on their stomach.

Where does the enemy speak? They place their hands on their heads.

Where do you believe about what both speak? They place their hands on their heart.

If intuitively people already know the answers to these questions, why in the world would anyone ever doubt God by wavering back and forth in their thoughts? Why would they choose and decide to believe in their heart what the enemy speaks to their minds versus what God speaks to their spirit?

In my own life and experience with others, the answer isn't that people don't have faith in God, *per se,* or don't want to believe in a God who is capable of miraculously saving them, in terms of healing, deliverance, or wholeness.

The primary issue is that most people have simply never learned an easy way to distinguish the voice of God speaking in their spirit from the voices of constant doubt in their mind.

But what if I could provide an easy way to never doubt again, as it relates to matters of salvation? What if by simply doing something even medical science validates and most people can do by three years of age ...

You could overcome all doubts,

You could cause your heart to believe at will,

You could abide in the kind of faith required to receive all the rewards of the gospel,

You could have the faith of God for yourself and others?

What if it required reorienting to the most frequently quoted verse of Scripture traditionally used to get people saved? Would you be willing to reorient?

# SAVED__RELATE

*Kevin, get up! You could spend the next thirty days begging Me to increase you in this area (faith for the impossible) and it wouldn't do as much good as one minute without your continued doubt, unbelief, and enmity in your heart toward Me because you think I am in control of this planet. If you only believed and quit doubting, nothing would be impossible for you!*

You may recognize elements of this statement as impacting some of what I shared in Chapter One about enmity and our part in co-laboring with God to see heaven expanded on earth. It was also the genesis of a profound but simple discovery I had about overcoming doubt and our part in receiving the grace of God to become superhuman.

Most importantly, however, this statement became the catalyst for a literal uprising in the life of my family and those around us who were contending for love's ideal but always falling short of it.

It all began ten days into a forty-day fast Michelle and I had begun in order to seek God about answers and the reasons why we were not personally seeing the mighty works that Jesus always demonstrated and proclaimed should be a reality in our own lives.

While we had faith in others' accounts about the nearly-too-good-to-be-true miracles God had done for or through them, at that point in time we had not yet personally witnessed or been a part of such things.

I am not saying we didn't see God do many good things for us. But practically speaking, miracles at this point were still very much a future-tense reality for us.

Even though we were fasting to hear God speak to us about these very things at the time, it's funny to me now how I was nearly shocked into a stupor that He actually did!

This alone should have been evidence that the things God was highlighting in His statement were true, but at the time it would have been nearly impossible to convince us that our own doubt and unbelief were the main problem.

After all, we loved God with all our hearts and had thought of ourselves as Spirit-filled believers for nearly fifteen years to that point. We also attended a great church of over twelve thousand other Spirit-filled believers and readily discussed the supernatural aspects of the kingdom. Sadly, however, we could count on less than one hand the number of legitimate supernatural miracles we had heard about occurring in our circles of friends, let alone having personally witnessed or participated in them.

When we began our so-called fast, we weren't so much focused on the traditional notion of eliminating food but rather other distractions like media, entertainment, and activities that hindered our ability to stay focused on hearing from God.

To begin our fast, we had written down four things that, in our minds at the time, were the potential reasons for our lack of results:

1. We were blowing it somehow.

2. God was holding out on us.

3. The enemy was resisting us.

4. All of the above.

While these were our beginning assumptions, honestly, we didn't much care what the problem was. We were desperate for the real thing and willing to do whatever it took to bring about better results. We were willing (and still are) to make any adjustment to our theology that was needed if it meant we could deliver the real rewards of the gospel and actually save ourselves and others in a more excellent way. Of course, I don't just mean save in terms of only going to heaven, but in terms of healing, restoring, and making someone completely whole like Jesus did.

After several days of immersive study about the anatomy of doubt and unbelief as it related to having faith for the impossible, we were convinced God was right: doubt was our real enemy. We quickly revised our problem set list to read:

1. Don't doubt!

2. Believe!

3. Have faith!

We even changed the name of our fast to the *"doubt fast"* and set our intentions to renew our minds by identifying and eliminating doubt wherever it existed.

We were convinced that if what we had discovered was true, simply getting clear in our spirits about the will of God and then eliminating doubt in our minds would automatically cause our hearts to more fully believe and, by default, allow faith for the impossible to be present.

And while this is true, our first attempts at eliminating all doubt proved more difficult than we ever imagined. It left us believing one thing for certain: doubt may be the most formidable opponent of all when it comes to man living fully alive and enjoying all that God has promised.

This is, of course, before we discovered a very simple approach to easily empower anyone to be victorious over the adversaries of doubt and unbelief. And as it turns out, it was much simpler than the traditional approaches with which we initially experimented.

The first few days of our newly proclaimed doubt fast were dedicated to simply jotting down every time we caught ourselves doubting or wavering between two thoughts, especially as it pertained to God's will to heal people. At this early stage, I was stunned to near silence to discover that virtually every thought I had seemed to contain elements of doubt.

For example, I remember arriving at my office one morning and hearing the phone. The caller ID identified the caller as my biggest client. I noticed my thoughts frantically and almost involuntarily vacillating between two extremes: *God, is this going to be something good or bad?*

Or in preparing to pray for the healing of a friend, I would find my mind shifting between two thoughts: *Will God or won't God heal this person?* Almost immediately, I noticed my mind scrolling through an index of possible scenarios. Thoughts like:

What if this doesn't work?

What if nothing happens?

What will they think?

What will I say in response?

What if they are disappointed in God?

What if they are disappointed in me?

What if they end up thinking I'm a fool?

What if I prayed "Your will be done, Lord" and took myself off the hook?

What if I relegate the outcome to the future with a "Well, sometimes healing takes time" disclaimer?

As our fast progressed and I continued to monitor my thoughts, I came to an unsettling realization: I rarely, if ever, had confidence in the answers to any of these questions.

By faith's very definition as being trusting, fully convinced, completely persuaded, and having full assurance, you might say I was a person of very little faith.

Sometimes I noticed that the wavering in my thoughts paralyzed me to the point of complete inaction. To compensate, I found myself hastily pushing forward like a good soldier while metaphorically, and sometimes literally, closing my eyes and hoping for the best.

If nothing less than determined at this point, believe it or not, we actually increased our prayers for people who needed supernatural breakthrough. We tried our best to push through our ever-growing mindfulness of doubt while those doubts were simultaneously re-inforced by our equally dismal track record of success.

During this brief period, we literally contended for dozens of friends and acquaintances alike who desperately needed breakthrough, but sadly with zero tangible results. The plight was maddening.

I remember thinking at the time, *How did I live for so many years thinking I was a person of great faith and confidence in God while overlooking the obvious doubts I had at the same time?* It seemed now that the only thing I believed for sure was that I was a constant and massive doubter!

I can see clearly now how even my prayers and fasting in the years leading up to this moment were more evidence of my doubt and unbelief than my faith in God and His ability and willingness to do these things. After all, why would a person need to pray and fast about something they were already completely convinced it was God's will and good pleasure to do?

In any respect, I felt we were on a mission and simply refused to relent or be deterred. If nothing else, I was at least convinced now more than ever that God was right. I could see my doubt and unbelief were a serious problem undermining my belief and keeping me from ever really being in a place of faith.

So with one last push, I concluded to do the only thing I knew how to do well at the time – try harder!

I spent many days, from sun up to sundown, trying to find the keys to breakthrough.

I researched articles online about how the human brain worked.

I researched how to reprogram engrained patterns of thinking.

I memorized key testament Scriptures on renewing the mind.

I studied every verse regarding doubt, unbelief, or faith.

I studied every verse that had roles in healing and deliverance.

I indexed healing verses with red tabs.

I indexed deliverance verses with orange tabs.

I indexed doubt, unbelief, faith, or lack-of-faith verses with green tabs.

Additionally, because several resources suggested the human mind applies less natural filters to a person's own voice, hence making it easier for people to believe their own self-talk, I began recording myself speaking these Scriptures in first-person, present-tense narratives, which I then listened to day and night for several weeks – even while I slept!

While this proved to be a worthwhile exercise for discovering and memorizing what the Bible said about these things, it proved virtually worthless for eliminating my mental doubts and producing tangible evidence of our reoriented definition of salvation.

After several weeks and near exhaustion from lack of adequate sleep – apparently a side effect from having an iPod playing my own voice in twenty-minute spoken-word Scripture loops in my ears all night – I was ready to resign myself to a life of doubt and uncertainty.

I felt like Doubting Thomas, whose nickname was said to be *didymus*, meaning two or double (John 20:24). While the name was apparently a reference to being born a twin, it quickly took on more ironic and prophetic implications for me, given he was arguably the most famous "duo-er," "doubter," and "double-minded" man in history.

In any respect, I felt I had more in common with Doubting Thomas at this point than Jesus and His disciples, who I was quickly concluding must have had some "faith for the impossible" gene that made them superhuman and which clearly I didn't possess.

Even though the entire goal of our fast was to live from hearts more fully alive, I could actually sense my heart shutting down. The discouragement from this pursuit without results was seemingly hardening my heart toward the very things we were pursuing – which, I would discover later, is the end result of prolonged doubt and unbelief. Jesus said prolonged unbelief results in "hardness of heart," which literally defined in the verse below means being "destitute of spiritual perception." In other words, and consistent with the anatomy of doubt, un-

RESOURCE
The nearly one-to-one relationship between red, orange, and green tabs on the edge of my Bible was enough to convince even the staunchest critic of the correlation between these things. To see a visual of the actual Bible used, visit the resource section for this chapter at www.thereorientbook.com.

belief, and faith illustration, a heart hardens to the things of God from not perceiving or being able to receive spiritual input.

> Afterward He ‹**Jesus**› *appeared to the eleven themselves as they were reclining at the table; and He reproached them for their unbelief and hardness of heart* ‹**destitution of spiritual perception**›*, because they had not believed those who had seen Him after He had risen.*
>
> ~ Mark 16:14, NAS

But just about the time I was ready to quit, admit defeat, resign myself to a life of disappointment, and leave the job of delivering the supernatural aspects of the rewards of the gospel to more spiritually gifted heroes of faith, I had a bright idea.

It was this: Maybe I should stop this obsessive striving to acquire head knowledge about how to keep my mind from doubting. Maybe I should get quiet and ask God to speak to my spirit and tell me how to overcome my doubts!

So after weeks of effort, I went back to the exact place in our home I had heard God speak previously and said out loud, "God, I give up! My mind seems hopelessly caught in this pattern of doubt and unbelief. I'm sorry. I don't know what else to do! Help me with my doubt and unbelief."

To my surprise and almost immediately, a simple but direct and resolute-sounding phrase came up inside me. I don't mean I heard an audible voice, but inside me, I heard, "Kevin, speak!"

*Speak.* I thought to myself, *What does that have to do with overcoming doubt and unbelief?*

Again I heard, *Speak, Kevin. What you speak with your mouth will affect what you believe in your heart!*

I instantly thought of what Paul said was required to be saved:

> *That if you* **confess with your mouth,** *"Jesus is Lord," and* **believe in your heart that** *God raised him from the dead, you will be* **saved.** *For it is with your* **heart that you believe**

*and are justified, and **it is with your mouth that you confess and are saved.***

> *~ Romans 10:9–10, **emphasis added***

I must admit that up to this moment, I had only thought of this verse in the context of a one-time proclamation that, for a reason unknown to me, God required in order for Him to save someone and grant them entrance to heaven. I never thought of speaking or confessing as an ongoing requirement to believing, let alone being saved. But then again, up to this point I had only thought of being saved in the context of a one-time event, too, and never as the kind of past-, present-, and future-tense realities we have been discussing in this book.

But what does speaking or confessing have to do with bringing about the benefits of salvation? Why does speaking or confessing something out loud with your mouth overcome doubt in the mind and help a person's heart to believe unto salvation?

Within hours of asking this question, an "aha moment" happened while Michelle and I were listening to a pastor who leads a congregation in Missouri and who we had learned about through a mutual friend. The pastor was apparently midway through teaching a multi-week series on the effects of doubt. In an incredible moment of serendipity, we logged on just as he was asking the congregation to join him in the following doubt exercise, which I would like to ask you to do with me now.

## THE DOUBT EXERCISE

Let me start by sharing the short seven-step exercise with you, and then you can take a moment and actually do the exercise for yourself.

1. Close your eyes.

2. Count to one hundred in your head without speaking the numbers out loud.

3. Count slowly (about 1 number per second).

4. While counting silently in your mind, prepare to speak out loud.

5. Speak out loud, "I am healed in Jesus' name," while still counting in your mind.

6. Speak this phrase repeatedly out loud while continuing to count silently.

7. Notice your counting while you speak out loud.

That's it. That's the exercise. Take a moment, close the book, and try it now on your own. Remember – first begin counting in your head and then speak out loud as described above.

Well, hopefully you did the exercise.

How did it go?

How did you do?

How difficult was it?

How simple was it?

How hard could it be, after all, to just count in your mind?

How hard could it be to just speak out loud?

How hard was it to do both simultaneously?

Did you find you had to stop doing one to effectively do the other?

If so, don't feel bad.

As it turns out, everyone does.

That's because, believe it or not, as simple as it is to do either one by itself, it is virtually impossible to do both together!

And the reason it's impossible is this: God wired humans in such a way that whatever we speak with our mouth overrides what we think in our minds every time – at least momentarily. In the midst of speaking, it's virtually impossible for a person to think one thing and speak another without causing some kind of physiological response – a kind of disconnect.

Now, think about this in the context of what I would like to now call the anatomy of the miracle of salvation illustration.

### The Anatomy of the Miracle of Salvation

God speaks to the human spirit in order that He might graciously influence a person's heart to believe and have faith in order to not only receive the rewards of the gospel and be saved but to become fully alive and empowered to co-labor with Him to extend His rule through us on earth as it is in heaven.

In contrast, the enemy speaks to the human mind in an effort to create constant doubts and unbelief in the heart. His goal is to undermine the will of God and the ability for a person to believe or receive the present-tense rewards of the gospel and operate in supernatural endowments of grace. God provides that to empower us to rise up, overcome the lies, and let God's love rule the earth through us once again.

Both God, who the Bible says has no plans to harm people but only to give us the hope of a prosperous future and to satisfy us with superabundant life (Jer. 29:11; John 10:10), and the enemy of God, whose sole purpose, the Bible says, is to steal, kill, and destroy that life, need the exact same thing to accomplish their objectives – the agreement of the human heart.

And while God only seeks to accomplish His objectives in knowing, willing, and voluntary lovers, the enemy endeavors to accomplish His aims through the willing, unwilling, knowing, and ignorant alike.

In this way, you might say that at any given moment, and depending on what a person hears, decides to believe, speaks, and acts upon, they are receiving and manifesting faith in one spirit or the other and agreeing to co-labor to advance the objectives of one kingdom or another at all times.

The key is having faith to manifest the literal "saving grace" of God and then co-laboring with Him to manifest His will on earth as the illustration suggests. The key is to simply hear about it in your spirit, believe it in your heart, and then speak it with your mouth and relentlessly contend for it until what God (who is love) speaks is a present-tense reality in your life and everyday realms of influence.

The only practical way to literally separate (you could even say sin) from God's will and the power of His gospel to transform any situation is to doubt it, choose not to believe it, and subsequently have no faith in it!

This is why I said earlier that doubt is the Goliath the enemy uses to taunt the heirs of salvation into retreat and erode their belief and undermine their faith to receive everything God has made available to them.

If a person will not doubt, because *nothing is impossible with God* (Luke 1:37), then *nothing is impossible for those who believe God* (Matt. 17:20). The key to not doubting is simply speaking what you clearly know to be the will of God. The reflexive way God made this work for those who voluntarily choose to do it ensures results.

The physical anatomy behind why it "just works" reminds me of a little game we play with our kids. It goes like this.

We ask them …

To sit in a chair.

To cross their right leg over their left knee.

To move their right foot around in circles in a clockwise motion.

To raise their left hand and draw the number six in the air.

To continue to move their right foot in a clockwise motion.


We love to watch the confidence on their face turn to amazement and eventually laughter as their foot involuntarily reverses direction whenever they make the six. No matter how hard they try, they simply are not wired to be able to do both simultaneously.

It's the same way thinking, speaking, and believing interoperate to produce physical results that are nearly automatic. In other words, what you speak not only has an effect on what you think, but it can also have dramatic effects on your anatomy and physiology, based upon their congruence.

To understand how and why something as simple as the way a mind thinks, a heart believes, and a mouth speaks can possibly interoperate to produce a physical or outward sign of salvation (i.e., a physical healing), I want to close this chapter by taking a quick look at some modern scientific breakthroughs that reinforce why this "just works!"

## WHY SCIENCE PROVES FAITH WORKS TO SAVE A PERSON

For an example of why this "just works," consider how a modern polygraph, or what is most often called a lie detector test, works.

The American Polygraph Association says they can measure the truth between what someone is saying versus what they are thinking and believing to be true with up to 98 percent reliability.[80] How do they do this? By using an instrument to measure a person's physiological state in terms of their pulse, respiration, blood pressure, and skin conductivity at the moment they are asked to speak out loud what they believe in their heart to be true or untrue answers to a series of questions.[81]

The premise is this. If a person says one thing but in their mind they know it's inconsistent with what their heart really believes, the polygraph will pick up the dissonance (the disconnect) by the degree of change in four specific physical manifestations – the person's ...

Pulse,

Respiration,

Blood pressure,

Skin conductivity

... when compared to base levels.

Ironically, each of the physiological indicators being measured is a direct function of the activity of the human heart. A sudden increase in a person's heartbeat will increase their pulse, which affects their breathing, changes their blood pressure, and eventually causes perspiration, which then affects the conductivity of the surface of their skin.

In short, speaking congruent answers to core beliefs produces little physiological change and a stable and steady graphing of each of these functions. In contrast, speaking incongruent answers causes drastic changes in the person's physiology and corresponding polygraph.

In a biblical context, you might say, this is why speaking congruent truth creates a sense of peace and speaking untruth can create anxiety, hypertension, or stress.

Maybe this is why Jesus ...

RESOURCE
For more on the heart science and what the Bible says about the human heart, consider the resource section for this chapter at www.thereorientbook.com

Who was called the Prince of Peace,

Who never told a lie,

Who only did what He knew His Father would do,

Who only spoke what He heard His Father say in His spirit,

Who was able to keep His mind stayed in perfect peace,

Who delivered the real rewards of the gospel as in heaven,

Who was completely saved in every way,

Who saved all those willing to speak out loud and believe as He did

... never doubted – not even once!

For us, knowing this information and being equipped with our newly discovered weapon against doubt led us to quit praying and fasting for these things to become a reality and begin reorienting our speech to have the faith of God until things actually came to be.

To our amazement, within just a few days, the results were nothing short of miraculous. Not only did we begin speaking with a new kind of resolve and assurance, but doubt no longer ruled our minds and faith in God for the impossible in areas of our own lives that still needed to be saved (i.e., healed, delivered, and provided for) was building.

Besides being personally healed (saved) of severe reactive hypogly-cemia, our daughter was healed (saved) of severe eczema which had tormented her since birth, and we began experiencing other miracles of provision that chance and circumstance could never explain.

Before long, these kinds of wins became near-daily recreational activity, allowing us to participate with God in literally hundreds of them over the next year.

As we began having more private victories within our own home and realms of influence, we began contending for others to do the same and developed a strong desire to equip people to not just receive but administer these things for themselves.

Sadly, though we encountered countless sincere people who not only received a miracle and readily admitted they believed such things were possible, their confidence to actually do this stuff themselves was small.

We heard responses like:

But I never saw miracles like that,

But I would have no idea where to even begin,

But I am afraid to even try,

But I don't know what to say,

But I am afraid to get rejected,

But what if I try and it doesn't work?

These were the most common responses we heard from people about why they had no confidence or faith for these things.

We immediately saw the need to develop new language to help others get saved, and to bridge the chasm between what people believe is possible in heaven and the reality of what they are willing to contend for on earth. We also saw the immense need to help people talk to others about it without the traditional weirdness and dogmas that so often have accompanied such pursuits.

RESOURCE
Several videos from people that benefited from some of these early "wins" are provided in the "You'll See" video section at www.thereorientbook.com.

# SAVED_REACT

Top three things you are taking away from this chapter:

........................................................................................................................

........................................................................................................................

........................................................................................................................

........................................................................................................................

........................................................................................................................

........................................................................................................................

........................................................................................................................

What action can you take now on what you've learned?

........................................................................................................................

........................................................................................................................

........................................................................................................................

........................................................................................................................

........................................................................................................................

........................................................................................................................

........................................................................................................................

........................................................................................................................

You said all the needy could come

You will always give them your best

You said all that labor could stop striving

And You would give them rest

You healed all who were sick

You freed all who were oppressed

You said above all we could

Think or imagine

You made "simple" for us to possess

- YOU SAID ALL -
*Lyrics by Kevin Weaver It's Feasible Publishing, LLC*

Download the complete lyrics and an .mp3 version of this
song in its entirety at www.thereorientbook.com.

# DOER

# What's your REACTION to the word?

⊕ Positive

⊖ Negative

◉ Neutral

# What does the word MEAN TO YOU?

_____

_____

_____

_____

_____

_____

_____

_____

_____

_____

# DOER_REDISCOVER

## OLD TESTAMENT HEBREW WORDS FOR DOER

USED  *More than 2600 times*

WORD  ASAH */aw-saw/*

DEFINITION  *To do, fashion, accomplish, make, act with effect*

---

## NEW TESTAMENT GREEK WORDS FOR DOER

USED  *6 times (root 518 times)*

WORD  POIETES */poy-ay-tace/*

DEFINITION  *Maker, producer, author, act, performer*

# DOER__RECOUNT

# DOER

OLD TESTAMENT USAGE
OF THE HEBREW WORD

## 2,286

MEW TESTAMENT USAGE
OF THE GREEK WORD

## 521

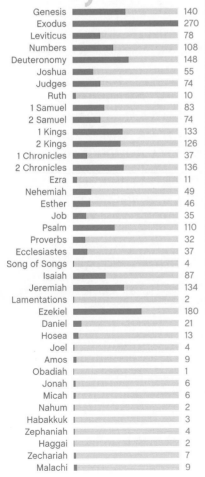

| Genesis | 140 |
| Exodus | 270 |
| Leviticus | 78 |
| Numbers | 108 |
| Deuteronomy | 148 |
| Joshua | 55 |
| Judges | 74 |
| Ruth | 10 |
| 1 Samuel | 83 |
| 2 Samuel | 74 |
| 1 Kings | 133 |
| 2 Kings | 126 |
| 1 Chronicles | 37 |
| 2 Chronicles | 136 |
| Ezra | 11 |
| Nehemiah | 49 |
| Esther | 46 |
| Job | 35 |
| Psalm | 110 |
| Proverbs | 32 |
| Ecclesiastes | 37 |
| Song of Songs | 4 |
| Isaiah | 87 |
| Jeremiah | 134 |
| Lamentations | 2 |
| Ezekiel | 180 |
| Daniel | 21 |
| Hosea | 13 |
| Joel | 4 |
| Amos | 9 |
| Obadiah | 1 |
| Jonah | 6 |
| Micah | 6 |
| Nahum | 2 |
| Habakkuk | 3 |
| Zephaniah | 4 |
| Haggai | 2 |
| Zechariah | 7 |
| Malachi | 9 |

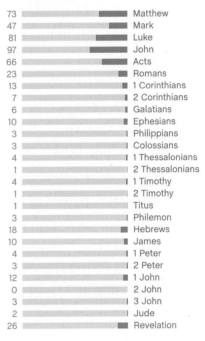

| 73 | Matthew |
| 47 | Mark |
| 81 | Luke |
| 97 | John |
| 66 | Acts |
| 23 | Romans |
| 13 | 1 Corinthians |
| 7 | 2 Corinthians |
| 6 | Galatians |
| 10 | Ephesians |
| 3 | Philippians |
| 3 | Colossians |
| 4 | 1 Thessalonians |
| 1 | 2 Thessalonians |
| 4 | 1 Timothy |
| 1 | 2 Timothy |
| 1 | Titus |
| 3 | Philemon |
| 18 | Hebrews |
| 10 | James |
| 4 | 1 Peter |
| 3 | 2 Peter |
| 12 | 1 John |
| 0 | 2 John |
| 3 | 3 John |
| 2 | Jude |
| 26 | Revelation |

*Graph is based on the highest
verse use and shown visually as
a percentage of the highest value.

# DOER__REORIENT

If you're arriving at this chapter after reading the previous eight, congratulations! You have officially begun to reorient and are what God calls a doer – at least in part.

What's a doer, exactly? It may not be the most frequently used word in this book, but it may be one of the most important.

We've come a long way since rediscovering love together in Chapter One and ending the journey by reorienting to what it really means to be saved in the last chapter. Are you seeing things differently?

The real question now, for each of us, is not what we know about the words to which we just reoriented, but what we will do with what we now know. In other words, will each us become a doer of these words, or a hearer and learner of them only?

> **"Well done, good servant,"** he replied; "because you have been faithful in a very small matter, be in authority over ten towns."
>
> ~ Luke 19:17, WNT, **emphasis added**

Isn't that what every sincere disciple wants to hear God speak over their life in the end: "Well done, good and faithful servant"?

If this is true for you, I want to pose a couple questions. What is the only way to ensure that we hear these words spoken over us? Or, more specifically, who are the only people who will hear God speak these words over them?

The answers are simple, of course.

The only way to ensure we will ever hear these words is to become a doer. That's because only doers – people who faithfully do well to serve the highest good and produce increase for the kingdom of God – are going to hear those words, "Well done!"

Furthermore, I am not aware of a single place in the Bible where God makes specific mention of rewarding something for having been:

Well heard,

Well understood,

Well studied,

Well theorized,

Well debated,

Well preached,

Well defended,

Well judged.

Like many things we have covered so far, this may seem like a simple distinction, but I assure you the implications are far reaching. Your own fate, the fate of your family, others you know, your community, and the world as we know it in this generation and the next may well depend on us being a doer of what we have learned!

So, then, considering the words we've reoriented to in this book, what would it mean to master the ability to be a doer of them instead of mastering the ability to understand, study, theorize, debate, preach, or defend them only?

Is it possible, for example, to be a ...

Doer of love,

Doer of life as though sin were no longer a problem,

Doer of religion,

Doer of church as it was originally intended,

Doer of things so supernatural and seemingly heretical,

Doer of a master-level discipleship,

Doer of the gospel,

Doer of getting saved?

Practically speaking, is it really possible for any of us mere mortals to become such doers of any of the above that even the Master Himself would say of us, "Well done, good and faithful servant"?

The answer is emphatically *yes*.

Furthermore, becoming a doer of these words is the essential component to bringing about the kind of real-world change we now know is possible but have not yet seen demonstrated on a significant level in our lifetime.

So, how exactly do we master the ability to be a doer of these things? What are the keys to becoming a doer?

For the answer to those questions – and to conclude this book and our first step toward an uprising of global proportions – let's consider one last golden text. Let's reorient to what it means to be a doer, all while measuring and tracking the fruit of a doer in the biblical sense of the word.

## WHAT EXACTLY IS A DOER?

The answer to this question can, as usual, best be understood by considering the actual meanings of the word.

The dictionary defines the word *doer* this way:

**Doer**

*noun*

1. a person or thing that does something, especially with vigor and efficiency
2. a person characterized by action, as distinguished from one given to contemplation
3. Australian: an amusing or eccentric person; a character

---

**RECONSIDER**

Fun with *doer* word usages:[82]

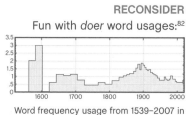

Word frequency usage from 1539–2007 in occurrences per 100,000 words per year

Phone Digits: (...) ...-3637

Anagram(s): redo, rode

Scrabble Score: 5

The Bible uses the term this way:

> But be you **doers of the word,** and not hearers only, deceiving your own selves.
>
> ~ James 1:22, AKJV, emphasis added

This famous verse, appropriately found a few verses after the core verse we used to conclude the "Saved" chapter about overcoming doubt and unbelief (James 1:5–8), is a powerful and straightforward directive that holds critical keys to becoming a doer and a person of superhuman faith.

The Greek word translated into English as *doer* in the verse from James is *poietes* (pronounced poy-ay-tace). The same Greek word is found at the root of our modern English word for *poet* and literally means "one who performs or acts."

The implications of the word is to perform or act in the same way we might think of a performer, poet, or actor doing so in the modern sense. In fact, this same Greek word is actually translated into English as *poet* in the book of Acts (Acts 17:28).

Notice how the word *doer* in our core text is used in direct contrast to the word *hearer*. The word *hearer* is derived from the Greek word *akroates* (pronounced ak-ro-at-ace') and translated into English to mean someone who only hears or spectates, as in an audience.

Inserting these amplified meanings into our core text would read as follows:

> But be you doers ‹**actual performers, as in a speaker or actor**› of the word ‹**something said; a motive, intent, reason**›, and not hearers ‹**hearing as spectators in an audience**› only, deceiving your own selves.

To draw upon an analogy from earlier in the book, the difference between a doer and a hearer in this biblical context is like that of a highly rewarded professional athlete, singer, actor, writer, or performer (doer) versus someone whose only reward is the joy that comes from listening to or watching others perform from a distance (hearer).

In this context, it's easy to see why being a doer or performer and not just a hearer or spectator is so critically important. Not only are the best performers the most highly rewarded, but they also play critical parts in every event that a hearer or spectator can't, and their individual performance affects the outcome of events in ways that hearers never will.

It's the same way in the kingdom of God and why highlighting this aspect of being a doer versus a hearer at the end of this book is so crucial – because it's the doers, those who do their part to faithfully master and perfect the ability to do the things we've reoriented to in this book, who will impact and affect the course of human events in ways that those who are only hearers never will.

As we've alluded to many times throughout this book, God designed virtually every aspect of manifesting the rewards of the gospel and advancing the kingdom of heaven on earth to depend on two parts: God being a doer of His part and us being doers of ours.

Though it's impossible for us to be doers of God's part, it's equally true that He has resolved never to be the doer of the part He has delegated for us to play. As a result, if we aren't a doer of our part, we will never experience the reality of God doing His part through us.

The good news, however, is that when we are simply doers of our part, we make it possible for God to be a doer of His part – and the combined result is nothing short of supernatural. It's natural, but in a super kind of way.

This is why the Bible says that with God, nothing is impossible (Matt. 19:26). While *God* is an essential aspect of that statement, so is *with*. While God can easily do the impossible all by Himself, He has chosen to do the impossible *with* us. Why God chooses to limit Himself in this way is a mystery, I am all but certain; however, love has something to do with it.

Thinking about it reminds me of a story I heard about a midwestern Amish farmer who was working in a field behind a horse-drawn implement pulled by two horses, one an extremely large work horse and the other a small Shetland pony. As the team approached one end of the field, another farmer stopped to ask, "Why have you bothered to hook two so unequally yoked horses together to pull the plow?" Didn't he understand that by doing so, he was actually causing the stronger horse to carry even more of a burden and hindering progress as a result?

"Yes, of course," the farmer replied, "but it's the craziest thing. You see, that little pony was born on our farm, and the two of them have been nearly inseparable ever since. Now in the mornings when I go to get my workhorse to work in the field, he won't even leave the barn unless I hitch him to the little pony. Even though the little guy is of no real use in terms of contributing substantial strength to pull the plow, the best I can figure is that the old work horse just likes having him around."

And so it must be for the all-powerful God of all creation to choose to co-labor with us to accomplish His aims. He could certainly do it without us, but obviously He desires that we have a part to play with Him along the way.

I guess He just likes having us around!

So, with this in mind, whenever I read a verse or get a new revelation from God, I try to ask myself four simple questions:

1. What is God's part?

2. What is my part?

3. Am I being a doer of my part?

4. How would I know for sure?

For example, let's apply these questions to Jesus' famous prayer, "Thy kingdom come, Thy will be done on earth as it is in heaven."

Applying the filter of my four questions, I would first ask myself what God's part is – or, in this case, whose part is it to do God's will in heaven. Of course, the answer to that is God, as clearly I don't rule heaven.

I would then ask whose part it is to do God's will on earth. Of course, that's clearly my part – as we have established, God delegated the rule of earth to us.

So the key question is, am I doing my part? And finally, if so, how would I know for sure? The simple answer is that if I am doing my part well, there would be evidence of God's kingdom's rule and love's ideal manifesting on earth through me, just as it is in heaven.

The same approach can be taken for many things we're instructed to do and not do in order for us to realize love's ideal.

For example, consider how God says things like:

Do not let your heart be troubled,

Do not fear,

Do not lie,

Do not cheat,

Do not covet,

Do not doubt.


Or how about what when He says:

Do believe,

Do have faith,

Do keep your mind stayed on Him,

Do guard your heart,

Do be of good cheer,

Do be at peace,

Do be strong,

Do be anxious for nothing,

Do choose life,

Do rejoice.

And these are just a few examples of a long list of things that we can either refrain from doing or choose to do in order to bring about God's kingdom reality in our life.

Think about it this way. Even though there are clearly no troubled hearts in heaven – no fears, lies, cheating, doubts, or anxieties – no matter how much a person might pray, fast, beg, or plead with God to take away, say, anxiety on earth, such begging and pleading will be of no avail if we don't first choose to be anxious for nothing.

But the nearly-too-good-to-be-true news is this. If a person simply chooses to be anxious for nothing, then God gives that person a peace that surpasses their own understanding:

> And the peace of God, which transcends all understand-
> ing, will guard your hearts and your minds in Christ Jesus.
> – Philippians 4:7

It works the same way for every promise God has made to mankind.

Choose life;

God gives life more abundantly.

Choose to not fear;

God gives supernatural courage.

Choose to be of good cheer;

God imparts the fullness of joy until a person's joy is complete.

Choose to not doubt and only believe;

009 · DOER · REORIENT

God imparts faith for the impossible.

You get the point. When we choose to be a doer and performer of our part, God, who never fails to be a doer of His part, can then work with us to do exceedingly abundantly above what we can ask or imagine on our own.

The key to seeing God do all these things and much more, however, is simply doing our part and choosing to become a doer first. The key to being a doer with a God for whom "nothing is impossible" is being someone who does their part in order to give God something and someone to do the impossible *with*.

While the Bible is true when it says that in ourselves, we are nothing (Gal. 6:3), it's equally true when it says that with Christ, we are the righteousness of God.

While the Bible is true when it says that in ourselves, we know nothing (1 Cor. 8:2), it's equally true when it says that with Christ we can know all things.

While the Bible is true when it says that in ourselves, we have nothing (1 Cor. 4:7), it's equally true when it says that with Christ, He gives us all things richly to enjoy.

While the Bible is true when it says that in ourselves, we can do nothing (John 15:5), it's equally true when it says that in Christ, we can do all things.

So the question is: Will we choose to become a doer and choose to do all things with Him, or will we choose to be a hearer only and merely a spectator of other doers?

## HOW TO BECOME A DOER

If you have resolved to be a doer, then the question becomes: How do we become doers and make sure we are at least doing our part so God can do His? For the answer, let's go back to our core verse one more time:

*But be you doers ‹**actual performers, as in a speaker or actor**› of the word and not hearers ‹**hearing as spectators in an audience**› only, deceiving your own selves.*

Notice the emphasis in this verse is on becoming doers and not just hearers of something the writer calls "the word." So, what is "the word," exactly, and how do we be doers of it?

For years I had a tendency to only think of the word of God as meaning the printed Bible. While that is true – the printed Bible contains the words of God – the definition of *word* in this verse is much broader in application, and I believe the key to becoming a doer of it is contained in its the expanded meaning.

The word translated into English as *word* in this verse is the Greek word *logos,* which means "something said containing an expression, a reason, a motive, or an intent." *Logos* is rooted in a similar Greek word, *lego,* which means "to break the silence and relate by having discourse."

So, in our core verse, being a doer of "the word" of God implies acting on or performing the intents, motives, and reasons God has for speaking and breaking silence to have discourse with us.

And therein lays the supernatural power of words and the entire purpose behind this book.

Our ability to empower God's words to accomplish His desires and achieve the purposes for which He said them (Isa. 55:11) is a direct result of traditional meanings and intent we give them and what we do to act on those meanings (Mark 7:13).

For instance, if sin is traditionally defined as bad behavior that separates us from God, then God's primary motive and intent behind eliminating sin is primarily an attempt to eliminate bad behavior so that we can connect with Him. If a person wants to please God by being a doer of His word in that context, they need to focus on managing, controlling, and eliminating bad behaviors (sins) if they ever hope to hear God say, "Well done, good and faithful servant – you're now sinless."

Unfortunately, while eliminating bad behavior is a good thing to do, seeing that as the sole meaning of the word *sin* assigns a reason and motive for eliminating sin that God never intended. And by doing so, it makes His real purpose for eliminating sin in the first place – that of eliminating the separation between Him and mankind, which causes us to keep missing the mark and not realize the highest good – of no effect in that area.

In this case, simply defining the word *sin* as bad behavior is, in and of itself, a significant sin, causing countless generations to miss the mark of God's ideal for them!

The same is true for love, religion, church, Christian, disciple, gospel, and saved – all the other words we've reoriented to.

The simplest and only way to see these "words of God" accomplish His intended purpose and not return void of impact is to become a doer of His words as He originally intended them to mean.

And the only way to become a doer, by definition, is to immediately and literally begin to act, speak, and perform them in ways that are consistent with God's original reason, motives, and intent behind them.

Like any highly rewarded professional athlete, singer, actor, writer, or performer, the only way to speak, act, or perform at a master level of competence is to exercise, rehearse, or practice your part in private. When the time comes to do that part in front of an audience, you're confident in your ability to do it in a way that's worthy of being seen and heard.

So, in short, the way you become a doer is – you guessed it – by *doing!*

And the only way to make sure you do something well is – you guessed it again – by practicing it until you can do it well.

> **" I don't fear the man who practiced 10,000 kicks one time. I fear the man who has practiced one kick 10,000 times. "**
>
> – BRUCE LEE –

Again, this may seem obvious, but in my experience it's one of the most-often overlooked aspects of people becoming disciples of Jesus. Because we so often equate knowing something with having done it, we often fail to continually practice doing it so as to become a sufficient master of it.

But if you want to be a disciple and make doing what Jesus did a permanent part of your nature, you will need to practice doing everything Jesus did until it becomes your second nature!

You may want to read that last statement a few times and let the implications sink in before moving on.

I say that because, for us, this was a monumental insight and shifted years we'd spent being focused on waiting, praying, fasting, and begging God to anoint us in a special way to do the mighty works Jesus did and that we knew were possible to actually dedicating ourselves to practicing and going about doing what Jesus did so God had something and someone to work with and anoint to do the impossible!

To our amazement, instead of waiting on an outpouring of some new supernatural endowment of grace by God for us to do this stuff, we discovered that it was actually by rising up and becoming a doer of that stuff that produced the greatest anointing to perfect it.

It appears that while many people spend years waiting on an outpouring of the Spirit of God to change the world as we know it, meanwhile God is at the same time waiting on an uprising of people to act on and be doers of what He has already poured out.

As this reality began to sink in, we realized that to perform at the highest level, we needed to train like those who perform at the highest level. Great singers, actors, soldiers, athletes, entrepreneurs, and performers don't perfect what they do by simply wishing they were better, praying they were better, or waiting on someone to magically anoint them to become great. Instead, they practice performing what is hard to perfect until they can perform the hard things perfectly and with ease.

> " *Knowing is not enough; we must apply. Willing is not enough; we must do.* "
>
> – JOHANN WOLFGANG VON GOETHE –

For us to reorient as a family, one of the first things we had to do was quit thinking of discipleship as something we accomplished by going somewhere on set days per week to hear others teach about things God historically did and performed through others and then think about how best to apply that knowledge to our everyday lives the rest of the week. Instead, we began setting aside times to train like athletes, soldiers, and other top-level performers to practice doing the things God did and not relent until we could do them well ourselves. Like doing anything at a high level of excellence, mastery takes lots of practice. Fortunately for us, along the way God was gracious to show us a few things and some simple methods that seem to make becoming a doer much easier.

## A FEW THINGS TO MAKE DOING EASIER

Remember, the goal of all instruction is doing, and, as the following proverb says, if you want to change the way you go about doing things, first and foremost it's important to began setting aside specific times to practice and train:

> Train ‹initiate or disciple› up a child ‹those who are at the infant or adolescent stage of development› in the

*way* *he should go: and when he is old ‹**more mature**›, he will not depart from it.*
> ~ *Proverb 22:6,* KJV, ***emphasis added***

As the Holy Spirit directed us, we found this training to be a critical aspect to helping anyone wanting to *disciple up* to do what Jesus did as a fully mature being but who may only be at an infant or adolescent stage of development themselves when they begin to contend for it.

The first step in terms of training was leveraging what we learned about the power of speaking as a method to transform our thinking and our beliefs and build our faith for the impossible. We literally needed to reorient and relearn how to speak the truth in love by incorporating everything we learned into the language of our everyday lives and realms of influence.

I can't underscore the importance of this enough.

> But ***speaking the truth in love, may grow up into him in all things, which is the head, even Christ.***
> ~ *Ephesians 4:15,* KJV, ***emphasis added***

Speaking is a critical component of both physical and spiritual development. In the same way the maturation and development of a child can be stunted by not learning to speak, so can the maturation of a disciple.

It became clear to us that changing the way a person speaks is a key to changing the way they think. Changing the way a person thinks can also have a profound impact on the way they do things – and, subsequently, the results produced from what they do.

Learning new ways to speak became a critical part of our regular training. Under what we sensed was the Holy Spirit's direction, we began listing some of the most frequently-used religious words and a few of the major concepts we needed to reorient to.

We then organized the words and concepts into tables alongside the reoriented meaning or original intent behind them and developed a kind of script for how they should be ideally performed.

For example, if we were to do this for each of the words and a couple major concepts we covered in this book, it might look like this.

| WORD(S) | ORIGINAL MEANING AND INTENT |
| --- | --- |
| Love | Contend for the highest good we can think or imagine until it's a present-tense reality. |
| Sin | Separation (no longer a problem) |
| Religion | Experientially reconnecting to God |
| Church | An uprising – our call to battle to confront any kind of oppression wherever it exists in the private and public realms of life. |
| Christian | Symbolic of the reproach we might face as we contend to demonstrate the supernatural and present-tense realities of the kingdom of God in every area of our private and public lives, just as Jesus did. |
| Disciple | One willing to endure hardness to become and perform just like the Master Teacher. |
| Gospel | The present- and future-tense rewards of the kingdom, which may sound like nearly-too-good-to-be-true news to those who hear about them. |
| Saved | Healed, redeemed, delivered, provided for, protected, and made whole now and in the future. |
| Faith | The state of being fully convinced, completely persuaded, and fully assured of a thing the evidence proves is substantive. |
| Repent | To think differently afterward |

Like young actors who just discovered their part and have been handed a fresh set of lines, we sensed the Holy Spirit directing us to practice speaking in new ways. At first, because of the traditional way we had learned to understand and speak about these things, it seemed very unnatural.

We missed it a lot early on, and God was faithful to help us. As a family, we found that especially in the midst of intensive training, it became critical to not point out where each person missed it but rather to lovingly reorient them when we noticed old patterns of speech and thinking emerging while simultaneously inciting them to continue to love and contend for the mighty works.

We also found it necessary for the more experienced to regularly model things for the less confident until each person was equally confident in their ability to perform a thing equally well.

Phrases like, "That was good, but not the most excellent I can think or imagine" or "What if we thought about this or that differently?" and "What would the evidence be if we were moving in the right direction?" became standard parts of our daily discourse.

As opposed to simply pointing out where someone was missing it, which has the potential to provoke strife, shame, or drive someone's heart into hiding, we found these kinds of phrases to be more excellent in helping each other reorient to a higher kind of good in terms of our thinking and speaking as a family.

As we began to master the speaking part as a family, again, like performers with a new script or playbook to learn, we began to notice something even more profound happening: *our hearts were changing.*

I remember thinking at the time, *This must be why so many actors end up believing they've fallen in love with each other on the set of a romantic movie.* Most people conclude it's just the result of spending so much time together or simply that "mysterious thing called love," which nobody can understand or control. What is more likely, however, is that the simple act of mastering their part and then speaking their lines to each other every day brought their hearts into agreement with the words they had been speaking. Which is why, sadly and far too often, after filming wraps and the actors are no longer speaking or acting the part of a couple in love, the feelings they once called love seem to deteriorate and they *fall out of love.*

There is no doubt, speaking is a powerful tool that can affect what the heart feels. For us, as we continued to master the speaking parts and our hearts became more fully alive, we sensed God directing us to slowly incorporate the truths we were now speaking and believing to be present-tense realities into the ways we were acting in our everyday lives.

Once again, the transition seemed awkward, as the words we were speaking didn't feel like our own yet. And now the process of making our actions line up with our new rhetoric seemed even more contrived and disingenuous at first.

In the early stages of reorienting, we felt at times as though we were speaking to things that weren't as though they were (Rom. 4:17). In one instance I remember being challenged to the core to speak and act differently while privately contending for our daughter's eczema to be healed. Intellectually, we had agreed there was nobody with eczema in heaven and had resolved it should be equally unacceptable for anyone to have eczema on earth. Intellectually, we began to share God's holy, violent hatred against these kinds of infirmities and the ways they ravage people's bodies. Intellectually, we were convinced that even though it sounded like nearly-too-good-to-be-true news, it no longer had to be this way because we were no longer separated from the present-tense reality of God, for the kingdom of God was near – literally within arm's reach.

Even though we were unwavering, convinced, completely persuaded, and had full assurance of our faith in God's ability and willingness to heal her, it was a constant battle at first to continue to think differently until we had tangible evidence or a witness of our daughter's healing from eczema.

As we practiced and exercised and endeavored to be doers of what we now knew was our part to do, we continued to relentlessly contend for the highest possible good we could think or imagine for her – love's ideal in this case was our daughter being saved from eczema – and we resolved as a family to not stop until this ideal was a present-tense reality!

For a time, our results didn't exactly match our rhetoric, and the temptation to lower our expectations to match our then-current reality was ever present. But by the supernatural grace of God, we finally did see improvement. It was small at first, and then more over time. Eventually she was nearly 90 percent healed with no other intervention except God's divine intervention.

Today, eczema is simply no longer a problem for her.

This was our first real "win," as we now like to call miracles like these, where love's ideal is victorious and prevails over the inferior but all-too-common adversaries of sickness, disease, poverty, lack, and oppression of any kind.

I know "wins" may sound like a funny term to assign such an event, but believe it or not, it's actually a biblically accurate way to describe such outcomes.

To be precise, the Bible uses the Greek word *nikao* to describe these kind of victories. It's a word that literally means "to overcome, subdue, conquer, prevail, get the victory over, or be victorious, as in having success."

In other words, today we might just say to *win!*

> *I write to you, fathers, because you have come to know (recognize, be conscious of, and understand) Him Who [has existed] from the beginning. I write to you, young men, because you are strong and vigorous, and the Word of God is [always] abiding in you (in your hearts), and you have been victorious ‹***have overcome, subdued, conquered, prevailed, and gotten the victory***› over the wicked one.*
>
> ~ *1 John 2:14*, AMP

> *For whatever is born of God is victorious ‹***has overcome, subdued, conquered, prevailed, and gotten the victory***› over the world; and this is the victory that conquers the world, even our faith.*
>
> ~ *1 John 5:4*, AMP

> *Who is it that is victorious ‹***has overcome, subdued, conquered, prevailed, and gotten the victory***› over [that con-*

591

*quers] the world but he who believes that Jesus is the Son
of God [who adheres to, trusts in, and relies on that fact]?*
*~ 1 John 5:5,* AMP

*He who is able to hear, let him listen to and give heed to
what the Spirit says to the assemblies (churches). To him
who overcomes ‹**subdues, conquers, prevails, and gets
the victory**› (is victorious), I will grant to eat [of the fruit]
of the tree of life, which is in the paradise of God. ‹**See
Genesis 2:9; 3:24.**›*
*~ Revelation 2:7,* AMP

*He who is able to hear, let him listen to and heed what the
Spirit says to the assemblies (churches). He who overcomes
‹**subdues, conquers, prevails, and gets the victory**› (is
victorious) shall in no way be injured by the second death.*
*~ Revelation 2:11,* AMP

*And he who overcomes ‹**subdues, conquers, prevails, and
gets the victory**› (is victorious) and who obeys My commands to the [very] end [doing the works that please Me],
I will give him authority and power over the nations.*
*~ Revelation 2:26,* AMP

*He who overcomes ‹**subdues, conquers, prevails, and gets
the victory**› (is victorious), I will grant him to sit beside Me
on My throne, as I Myself overcame (was victorious) and
sat down beside My Father on His throne.*
*~ Revelation 3:21,* AMP

*He who is victorious ‹**overcomes, subdues, conquers, prevails, and gets the victory**› shall inherit all these things,
and I will be God to him and he shall be My son.*
*~ Revelation 21:7,* AMP

In the same way winning and being victorious is the ideal outcome
for any great athlete who has committed himself or herself to the
required training to be great, being victorious should be the goal of
anyone committed to discipling up, becoming doers, and training in

such a way as to master the ability to emulate Jesus in this life, who Himself was ultimately victorious in all these areas.

*If we pull this off,*
*we change the game.*
*We change the game for good.* "

- BILLY BEAN, THE MOVIE *MONEYBALL* -

For us, the single win over our daughter's eczema was part of the initial victories God used to build our confidence in our ability to co-labor with Him to administer the present-tense rewards of the gospel and to bring about even greater victories.

Shortly thereafter, we found safe places among people in our immediate family and friends where speaking about and rehearsing the things we had been practicing in private wasn't met with shame, ridicule, or scorn if we fell short of performing to perfection. We didn't always get the results we wanted, and the results we did get weren't always spectacular, but we were getting wins on a more regular basis.

For example, the wins in terms of healings we experienced at first mainly consisted of relief from minor ailments and discomforts like headaches, backaches, sprained ankles, and the like.

Regardless, one thing was for sure – we were slowly becoming doers of what Jesus did, and we were pumped! And not because we were able to do the stuff to be impressive but because we were able to see the love of God do what the love of God does best – restore people – and that seemed to leave a lasting impression with people!

It was just a short time later, though, that while engaged in a brief conversation with a friend, we got to experience God doing the impossible in an even greater capacity for the first time.

In retrospect, we can now see that in this one moment, that which we once had only hoped was possible was now not just possible but was becoming a near daily reality and a natural, effortless part of our

009 · DOER · REORIENT

everyday life. It was also the moment we realized we were no longer just spectators, practicing to play the metaphorical game of life with God at a higher level, but were actually in the game and doing it – able to deliver the present-tense rewards of the gospel for real!

We had truly been reoriented!

The key moment happened while in a conversation with a friend and a few of their relatives. All of a sudden, in what was otherwise a normal conversation, I sensed a leading in my spirit to ask the relative, who we did not know well at the time, what was wrong with their eye.

There was nothing visibly wrong with their eye that I could tell, but nonetheless, I figured it was harmless to inquire.

Though it didn't seem germane to the conversation, I asked, "Hey, is your eye okay?"

"Which one?" they asked.

"The left one," I responded.

They immediately revealed they had been completely blind in their left eye for more than thirty years.


Almost reflexively, I said:

*That's unacceptable!*

*I hate that!*

*I am completely convinced, completely persuaded, and have total confidence in the good news that it does not have to be that way!*

*I bet if we just thought differently, the answer is within arm's reach!*

*In fact, if I spoke over your eye and it was completely healed right now, what would be the evidence?*


They immediately said, "Well, I would be able to see, of course!"

I asked if I could speak over their eye, and they agreed.

Moments before speaking, I invited them to simply concentrate on the highest good they could think or imagine would result from this as I spoke.

They agreed, and I simply said, "Eye, be right in Jesus' name – so be it!"

"That's it?" they asked, as if expecting a much longer or more impassioned prayer.

"That's it," I replied, and I asked them to cover their good eye and tell us if they noticed any improvement in the vision of the blind eye.

At first there was no noticeable improvement, so we spoke again: "Eye, be right – so be it!"

Everyone standing in the room, which now included several others who had apparently overheard the exchange and gathered around, erupted in concert with gasps of awe and excitement when, all of a sudden, a single teardrop squeezed past the inside corner of the person's blind eye and they whispered – in hesitation at first:

"I can see!"

We began gathering items with small print from the nearby kitchen in our home for them to read. To everyone's astonishment, the person was now reading labels on canned goods and vitamin bottles from 15 feet away with what was previously a blind eye of thirty-plus years.

It was a glorious happening for everyone involved. The person healed left our home with a profound gratefulness to God and a renewed sense of awe of His love for them.

For the marginally skeptical and those who were only spectating that day, they seemed to leave with a newfound sense of curiosity about the things of God and the reality of His kingdom.

For us, it was a single moment of immense triumph over a hated adversary – sickness, disease, and oppression wherever it existed. This single victory, though small in the scheme of global events, was a huge victory for us and a catalyst for even greater things to come.

This single moment of divine manifestation and tangible expression of the love of God in the form of a simple healing for a friend was, for us, a moment of convergence.

It was the moment that, following months of awkwardness of struggling to learn new ways of thinking, speaking, and acting on the gospel, our intentional preparation seemed to effortlessly converge with the will of God to produce a result that was truly greater than we had previously imagined was possible.

In the afterglow of this initial miracle, we began noticing a confidence for the supernatural we hadn't experienced before. Within days we were introduced to a relative of the same person God had healed of the blind eye, and an equally stunning miracle resulted.

This individual, who was in their mid- to late teens, had been born partially blind in one eye and deaf in one ear. Within seconds of learning of the infirmity, reflexively, my wife Michelle responded:

*That's simply unacceptable!*

*I hate that!*

*I am completely convinced, persuaded, and have total confidence in the good news that it doesn't have to be that way!*

*If we just think differently, I know the answer is within arm's reach!*

*In fact, if I spoke over your eye and it was completely healed right now, what would be the evidence?*

In the same way that only days earlier God had healed the blind eye of their cousin, this person's eye and ear were completely restored and made whole, instantly!

In less than ten minutes, and before Michelle left that day, the person was having an ecstatic exchange with their family about the miracle they had just received – with a cell phone held up to what was only moments before a totally deaf ear.

As Michelle and I both reflected with gratitude to God on these two stunning manifestations of His love toward our friends and marveled at the seemingly effortless way they came about through simple conversations, we noticed something profound.

As the following table parallels, what we had spoken reflexively was actually the meaning and definition of some of the more prominent biblical words and precepts to which God had been reorienting us.

What we were now speaking out of our hearts with confidence, we had previously only known in theory!

| CONVERSATION | BIBLICAL PRECEPT |
| --- | --- |
| Unacceptable | On earth as it is in heaven |
| I hate that | Enmity |
| I am convinced | Faith |
| The good news | Gospel |
| Think differently | Repent |
| Within arm's reach | No sin; the kingdom is near |
| Speaking | Pray |
| Evidence | Witness |
| The highest possible good | Love |
| Be right | Righteous |
| So be it | Amen |

These words and concepts were now so much more; they were becoming alive in us and an integrated part of our everyday lives. Saying *that's simply unacceptable* was just a conversational way to declare God's will on earth as it is in heaven!

*I hate that* was just another way of exercising enmity and unleashing the nuclear force behind *agape* love.

*I am completely convinced, persuaded, and have total confidence* was just another way of saying *I have faith for this!*

*The good news is, it doesn't have to be that way* was just a simple declaration of the gospel!

Asking them to *think differently* was establishing the literal need to repent.

*The answer is within arm's reach* was a conversational way to declare sin no longer a problem and that God's kingdom is actually near!

Speaking with authority for us had begun to replace praying with uncertainty about the outcome, which would now inevitably result. Witnessing took on a whole new meaning. Instead of thinking about witnessing as converting someone to have faith in God in order for them to be saved and go to heaven when they die, it now meant contending for the actual evidence of the gospel's full effect that brings about the benefits of salvation now.

Having the person meditate on love's ideal became the way we invited people to agree with us and created an atmosphere for real faith in the impossible to work.

Commanding something to be right was just another way of saying the word *righteous,* which means "to bring something into right standing with God."

And lastly, *so be it* was just another way of saying *amen!* Within a short time of these initial miracles, as a family we began looking for ways to practice and exercise "doing this stuff," as we called it, in more public ways.

Using the same conversational framework (what we would later call our "treasure-hunting script"), a simple trip to our local Wal-Mart, Target, or coffee shop became a training ground for finding ways to see God treasure people in public arenas of life where the need for tangible demonstrations of the love of God were equally great.

We began scheduling regular treasure-hunting adventures with our family and friends, resulting in an avalanche of more than two hundred miracles we personally recorded over the next year.

Breaking down the truths and forming new ways to speak about them became the primary way God matured us in these things. In retrospect, I am in awe of the way God used this simple script, for lack of a better term, to integrate profound supernatural biblical principles into what otherwise could have been mundane normal events and interactions with people.

What previously seemed to us only a verbal reflex to our near-constant immersion and reorientation to some key biblical words and concepts, God made a part of our nature. The way He led us to organize these concepts into everyday terms and ways of speaking to people accomplished two things: it kept us from doubting in faith for the impossible, and it set the stage for God to do above what we thought was possible in every situation.

This simple treasure-hunting script turned a simple "Hello, how are you?" into an opportunity for daily recreational miracles that are now too many to mention.

At a store, if I asked, "How are you?" and a person replied, "I would be fine if my back didn't hurt so badly!" my response became:

*That's simply unacceptable!*

*I hate back pain!*

*But you know what? I am completely convinced, persuaded, and have total confidence that the good news is, it doesn't have to be that way!*

*I bet if we just thought differently, the answer is within arm's reach!*

*In fact, what if I spoke over your back and it was completely healed right now – what would be the evidence it worked?*

If they agreed to let me do that, I simply asked them to imagine love's ideal and spoke over their back. I would say, "Back, be right – so be it!"

Miracle after miracle has resulted.

And even more amazingly, unlike our previous approach of asking a person if we could pray for them, which statistically yielded marginal results for us, I rarely met a person who resisted me because I hated their infirmity with them. In fact, that was usually the one thing we could always agree on – we both hated the thing that was hurting them!

It didn't seem to matter where, when, or what type of situation it was, if a fruit was less than love's ideal and required divine intervention to bring about a higher kind of good, the same approach worked.

In my business, if a client would complain of a near-impossible problem, we approached it the exact same way. Our response to most every problem that was less than love's ideal was simple:

*That's unacceptable!*

*We hate it!*

*We are completely convinced, persuaded, and have total confidence that the good news is, it doesn't have to be that way!*

*I bet if we just thought differently, the answer is within arm's reach!*

*In fact, what is the highest possible good you can think or imagine as the result if I spoke to this situation and God changed it right now?*

*What would be the evidence it worked?*

It didn't seem to matter what the situation was – poverty, sickness, disease, strife, oppression, pain, and more – we saw God do the impossible over and over again when we simply did our part and then had faith in Him to do His.

Did it work out instantly and perfectly every time? No. Was everyone instantly healed every time and in every situation? No, nor were they when Jesus did it.

But our results are certainly improved over the zero results we got before. And if you continue to practice and commit to becoming a doer of these things, so will yours.

My point is simply that this script, which we have now taught thousands of people to use, will help you make the transition between being a hearer and doer of these things, as it has done for those we have taught.

But as you master it, remember: It's not that a script, in and of itself, has any real power, nor do the exact words or ways you choose to express the truths God shows you in this book.

Instead, it's the very nature of God Himself, whose Spirit empowers the intent and purposes behind these truths, that brings them about when we speak and act in faith.

But before any of these things can become a constant reality for you or me, we simply must commit to being a doer or performer of them first, and not just hearers or spectators of them only.

## CLOSING EXHORTATION

Let me encourage you to commit first and foremost to not just using what you learned in this book to reorient, but to becoming a doer of what you have reoriented to!

If needed, by yourself or with your small group, go chapter by chapter or precept by precept and ask the questions:

Do I/we know this?

Am I/are we doing this?

If so, how would I/we know it for sure?

What would be the evidence?

**RESOURCE:**
Want to begin treasure hunting? Want some tools to help? Consider the print or video resources we've developed in the resource section for this chapter, www.thereorientbook.com.

If you are not yet a doer, keep reorienting, training, and practicing to become a doer of that which you desire more of!

Be a doer of love. Go back to Chapter One and immerse yourself in what it really means to contend for love's ideal in every situation, and then begin applying it to every area of life until your default response is going for the highest good in every situation and relentlessly contending for it until it is present-tense reality! Become a doer of love until it's such a part of you and your family or small group ethos that anything short of love's ideal is unacceptable.

Be a doer. Do not let sin be a problem any longer. Let nothing separate you from God.

Be a doer. Do not let anything take the place of true religion. Experientially connect and reconnect yourself and others to God – now, in the present tense.

Be a doer. Forget trying to be a church and focus instead on being an *ekklesia*. Reorient to what it would look for you, your family, your small group, or your congregation to rise up together and battle oppression wherever it exists, in every area of public life and realm of influence God has placed you.

Be a doer. Like Jesus' first disciples, who were first called Christians, don't concern yourself with the labels placed on you by those who will mock and ridicule you in order to drive your heart back into a place of hiding. Focus on maturity to do the stuff He did so that whatever others call you is based on the supernatural fruit you produce, not simply the ideas you claim to espouse.

Be a doer. Like going to the gym, prepare to exercise and endure whatever hardness is necessary to disciple up and do everything Jesus did – and even greater works – because He did what He did. Like a special-forces soldier, Olympic athlete, or successful farmer, don't relent until you can do and perform and produce the same fruit He produced, and equally well.

Be a doer. Learn to administer the supernatural endowments of grace God has made available to you in order to send you into the world and bring about the real present-tense rewards of the gospel to everyone and every situation that needs it.

Be a doer. Go back and reorient, if needed, to what it really means to be saved, focusing first on learning to receive the benefits of salvation yourself, then bringing them about in your own family and helping others who need and want to receive it.

Commit to being a doer. Together, let's rise up, battle for love, and reorient the world to what it really means to be a disciple of Christ. Let's reorient the world to a new definition of the gospel and what it really means to be saved now and in the future tense.

Commit to not becoming weary of doing good, and rise up with me with a holy, violent enmity against evil wherever it exists and in every situation until the highest good we can think or imagine – the whole world being saved – is a present-tense reality (Gal. 6:9).

As lofty and ambitious as "saving the world" may sound, I want to provide one last closing illustration that I believe highlights just how doable this really is if we reorient our thinking in terms of how to go about it.

As Jesus originally modeled and the following mathematical reality supports, the key to saving the world, as we know, is not found in the greatness of some ambitious crusade to evangelize the world and compel them to covert to becoming Christians, *per se*.

Instead, the mission can only be accomplished by making disciples and simply doing it two by two! The greatness of what Jesus modeled and deployed to change the world as we know it is still, to this day, found in the smallness of just one person becoming a real disciple and then mastering the ability to equip two others to do the same.

So, assuming I am a disciple and capable of equipping just two more people to disciple up and to do the same, in just thirty-three short iterations, we could save the whole world as we know it! And amazingly, all without a single tent meeting or global evangelistic crusade – just one person reorienting and mastering the ability to do the stuff that Jesus did and then equipping two more to do the same.

And just in case it this sounds too simple and too good to be true, here is the math:

I Am 1
2
4
8
16
32
64
128
256
512
1,024
2,048
4,096
8,192
16,348
32,768
65,536
131,072
262,144
524,288
1,048,576
2,097,152
4,194,304
8,388,608
16,777,216
33,554,432
67,108,864
134,217,728
268,435,456
536,870,912
1,073,741,824
2,147,483,648
4,294,967,296
8,589,934,592
World Saved

So, rise up as I Am,

and let's do our part and not stop until we can each say, just as Jesus did and as I will to end this book,

*My job is done – it is finished – it is complete!*

# DOER__REACT

**What are the top three things you are taking away from this chapter?**

\
\
\
\
\
\
\
\
\
\
\

**What action can you take now on what you've learned?**

\
\
\
\
\
\
\
\
\
\

"It's not God people reject

when they reject Him as savior

but wrong ideas about Him

From all the bad … Christian … behavior

He called us out to rise up

It's what church should really mean

To battle for love and reorient

A world to more than they see"

– REORIENT: BAD CHRISTIAN BEHAVIOR –

*Lyrics by Kevin Weaver It's Feasible Publishing, LLC*

Download the complete lyrics and an .mp3 version of this
song in its entirety at www.thereorientbook.com.

# REVIVE

Go!

Go and reorient the world as we know it.

Go and relentlessly contend for love's ideal.

Go and never again be separated from God.

Go and experientially connect yourself and others to God.

Go and answer the summons to rise up and battle for love's ideal in every realm of life.

Go and mature into the very likeness of Jesus Himself.

Go and disciple up to do everything Jesus did and even greater works.

Go and deliver the present-tense rewards of the gospel.

Go and be made perfectly whole and help others to do the same.

Go and be a doer and not just a spectator.

Go and reorient the world as we know it.

Go!


But as you go, be advised...


Reorienting the world is essential to save the world as we know it. However, saving the world may not immediately change the culture of the world as we know it! Changing culture will take more than just reorienting; it will require a new kind of revival!


What kind of revival exactly?


You'll see!


To be continued at www.therevivebook.com

Because nothing is impossible

And what Jesus said is true,

We could do greater works

Than even He can do.

POSTLUDE TO
- GREATER WORKS -
*Lyrics by Kevin Weaver It's Feasible Publishing, LLC*

Download the complete lyrics and an .mp3 version of this
song in its entirety at www.thereorientbook.com.

ENDNOTES

# ENDNOTES

1.  Props to Johnny Lee for this one. See "Johnny Lee," Wikipedia, last modified October 4, 2011, http://en.wikipedia.org/wiki/Johnny_Lee.

2.  "Love Shack," Wikipedia, last modified December 17, 2011, http://en.wikipedia.org/wiki/Love_shack.

3.  "Love Bites," Wikipedia, last modified December 30, 2011, http://en.wikipedia.org/wiki/Love_Bites_(song).

4.  Ironically, written by a band called Nazareth. See "Love Hurts," Wikipedia, last modified January 14, 2012, http://en.wikipedia.org/wiki/Love_Hurts.

5.  That's for all you Beatles' fans. See "All You Need Is Love," Wikipedia, last modified January 12, 2012, http://en.wikipedia.org/wiki/All_You_Need_Is_Love.

6.  Provided by Wolfram Mathematics on its WolframAlpha computational knowledge engine, accessed at http://www.wolframalpha.com.

7.  Provided by Wolfram Mathematics on its WolframAlpha computational knowledge engine, accessed at http://www.wolframalpha.com.

8.  To preview the survey results taken from a survey audience of more than 300 people, go to www.thereorientbook.com.

9.  "Hamartiology," Wikipedia, last modified January 3, 2012, http://en.wikipedia.org/wiki/Hamartiology.

10. Austin Cline's blog is located at http://atheism.about.com.

11. Austin Cline, "What If Atheists Are Wrong? Aren't You Afraid of Hell? Can You Take the Chance?"

Agnosticism/Atheism blog, http://atheism.about.com/od/atheismquestions/p/FearHellWrong.htm.

12. Frank Viola and George Barna, *Pagan Christianity? Exploring the Roots of Our Christian Practices* (Carol Stream, IL: BarnaBooks, 2008).

13. Provided by Wolfram Mathematics on its WolframAlpha computational knowledge engine, accessed at http://www.wolframalpha.com.

14. For an example of "old-time religion," see the videos posted at http://www.youtube.com/watch?v=f68TdgErXkE and http://www.youtube.com/watch?v=aQq9F3TacoM&feature=related.

15. http://www.christianitytoday.com/ct/2001/februaryweb-only/43.0b.html

16. Provided by Wolfram Mathematics on its WolframAlpha computational knowledge engine, accessed at http://www.wolframalpha.com.

17. "Kirk," Wikipedia, last modified January 27, 2012, http://en.wikipedia.org/wiki/Kirk.

18. "Lord," Wikipedia, last modified January 20, 2012, http://en.wikipedia.org/wiki/Lord.

19. Found in book 3, chapter 11, of Clement of Alexandria's book, *The Instructor*.

20. "Theodore Beza," Wikipedia, last modified December 24, 2011, http://en.wikipedia.org/wiki/Theodore_Beza.

21. "William Tyndale," Wikipedia, last modified January 21, 2012, http://en.wikipedia.org/wiki/William_Tyndale.

22. Strongs numbers 1537 and 2564

23. Provided by Wolfram Mathematics on its WolframAlpha computational knowledge engine, accessed at http://www.wolframalpha.com.

24. Statistics provided by www.worldchristiandatabase. org.

25. Statistics provided by www.religioustolerance.org.

26. "List of Christian Denominations by Number of Members," Wikipedia, last modified January 3, 2012, http://en.wikipedia.org/wiki/List_of_Christian_ denominations_by_number_of_members.

27. Phil Vaz, "The Facts and Stats on '33,000 Denominations,'" Evangelical Catholic Apologetics, August 28, 2007, http://www.bringyou.to/apologetics/ a106.htm#Independents.

28. David Kinnaman and Gabe Lyons, *unChristian: What a New Generation Really Things About Christianity ... and Why It Matters* (Grand Rapids, MI: Baker Books, 2007), 26.

29. http://en.wikipedia.org/wiki/Crete

30. Associated Press, "Justice Antonin Scalia: Proud to Be a Cretin, Supreme Court Justice Removes All Doubt," April 10, 1996, as quoted at http://www. positiveatheism.org/writ/biblesays.htm.

31. Kahal Yahweh, "The Chi Rho: Ancient Symbol," http:// kahalyahweh.net/Articles/chirho.htm.

32. "Bar and Bat Mitzvah: Responsibilities," Wikipedia, modified January 21, 2012, http://en.wikipedia.org/ wiki/Bar_and_Bat_Mitzvah#Responsibilities.

33. Luke 1:27, which uses the word *virgin* in many English translations, *virgo* in Latin, means "a young woman of marriageable age." Translation from the Greek *parthenos* and Arabic *almah* means "a young woman considered old enough for marriage."

34. "Shepherding Movement," Wikipedia, last modified August 29, 2011, http://en.wikipedia.org/wiki/ Shepherding_Movement.

35. Data provided by Wolfram Mathematics on its WolframAlpha computational knowledge engine, accessed at http://www.wolframalpha.com.

36. Brian Knowles, "The Hebrew Mind vs. the Western Mind," Godward.org, http://www.godward.org/Hebrew%20Roots/hebrew_mind_vs__the_western_mind.htm.

37. *http://en.wikipedia.org/wiki/Kung_Fu_(TV_series)*

38. *http://en.wikipedia.org/wiki/The_Karate_Kid_(1984_film)*

39. http://en.wikipedia.org/wiki/Star_wars

40. *http://en.wikipedia.org/wiki/The_Matrix*

41. "University," Wikipedia, last modified on January 28, 2012, http://en.wikipedia.org/wiki/University.

42. Adherents.com, "Major Religions of the World Ranked by Number of Adherents," http://www.adherents.com/Religions_By_Adherents.html.

43. Malcolm Gladwell, *Outliers* (New York: Little, Brown and Co., 2008), 40.

44. To view or download the 2009 report, visit http://blog.nielsen.com/nielsenwire/wp-content/uploads/2009/09/3ScreenQ209_US_rpt_090209.pdf.

45. Jane McGonigal, "Gaming Can Make a Better World," TED Talks, http://www.ted.com/talks/lang/en/jane_mcgonigal_gaming_can_make_a_better_world.html.

46. SpecialOperations.com, "The Special Forces Soldier," http://www.specialoperations.com/Army/Special_Forces/SF_Info/Soldier.htm.

47. See, for example, "United States Army Basic Training: Daily Schedule," Wikipedia, last modified January 29, 2012, http://en.wikipedia.org/wiki/United_States_Army_Basic_Training#Daily_schedule.

48. Learn more at www.jerryboykin.com.

49. Flying Ace http://en.wikipedia.org/wiki/Ace_fighter_pilot

50. "Corslet," Wikipedia, last modified on September 9, 2010, http://en.wikipedia.org/wiki/Corslet.

51. "Ancient Olympic Games", Wikipedia, last modified January 30, 2012, http://en.wikipedia.org/wiki/Ancient_Olympic_Games.

52. "Michael Phelps," Wikipedia, last modified on January 20, 2012, http://en.wikipedia.org/wiki/Michael_Phelps.

53. Kathleen M. Zelman, "The Olympic Diet of Michael Phelps," WebMD.com, August 13, 2008, http://www.webmd.com/diet/news/20080813/the-olympic-diet-of-michael-phelps.

54. You can read the full text of *An Introduction to the Old Testament Template* online at http://templateinstitute.com/2011/09/read-the-old-testament-template-book-online/.

55. Learn more about Landa Cope and the Template Institute at www.templateinstitute.com.

56. Landa Cope, *An Introduction to the Old Testament Template,* chapter 1, viewable at http://templateinstitute.com/the-old-testament-template-book-chapter-1/

57. Data provided by Wolfram Mathematics on its WolframAlpha computational knowledge engine, accessed at http://www.wolframalpha.com.

58. "Paul Revere," Wikipedia, last modified on December 23, 2011, http://en.wikipedia.org/wiki/Paul_Revere.

59. Andrew Wommack, "Romans," Andrew Wommack Ministries website, http://www.awmi.net/extra/article/romans.

60. R. C. Sproul, "The Proto-Gospel," as quoted at http://www.oocities.org/heartland/9170/SPROUL6.HTM.

61. "Marathon," Wikipedia, last modified on February 1, 2012, http://en.wikipedia.org/wiki/Marathon.

62. John L. McKenzie, *Dictionary of the Bible* (New York: Touchstone, 1995), 480; R. T. France, *Matthew: An Introduction and Commentary,* Tyndale New Testament Commentaries Series, (Leicester, English: Inter-Varsity Press, 1985; reprinted 2008), 49.

63. Richard W. Chilson, *Yeshua of Nazareth, Spiritual Master: The Spirituality He Lived and Taught* (Notre Dame, IN: Sorin Books, 2001).

64. Frank Viola, "Rethinking the Five-Fold Ministry," Beyond Evangelical (blog), October 27, 2010, http://frankviola.org/2010/10/27/rethinking-the-five-fold-ministry/.

65. *Word in Life Study Bible* (Nashville: Thomas Nelson, 1994), note on page 127.

66. Strongs G5485, 5486

67. http://dictionary.reference.com/browse/CADRE

68. Frank Viola, *Who Is Your Covering? A Fresh Look at Leadership, Authority, and Accountability* (Gainesville, FL: Present Testimony Ministry, 2001), 53–54.

69. Paul Vitello, "Taking a Break from the Lord's Work," August 1, 2010, *New York Times,* http://www.nytimes.com/2010/08/02/nyregion/02burnout.html?_r=1.

70. PastorBurnout.com, "Pastor Burnout Statistics," http://www.pastorburnout.com/pastor-burnout-statistics.html.

71. Barna Group, "A Profile of Protestant Pastors in Anticipation of 'Pastor Appreciation Month,'" September 25, 2001, http://www.barna.org/

barna-update/article/5-barna-update/59-a-profile-of-protestant-pastors-in-anticipation-of-qpastor-appreciation-monthq.

72. *Word in Life Study Bible,* 474–475.

73. Provided by Wolfram Mathematics on its WolframAlpha computational knowledge engine, accessed at http://www.wolframalpha.com.

74. David B. Barrett and others, *World Christian Trends, AD 30–AD 2200: Interpreting the Annual Christian Megacensus,* volume 1 (n.p.: William Carey Literary, 2003).

75. David H. Stern, *Jewish New Testament Commentary* (n.p.: Messianic Jewish Resources International, 1992), 86.

76. Harry E. Boer, *Pentecost and Mission* (London: Lutterworth Press, 1961), 18–20.

77. Gospel Fellowship Association, "Baron Justinian Welz (1621–1668)," http://www.gfamissions.org/missionary-biographies/welz-baron-justinian-1621-1668.html.

78. "Hudson Taylor," Wikipedia, last modified on January 29, 2012, http://en.wikipedia.org/wiki/Hudson_Taylor.

79. Ki Mae Heussner, "Stephen Hawking on Religion: 'Science Will Win,'"June 7, 2010, ABC World News, http://abcnews.go.com/WN/Technology/stephen-hawking-religion-science-win/story?id=10830164&page=1#.Ty3HteNrOFg.

80. See www.polygraph.org for more information on polygraphy.

81. "Polygraph," Wikipedia, last modified on January 29, 2012, http://en.wikipedia.org/wiki/Polygraph.